Japan's Security Relations with China since 1989

The Japanese–Chinese security relationship is one of the most important variables in the formation of a new strategic environment in the Asia-Pacific region which has not only regional but also global implications. The book investigates how and why since the 1990s China has turned in the Japanese perception from a benign neighbour to an ominous challenge, with implications not only for Japan's security, but also its economy, role in Asia and identity as the first developed Asian nation. Japan's reaction to this challenge has been a policy of engagement, which consists of political and economic enmeshment of China, hedged by political and military power balancing.

The unique approach of this book is the use of an extended security concept to analyse this policy, which allows a better and more systematic understanding of its many inherent contradictions and conflicting dynamics, including the centrifugal forces arising from the Japan–China–US triangular relationship. Many contradictions of Japan's engagement policy arise from the overlap of military and political power-balancing tools which are part of containment as well as of engagement, a reality which is downplayed by Japan but not ignored by China. The complex nature of engagement explains the recent reinforcement of Japan's security cooperation with the US and Tokyo's efforts to increase the security dialogues with countries neighbouring China, such as Vietnam, Myanmar and the five Central Asian countries.

The book raises the crucial question of whether Japan's political leadership, which is still preoccupied with finding a new political constellation and with overcoming a deep economic crisis, is able to handle such a complex policy in the face of an increasingly assertive China and a US alliance partner with strong swings between engaging and containing China's power.

Reinhard Drifte has held the Chair of Japanese Studies at the University of Newcastle upon Tyne since 1989. In recent years he was Visiting Professor at the University of Tokyo and Visiting Professor at the University of Beijing. His most recent books are *Japan's Quest for a Permanent Security Council Seat* and *Japan's Foreign Policy for the 21st Century*. For further information see his home page: http://www.staff.ncl.ac.uk/r.f.w.drifte/

The Nissan Institute/RoutledgeCurzon Japanese Studies Series

The Japanese Numbers Game: The Use and Understanding of Numbers in Modern Japan
Thomas Crump

Ideology and Practice in Modern Japan
Edited by Roger Goodman and Kirsten Refsing

Technology and Industrial Development in Pre-war Japan: Mitsubishi Nagasaki Shipyard, 1884–1934
Yukiko Fukasaku

Japan's Early Parliaments, 1890–1905: Structure, Issues and Trends
Andrew Fraser, R.H.P. Mason and Philip Mitchell

Japan's Foreign Aid Challenge: Policy Reform and Aid Leadership
Alan Rix

Emperor Hirohito and Shwa Japan: A Political Biography
Stephen S. Large

Japan: Beyond the End of History
David Williams

Ceremony and Ritual in Japan: Religious Practices in an Industrialized Society
Edited by Jan van Bremen and D.P. Martinez

Understanding Japanese Society, Second Edition
Joy Hendry

The Fantastic in Modern Japanese Literature: The Subversion of Modernity
Susan J. Napier

Militarization and Demilitarization in Contemporary Japan
Glenn D. Hook

Growing a Japanese Science City: Communication in Scientific Research
James W. Dearing

Architecture and Authority in Japan
William H. Coaldrake

Women's *Giday* and the Japanese Theatre Tradition
A. Kimi Coaldrake

Democracy in Post-war Japan: Maruyama Masao and the Search for Autonomy
Rikki Kersten

Treacherous Women of Imperial Japan: Patriarchal Fictions, Patricidal Fantasies
Hélène Bowen Raddeker

Japanese–German Business Relations: Competition and Rivalry in the Inter-war Period
Akira Kudô

Japan, Race and Equality: The Racial Equality Proposal of 1919
Naoko Shimazu

Japan, Internationalism and the UN
Ronald Dore

Life in a Japanese Women's College: Learning to be Ladylike
Brian J. McVeigh

On The Margins of Japanese Society: Volunteers and the Welfare of the Urban Underclass
Carolyn S. Stevens

The Dynamics of Japan's Relations with Africa: South Africa, Tanzania and Nigeria
Kweku Ampiah

The Right to Life in Japan
Noel Williams

The Nature of the Japanese State: Rationality and Rituality
Brian J. McVeigh

Society and the State in Inter-war Japan
Edited by Elise K. Tipton

Japanese–Soviet/Russian Relations since 1945: A Difficult Peace
Kimie Hara

Interpreting History in Sino-Japanese Relations: A Case Study in Political Decision Making
Caroline Rose

Endô Shûsaku: A Literature of Reconciliation
Mark B. Williams

Green Politics in Japan
Lam Peng-Er

The Japanese High School: Silence and Resistance
Shoko Yoneyama

Engineers in Japan and Britain: Education, Training and Employment
Kevin McCormick

The Politics of Agriculture in Japan
Aurelia George Mulgan

Opposition Politics in Japan: Strategies Under a One-Party Dominant Regime
Stephen Johnson

The Changing Face of Japanese Retail: Working in a Chain Store
Louella Matsunaga

Japan and East Asian Regionalism
Edited by S. Javed Maswood

Globalizing Japan: Ethnography of the Japanese Presence in America, Asia and Europe
Edited by Harumi Befu and Sylvie Guichard-Anguis

Japan at Play: The Ludic and Logic of Power
Edited by Joy Hendry and Massimo Raveri

The Making of Urban Japan: Cities and Planning from Edo to the Twenty First Century
André Sorensen

Public Policy and Economic Competition in Japan: Change and Continuity in Antimonopoly Policy, 1973–1995
Michael L. Beeman

Modern Japan: A Social and Political History
Elise K. Tipton

Men and Masculinities in Contemporary Japan: Dislocating the Salaryman Doxa
Edited by James E. Roberson and Nobue Suzuki

The Voluntary and Non-Profit Sector in Japan: The Challenge of Change
Edited by Stephen P. Osborne

Japan's Security Relations with China since 1989: From Balancing to Bandwagoning
Reinhard Drifte

Japan's Security Relations with China since 1989

From balancing to bandwagoning?

Reinhard Drifte

RoutledgeCurzon
Taylor & Francis Group

LONDON AND NEW YORK

First published 2003
by RoutledgeCurzon
11 New Fetter Lane, London EC4P 4EE

Simultaneously published in the USA and Canada
by RoutledgeCurzon
29 West 35th Street, New York, NY 10001

RoutledgeCurzon is an imprint of the Taylor & Francis Group

Typeset in Baskerville by Taylor & Francis Books Ltd
Printed and bound in Great Britain by Biddles Ltd, Guildford
and King's Lynn

British Library Cataloguing in Publication Data
A catalogue record for this book is available from the British Library

Library of Congress Cataloging in Publication Data
Drifte, Reinhard.
Japan's security relations with China since 1989 : from balancing to
bandwagoning? / Reinhard Drifte.
(Nissan Institute/RoutledgeCurzon Japanese studies series)
Includes bibliographical references and index.
1. National security–Japan. 2. National security–China.
3. Japan–Relations–China. 4. China–Relations–Japan. 5. East
Asia–Relations–United States. 6. United States–Relations–East Asia. I.
Title. II. Nissan Institute/Routledge Japanese studies series.

UA845 .D75   2002
355'.033052–dc21   2002068241

ISBN 0–415–30507–1

To Collette

Contents

List of tables	xii
Preface	xiii
List of abbreviations	xiv

Introduction 1

Security in the post-Cold War era 1
Methodology and questions to be addressed 2
The complex nature of engagement policy 5
Restraint and deference 6
The dynamics of engagement 7
Summary of chapters 10

1 Japanese–Chinese relations under Cold War conditions 12

Introduction 12
An overview of Japanese–Chinese history 12
The role of the past 14
Deference to China 18
The impact of the alliance with the US 19
Normalization of relations, 1972 21
The anti-hegemony phase of the 1970s 23
The resurgence of Chinese security concerns 26
Japan as a civilian power engaging China 28
Tiananmen 1989 as a test of engagement 29
Conclusions 32

2 The rise of traditional and non-traditional security concerns 33

Introduction 33

PART 1: THE BACKGROUND TO CHINA'S SECURITY POLICIES 33
China and the post-Cold War environment 33
Japan's place in China's 'multipolar world' 36
China's military modernization 40

PART 2: JAPAN'S EMERGING TRADITIONAL SECURITY
CONCERNS ABOUT CHINA 43
China's military modernization 43
China's nuclear deterrent and testing 44
Territorial disputes 48
The 1995–6 crisis in the Taiwan Strait 64

PART 3: NON-TRADITIONAL SECURITY CONCERNS 70
Introduction 70
Competition for access to natural resources 71
The environmental impact of China's economic growth 72
Crime and refugees 72
Challenging Japan's identity as an economic power? 74

PART 4: INTERNATIONAL AND DOMESTIC CHANGES
AND JAPAN'S CHINA DEBATE 76
International and domestic changes 76
The debate about the 'China threat' theory 80
Conclusions 83

3 Between power balancing and enmeshment policies   **84**
Introduction 84

PART 1: MILITARY AND POLITICAL POWER BALANCING 85
Japan's military force structure and China 85
The National Defence Programme Outline of 1995 88
The Nye Initiative: don't mention the C-word! 89
The 1996 Joint Japan–US Declaration 91
The background to Japan–US cooperation on TMD 93
The Japanese–Chinese debate on Japan's new security policy 94
Political power balancing of China 101

PART 2: POLITICAL AND ECONOMIC ENMESHMENT 110

A. Bilateral and multilateral security dialogues 110
Introduction 110
Bilateral security dialogue and military exchanges 112
Multilateral security dialogue and exchanges 121
The evaluation of security dialogues 131

B. Economic enmeshment 133
Introduction 133
Trade 134
Investment 135
ODA 136
Multilateral economic involvement 137

Japan and China's export- and FDI-led strategy 138
Conclusions 139

4 The dynamics of engagement **140**
Introduction 140
Open issues of political and economic enmeshment 140
Rivalry and competition 147
Triangular dynamics: challenges arising from the US context 157
Japan's deference and restraint 170
Conclusions 172

Conclusions **174**
Challenges 178
Scenarios 180
Policy recommendations 182

Notes 187
Index 237

Tables

2.1	Official figures for China's defence spending 1985–2002	42
2.2	Intrusions by Chinese 'research vessels' into Japan's EEZ	57
3.1	The chronology of the security dialogue	114
3.2	Japanese–Chinese trade (in US$ billion)	135
4.1	A poll on the following question: Thinking of all Asian countries, which country in this region do you think is the most important partner of the US?	165

Preface

Thanks have to go, first to all, to those who contributed both to my buyout from teaching and administration in the Department of Politics of the University of Newcastle and to my research funding during the course of this book project, from January 1999 to March 2002. I am particularly grateful to Jürgen Paleit, Managing Director of URENCO Ltd and now a member of its board, which company financed the buyout. I am indebted to the Japan Society for the Promotion of Science, which funded five weeks' field research at the Faculty of International Relations of Shizuoka Prefectural University in April–May 2000, and to the Social Science Institute of the University of Tokyo for inviting me as Visiting Professor from January to April 2001. I am also particularly grateful to Professor Hirowatari Seigo, its director at the time, and Professor Ishida Hiroshi. Other field research in Japan, as well as three weeks as Visiting Fellow at the John Sigur Center, George Washington University, Washington, DC, in October–November 1999, was funded by a combination of my own means, expanded conference invitations and a surplus from an earlier buyout.

I am grateful to many academics, diplomats, businessmen and journalists who gave me their precious time for interviews and for providing information. Thanks have to go to Taki Tomonori, Dr Christopher Hughes, Dr Hanns Guenther Hilpert and Professor Takahara Akio, who all read specific parts of my manuscript and provided valuable comments. Comments by two anonymous reviewers were also helpful in making this, I hope, a better book. Special thanks have to go to Professor Asano Ryoota and Dr Rex Li, who read the whole manuscript and shared their expertise with me. I would also like to thank Professor J.A. Stockwin for including the book in his series. Thanks have also to go to Morimoto Nami (Waseda University), Kusumi Noriko (Aoyama University) and Iiyama Miyuki (Tokyo University), who helped me with finding research material.

Above all I have to thank my wife, Collette, for her patience with my long absences from home and my mental absorption with this project!

Catton, Northumberland, April 2002

Note: For East Asian names I have followed the usual convention of putting family names first. In the case of references I have tried to follow the naming convention used in each individual publication.

Abbreviations

ABM	anti-ballistic missile
ACSA	Acquisition and Cross-Servicing Agreement
ADB	Asian Development Bank
APEC	Asia-Pacific Economic Cooperation
ARF	ASEAN Regional Forum
ASDF	Air Self-Defence Force
ASEAN	Association of Southeast Asian Nations
ASEAN–ISIS	ASEAN Institutes of Strategic and International Studies
ASEM	Asia–Europe Meeting
BMD	Ballistic Missile Defence
CASS	Chinese Academy of Social Sciences
CCP	Chinese Communist Party
CEP	circular error probable
CIIS	China Institute of International Studies (*Zhongguo Guoji Wenti Yanjiusuo*)
CNOOC	China National Offshore Oil Corporation
CNPC	China National Petroleum Corporation
COCOM	Coordinating Committee (on export controls)
CSCAP	Council for Security Cooperation in Asia-Pacific
CSIS	Center for Strategic and International Studies
CTBT	Comprehensive Test Ban Treaty
CWC	Chemical Weapons Convention
DPJ	Democratic Party of Japan
DPRK	Democratic People's Republic of Korea
EASI	East Asia Strategy Initiative
EASR	East Asian Strategy Report
ECAFE	UN Economic Commission for Asia and the Far East
EEZ	exclusive economic zone
EU	European Union
FDI	foreign direct investment
FY	fiscal year (1 April to 31 March of the following year)
GITIC	Guangdong International Trust and Investment Corporation
GDP	gross domestic product

GNP	gross national product
GSDF	Ground Self-Defence Force
ICBM	intercontinental ballistic missile
IDA	International Development Association
IFANS	Institute of Foreign Affairs and National Security
IMB	International Maritime Bureau
IMET	International Military Education and Training
IMF	International Monetary Fund
JCIE	Japan Centre for International Exchange
JETRO	Japan Export Trade Organization
JICA	Japan International Cooperation Agency
JIIA	Japan Institute of International Affairs (*Kokusai Mondai Kenkyusho*)
JSP	Japan Socialist Party (since 1991 Social Democratic Party of Japan, while retaining its Japanese name *Nippon shakaito*, which was changed to *Shakai Minshuto* in 1996)
KEDO	Korean Peninsula Energy Development Organization
LDP	Liberal Democratic Party
LNG	Liquified Natural Gas
LSE	London School of Politics and Economics
LWR	Light–Water Reactor
MFN	most-favoured nation
MIRV	multiple independently targetable re-entry vehicle
MITI	Ministry of Trade and Industry, Tokyo
MOF	Ministry of Finance
MOFA	Ministry of Foreign Affairs (Japan)
MPLA	Maritime People's Liberation Army
MSA	Maritime Safety Agency
MSDF	Maritime Self-Defence Force
MTCR	Missile Technology Control Regime
NATO	North Atlantic Treaty Organization
NDPO	National Defence Programme Outline
NEACD	Northeast Asia Cooperation Dialogue
NIC	National Intelligence Council
NIDS	National Institute for Defence Studies
NIO	New International Order
NMD	National Missile Defence
NPA	National Police Agency
NPCSD	North Pacific Cooperative Security Dialogue
NPO	non-profit organization
NPT	Nuclear Non-Proliferation Treaty
NSC	New Security Concept
NTWD	Navy Theater Wide missile defence
ODA	Official Development Assistance
PECC	Pacific Economic Cooperation Council

PKO	Peacekeeping Operations
PLA	People's Liberation Army
PMO	Prime Minister's Office
PPP	Purchasing Power Parity
PRC	People's Republic of China
RimPac	Rim of the Pacific (naval exercise)
RIPS	Research Institute for Peace and Security, Tokyo
ROC	Republic of China (Taiwan)
ROK	Republic of Korea
SALT	Strategic Arms Limitation Treaty
SDF	Self-Defence Forces
SDI	Strategic Defence Initiative
SDPJ	Social Democratic Party of Japan
SLOC	sea lanes of communication
SLORC	State Law and Order Restoration Council
SSPC	Sinopec Star Petroleum Corporation
TMD	Theatre Missile Defence
UN	United Nations
US	United States
UNCLOS	United Nations Convention on the Law of the Sea
UNTAC	United Nations Transitional Authority in Cambodia
WESTPAC	West Pacific
WPNS	Western Pacific Naval Symposium
WTO	World Trade Organization

Introduction

The Japanese–Chinese security relationship is one of the most important variables in the formation of a new strategic environment in the Asia-Pacific region which has not only regional but also global implications. The management of China's rise to great-power status by Japan will be of crucial importance for regional and global stability and for access to the most populous market of the future. The outcome will have an important bearing on whether and how the international system can accept a new great power that is advancing and developing as fast as China, but which is also beset with many domestic and foreign policy problems.[1] Referring to the similar situation of the US in facing China, Alastair Iain Johnston and Robert S. Ross described this challenge as 'how to respond to a rising power in a manner consistent with both their countries' short-term parochial national interests and their instrumental and/or normative interest in global order, particularly the absence of great power war'.[2]

As the second largest economic world power, Japan's influence on China's rise to great-power status and on contributing to an outcome which is benign to the world system is considerable. Japan's relevance is emphasized by its geographic contiguity to China, its willingness to help China with its economic and social development for economic as well as political reasons, and its position as America's major Asian alliance partner. The Japan–US comprehensive relationship is simultaneously exerting influence on Japan's ability to influence and mediate China's rise to great-power status as well as impacting on China's most important bilateral relationship, i.e. the Sino-American relationship.

Security in the post-Cold War era

The concept of security has until now mostly been defined by realists for whom the referent is the state, whereas the content is narrowly related to military security. Particularly since the end of the Cold War, this neo-realist understanding has been increasingly challenged, and security now includes for many the survival of human collectivities (rather than just the nation-state), but also the conditions of existence, which are affected by political, economic, societal and environmental factors in addition to military factors.[3] These non-traditional conditions may not directly result in a military clash, but they may create an environment in which such a clash becomes more likely.

In this book the main referent of security is still understood to be the state, but security is taken as encompassing international and intra-state security. As we will see, a considerable part of Japanese security perception of China is formed by the impact of issues related to national identity, political legitimacy and distributive justice on China's internal stability. There is concern among many Japanese observers that the consequences of China's possible economic and social failure may constitute a more realistic threat to Japan than the likelihood of military aggression. National independence and territorial integrity are still core values of security in Japan and China, but so are the acquisition and/or protection of 'rank, respect, material possessions, and special privileges', and the question is very much, for Japan as well as China, the perception of the degree to which the other side requires national self-extension for national self-preservation.[4]

Economic strength and resilience have been included in the concept of security for a much longer time in Asia than in Europe or the US. Since the beginning of the 1980s Japan has been using the concept of comprehensive national security, and China has adopted it since its economic opening.[5] The following statements can be made about its relevance to security:

- economic strength is directly related to the power and the security of a state;
- economic well-being is part of the essential values of the state and serves as a crucial factor for the state's legitimacy and stability;
- economic means are used to achieve important ends of the state at the national as well as the international level;
- the means of securing and protecting the material resources for economic development range from economic ones to diplomatic and military ones;
- the ecological consequences of economic growth impact on the national as well as the regional/international level.

This author agrees, therefore, with the generic definition of security as provided by Alagappa: 'the protection and enhancement of values that the authoritative decisonmakers deem vital for the survival and well-being of a community'.[6]

Methodology and questions to be addressed

With this understanding of security, the book analyses the changing Japanese perception of China's security since 1989 and how it has been reacting. The year 1989 has been chosen because it is associated with a major shift in international politics, i.e. the end of the Cold War. The June 1989 Tiananmen repression provided a further break in the relationship between China and the international environment. This research includes China's military policies, but will also touch on the impact of China's economic development on issues which are considered critical for Japan's security, ranging from China's military modernization to

China's response to territorial issues (oil extraction, protection of sea lanes), the positioning of the two countries in the East Asian hierarchy (leadership competition), ecological issues and China's domestic stability. While the focus is on Japanese perceptions (and the resulting policies) because of my expertise and language abilities, I have tried to contrast these perceptions with those held by their Chinese counterparts.

Japan, like any other concerned state, has to deal with its own perception of what China is now and may become in the future, as well as with China's projection of itself. The formation of these perceptions on both sides is influenced by many variables, including historical experience, tactical considerations and domestic politics. China's impact on regional security is still based less on its comprehensive national power (in terms of actual economic and military capabilities) than on how its leadership manipulates the perception by outside powers of its size, geographic location, resources and potential economic and military power, as well as intentions to mobilize these resources. The message which is coming across indicates that China wants to overcome its military, economic and social backwardness, maintain its mixture of socialism and free-market economy, achieve territorial integrity (reunification with Taiwan, realization of territorial claims), and play a regional and global role commensurate with what it considers its rightful historical place, from which it was pushed by colonialism and Western aggression. Some of these revisionist goals and their mode of implementation are rather vague, and they are backed up by an old-fashioned Realism, which has led some outside observers to speak of a 'China threat'. For Japan, these revisionist goals raise fundamental issues of Japan's own future role and position in Asia.

In order to influence China so that it realizes its goals in a peaceful way – despite the country's territorial and ideological revisionism, and despite its difficulties in reconciling its rapid economic growth with a stable domestic political situation and environmental sustainability – Japan has chosen a policy of engagement which is based on providing China with economic and political incentives, hedged by military balancing through its own military force and the military alliance with the US. This author is therefore rejecting structural realism as an explanation for Japan's policy towards China, as well as the assertion that Japan has accepted 'all the assumptions of realism but applied them purely in the economic realm'.[7] Instead, it is argued that Japan has moved from publicly downplaying the military component of its China policy and exhibiting an inclination to accommodation and deference to China on many bilateral issues, towards a position where military as well as economic China policies are increasingly linked to expectations of Chinese policy that are in line with Japanese national interests and internationally accepted rules.

China's territorial and ideological revisionism raises the challenge for Japan (and other involved countries) of how to prevent a situation where many Chinese policies which seemingly respond positively to engagement are merely a temporary or tactical accommodation, which aims to extract maximum benefit from the economic support strategy of powers like Japan, until China feels strong enough to secure its objectives in a way which is less compatible with maintaining a peaceful and stable world. In addition, there is concern that even successful economic modernization of China may fragment its social fabric and/or destroy the environment to such an extent that destabilization of this huge country threatens the security of neighbouring countries by way of refugee streams, cross-border crime and transboundary pollution.

Engagement is often one-sidedly associated with the Liberal school of international relations, which does not do justice to the complex nature of what engagement actually entails. This author proposes a dynamic model of engagement which is based on elements of Realism, Liberalism and Constructivism. While the first and second elements explain Japan's power balancing (based on its bilateral military deterrent with the US) and its economic policies (notably its huge official development assistance (ODA) programme for China), the latter is helpful in explaining why Japan is not, for example, fully using its military, political and economic power resources towards China, often showing deference in its relationship with China. The model is a dynamic one because a close examination of the policies based on the three theories reveals that there are inherent constructive as well as destructive dynamics in addition to those created by the regional/international environment. The fundamental questions raised in this book are therefore what kind of engagement Japan is pursuing with China, and how feasible and sustainable it is. Based on this investigation of a dynamic model of interaction, it is possible to develop several scenarios of the future of Japanese–Chinese security relations and propose some policy recommendations.

The book analyses Japan's engagement policy towards China on the bilateral level (Japan–China), the alliance level (Japan–US), and the multilateral level (e.g. Association of Southeast Asian Nations Regional Forum). The Japanese–American comprehensive alliance is shaping Japan's security relationship with China, and at the same time this alliance is being shaped by that relationship. Both Japan and the US profess to pursue an engagement policy towards China, and they rely on each other to do so to varying degrees. A central question pursued in this book is the impact of Japan–US asymmetries in power, interests and policy tools, as well as of differences in their domestic environment, on their engagement policy. Are these interests and policy tools compatible, and, if so, are they adequate?

Japan's regional and multilateral engagement of China has not yet been well documented in the literature because of its short history. It is, however, important to ask to what degree Japan is supplementing its bilateral and alliance approaches to China's security challenges with multilateral approaches, and what the conditions shaping them are. The outcome is not only highly relevant to the professed goal of making China a shareholder in a peaceful and open world system, and of providing a mechanism for checks and balances as well as addressing transnational problems such as environmental degradation, but it will also be a crucial test for the future of multilateralism since multilateralism may not survive if China does not embrace it.

The complex nature of engagement policy

The misunderstanding of the policy of engagement gives rise to considerable confusion because it obfuscates the Realist elements of engagement, i.e. the role of force to effect balancing and hedging. In order to propose remedies to perceived deficiencies of engagement, qualifying adjectives to 'engagement', or even the coinage of new words, have been proposed which make an appropriate understanding of engagement policy even more difficult. Definitions range from unconditional engagement, conditional engagement, comprehensive or constructive engagement, robust engagement, congagement, coercive engagement, to constrainment.[8] The resulting definatory maze cannot fail to make the pursuit of engagement difficult at a national level, let alone in tandem with another country. In fact engagement relies as much on Realist foundations, with their deterrence and balance-of-power elements, as on Liberal foundations, which stress the positive forces of increasing international economic interdependence and integration, the spreading of international norms, the establishment of rules and institutions to regulate and enable peaceful cooperation between nations.

The power-balancing and deterrence elements in engagement policy follow the Realist teaching that war can be avoided if there is a stable power balance, but that the shift of power relations (which China drives forward through its economic and military strengthening) is particularly dangerous for the maintenance of peace. The systemic issues for hegemonic stability are how to maintain such stability and how to accommodate change. Realists will point out that multipolar systems like those in Asia are less stable than unipolar systems. The situation in Asia has been depicted as a five-power balance-of-power system, as 'ripe for rivalry', and as heading for instability.[9]

The following definition of engagement by Alastair Iain Johnston and Robert S. Ross probably describes best the dualistic character of this policy: 'The use of non-coercive methods to ameliorate the non-status-quo elements of a rising power's behaviour. The goal is to ensure that this growing power is used in ways that are consistent with peaceful change in regional and global order'. The authors explicitly state that amelioration of the rising power's behaviour does not seek to limit, constrain or delay the newcomer's power, nor to prevent the development of influence commensurate with its greater power.[10] They attach four conditions that will make a policy of engagement effective:

1   the new rising power has only limited revisionist aims and there are no irreconcilable conflicts of interests with the established powers;
2   the established powers are strong enough to mix concessions with credible threats, i.e. a sticks and carrots policy;
3   engagement is a complement and not an alternative to balancing;
4   the established powers must live by the same principles they demand of the new rising power[11]

When we look carefully at this statement it becomes clear that, for the rising power, 'coercive means' must still be considered in its calculation of the established powers despite their goal of the non-use of 'coercive methods'. Not only is this related to the established powers' Realist objectives (i.e. balancing and hedging) *vis-à-vis* conceivable intentions of a rising power, but it is also, in the first instance, due to the simple fact that all the established powers, including Japan, maintain considerable military forces and are involved in military alliances to cater for a whole range of challenges to their security. The crucial issue for a correct understanding of Japan's engagement policy (and this would apply to the engagement policy of any other country) is to clarify the emphasis and the robustness with which some rather than other goals associated with engagement are pursued, as well as the mix of policy tools used; one needs to consider issues such as no unilateral use of offensive military force, peaceful resolution of territorial disputes, respect for national sovereignty, transparency of military forces, cooperative solutions for transnational problems or respect for basic human rights.[12]

Restraint and deference

Theories of Realism and Liberalism are not sufficient to explain human behaviour, including state actions, which are fundamentally shaped by socially shared understandings of the world. The Constructivist school of international relations addresses these understandings, which 'alternatively can be called cultures, mentalités or discourses' and which 'are not simply reflections of an objective material reality, but rather emerge out of communicative and social processes, socialization, debate and sometimes coercion'.[13]

As we will see in the following chapters, one prominent feature of Japan's China policy (but also of policies towards other countries) which is difficult to explain purely in terms of Realism or Liberalism is Japan's restraint in exercising its considerable power in interest conflicts with China. Instead, Japan has often reacted to China with what may be called deference or restraint, although it has had the upper hand in terms of power and/or although resisting would not have involved much political cost. Of course any economically, politically or militarily strong state encounters limits to its ability to deploy economic, political or military power. The amount of power necessary to achieve the intended goal may surpass the available power resource, or there may be insufficient domestic support (e.g. competing demands, fear of counterproductive results, a low level of interest, etc.). However, there are cases in Japan's China policy which are beyond obvious or straightforward power calculations and which are better explained from a Constructivist perspective. While some authors already speak of a strategic Japanese–Chinese rivalry, Japan often seems to be waging this rivalry in a very restrained way, whereas China maximizes its relatively inferior power resources.

To explain this Japanese inclination to deference and restraint in the bilateral relationship with China, Constructivist approaches seem to be particularly useful. Constructivist scholars have notably investigated those norms and behaviours which account for Japan's post-war pacifism, which is one source of

Japanese deference and restraint.[14] There are, however, other sources as well which are either China-specific or not (e.g. cultural affinity, war guilt and a general tendency towards conflict avoidance), and which often reinforce each other (war guilt, pacifism, the sympathy of the Japanese Left for Chinese Communism). As a specialist of Chinese history Yokoyama Hiroshi refers to China's demand for 'kowtow diplomacy' (*dogeza gaiko*) from Japan, which reinforces Japan's deferential inclinations.[15]

As the following chapters will show, deferential and restrained behaviour can be found across the whole spectrum of the Japanese–Chinese relationship, ranging from even officially avoiding the use of the word 'engagement' because of some negative connotations for the Chinese (e.g. changing the nature of China's regime; Japanese–American security alliance) to granting China ODA in accordance with Beijing's five-year economic plan rather than Japan's own regulations, which allow ODA planning only for one year. Deferential behaviour towards another country occurs in many bilateral relationships, but the point to be made in this book is that in the case of Japanese–Chinese relations the frequency of such behaviour is particularly obvious and enduring, despite power asymmetries in Japan's favour.

The dynamics of engagement

These approaches to the analysis of engagement inspired by Realism, Liberalism and Constructivism alone would not explain the shift in Japan's China policy towards greater emphasis on Realist principles (in reaction to, for example, Chinese military modernization or intrusions into Japan's Exclusive Economic Zone (EEZ)); one must also analyse the dynamics which are set free by the various engagement policies. These dynamics are created by the interaction between the engagement policies and China's perceptions and discourses, as well as by tensions inherent in the different approaches to engagement.

First, we have to consider the impact of Realist approaches on China. China's perceptions and discourses are shaped by its historical experience, political and economic system, tactical calculations, ideology and national goals. Three features need particular mention and will be elaborated in greater detail in the following chapters. One is the deeply engrained foreign-policy Realism of the political leadership, which inclines to a strong belief in power balancing, foreign and security policy being a zero-sum game, and a historical determinism that assumes that economic power leads to military power. A second feature is the deep distrust of Japan, shared by a majority of Chinese, because of Tokyo's past aggression against China and its unwillingness to come to terms with it. A third feature is the ability of the small and relatively coherent political leadership to develop and implement foreign policies in a much more consistent way than an open democratic political system can, allowing the optimum use of even small tactical advantages or ploys. Against this background, the Realist element of engagement may ultimately encourage and facilitate the more aggressive impulses of China, rather than balance or restrain them.[16] This could therefore enhance the risk of miscalculation leading to military confrontation which is inherent in military power balancing.

Second, the Liberal element of engagement also has negative dynamics. China is benefiting hugely from the liberal-institutional element of engagement (i.e. ODA, trade, technology transfer) because it helps to enhance its national power. But this element also has the potential to produce negative dynamics working against the prospect of a stable and peaceful future China.

The liberal-institutional element of engagement has a sting for China's leaders because it is regarded 'as a means for the West to bring about a peaceful transformation of China's international and domestic behaviour in accordance with rules and norms set by the West and endangers Chinese regime stability' (socialization).[17] Chinese leaders particularly dislike Western insistence on values like human rights and national self-determination (e.g. for Taiwan or Tibet). The negative reaction of these leaders to this 'socialization approach' could potentially reinforce their Realist inclinations towards international relations. Moreover, China's economic strengthening is not just creating a dynamic force which in time may change its political system and make it a peaceful player, but, at least in the medium term, it is creating one that allows the current leadership to strengthen the country's military potential, which may in the long run construct a less peaceful mentality.[18] There is therefore some tension between the 'socialization' approach and the 'economic interdependence' approach (through trade, ODA, foreign direct investment (FDI)), although they have many complementarities.

Japan is more inclined to follow the 'economic interdependence' approach (in contrast to the US, with a greater emphasis on 'socialization' leading to the acceptance of Western values) because of its economic advantage, its civilian power mentality and the fact that it shares Chinese feelings about traditional norms/Western superiority. This can only further complicate alliance relations with the US. While China prefers the 'economic interdependence' approach because of its pragmatic agenda, it resents Japanese leadership and continuous economic superiority. At the same time, a successful 'economic interdependence' approach may give Japan a considerable future economic competitor, and perhaps also a strategic one. There is also the risk of political and economic destabilization, particularly during democratization and economic development, as a result of fostering economic interdependence. For this reason we will have to investigate the impact of new security issues like environmental degradation, transboundary crime and migration on Japanese–Chinese security relations.

Liberal-institutional approaches in the multilateral sphere can give China unfair advantages. China's tactical adoption of multilateralism (rather than normative adoption) would create a 'time spanner': China attempts, for example, to exclude issues from multilateral fora which it dislikes. In the case of the ARF, membership allows China to influence the agenda and to prevent, for example, the progress of deliberations on preventive diplomacy and to address its territorial demands in the South China Sea in a multilateral forum. Although China may in the end have to compromise on some issues, its initial obstructionist position may help it to gain valuable time so as later to be in a more powerful position. One has also to consider that the growing forces of Liberalism in Asia suffered a certain setback in 1997 due to the East Asian economic crisis, which has weakened Japan's economic role in the region, destabilized several regimes in the region and shown the Association of Southeast Asian Nations' (ASEAN) ineffectiveness in the face of conflict (e.g. East Timor) and in driving forward political and economic integration.

Third, Japan's deference also may set free negative dynamics. These attitudes may encourage China to push its interests even more strongly. Also, China's actions may gradually reduce or even destroy the normative foundations on which Japanese accommodation and deference stand. This can be argued, for example, with regard to Japan's astonishing reconfirmation (the Chinese speak of expansion) of the Japanese–American security relationship in 1996 and the revision of the guidelines for Japanese–American security cooperation in 1999 as regards Japan's pacifism. Ultimately it may lead to Japan becoming a military power commensurate with its economic power, including nuclear power, particularly if the country perceives the US security guarantee as no longer reliable. On the other hand, the difficulty involved in such an extreme change may instead lead to Japan accepting Chinese hegemony in Asia.

Dynamics arising from the alliance and triangular relations

Other negative dynamics result from the interaction between the Realist approach, on the one hand, and the Japan–US alliance and Japan–China–US triangular relations, on the other. The Realist policies of balancing and hedging are driven as well as checked by what are referred to as the two kinds of fears inherent in the 'alliance game': abandonment and entrapment.[19]

Whereas until the end of the Cold War Japan's main fear was entrapment, with the Korean War and the Vietnam War being the most critical events, Japan is now facing both entrapment and abandonment. The Revisionists in the US argue that the end of the Cold War make the Japanese–American security treaty redundant, while a virtual coalition of leftists and rightists in Japan might welcome such an outcome. The sudden reversal of US China policy under President Nixon in 1972 was a minor form of abandonment by an ally and is still very much on the mind of Japanese decision-makers and analysts. Fears of abandonment were also raised by certain pro-China actions and statements during the Clinton administration.

In order to counteract the uncertainties of the post-Cold War era (particularly in view of the uncertainties about China's future path) Japan deepened the military alliance in 1996 and 1999, as mentioned before. These moves, as well as a greater assertiveness of American unipolar power, dashed China's hope of a more multipolar world, which would have eased its own emergence as a new rising power. China became particularly upset about the intentional ambiguity in the 1999 revised guidelines concerning their applicability to Taiwan, which touches on China's greatest security interest. If, despite considerable financial, technical and political concerns, Japan and the US go ahead on Theatre Missile Defence (TMD), it will propel Japanese–American military cooperation to a much higher level in order to deal with the real-time requirements of a missile defence system. In view of China's animosity to TMD and closer Japan–US cooperation in general, the consequences of Japan's fear of abandonment would set free even greater dynamics, propelling China to increase its military power and take an even more hostile attitude towards Japan. On the other hand, given the deep contradictions between the US and China over Taiwan (but not between Japan and China!), which may possibly degenerate into 'irreconcilable conflicts of interests' as mentioned in the first condition for engagement, Japan's fear of entrapment may cause it to be more accommodating to China, with all the possible negative consequences for the viability of the Japan–US relationship.

These dynamics arising from the abandonment–entrapment dilemma must also be linked to those inherent in the complexities of triangular Japan–US–China relations, i.e. three sets of relations – that is, between Japan and China, between China and the US and between Japan and the US. In theory there is always the possibility that two may gang up against the third and that the third may play the two others against each other.[20] Another possibility is for one power to engage in offshore balancing or to act as a balancer of last resort; this finds favour not only with some traditional Realists, like Richard Holbrooke and Christopher Layne[21], but also with a Revisionist like Chalmers Johnson. Looking at the Japanese–Chinese–American triangular relationship, we have to state that it is most certainly not an equilateral triangle, as it is not a three-way strategic partnership or a big-power condominium.[22] Two of the countries (Japan and the US) have a relationship with each other which cannot be rivalled by China's relationship with either the US or Japan. There is therefore an inherent and an a priori two-against-one triangular relationship. The challenge for China is to find out the degree of shared Japan–US concern about China and how far Japan and the US can work together on meeting the perceived challenge from China, and to weaken such a common front. It is therefore not surprising that China exploits, for example, the US's difficulty in '[sending] consistent and coherent signals' to China, trying to play one against the other.[23] China has only to play on Japan's fears of entrapment. Under these circumstances, it is not, for example, in China's interest to give the appearance that it could be convinced that a strengthened Japanese–American security alliance is not directed against it. As we will see later, however, the dynamics involved in the three sets of relationship go beyond any single option of the game-theory approach to triangular relations. The interdependence of all three actors has gone very deep and is recognized by all.[24]

Summary of chapters

Chapter 1 is a short historical overview of Japanese–Chinese security relations from 1945 to the 1989 Tiananmen massacre. It describes the move from containment of China to the beginning of Japan's engagement after the normalization of diplomatic relations in 1972. After an exploration of Japan's place in China's post-Cold War foreign and security policy, Chapter 2 analyses the changes in Japanese security perceptions of China against the rise of traditional and non-traditional security challenges from China, ranging from territorial disputes in the East China Sea to increasing illegal immigration from China. Chapter 3 details the various elements of Japan's engagement, with an emphasis on the strengthening of Japanese–US military cooperation since around 1995. It also contains a description of Japan's bilateral and multilateral efforts to engage China politically, at official and non-governmental level. In Chapter 4 I look in more detail at various dynamics resulting from Japan's economic enmeshment and its cooperation with the US.

1 Japanese–Chinese relations under Cold War conditions

Introduction

This chapter describes the setting for Japan's post-war security relationship with China against the background of its overall security policy, which has been dominated by the dichotomy between its post-war pacifism and the comprehensive alliance with the US.[1] It allowed Japan to engage China through economic interaction, particularly once China opened itself up to the outside at the end of the 1970s. This led to a flourishing economic relationship, while Japanese development assistance greatly contributed to China's modernization. China, however, never lost sight of Japan's close military relationship with the US and its growing defence potential, although the impact of these on its policy towards Japan fluctuated. Moreover, Japan's past aggression against China and its inability to come to terms with it in a more convincing way bedevilled the Japan–China security relationship beyond the confrontation brought on by the Cold War era.

An overview of Japanese–Chinese history

History plays an important role in the bilateral Japanese–Chinese relationship and has an enduring impact on the perceptions, policies and future outlook of both sides. Historical experience shapes identities, but it is also instrumentalized for pressure on the other side. Depending on the prevailing political situation at a given time, Japan and China have found reasons for optimism or pessimism about their relationship.

Geographic contiguity has encouraged links between Japan and China since ancient times and allowed Japan to benefit from China's advanced civilization and culture in order to develop its own. This closeness and China's geographic size (it is twenty-five times larger than Japan) have never (except during the failed Mongol invasion attempts in the thirteenth century) constituted a threat to Japan. For hundreds of years until the last century the Chinese considered Japan a tributary state. While the Japanese rulers did not quite accept this claim, they went along with it because they realised how much they could learn and benefit from accommodating China, which had no expansionist desires. Relations had phases of lesser intensity, notably during Japan's period of seclusion between 1600 and 1867, but trade, cultural exchanges and political contacts were never totally interrupted.

The security aspect of the bilateral relationship changed dramatically after Japan was forced by Western powers to open up to the outside and to modernize according to Western models. Japan observed Western aggression against China and the failure of China's policy of isolation to provide an adequate response. The Chinese failure to modernize and to develop what the Western powers considered to be normal relations with the outside world made it an easy victim of Western imperialism. The Meiji leaders were concerned that they might be next if their country did not modernize quickly. Another conclusion from China's experience, however, had very negative consequences for Japan's relationship with China: China's weakness was perceived as a threat to Japan's security, and its leaders decided to react with their own version of belated imperialism. It is worthwhile remembering this concern about Chinese weakness, because today some Japanese are more, or at least as much, concerned about the security implications of a possible failure of China's economic modernization programme as they are about China becoming a military threat.

At the end of the nineteenth century China's perceived weakness led to Japanese designs over Korea, which was still under Chinese suzerainty and which the Japanese rulers considered in strategic terms as a 'dagger pointing at Japan's heart'. To forestall any threat to its 'line of interest' (as Yamagata Aritomo formulated it in 1890) on the Asian continent, which included the Korean peninsula, Japan clashed with China over Korea in 1894 and achieved its first victory in its imperialist expansion. Despite Chinese resentment of Japan, after the war the victor became a role model for China's adaptation to the modern Western world, and many Chinese students went to Japan to learn about the West through Japanese textbooks and Japanese eyes. But Japan's military expansion had only just begun and it gradually consolidated its control over the Korean peninsula after defeating Russia in 1905. China became the main victim, losing control over not only Korea but also Taiwan. In 1931 the Manchurian incident led to further Japanese encroachments in China; the following year saw the establishment of the puppet state Manchukuo; and the Marco Polo Bridge incident in 1937 opened the way to an all-out war against China, which ended only in 1945 with Japan's surrender to the Allied forces.

After Japan's defeat in 1945, the security issue in Japanese–Chinese relations stayed in the background until the end of the US–Soviet confrontation because of Japan's protection by the Japanese–American security alliance, the weakness of China and the promising emerging economic relationship with its giant neighbour, notably since the opening in 1978. In 1945 Japan was occupied by the Allied forces under American leadership. These forces incidentally included troops from the Guomindang regime, which was then still ruling China. The Guomindang had to withdraw to Taiwan and some adjacent islands in 1949 when the Chinese Communists won victory in the civil war. The US forced Japan to recognize the Guomindang regime, which established the Republic of

China (ROC) on Taiwan. Yoshida Shigeru, then prime minister of Japan, was no friend of the Chinese Communists, but he knew that Japan's larger economic interest had traditionally always been on the mainland and he would have preferred not to make any decision at that point on which Chinese government to recognize. Before the war, trade with China had accounted for more than 25 per cent of total Japanese foreign trade. Following its surrender in 1945, Japan became totally dependent on the US as a market and source of imports. Strangely reminiscent of Japan's contemporary strategy of engagement towards the People's Republic of China (PRC) is what Yoshida Shigeru told the US, that Japanese businessmen, as a result of their experience with the Chinese, would be the 'best fifth column for the democracies against the Chinese Communists'.[2] He even suggested that the US to act as a mediator through direct Japanese–Chinese negotiations to dissuade China from accepting 'domination by the Soviet Politburo'.[3] Moreover, Yoshida held the view that in the long term Communism in China stood no chance against deeply embedded elements of Chinese culture.

Against a background of growing anti-Communism in the US and China's intervention against the United Nations (UN) in the Korean War, Japan stood no chance of prevailing and on 28 April 1952 Japan signed a peace treaty with the Guomindang. The only concession Yoshida was able to extract consisted in restricting the effectiveness of the treaty to those areas of China actually under the control of the ROC at the time of its conclusion. In a letter of 24 December 1951 to John Foster Dulles, the special representative of President Truman for the conclusion of a peace treaty with Japan, Yoshida Shigeru justified the recognition of the ROC by referring to the UN condemnation of the Chinese Communists as aggressors in the Korean War, as well as to Japanese obligations to support UN actions. He also mentioned the Sino-Soviet Treaty of Friendship and Alliance of January 1950 and Chinese support of the Japan Communist Party as grounds for rejecting a bilateral peace treaty with Beijing.[4]

Until 1972 Japan thus recognized only the Guomindang regime on Taiwan and closely followed the US in its relationship with the People's Republic of China (PRC). Japan was able to revive its economic relationship with the Chinese mainland, but only under difficult political circumstances, which arose from its alliance with the US and China's policy of using economic incentives to separate Japan from the US and extract political concessions from Japan. However, before dealing with the more recent post-war history of Japanese–Chinese security relations we have to assess the impact of two important and interlinked factors in this security relationship: the role of the past and the Japanese–American security relationship.

The role of the past

Japan's past aggression against China and its inability to deal with it in a way considered appropriate by China (but also by other Asian countries) has influenced the bilateral security relationship up to the present day. From a

Constructivist perspective, the discourse of the Japanese on China and that of the Chinese on Japan is clearly shaped by their shared historical experience. The brutal Japanese war campaigns, massacres like that of Nanjing in 1937 and forced Chinese labour left deep scars in China's historical memory which impact on Japan.[5] There are still many current policy issues which force both countries to deal concretely with the legacy of this period. These issues include warped perceptions of past misdeeds held by many Japanese. This is regularly demonstrated by so-called 'slips of tongue' by conservative politicians; newly published textbooks with biased historical accounts; visits by government ministers to the Yasukuni war memorial shrine; the disposal of chemical weapon munitions left by Japan in China, which started only in 1999; and the fate of Japan's former colony Taiwan, which is still not settled (on Taiwan, see Chapter 2).[6] The past makes it difficult for many Chinese to recognize the fundamental changes which have taken place in post-1945 Japan and to trust Japan's intentions. This distrust is a logical reflection of the trauma inflicted upon China, but for China it is often also a convenient tool in the battle of national interests and sustaining the power of the Communist regime. Without knowing about China's perception of the past, it is even more difficult to understand its contemporary suspicion about Japan's Taiwan policy or its resistance to Japan's involvement in the US-promoted TMD (which is analysed in Chapter 3).

Japan's inability properly to acknowledge the historical facts (*rekishi ninshiki*) and apologize to China in a way recognized by China as convincing is casting a shadow over the overall relationship, and it particularly affects the security relationship, which is singularly sensitive to perceptions of intentions and to manipulations of these perceptions. At the most basic level, many Chinese fear that an unrepentant Japan is bound to repeat its past aggression, echoing the widespread historical deterministic idea of many Chinese that a country that does not acknowledge past misdeeds 'correctly' is bound to repeat them. The Japanese–American security alliance is, depending on China's mood, considered a smokescreen, or at least a crumbling wall, behind which Japan may transform its huge economic power to become a future military superpower with ill intentions towards China.

There are many circumstances on both sides which make reconciliation over this historical legacy very difficult. At a structural level, reconciliation is complex between countries with very different political systems (democratic versus authoritarian regimes), and this inhibits the ability of both to address the issue because of a failure to grant full legitimacy to the other system (for example an absence of normal diplomatic relations) and the delay in developing common interests. This difference also became apparent in the much earlier reconciliation of Germany with Western countries than was the case with countries under Communist rule in Eastern Europe.[7] The alliance with the US has only reinforced this structural problem. The US, as Japan's former enemy and victim of aggression, absolved Japan from guilt to a much greater extent than was the case between Germany and the Allied powers. American anti-Communism and anti-China deterrence objectives led to Japan's insulation from China and other

Asian countries directly after Japan's defeat in 1945. China's legitimate grievances are also undermined by the features of its repressive Communist regime, which include distortion of historical facts in its own textbooks and the huge human sacrifices of its domestic policies over the last fifty years. Finally, the Japanese political system is rather inward-looking and parochial, encountering deep problems of perception when it comes to foreign views and sensitivities.

Other inhibiting factors are of a more direct psychological character. There is a Japanese propensity to avoid conflict which is much stronger than we find in most Western societies and which prevents the Japanese from tackling such a contentious issue as the recognition of the past, and this goes far beyond the humiliating or at least hurtful process this would engender. Japanese leaders are concerned that a critical and honest approach to their country's history in school textbooks may alienate children from their country and harm social cohesion at all societal levels. Only strong political and moral leadership could overcome these attitudes and inclinations, but Japan's cultural make-up is also known for a lack of strong leadership, and the attitudes are too much shared by these leaders. There is also the general phenomenon that the memory of the victim is much better than that of the victimizer. The victimizer also has a preference 'to look ahead', which meant, in Japan's case, concentrating on economic relations and benefits with its former victims. This was encouraged by China in 1972 when it waved demands for reparations and instead accepted Japan's economic development aid because it wanted to rehabilitate its economy and win sympathy with the Japanese public, in the same way as Taiwan's president Jiang Jieshi had done in 1952. Faced with much less developed Asian neighbours, its rapid economic rehabilitation provided Japan with ample means to insist on such an approach. The growing Japanese self-confidence and nationalism which resulted from its economic success, and the failure of the war generation to pass on knowledge of the past to the younger generation compound the relationship further, since the younger generation now shows an astonishing degree of insensitivity and ignorance about the past, and as a result it is very frustrated and annoyed by China's insistence on issues of the past. Unrepentant old diehards in high political office regularly make insensitive remarks which reopen the issue. All this has made it very difficult for Japan to utter an acceptable apology to its former victims. When the government tries to do so the issue tends to become so politically contentious that it almost cancels out the original good intention.[8] The emperor's apology on his first visit to China in 1992 said at least as much about Japan's unwillingness to come to terms with the past as it did about a new beginning.[9]

Other circumstances based on Japan's domestic political system further reinforce psychological and structural resistances to addressing the past in a more satisfying way. In addition to the lack of political leadership already mentioned, there is the Japanese government's rigid legalistic approach to issues of compensation, which precludes generosity. For example, the government was reluctant to offer official compensation to former forced war prostitutes for fear of reopening the reparation issue. According to the official version, the conclusion of agreements on reparations

– or, in the case of China, Beijing's waver of reparation claims in 1972 – had closed the door to them.

But the Chinese side is just as guilty of making it more difficult for Japan to cope appropriately with its historical legacy. It has been easy and beneficial for the authoritarian and economically less developed regime to manipulate Japan's guilt to advance its economic interests and enhance its increasingly shaky political legitimacy. This explains to a large extent why President Jiang Zemin, apart from personal reasons, considerably damaged the outcome of his state visit to Japan in November 1998 by constantly harping on the issue of the past.[10] But playing the 'history card' and increasing over time the official number of victims of Japan's aggression only further reduces the legitimacy of China's grievances in the eyes of an increasingly self-confident Japan.

As we will see in the next chapters, it is often difficult to know whether the Chinese side raises the past in the context of security problems for reasons of opportunism ('historical card') and in order to keep Japan in an inferior position, or because it truly believes that the Japanese will repeat their aggression, or at least that constant reminders are essential to prevent this while China is militarily still weak.[11] It is obvious that Chinese attacks on Japan over historical issues are also intended to weaken the degree of Japanese–American security cooperation. Other factors are a feeling of rivalry with Japan and a sour reaction to the fact that Japan is not only more advanced than the 'culturally superior China', but also economically dominating it. One can assume overlapping policy constituencies which favour either one or several of these opinions-cum-tactics. However, even Japanese observers favourably inclined towards China question whether China appreciates the damage the 'historical card' is doing to Chinese public opinion towards Japan.[12] Over the years the Japanese have become increasingly resentful of how the Chinese regime can manipulate public outcry at home over yet another slip of the tongue by a Japanese politician or yet another alleged falsification of historical facts in Japanese textbooks.[13] While the excesses of the Cultural Revolution did not have a lasting absolving impact on Japan's feelings of war guilt, the repression in Tiananmen Square in 1989 did speed up the process by reducing the legitimacy of the Chinese regime in Japan's eyes.[14]

In the 1990s the Chinese leadership also lost an important ally in the Japanese political system. The legacy of the past had been kept alive by leftist forces in Japan, who instrumentalized it to sustain the country's post-1945 pacifism, opposing consecutive Conservative cabinets with their US-oriented foreign and security policy.[15] The irony is that this pacifism would not have lasted so long without the comfort provided by the US security guarantee, as invoked during the Korean War when the US intervened to protect Japan. The main political force for Japan's pacifism had for a long time been the Japan Socialist Party, until it lost much of its vigour in the 1990s. The PRC could always rely on these opposition forces to put pressure on the Japanese government. But China contributed to their disappearance by increasingly abandoning its revolutionary appeal in favour of more pragmatic policies, and later in the 1990s it pursued security policies towards Japan which severely tested their pro-China feelings.

Deference to China

The social processes associated with the legacy of Japan's past aggression against China also partially explain Tokyo's restraint in exercising its considerable power in conflicts of interest with China. Put simply, refraining from criticizing China (at least until China's security policies became more challenging in the 1990s) was psychologically easier than facing squarely past misdeeds during the war, but this kind of behaviour has contributed to the rise of behaviour which ranges on a continuum from politeness, restraint, procrastination, to deference to China. Additional sources of this Japanese deference range from systemic to psychological ones; they are only partly China-specific and they often reinforce each other. Individual decision-makers or policy-making constituencies may be affected by only some of these understandings, feelings and behavioural patterns, but they may reinforce other motivations which are based more on simple power calculations and reflect an objective material reality. Often these understandings not only shape individual policies (which will be examined in Chapter 3), but – in an ironic twist – have become part of the dynamics facilitating changes in Japan's perceptions and policies towards China since the beginning of the 1990s.

The main reason for this deference is the way Japan attempts to deal with its past aggression against China and with China's reactions. Japanese leaders sometimes try to compensate by showing greater deference to Chinese interests. This has often been easier for Japanese policy-makers than going through the more long-term, humiliating and painful process of squarely facing up to the legacy of the past – a process requiring leadership. China has made particular use of this situation to get concessions from Japan in all areas of the bilateral relationship, and other Asian countries have done so as well. We will see below that Japan's reluctance to join Western sanctions against China in the wake of the Tiananmen repression was officially partly justified by Japan's past record in China.

This 'historical card' would not have been so effective without the existence of a generation of policy-makers, supported by the media and public opinion, who feel a cultural indebtedness to China, as well as a cultural affinity. This belief may sometimes be reinforced by Japan longing to find its cultural mooring as an Asian country, becoming a leader of Asia based on its economic power, and/or by resistence to US aggressiveness in spreading 'Western values'. Japanese deference can also be partially explained by a culturally bound inclination towards harmony (even if only at a superficial level), which again would be reinforced by the above motivations. The Chinese tend to be more willing to risk harmony in order to show their feelings and promote their interests, particularly in a situation where they feel the other side to be historically wrong, as well as in need of remorse and 'preventive reminding'. Japanese reluctance, until recently, to challenge these behavioural patterns and perceptions has been bound to reinforce them.

The above feelings and behavioural patterns may also occasionally reinforce or rally other policy constituencies, resulting, for example, in Japan's abstention from certain criticism of China, although the main reason may lie more with genuine differences, even if of a tactical or strategic nature. Criticism of China's non-democratic system and forceful representation of its own interests *vis-à-vis* Japan has been muted by doubts in Japan about the appropriateness of Western democracy for a country with such huge potential for instability.[16] Japanese political and economic leaders believe in China becoming more agreeable to the Western world as a result of economic development, but not necessarily in a short time or thanks to the structural adjustment policies of the World Bank or as a result of the West pressuring China to adopt Western concepts of democracy. On the former, Sato Hideo points out:

> [T]he more leaders are inclined to believe in the ultimately salutary effect of economic development on political stability and international convergence, the more they are willing to take a long-term perspective and gradualist approach on different Chinese behaviours and violations of international norms and be more accommodative. This seems to be the case with Japan and less so with the US'.[17]

Deference has also found some institutional footholds in Japan. The Gaimusho (Japan's Ministry of Foreign Affairs) was, until the 1990s, mainly in charge of Japan's China policy. Only on rare occasions, like the highly politicized decision in 1972 to recognise China, have politicians been in the driver's seat. Within the Gaimusho, the China Division has been responsible for the day-to-day relationship. Led by the 'China School' diplomats (i.e. diplomats who were trained in the Chinese language), there has been a tendency for it to be particularly understanding of China, in contrast to the Soviet School, which distinguished itself by its anti-Soviet views.[18] There are about 100 diplomats who have received training in the Chinese language. Whereas the first post-war generation received such training in Taiwan, the second received it initially in Taiwan and then in the PRC; and since the third generation Chinese-language training has taken place in the PRC.[19] Another institutional feature which may sometimes have encouraged deference to Chinese interests is the fact that Japan's policies towards China are often not well coordinated, running often on separate economic, political and security tracks, which deprives individual policies of leverage and coherence.

The impact of the alliance with the US

The outcome of the Chinese civil war and Japan's total integration into the US anti-Communist strategy created a very difficult relationship between Japan and China. In 1950 China had felt forced to ally with the Soviet Union, which was perceived by the US and its allies as the greatest danger to Western security. Differences between China and the Soviet Union were noticed by Secretary of State Dean Acheson, but he had to abandon his cautious policy of trying to separate the Chinese Communists from Moscow in favour of political self-preservation after the start of the Korean War in 1950.[20] As a result, the first official meeting between representatives of Japan and the PRC took place only in April 1955, on the occasion of the Bandung Conference in Indonesia, when Zhou Enlai met with Takasaki Tatsunosuke, who represented Japan as Secretary of the Economic Planning Agency because the foreign minister, Shigemitsu Mamoru, did not want to attend.[21]

But, as Iriye Akira points out, although Japan and China were fully incorporated into their respective alliance system, their respective military power may have played a lesser role than other factors, notably economic interests on both sides.[22] Japan aligned itself with the US and its policy of containing the new Chinese Communist rulers, but took pains not to become militarily too directly involved. From a Chinese perspective, however, Japan supported the US policy of thwarting China's drive to complete the liberation of the whole country when it recognised Taiwan, whatever Yoshida's preference had been.[23] In addition, Japan allowed the continued stationing of American troops on its territory (at considerable cost to its sovereignty and domestic security consensus), which was an important condition for US forward deployment in Asia, notably against China.

The Japanese–American security treaty created a deep rift between Japan and China, and extended China's perception of Japan as an adversary. It is also true, however, that the US security umbrella allowed Japan to nurture its pacifism, and inhibited the country from seeing China as a threat despite security policies aimed at reuniting with Taiwan, expelling the US from Asia and supporting liberation struggles in the Third World. When China tested its first nuclear device in October 1964, in public the Japanese government reacted very calmly and played it down, hinting at the protection given by the US nuclear umbrella.[24] Feeling secure under the American conventional and nuclear umbrella, Japan was not overly concerned about China becoming a nuclear power in 1964.[25] This was also helped by the strong political polarization in Japan between conservatives and 'progressives', the latter having considerable sympathies with Communist China because of shared anti-American feeling. The conservative political leaders did not want to aggravate this polarization further, particularly after China's break with the Soviet Union, which gave some credence to Yoshida's thinking and to hopes about economic opportunities. Moreover, China's weakness – notably in comparison with that of the Soviet Union, the main focus of the East–West confrontation – and positive feelings towards China, nurtured by cultural links and war guilt, had a positive impact on Japan's perception of China and offset fears about security.

The Japan–US security treaty fostered an emphasis in Japanese post-war diplomacy on 'economics first', the so-called Yoshida line. When Prime Minister Yoshida travelled to Europe in 1955 he indirectly criticised the USA's confrontational approach to Asian Communism by stating in a policy paper that 'in fighting communism, political and economic strength was as important as military might, if not more so'.[26] He still believed in a long-term policy of detaching China from dependence on the Soviet Union, relying on trade relations. Naturally this position was nurtured by concrete Japanese business interests, but Yoshida also knew that without 'economics first' Japan would continue to be heavily dependent on the US. The Yoshida line, Japan's emphasis on stability and economic interests in China, would later prove to be the conceptual as well as material backbone of the strategy of engagement, once Japan had normalized relations with the PRC.

Against this background, Japan tried gradually to improve at least its commercial relations with the PRC through various kinds of agreements. Although trade resumed with China in August 1950, it was restricted by the imposition of controls by the Coordinating Committee on export controls (COCOM) which were intended to deprive China's developing economy of the benefits of Western advanced products. China cleverly exploited Japan's interest in increasing the trade flow by linking allegedly 'private' trade agreements with political demands, whereas the Japanese government hoped to insist on the separation of politics from economics (*seikei bunri*). These political demands aimed at playing the pro-China forces in Japan off against the conservative government, with the ultimate aim of making Japan switch diplomatic recognition from Taibei to Beijing. In 1962 these trade agreements moved from 'Friendly Trade' to a semi-official, long-term agreement (five years) referred to as L-T Trade, which made Japan the only country in the world to trade with both Taiwan and the PRC with considerable freedom.[27]

These negotiations for trade agreements allowed Beijing's leaders to put considerable pressure on the ruling Liberal Democratic Party (LDP) and counterbalance to some extent Japan's allegiance to the strict US line on the PRC. In the Sato–Nixon Joint Communiqué in 1969, Prime Minister Sato Eisaku went as far as declaring that the security of both Taiwan and South Korea was essential to that of Japan and that Japan would 'fulfill its obligations in regard to "the peace and security of the Far East" '.[28] This statement still haunts Japanese–Chinese relations today. On the one hand, it is natural that war over Taiwan would affect Japan's security since its lines of communication pass over the island, it has considerable commercial interest in Taiwan, and as an alliance partner it is under some obligation to support US military countermeasures. On the other hand, the question arises of to what extent Japan's normalization of diplomatic relations with the PRC in 1972 and its 'understanding' of the PRC's view that there is only one China have changed the foundations for the 1969 Communiqué.

Normalization of relations, 1972

Until 1972 Japan withstood Chinese pressure to switch its diplomatic recognition from Taibei to Beijing. Its close alliance with the US did not give it much choice but to pursue a policy of military containment of China and to thwart the reunification of China on the conditions of the Beijing regime.[29] Every year in the autumn, until 1971, Japan continued to support US efforts to forestall the PRC taking over the ROC's seat in the UN General Assembly and in the UN Security Council. It was the change in Sino-American relations in 1971 that finally led to the normalization of diplomatic relations.

The switch of recognition did not occur without its ambiguities, which today still cast a shadow over Japanese–Chinese relations. Soeya Yoshihide calls it a 'de facto "two Chinas" policy'.[30] The move was made after a long drawn-out confrontation between the pro-Taiwan and the pro-PRC lobbies in the ruling LDP, but domestic opinion and trade interests had been so well nurtured by the PRC that it speeded up the change and helped to overcome resistance within the LDP.[31] In the document finalizing the normalization of diplomatic relations in 1972 Japan merely 'understands and respects' China's position that Taiwan is a part of the PRC. Officially, Japan maintains that it surrendered Taiwan under Article VIII of the Potsdam Declaration and it can therefore not pronounce on the legal status of the island.[32] However, Japan's obstinacy in sticking to this legal ambiguity about Taiwan's status also owes much to the strength of the pro-Taiwan forces in Japan. US pronouncements relevant to the legal status of Taiwan during the Clinton administration (see Chapter 4 for the three 'Nos') have made Japan's legal stance appear more hardline.

With this ambiguous Japanese stance on the legal status of the island, the Taiwan issue was bound to become a bone of contention again in the Japanese–Chinese security relationship when China started to witness closer relations developing between Tokyo and Taibei . It has only reinforced Chinese perceptions that Japan, as a former colonial power, is even more committed to an independent Taiwan than the US, or even that it is intent on regaining control over it.[33] Deng Xiaoping is quoted as saying that if China does not get hold of Taiwan, than someone else (meaning Japan!) will do so in the future.[34]

Direct, official, intergovernmental contact became impossible after 1972, but Tokyo as well as Taibei devised institutions and means with varying degrees of governmental support to substitute for the pre-1972 official channels.[35] Japan and Taiwan continued to maintain offices in each other's capitals for unofficial links, and until the 1990s economic links surpassed those between Japan and the PRC. Still, the Ministry of Foreign Affairs has been very assiduous in main-taining a very consistent stance on excluding official links in order to keep the Taiwan issue out of domestic politics and to avoid arousing further Chinese suspicion. Officially, Tokyo pursues only 'non-governmental regional or working exchanges' which are below the rank of ministers.[36] But Taibei does not seem to have given up using every means available to notch up relations and to maintain as high a profile in Japan as possible. The very fact that the Japanese occupation of 1895–1945 did not create anything similar to the hatred found on the Chinese mainland after Japan's brutal occupation during a much shorter period is not only incomprehensible to mainlanders but fuels their suspicions that Japan harbours new colonial intentions towards Taiwan. Taiwanese textbooks today even appreciate that the infrastructure developed during Japan's occupation contributed to the rapid modernization of Taiwan after 1945.[37] We will see in Chapter 4 how the closer relationship between Japan and Taiwan in the 1990s became a major source of conflict between Japan and the PRC.

In 1972 Beijing accepted Japan's reluctance to be more explicit about Taiwan because it needed allies for strategic and economic reasons, and because it put greater weight on relations with the US and on its ability to keep the Japanese at bay in Asia. Recently released records of US–Chinese talks in 1972 reveal how much the PRC was concerned that a reduction of American influence in Taiwan and South Korea might lead to greater Japanese influence there, or that after withdrawal from Taiwan the US troops might be replaced by Japanese troops.[38] We will see in Chapter 4 that such concerns have not yet totally disappeared from the minds of China's leaders.

Those interested in an increase in economic interactions on both sides were not disappointed by the change in 1972. Trade expanded dramatically and became the most positive foundation for the Japanese–Chinese relationship. This was facilitated by Chinese politics, which shifted from an ideological focus to economic modernization and pragmatism. From 1977 to 1981 two-way trade tripled, reaching more than US$10 billion. In 1975 Japan became China's principal trading partner. During much of the 1980s Japan was China's second-largest trading partner, beaten only by Hong Kong. Even more beneficial for China was Japan's development aid in the form of loans and grants. Japanese investment was encouraged by the high complementarity of the two economies, between Chinese raw materials and Japan's ability to supply capital goods and technology. In 1983 Japanese investment in China amounted to only US$3 million, but it reached US$100 million in 1985, US$1.2 billion in 1987 and US$2.8 billion in 1990.[39] The investment climate improved with the conclusion of a bilateral tax treaty in 1983 and the provision of trade insurance by the Ministry of Trade and Industry (MITI) in November 1985.[40] The real turning point was the need to replace exports by manufacturing abroad in the wake of the 1985 revaluation of the yen against the dollar. An investment protection treaty was finally signed in August 1988. However, despite the increase in Japanese investment in China the Chinese government always pointed to Japan's relative low share of FDI in China compared with the US, as well as to Japan's reluctance to transfer technology.

The anti-hegemony phase of the 1970s

The security relationship during the 1970s was characterized by an unprecedented convergence of strategic interests which stood in marked contrast to the situation before and afterwards. Due to China's fear about Soviet military intentions, Japan and China shared with the US an important security concern which dominated the relationship in the first decade after the normalization of relations. In addition, the normalization of diplomatic relations seemed to have unblocked an unnatural barrier between two culturally close countries, and the catch-up effect sustained a very strong Japanese euphoria towards China. Finally, China still looked weak and non-threatening.

China's leader, Deng Xiaoping, called 1972–4 a period where both sides could trust each other, although the circumstances of the normalization of diplomatic relations may be interpreted differently.[41] It was a period of unusually strong political leadership in Japan, which overcame bureaucratic bickering, thus facilitating communication with a Chinese regime in which a small group of key people ran the country's external relations. By 1978 Japan and China shared a concern about the Soviet Union which found its expression in the anti-hegemony clause of the Treaty of Peace and Friendship, concluded the same year. The intensity of this interest was much smaller on the Japanese side, but it was accepted as the price of improved relations with China. Moreover, Japan was concerned that agreement with the Chinese position on the Soviet Union might damage its chances of recovering the Northern Territories and make its relations with Southeast Asia more difficult. As a consequence, the negotiations on the Treaty of Peace and Friendship had started in 1974 but were concluded only in 1978, when stronger political leadership in Japan was confident enough to live with the outside perception, fanned by China, that the proposed so-called 'anti-hegemony clause' was directed against the Soviet Union. In a sign of what was to come later, the Chinese leadership instigated a conflict over the Senkaku Islands, sending Chinese fishing boats into Japan's territorial waters around the islands in order to speed up a compromise over the treaty (for the territorial dispute, see Chapter 2). The territorial problem over the Senkaku/Diaoyu islands was then shelved, but intrusions by Chinese boats into the surrounding waters kept the issue alive and reminded the Japanese of China's territorial claim, which it could bring up at any time it judged convenient and useful.

China's anti-hegemonic posture against the Soviet Union, its economic success since the opening of the country in 1978 and the growing importance of the economic relationship for China's economic modernization eased Chinese concerns about Japan's military and security policy and the security alliance with the US. In September 1972 Zhou Enlai declared that China no longer opposed Japan's security treaty with the US.[42] China even expressed support for Japan's territorial claim to the Northern Territories since it allowed Beijing to express its anti-Soviet feelings.[43] China moved to a neutral position only after the demise of the Soviet Union in 1991. Japan's leadership reciprocated China's support by expressing confidence in China's security policy. For example, in 1973 Prime Minister Tanaka publicly refuted the possibility of Japan being attacked by China with nuclear arms, and this was repeated by his successor in 1975.[44]

On various occasions, meeting with the Japanese, Chinese leaders also expressed acceptance of Japan's defence efforts and the Japanese–American security alliance. In September 1978 Deng Xiaoping told a Japanese delegation that he was in favour of the build-up in Self-Defence Forces (SDF).[45] In May 1980 Hua Guofeng became the first head of the Chinese government to visit Japan. At a press conference he stated that '[a]n independent and sovereign state should have the right to maintain its own defense so as to safeguard its independence and sovereignty. As to what Japan will do, we do not interfere in its internal affairs'.[46] He was even quoted as saying to Prime Minister Nakasone that the Japanese air force should be expanded to protect shipping routes. In 1980 the deputy general chief of staff, Wu Xiuquan, recommended to Nakasone, before he became prime minister , that he should raise the percentage of the gross national product (GNP) allotted to defence from 1 to 2 per cent.[47] In

November 1982 Deng Xiaoping, then chairman of the Central Military Commission, made a similar statement.[48] He also declared that '[w]e appreciate Japan's efforts to strengthen its alliance with the US'.[49] In private conversations China's leaders expressed the opinion that it was for the Japanese and American people to define their own security relationships.[50] In July 1984 the visiting defence minister, Zhang Aiping (on an unofficial visit), told his Japanese counterpart, Kurihara Yuko, that China agreed as a matter of policy with Japanese–US defence cooperation. 'Each country has the right to protect itself. For this purpose strong defence power is necessary'.[51] But when Japan's military spending increased rapidly during the Nakasone era, the Chinese foreign minister, Wu Xueqian, after repeating the Hua statement, added in a meeting with Japanese special envoy Nikaido Susumu that 'such an armed force should be defense-oriented and of appropriate size so it does not constitute a threat to its friendly neighbours'.[52] While they were willing to accept greater autonomy in Japanese diplomacy – which, after all, in China's view provided a welcome balance against Japan–US relations becoming too close – Beijing's leaders warned against 'a handful of Japanese' promoting Japan's militarism. In 1983, for the first time, Chinese commentators referred to Japan as moving from the status of economic big power to that of political big power and wanting to expand its influence on the global economy and global politics to become 'one pole of the world'.[53]

A high point in the relationship and in trust between the two countries was reached with the visit of Hu Yaobang, the general secretary of the Chinese Communist Party (CCP), to Japan in 1983. He admired Japan for its post-war economic performance and expressed his confidence that Japan would never again invade China, even if Japanese military power were to expand.[54] Earlier, in May 1982, Premier Zhao Ziyang had visited Japan and announced three principles for the bilateral relationship: peace and friendship, equality and mutual benefit, and long-term stability. During Hu's visit in November 1983 'mutual trust' was added to the three principles and both sides agreed to establish the Twenty-First Century Committee.[55] At this time the economic relationship blossomed and measures were taken to improve relations at all levels. The 1983–4 period was therefore referred to as the best in the 2000-year history of Japanese–Chinese relations.[56]

At the same time, Japan's leaders became concerned about some security aspects of improved Sino-American relations. While Japan shared America's anti-Soviet line, there were differences. Japan had never considered the Soviet threat as menacing as had the US since it was much more aware than the US of the Soviet Union's intrinsic economic weakness. American arms deliveries to China might increase the military power of China too much. Japan had much greater understanding of the wish of Southeast Asia not to burn all its bridges with Vietnam because they saw it as a future barrier against China.[57] Still, China tried very hard to win Japan over to some military cooperation, in terms of exchange of military officers and other defence officials, to reinforce the anti-hegemony policy against the Soviet Union.[58] Military attaches were posted by each country in the other's embassy in 1974 at the urging of Japan.[59] But in 1979 Prime Minister Ohira ruled out the extension of military assistance to China. Later, reluctance to expand military personnel exchanges grew on both sides, particularly when compared to the much wider scope of exchanges at various levels between the US and China. The Japanese government was concerned about China's emphasis on anti-hegemony and placed limits on further military exchanges. Not until May 1987 did a director-general of the Defence Agency (Kurihara Yuko) visit China – after his Chinese counterpart, the defence minister, Zhang Aiping – had visited him in July 1984. This reluctance was reinforced when China once again reverted to criticism of Japan's military efforts.[60] In 1987 the Defence Agency was reported to be reluctant to accept informal requests by Beijing for officer candidates to attend the Defense Academy.[61]

The resurgence of Chinese security concerns

It is clear today that China's anti-Soviet stance of joining up with Western countries was only a transient phase in Beijing's diplomacy and security policy. When China realised the diplomatic costs of this policy – in terms of vulnerability to being used as a card by the US, jeopardizing other important security interests (notably national reunification) – and when the immediate danger of a Soviet attack had disappeared, China's leaders reverted to a more aloof and independent line. The shift in the Chinese international 'united-front' policy against the Soviet Union to the line of 'independence and autonomy' was publicized at the Twelfth Party Congress in September 1982. In 1985 Hu Yaobang declared that China would 'never attach itself to, nor foster strategic relations nor an alliance with, any big power or bloc of power'.[62] China's relationship with the US soured over Taiwan and Reagan's military build-up. As a result, China's strategic entente with Japan and the US weakened, and Beijing pursued again an independent and non-aligned stance. But the manifestations of this change were not consistent during the 1980s and still allowed positive developments like the visit of the director-general of the Defence Agency in 1987.

However, old fears about Japan's future direction were once again voiced publicly more often. Concern was expressed about Japan becoming a 'political big power' as the preceding stage to being a 'military big power'.[63] The most important problems that shaped the Chinese perception of Japan in the 1980s were, once again, the fear of a possible resurgence of Japanese militarism, which was fanned by closer defence cooperation with the US and Japan's inability to come to terms with the past, growing imbalances in the bilateral economic relationship, Japan's ambiguity about the status of Taiwan, and the dispute about the Senkaku/Diaoyu islands.[64]

China voiced its concerns about what it saw as rising nationalism in Japan, and the revival of militarist tendencies as allegedly expressed by the sanitizing of Japanese history books on items related to Japan's past militarist expansion and to government officials visiting the Yasukuni Shrine in Tokyo. In 1985 the prime minister, Nakasone Yasuhiro, visited the Yasukuni Shrine for the war dead on the fortieth anniversary of Japan's surrender, which led to Chinese government protests, but also to student protests that Japan's economic 'invasion' of China was linked to the issues of the past.

In summer 1982 China launched a strong attack against Japan's alleged move to whitewash Japan's past aggression against China in textbooks screened by the Ministry of Education by replacing the word 'invade' (*shinryaku*) with 'advance' (*shinshutsu*). Later it turned out that the alleged changes in Japan's textbooks were based on an incorrect report.[65] While the official campaign against Japan was certainly supported by a latent distrust towards Japan, the delayed start and the sudden end of the campaign (before Prime Minister Suzuki's visit to China) also demonstrated the manipulation of the issue by the Chinese leadership for domestic as well as bilateral purposes. Before 1982 China had never shown any interest in the long-running disputes in Japan over the presentation of the country's aggressions before 1945 in its history textbooks. The start of China's textbook campaign coincided with a Japanese trade mission to Taiwan, which was headed by Esaki Masumi, chairman of the LDP's International Economic Policy Special Research Committee. Its purpose was to find ways of reducing the high Taiwanese trade deficit with Japan, but Beijing was concerned about the high-level political and economic character of the delegation. In the agreement of the Esaki mission, the word 'country' was used in reference to Taiwan, which raised fears about Japan's two-China policy.[66] The Taiwan issue was also raised later, in 1986, when a Japanese court ruled in favour of the ROC in the case of the disputed ownership of a student dormitory in Kyoto (*kokaryo*), betraying China's ongoing concern about Japan's true intentions towards Taiwan.[67]

In response to changes in the international environment in the 1970s, Japan conceptualized its foreign and security policy on the basis of the Report on Comprehensive National Security.[68] Recognizing the 'termination of clear American supremacy in both military and economic spheres', the report proposed diplomatic, military and economic efforts. The Ohira government, which had commissioned the report, abandoned the omnidirectional diplomacy which previous cabinets had unconvincingly proclaimed. It laid the foundation for increased Japanese defence expenditures and closer security links with the US, which, as we have seen, were initially accepted by China, but then criticized when it abandoned its anti-Soviet campaign. Prime Minister Nakasone became the main promoter of increased defence efforts. The discussion of roles and missions led to a tightening of the Japanese–US security alliance and an announcement in early 1987 that Japan's defence expenditures could break through the ceiling of 1 per cent of Japan's GNP. Under Nakasone's premiership Japan assumed a much more nationalistic posture, helped by the booming 'bubble economy'. These developments led to Chinese warnings, which increased in tone over the next few years. In August 1985 Vice-Premier Yao Yilin said that Japanese defence preparations that went beyond the requirements of self-defence would 'arouse and upset Japan's neighbours'.[69] Japanese–Chinese relations suffered a further setback in January 1987 when Hu Yaobang suddenly resigned. He was considered in Japan as the Chinese leader most sympathetic towards Japan, and it worried many that Hu's favourable attitude might even have played some role in his fall from power.[70]

Japan as a civilian power engaging China

By the end of the 1980s Japan had become an economic superpower. This was the successful outcome of Yoshida's focus on economic rehabilitation, followed by economic expansion. What may have been an expedient after the crushing defeat in 1945 had become the main focus of Japan's domestic and foreign policy. The 1973 and 1979 oil crises only reinforced the emphasis on economic diplomacy. Economic power had also become an important diplomatic tool to achieve economic and diplomatic goals. It was the security assurances accompanying the Japanese–American security alliance and the gradual increase in the military responsibilities of the SDF against the background of growing US requests for burden sharing that had made such a policy feasible.

As a result of its successful economic and political development, Japan has been called a 'civilian power' (*minsei taikoku*) or 'global civilian power', to characterize its (as well as Germany's) power position in the post-war period.[71] Richard Rosecrance has coined the term 'trading state' to define this new paradigm of the civilian state.[72] Comparing Japan and Germany, Hanns Maull speaks of the two countries as prototypes of 'civilian powers' and defines 'civilian power' thus:

1   acceptance of the necessity of cooperation with others in the pursuit of international objectives;
2   concentration on non-military, primarily economic, means of international interaction;
3   a willingness to develop supranational structures to address critical issues of international management.[73]

In the 1980s it became apparent that Japan was increasingly translating its economic power into political power.[74] This strategy has been particularly emphasized in Japan's relations with developing countries, which are especially susceptible to what Japan has to offer in terms of market, development aid, capital and technology. Political and strategic aims were originally rarely involved, but since the 1980s the US has pressured Japan to make its aid more politically conditional and to increase aid to 'strategically important countries' in Indochina and the Middle East, including also the Philippines from 1989 onwards.

It is not surprising that Japan has tried to maximize its relative advantage as a global civilian power and seized the opportunities of China's opening since 1978 to benefit economically from the complementarity of both economies. At the same time, Japanese political leaders soon became aware of the political and strategic implications of economic interactions and, notably, development aid. Official support for Japan's trade and investment with China became motivated by the desire to stabilize China through economic development, while the military aspects of Japan's China policy were entrusted to the Japanese–American security alliance. Moreover, in the 1980s economic aid became a convenient policy tool to overcome the various political disputes centring mostly around China's criticism of how Japan approached the legacy of its past aggression in China.[75] Japan's China policy has therefore always contained the two basic ingredients of engagement – that is, on the one hand, political and economic diplomacy and, on the other, military power for the purposes of power balancing and hedging.

Engagement, as understood here, seemed the ideal mix of policy tools to enhance the chances of China's modernization policy; not only did it stabilize China's economy and enable it to feed its people, but it also induced a peaceful change from a Communist regime to a more democratic system, without giving up the tools of military balancing. China's focus on opening the country and relying on foreign input to improve its weak economic basis thus blended perfectly.

Tiananmen 1989 as a test of engagement

While since 1978 China had embraced the economic opportunities offered by the West's policy of engagement, it was at the same time aware of the 'subversive' aspects of this policy and their threat to the stability of the Communist regime. This realization could not fail to have the contradictory effect (from a Western perspective) of reinforcing the Realist frame of mind of China's Communist leaders, while an ideological softening was going on as a result of dramatic economic changes. The brutal repression of the demonstration in Tiananmen Square in June 1989 showed that China's leaders were willing to use force and to withstand the resulting international opprobrium to maintain their rule. The incident may be called a first test of the viability of Japan's engagement at the close of the Cold War era, not so much for the negative reaction in Japan against China, but for the difference of Japan's official reaction in comparison to that of other Western countries, which affected the emphasis of policy tools.

While the Tiananmen massacre of 3–4 June 1989 ended the dreams of many Western leaders about China's unstoppable move towards democracy and economic stability, Japan's policy-makers had much fewer expectations and less hope to lose. Japan was relying more on the quiet forces of greater economic exchanges and transformation, while notably its American alliance partner was more verbal about its hopes of transforming China's political and economic system through the policy of engagement.[76] True, China fell in its poll rating in Japan as a liked country from 17.3 per cent in May 1989 to 4.9 per cent in June, while those who expressed a dislike for China rose from 5.4 per cent to 27.1 per cent during the same short period.[77] But Japan's leaders had never shared the USA's often expressed wish for a strong China; they were more interested in a 'stable and slowly modernizing China'.[78] Japan's leaders had much more sympathy with the Chinese leaders' concern about internal tumult, which would not only result in a loss of business for Japan and endanger the 8,300 nationals in China, but would also mean streams of refugees coming to Japan's shores. Punishing China with economic and political sanctions might push China over the edge and invite greater disaster than the killing of a few hundred protesters.[79] However, Japan's muted reaction to the Tiananmen massacre did not just come from a cool strategic calculus and commercial interests. Immediately after the event officials explained Japan's reluctance to take stronger measures of protest: the burden of Japan's past would not allow it to take a strong moral position.[80] Prime Minister Uno declared that, because of the past, Japanese–Chinese relations are different from US–Chinese relations.[81] In the end the Japanese government avoided straightforward reference to human rights and instead pointed to the practical difficulties of conducting ODA negotiations under the 'confused conditions' following the Tiananmen killings.[82]

Western indignation was particularly high in the US, and economic and political sanctions were imposed. Significant were the ending of military exchanges and the sale of American military hardware to China.[83] However, Japan's initial official reaction was not to impose sanctions.[84] It finally relented under the pressure of the other major Western countries and suspended a US$5.2 billion loan package announced a year earlier, warned Japanese tourists, halted high-level visits and discouraged Japanese businessmen from 'undue haste'.[85]

At the same time, Japan's government actively tried to reduce international criticism of China and to end international sanctions.[86] Yasutomo even speaks of Japan exhibiting 'a rare aggressiveness in distinguishing its views from those of other G-7 nations'.[87] Although it joined the G-7's statement condemning China in Paris in July 1989, it also argued for the inclusion of a passage on the importance of not isolating China (supported by President Bush) and for limiting the sanctions mentioned in it to the ones already in place.[88] The Japanese government was instrumental in avoiding any mention of 'joint sanctions against China' in the Paris Summit declaration.[89] At the summit it used the issue of environmental aid (also within the framework of the World Bank) to soften the support for sanctions against China in the aftermath of the Tiananmen incident. Since environmental degradation was an issue for many countries, notably China, it appeared as a logical target of green funds.[90] After the Paris Summit the Japanese government lifted its ban on business travel in China and the freeze on the Second Yen Loan of ¥470 billion. By the end of 1989 Japan had ended all its restrictions except the Third Yen Loan and the ban on minister-level contact.[91] At the G-7 Summit in Houston in August 1990 Japan took the lead among the G-7 countries in ending sanctions and resuming its full loan and other development programmes. Before the summit some Chinese leaders had warned Japan about the damage to Chinese–Japanese relations if the yen loans were not resumed.[92] In 1991 Japanese–Chinese ties were fully restored and Prime Minister Kaifu visited China in August. This was followed in October 1992 by the first visit of a Japanese Emperor to China, an event very much desired by China but which faced some difficulties in Japan from rightists, who were concerned about an inimical reception and about the government's plan for a war apology.[93] Although trade relations immediately after the momentous events in Tiananmen Square suffered, overall trade reached US$29 billion in 1992. Investment showed dramatic increases after 1992. As Whiting and Xin point out, Japan's decline in FDI to China from US$515 million in 1988 to US$356 million in 1989 (making Taiwan's investment of US$400 million on the mainland surpass that of Japan in 1989!) had more to do with the deteriorating investment climate than with sanctions.[94] In 1992 Japan's ODA constituted 46 per cent of China's total bilateral ODA, and 29 per cent of its entire ODA.[95]

While Japan was attacked for being too willing to resume contacts with China, the administration of George Bush Snr tried to do the same with more circumspection in the face of a very strong domestic reaction to China's human rights violations. The rationale was very similar to that of Japan, but in addition the administration wanted to soften the impact of rising anti-China feelings in the US. Bush sent Brent Scowcroft, his national security adviser, on two missions to China in 1989 and personally met the foreign minister, Qian Qichen, in early 1991; this was followed by the visit of Secretary of State James Baker to Beijing in November of the same year.[96] Between 1990 and 1994 the debate over according China another year of most-favoured nation (MFN) status became very acrimonious between the administration and Congress, and in 1990, 1991 and 1992 President Bush vetoed legislation that would have linked MFN status with an improvement of Chinese human rights policies. As presidential candidate, Bill Clinton attacked the Bush administration's 'coddling of dictators', but when he got into power he also unlinked human rights from MFN status because of the interests of US business in China and the overriding concern of Chinese leaders about domestic stability.[97] China was no longer the indispensable bulwark against the Soviet Union, but its rising power and growing role in the proliferation of weapons of mass destruction, apart from strong sectoral business interests, had become the new motivation of successive US administrations for maintaining goods links with China. Still, it took the new Clinton administration until September 1993 to lift all economic sanctions and to reach the same level which Japan had reached in August 1991.[98]

Japan managed to walk the fine line between isolation among its Western allies and angering China. Japanese writers point out that Japan's post-Tiananmen countermeasures were not much different from those of other Western countries, and the chronology of sanction relief offers some proof.[99] However, in public Japan's position looked different and it was more vocal about the need to end sanctions and to avoid China's isolation. Whiting and Xin called unprecedented the 'degree of sophistication and sensitivity' with which Japan and China handled the fallout from the massacre.[100] As a result of Japan's active anti-sanction policy, relations with China improved rather than deteriorated and briefly enjoyed another rise. The Chinese government appreciated Japan's restraint and some leaders revealed 'privately their understanding of the Japanese situation and expressed remorse'.[101] China did not directly attack Japan for the sanctions it had joined in, but it did so with other countries, notably the US.[102] After the Tiananmen incident China found itself in a difficult diplomatic position. Not only did it have to overcome economic and political isolation as a result of Western indignation over the events in Tiananmen Square, but the collapse of Communism in Eastern Europe and the Soviet Union, the move towards US unipolarity in the wake of the Soviet demise and US leadership during the Gulf War, as well as Russia's initial policy of leaning to the West, reinforced this Chinese perception. Reacting to international isolation, China decided once again to devote more attention to the Third World, and to Asia in particular.[103] Japan, as an Asian nation and a country trying to prevent China's international isolation, therefore became particularly important for China's post-Tiananmen foreign policy.[104]

Conclusions

At the end of the Cold War and the beginning of the post-Cold War era the Japanese government had established a consistent policy of engagement towards China which aimed at integrating China into a rules-based international community because of Beijing's regional power and its potential to cause instability, while at the same time relying on its own military deterrent and the Japanese–American security alliance for power balancing and hedging. Many economic and political problems appeared in the Japanese–Chinese relationship between 1972 and 1989, but the framework of shared concerns about the Soviet Union, US support of a positive Japanese–Chinese relationship and the existence of influential mediators in the political establishment on both sides did not allow problems to seriously hurt the Japanese–Chinese relationship. Japan's reactions to the Tiananmen killings, which were, at least at the public government level, significantly different from those of its allies, notably the US, showed how Tokyo managed to equilibrate the diverse dynamics of engagement, notably differences with the US. The changed situation in the latter part of the 1990s – that is, the end of the Cold War and greater Chinese military assertiveness – was to demonstrate that this would not be so easy in the future.

2 The rise of traditional and non-traditional security concerns

When a young American visitor to the premier Zhou Enlai expressed his belief that China will never become a 'hegemonic power', Zhou replied: 'Do not count on it. China could embark on a hegemonic path. But if it does, you should oppose it. And you must inform that generation of Chinese that Zhou Enlai told you to do so.'[1]

We still don't stand for anything. We are not a democracy, we're not communist. We're just big.'[2]

Introduction

The 1990s led to a profound change in Japanese perceptions of China's security policies. This change is explained, in this chapter, as the result of the rise of traditional as well as non-traditional security concerns relating to China, and shifts in Japan's international and domestic environment as well as China's economic and political development. The end of the Cold War refocused Japan's security concerns from the Soviet Union to other concerns, and created strategic uncertainties about China's development and US security commitments to Asia. China has been considerably increasing its defence expenditures since 1989 and had become more assertive in its desire to promote a multipolar world. At the same time, China has again become deeply ambivalent about the security policies formulated by Japan in response to the above. Domestically, generational changes in Japan's political and bureaucratic leadership and Japanese self-assertiveness have eroded the previous cautious approach to China, which had been prevalent since the end of the 1970s.

PART 1: THE BACKGROUND TO CHINA'S SECURITY POLICIES

China and the post-Cold War environment

The end of the Cold War initially led in China to the hope of a world where American influence would be diminished thanks to the emergence of a multipolar power structure, which would give China greater autonomy. Immediately after 1989 the breakdown of the Yalta regime and the relative weakening of US power seemed to herald the emergence of such a structure, in which the American pole would be weakened by greater Japanese and European autonomy.[3] Reflecting the Realist balance-of-power approach to international relations of Chinese strategists, Yan Xuetong, director of the Centre for China's Foreign Policy Studies of Contemporary International Relations, wrote that China's leaders considered that the trend toward a multipolar world could help prevent a new world war.[4] The idea that a more multipolar world would be more stable than a world system based on multilateralism and cooperative security is, of course, strongly contested.[5] Moreover, the world was and still is very far from multipolarity if one differentiates between multipolarity in terms of the distribution of economic and military power (actual capabilities) and in terms of potential.

To speed up the advent of a multipolar world Chinese leaders and foreign-policy experts highlighted the conflicts between Japan and the US, either because of growing dependence by the US on support from Japan to maintain its hegemonic position or because of sharpening economic conflicts between the two countries. A secret CCP document is alleged to have encouraged the Chinese media in 1992 to enhance its coverage of conflicts and compromises among the US, Western Europe and Japan.[6] The Chinese noted that after the end of the Cold War Japan's economic rise and greater political assertion replaced the 'Soviet threat' for many Americans.[7] In 1992 Zhou Jihua, a leading Japan specialist in the Chinese Academy of Social Sciences, detected two main features of the immediate post-Cold War period: one being that competition in economic and national strength would replace military and ideological confrontation; the other being the growing tendency of economic and political pluralism. He named Japan and Germany, with their strong economies, as the main winners of the Cold War.[8]

Up to the summer of 1995 China believed that because of the escalation in the Japanese–American trade conflict, which was then focusing on Japan's opening of its automobile market, Japanese–US relations would not survive in the post-Cold War era, and felt encouraged in its belief that multipolarity was around the corner. It made many Chinese believe that China might hold the pivotal position in a new US–Japan–China triangle which replaced the Russia–China–US triangle.[9] From around 1995, however, Chinese observers became concerned that the security alliance was giving Japan a regional security role and was directed against China (see Chapter 3 on the Nye Report and the Hashimoto–Clinton Japan–US Joint Declaration in April 1996).

It soon became obvious that the American position after the Gulf War in 1991 and the end of the Soviet Union in 1992 signified that the advent of a multipolar world in the Chinese sense would be delayed and the predominance of the US would still last for some time. Some Chinese scholars recognised, therefore, that the world-power configuration after the Gulf War was still more 'one superpower and four big powers', the latter including Japan.[10] At the same time the Chinese took comfort in a gradual weakening of the US hegemon and in the 'development of various world forces experiencing new splits and realignments'.[11]

Once China's leaders realized this delay and even observed a strengthening of the Western camp – for which, implicitly or explicitly, the challenge emanating from a rising China was often used as an incentive ('China threat') – they started to promote a foreign policy which openly opposes military alliances, selectively supports multilateralism and creates various versions of 'partnerships'. In its official declarations, China's leaders have been warning against the 'containment' and 'interference' elements of the West's engagement policy. Military alliances are declared confrontational and out of date in the post-Cold War era. Seen from China's own historical experience, it is argued, US alliances have always been directed against China. As a Chinese academic put it, '[f]or Chinese strategists, the traditional concept of alliances is always threat based, or interpreted as a hedging strategy'.[12] As we will see later, this is one of the reasons why China vehemently opposes the redefinition of the Japan–US military alliances, as it occurred after the Nye initiative in 1995 and the April 1996 Japan–US Joint Declaration.

Although a multipolar power structure has not yet materialized, there is agreement among Chinese experts that the post-Cold War strategic environment is more benign than before. But due to their combination of realism, nationalism and a desire for regime maintenance, this has not stopped them perceiving the international environment as inimical to China's security concerns. As David Armstrong explains, the Chinese discussion of the 'new world order' in the post-Cold War era still 'rests upon a theoretical/conceptual framework that combines Marxist analytical categories, Western realist thought and traditional Chinese wisdom'.[13] In view of China's historical experience and Marxist background, a balance of power is therefore seen as the most appropriate approach to international relations, and the assumption is that this will provide the space to develop China economically.[14] The negative historical experience has become a source of nationalism, which in the post-Mao period is in turn also instrumentalized by the Chinese leadership to cover a growing ideological void and to maintain regime stability. This kind of 'defensive nationalism', with its urge to regain China's 'rightful' place in the world, strengthens the perception abroad that China is a revisionist power, leading some to argue that, now or in the future, China constitutes a threat.[15] With China's Realist approach to international relations, its revisionist goals, its historical experience of weakness since the nineteenth century, the majority of Chinese analysts and decision-makers still feel that international relations is a zero-sum game and that China is more secure if other states are weaker.[16]

Michael Pillsbury broadly divides the thinking of China's military specialists into three schools of thought. One school views the US as a major threat and proposes developing weapons to confront it. Another sees the US as a declining power and looks towards Japan as a future threat to China. The third believes the People's Liberation Army (PLA) has enough time to engage in high-technology weapons development over the long term and is engaged extensively in using advanced technology to radically change future warfare.[17]

China's security concerns are diverse. The West's engagement policy is seen as supportive of China's economic modernization and strengthening, but at the same time also as intent on undermining and transforming the Chinese political system under the banner of 'peaceful evolution'.[18] The insistence by the West on a peaceful solution to China's division is considered an interference in the country's domestic affairs that leads to a perpetuation of that division. Western endeavours to make China a responsible power which adheres to Western concepts like human rights or nuclear non-proliferation, either by positive or negative incentives, are seen as offensive. The continued existence of conflicts, even near China's borders, are a potential threat. Finally, China has several territorial disputes, notably those related to its claims to the whole South China Sea. In a Chinese paper submitted in 1996 to an ARF workshop in Tokyo, these security concerns were summarized in the following way:

- external imposition of values and ideologies;
- 'splitting' China;
- indiscriminate sanctions v. China on international issues;
- conflicts and wars in some regional countries;
- China's sovereignty, maritime rights and interest are still being encroached;[19]

Against this background of threat perception and a combination of realism, nationalism and regime maintenance, Muthiah Alagappa distilled the following elements from Beijing's foreign and security policies:

1   pursuit of balance among the major powers in Asia;
2   good-neighbour policy with all Asian neighbours;
3   build-up of military strength;
4   mobilization of international support for economic modernization;
5   projection of China as an indispensable and responsible regional player.[20]

Japan's place in China's 'multipolar world'

Japan does not fit easily into this complex set of perceptions and policies because it presents China's Realists with a dilemma. As a result, China finds it difficult to develop a consistent policy which is less US-fixated and does not invite the very response it fears most by threatening Japanese security concerns.

For China, security cannot be discussed in a Japan–China framework because of the close Japan–US links and China's overriding concerns with the US in its security evaluation. Since China opposes US preponderance in Asia, and therefore also the alliances on which this preponderance is based (but at the same time is ideologically against the dependence for security of one country on another), China will have to encourage Japan to become more independent from the US and to have a security policy commensurate with its economic power. Moreover, since Japan is, after the US, China's most important economic partner, and since it relies on Japan to regain its due status as a great power, good relations with a prosperous Japan should be important.

However, as Realists they also are convinced that big economic powers inevitably become big military powers, although this historical determinism is called into question by Japan's rise as a global civilian power because of the gap between, on the one hand, Japan's economic might and performance and, on the other, its military might and willingness to use it. Moreover, potential is equated with intention, and many Chinese experts just think it inevitable that having the potential will sooner or later result in the willingness to exploit it.[21] Even the Japanese economic crisis which started in 1990s does not reassure but is interpreted by some as water on the mills of the hawkish Japanese who fan nationalism, harming Japan–US relations as a dam against an independent Japanese military power. While Chinese observers concede the damage done to Japan's economy by the crisis, they point out that the high-technology industry is not affected.[22]

Obviously China does not want to follow its own Realist prescriptions in Japan's case and encourage Tokyo's independent military growth (the period of anti-hegemonic struggle in the 1980s was somewhat an exception); nor does it want to hasten the realization of its historical determinism about Japan's future path because of its own national ambitions, its concern about strong Japanese–American links inhibiting the advent of a multipolar world and its deep distrust of Japan because of the past.

But by working towards the end of the Japanese–American security alliance and/or threatening Japan with a rapid and non-transparent build-up of conventional and nuclear military forces, as well as with destabilizing acts to assert its territorial claims, China risks the unwanted scenario of either a stronger Japanese–American military alliance or a stronger independent Japanese military power.

Even if China's political and strategic leaders abandoned their historical determinism, as some have done, ending the Japan–US alliance would force Japan to overcome its hesitancy towards military force and nuclear armament, at least from the Realist point of view which is so entrenched with Chinese strategists.

Reflecting this dilemma and ambivalence, Chinese writing on Japan ranges from the more pessimistic assumptions about Japan's future path to the optimistic view that Japan will need China's support to become an Asian power. Chu Shulong concludes that '[d]ifficulties and problems in Sino-Japanese relations always tend to be exaggerated. In fact, there are few problems between Japan and China and most of them are conceptual or symbolic problems rather than real policy differences'.[23] The defence minister, Chi Haojian, was quoted as saying during the defence officials talks in Beijing in November 1999 that as a result of his visit to Japan he was able to confirm for himself that contemporary Japan was not militaristic.[24]

But incidents like Prime Minister Hashimoto's visit to the Yasukuni Shrine in July 1996, textbook crises, Japanese reassertion of its sovereignty over the

Senkaku Islands, Japanese moves which in Beijing's view complicate reunification and the strengthening of Japanese–US defence cooperation lead immediately to the predominance of statements and writings which are closer to the pessimistic view of Japan, although in most cases they may only have a tactical or warning intention or may just reflect the bluster of China's increasingly commercial mass media. The latent suspicion towards Japan in Chinese public opinion is so strong and can be so easily mobilized by official propaganda that the government has to take care lest public opinion may eventually turn against the regime itself.

Chinese public opinion regarding Japan has traditionally been negative because of the past, Japan's political and economic ascendance, the lack of knowledge about contemporary Japan and a constant stream of bilateral political and economic frictions.[25] It is particularly worrying that generational change does not seem to make much difference. According to the results of a 1997 PRC survey on young people's attitudes towards Japan, only 14.5 per cent had a favourable impression of Japan, with 41.5 per cent claiming an unfavourable impression.[26] Polls by the *Yomiuri Shimbun* confirmed a deterioration of perceptions between 1995 and 1999. Even among those in their thirties, who are most positive toward Japan, 43 per cent of respondents had negative opinions.[27]

The more academic literature reflects the dilemma of China's thinking and policies in a more sophisticated way. One of the key problems for Chinese international relations specialists is the strong focus on the inter-state level. As a consequence they overestimate the role of the Japanese state (as well of their own central government).[28] Although the Chinese academic literature in general no longer supports the thesis of the historical inevitability of Japan's future militarism or that Japan now is once again a militaristic nation, suspicions of Japan are strong and still evoke considerable emotion. There is concern that any further move towards a more 'normal' defence posture (which these scholars would have to advocate if they consistently applied their Realist approach) or a particular new advanced-weapon system (for example air tankers or TMD) would break the dam which holds Japan back from becoming a militarist country again.[29] At the very least it would keep the balance of power in Japan's favour. Thus, while these scholars from a Realist/nationalist point of view would not agree with the constitutional restraints on Japan's defence posture and their leftist advocates in Japan, they watch with concern any further erosion of these constraints by ever more expansive interpretations of the constitution by the Japanese government. An example of this suspicion is an article published in 1994 in a Chinese military journal, *Xiandai Jianchuan*, which asserts that Japan's naval strategy has evolved from the defence of home waters in the 1960s and 1970s to active defence of distant waters since the early 1980s. It gives as examples Japan's participation in UN peacekeeping operations (PKO), sending minesweepers to the Gulf in 1991 and participation in RimPac (Rim of the Pacific) exercises with the US and its allies.[30] On the other hand, China and Japan both participated in PKO for the first time when they sent troops to the United Nations Transitional Authority in Cambodia (UNTAC). Japan's deployment was initially criticized by the Chinese government, and in 1992 Jiang Zemin called it a 'delicate problem' (*bimyo na mondai*), but then in 1993 Foreign Minister Qian Qichen spoke positively about it.[31] The outdated Chinese perception of some PLA members in UNTAC was also symbolized by the expectation after one Japanese UNTAC policeman was killed that the SDF soldiers would now burn villages in retaliation.[32] The slogan of the revival of Japanese militarism is still used by many academics, at least in the context of trends to be watched or in order to caution Japan.[33]

China's central focus is on the Japanese–US relationship, but still as a dependent variable of the China–US relationship. In China's perception, Japan supports a world order, together with the US, which is not considered as congruent with China's interests. This world order is

one in which international regimes and institutions, often reflecting US interests and values, limit the proliferation of certain conventional weapons and weapons of mass destruction, constrain mercantilist economic policies that interfere with free trade, and limit sovereignty by promoting universal norms of human rights.[34]

While there is some tolerance for US forces in Japan because of their constraining influence on Japan's alleged military ambitions, feelings are very mixed because the constraints go with US encouragement of greater Japanese military efforts which in the end may lead to a decoupling from the US, while Chinese security specialists are in any case opposed to the US military presence in Asia and to alliances in particular.[35] After enumerating all the developments in Japan's security policy which worry China, Wu Xinbo concluded, in an article in 2000, that most policy and academic elites in China do not embrace the idea that Japan will become militarized and aggressive, but rather that their concern is

that the increase in Japan's military capabilities will shift the balance of power in Japan's favor. A militarily powerful Japan is more likely to invoke its alliance with the US to intervene should a military conflict arise in the Taiwan Strait.[36]

Michael Pillsbury summarizes the thinking of Chinese authors on Japan's future policies in the following way:

- will achieve CNP (Comprehensive National Power) equal to the United States by 2010;
- wants to restrain China's rising influence;
- seeks to foment conflict between the United States and China;
- will continue to have a militaristic, strategic culture;
- will struggle for resources in Central Asia and Siberia against the United States and Russia;
- will have ever-increasing conflicts with both Europe and the United States;

- will develop nuclear weapons eventually, earlier if Korea obtains them;
- will face a dangerous environment of potential conflict with Russia, Europe, and the United States;
- seeks (covertly) to become the military equivalent of the United States.[37]

Even if only half of these future possibilities are considered likely, China finds itself in a strategic rivalry with what it now considers the US hegemony supported by Japan, which may possibly lead to a direct rivalry with Japan. In view of China's historical experience with Japan, Thomas Christensen wrote that 'Chinese elites and the Chinese public view Japanese power as more threatening than any other nation's power'.[38] In another context he clarified that Chinese analysts recognize the military superiority of the US, although the negative feelings towards Japan are stronger: 'Although Chinese analysts presently fear US power much more than Japanese power, in terms of national intentions, Chinese analysts view Japan with much less trust and, in many cases, with a loathing rarely found in their attitudes about the US'.[39] Allen S. Whiting and Xin Jianfei showed that Chinese writing about Japan's military equipment and defence developments tends to exclude countervailing arguments, preferring instead to quote foreign publications that express concern about Japan's rising military and political might.[40]

With all these emotional, strategic and tactical elements sometimes fused into each other and sometimes separately guiding individual decision-makers and analysts, it is difficult to make any definite generalizations about China's evaluation of Japan's position in the 'new world order'. Moreover, Chinese projections of Japan's future path depend on assumptions about the national strength of China, Japan and the US, and on whether they look at the regional or global level. If Chinese analysts assume that sooner or later the US will go into decline and Japan will lose its will to support US hegemony, then Japan certainly looms as the longer-term threat. This understanding was moderated in the 1990s by the ups and downs in the perception of US strength and of Japan's deepening economic crisis. Depending on whether one focuses on the regional or global level, Japan looms larger on the former. But, for the time being, China's goal of parity in national comprehensive strength aims at a US exercising hegemony in Asia and supported by Japan.

China's military modernization

Against this background of perceptions of the post-Cold War world, China's leaders reviewed the country's strategy, defence doctrine and force structure in the 1990s. At the 14th National Party Congress in October 1992 China's leaders emphasized the importance of military strength and the defence of territorial sovereignty. Shambaugh mentions that China has expanded its strategic frontiers from continental to regional definitions. He comments that since about 1991 Chinese strategists have been referring to the strategic value of Southeast Asian shipping lanes and the Straits of Malacca for China's foreign trade, in addition to their claims to the South China Sea. India should not become the dominant power of South Asia or the Indian Ocean.[41] Bitzinger and Gill mention, in particular, the role of Taiwan in China's new emphasis on projecting naval and air power.[42]

The success of the Allied powers in the Gulf War led the Chinese to emphasize high-technology warfare.[43] Accordingly, the 15th National Party Congress in 1997 basically reaffirmed the strategy of 'Qualitative Army against Limited and High-Tech Warfare' which had been adopted by Deng and other party and military leaders since the late 1980s.[44] In line with Deng's policy China has been devoting considerable funds to the modernization of its military forces, but it has also reduced their size to achieve a more professional armed force.[45] Weapon systems and technologies of particular interest to the Chinese include C3I systems, cruise missiles, satellite-based navigation systems, advanced radar, lasers, precision-guidance and thermal imaging and guidance.[46]

The Chinese stress the need for 'comprehensive security' (*zonghe anquan*) or 'comprehensive national strength' (*zonghe guoli*), concepts which China has copied from Japan's comprehensive security policy. This became China's official approach to security after Deng Xiaoping advocated the concept of 'comprehensive national power' at the beginning of the 1980s.[47] Accordingly, Jiang Zemin confirmed in 1992 that the pace of military modernization was to be raised to a level commensurate with the country's economic growth.[48]

In 1988–9 China's military budget started to increase above 10 per cent annually. Official defence spending increased from Yuan91 billion (US$11 billion) in 1998 to Yuan105 billion (US$12.6 billion) in 1999. In March 2001 the Chinese government announced a 17.7 per cent increase for the fiscal year 2001, the largest expansion in real terms in the last twenty years, which brings the defence budget to US$17,195 billion.[49] While this was slightly less than the 19.8 per cent increase in overall spending, it was noted with concern in Japan.[50] Official defence-budget figures, however, do not include many other allocations and benefits accruing to China's armed forces.[51] The real level of military expenditure was estimated by Japan's National Institute for Defense Studies in 1998 at more than US$37 billion.[52] Kokubun Ryosei, a China expert at Keio University, points out, however, that the share of military expenditures in China's overall budget was actually much higher in the 1980s, at one point reaching 15 per cent, compared with around 9 per cent in the 1990s. However, not only was China's military was less powerful in the 1980s, but the West and China were facing the Soviet Union as a common enemy.[53]

Attention on China's efforts to modernize its armament have particularly focused on the expansion of weapons imports from Russia. In 1992 China imported from Russia twenty-six SU-27 fighter aircraft and four sets of S-300 surface-to-air missiles, followed by ten IL-76 transporters in 1993, four Kilo-class submarines between 1995 and 1999, and twenty-two SU-27 in 1996. Since 1997 licensed production of the SU-27 has started in China, which is to total 200 aircraft. In July 2001 it was reported that China had signed an agreement to import thirty-eight SU-30.[54] In December 1999 China received delivery of the

Table 2.1 Official figures for China's defence spending 1985–2002

Year	Amount (millions of yuan)	Share in Gross Expenditures (%)	Growth rate (%)
1985	19,153	10.4	6.0
1986	20,075	8.6	4.8
1987	20,962	8.6	4.5
1988	21,800	8.1	3.9
1989	25,146	8.3	15.4
1990	29,031	8.4	15.5
1991	33,031	8.7	13.8
1992	37,786	8.6	14.4
1993	42,580	8.1	12.7
1994	55,071	9.5	29.3
1995	63,672	9.3	15.6
1996	72,006	9.1	13.1
1997	81,257	8.8	12.8
1998	92,857	8.6	14.3
1999	104,650	8.5	12.7
2000	120,500		12.7
2001	141,000		17.7
2002	166,000		17.6

Source: *East Asian Strategic Review 2000*, Tokyo: National Institute for Defense Studies, 2000, p. 217; for 2000: *China Daily*, 8 March 2000; for 2001, 2002: *Reuters*, 4 March 2002

first of two Sovremenniy class destroyers; the second followed in November 2000. Included in the destroyer deal are anti-ship 3M-80E 'Moskit' missiles, which are particularly feared for their capabilities by the US navy. Other arms deals are currently negotiated and executed. Since 1992 Chinese weapons imports from Russia amount to about US$1 billion per year.[55]

In conclusion, one can say that China's military modernization has made significant progress since the beginning of the 1990s and, with the help of weapon imports from Russia, has created some pockets of excellence. However, the general technical level of hardware is still about ten to fifteen years behind the standard of the most advanced Western weapons systems, military education and training have suffered from the PLA's involvement in economic activities, and the cooperation between the various forces is underdeveloped.[56] These deficiencies are addressed with various degrees of success. Future prospects of this modernization are unsettling and China knows how to maximize limited resources politically. This is particularly obvious in the case of China's strategic nuclear forces, which by their nuclear nature evoke terrorizing perceptions. In addition, China wants to offset its backwardness in conventional weaponry by developing information-technology warfare. As a result the maintenance of US military predominance in Asia has become more difficult and costly.[57]

PART 2: JAPAN'S EMERGING TRADITIONAL SECURITY CONCERNS ABOUT CHINA

China's military modernization

The traditional security concern most consistently raised by Japan in the 1990s was the steep rises in China's military expenditures and their non-transparency.[58] Japanese academic writing did not fail to point out that while the modernization of the military had taken a back seat to economic development, this changed at the beginning of the 1990s. Without China's startling economic growth and the explicit link to 'comprehensive national power', Japanese concerns about China's rapid and non-transparent military build-up and security policies would have been much less pronounced.[59] The insertion of an article in China's Constitution about aiming for 'wealth and strength' has further enhanced this link between economic development and military build-up in particular.[60] Nakai Yoshifumi, China expert at the Institute of Developing Economies, a semi-governmental body, commented that the higher priority assigned to military modernization was 'an important change'.[61] Japanese observers were particularly concerned about the link between the build-up of the navy and China's assertion of its territorial claims in the South China Sea and the East China Sea.[62]

Even before the LDP lost its power in 1993, for the first time since 1955, the consistency and speed of China's budgetary increases for military expenditures had led to the first public critical statements by leading government figures. Moreover, Japanese complaints established a link between China's willingness to increase defence expenditures and the role of Japan's ODA to China which touched on the very foundation of Japan's engagement policy and its political support base (see Chapter 3). In March 1991 the chief cabinet secretary, Sakamoto Misoji, declared that Japan was undecided on whether to curb economic aid to China following Beijing's announcement of a sharp increase in defence expenditures.[63] Nothing further happened in this regard, partly also because the government had just successfully extracted itself from the Western sanctions against China in the aftermath of the Tiananmen incident. But the unease about China's military budget continued to find public expression and was also taken up in bilateral talks. Japanese comments have particularly noted the non-transparent character of China's military spending, which is made even more ominous against the background of uncertain political conditions in China.[64] In 1992 the vice-foreign minister, Kakizawa Koji, warned China about buying a Ukrainian-built aircraft carrier.[65] In 1993 a leading member of the ruling LDP, Mitsuzaka, expressed concern about the modernization of China's military and the increase in China's defence spending.[66] In August 1994 a special non-governmental advisory panel on defence, which had been set up under Prime Minister Hosokawa, published a report (the Higuchi Report) which obliquely referred at several points to China's military challenge.[67]

The White Paper on Defence originally took a very cautious approach to China's rising defence expenditures, but this changed towards the end of the 1990s. A senior civilian official of the Defence Agency explained this initial cautious approach by pressure from the cabinet, but he noted that in 1996 a change occurred in the wording of the White Paper.[68] Since 1996 Russia has been portrayed as a diminished threat and the PRC as, at least potentially, an increasing one. While noting the drastic increases in the Chinese military budget since 1988–9, it always qualified this information by pointing at the high inflation, budgetary constraints and the priority of economic reconstruction.[69] From 1995 the White Paper added, however, that items like research and development are not included in the official defence budget, and that there were indications that China used revenue from arms exports for its military modernization which are not included in the official Chinese figures.[70] In the 1998 edition reference is made to the bilateral security dialogue in December 1997, during which China explained that its defence spending is set at around 1 per cent of GNP.[71] The editions from 1996 onwards contain an increasing number of tables about China's military and warn that Japan would have to watch Chinese actions (*chumoku shite iku hitsuyo ga aru*) such as modernization of its nuclear forces, naval and air forces; expanding its scope of activities in the high seas; and growing tension in the Taiwan Strait caused by its military exercises.[72] In the 2000 Japanese edition the White Paper increased the coverage on China to eight pages (compared with eight pages on North Korea and three on South Korea), and for the first time the White Paper mentioned that Japan was within striking distance of Beijing's medium-range ballistic missiles.[73] In the 2001 Japanese edition twelve pages were devoted to China (compared with ten pages to North Korea) and it said that '[t]he objective of modernization needs to be carefully determined to check it does not exceed the needs for the defense of China', an interesting echo of the wording of China's warning against Japanese defence efforts. Moreover, for the first time the paper compared the military capability of China and Taiwan.[74]

China's nuclear deterrent and testing

China's resumption of nuclear tests in the middle of the 1990s touched a very emotional point in Japan, in addition to highlighting the existence of a weapon system which Japan cannot directly counter.

Between May and September 1992 and in October 1993 China conducted a series of nuclear tests, bringing their total number to thirty-nine. Another series of tests took place in June and October 1994. While these tests were criticised in

Japan and also in the US, this criticism did not go beyond official expressions of regret.[75] But with the beginning of a new Chinese nuclear test series in May 1995 the situation had reached a critical stage. The tests occurred at a sensitive moment in global efforts to enhance the nuclear non-proliferation regime; they further added to the negative impact of China's rising military budget and they drew attention to China's growing nuclear deterrent and missile exports. Nuclear weapons have always been a very emotional issue in Japanese domestic politics because of the nuclear bombing of Hiroshima and Nagasaki at the end of the Second World War. However, because of the official policy of putting Japan under the USA's nuclear umbrella as part of the Japan–US security alliance, a dichotomy developed between the public's wish for a more active anti-nuclear weapon policy and the government's actual nuclear-deterrent-based defence policy.[76] As I mentioned in Chapter 1, publicly the Japanese government had not voiced too much concern about the emergence of a Chinese nuclear deterrent in the 1960s, although behind the scenes this was used to extract a nuclear guarantee from the US. In addition to the comforting feeling of the security provided by the US nuclear umbrella, the Chinese nuclear-weapon programme weakened the left-wing forces in Japan which were militating against nuclear weapons. Many of them viewed a nuclear deterrent by Communist China opposing American hegemony as qualitatively different and more acceptable. This even led to a split in the anti-nuclear movement.

China's leaders have always considered a 'limited nuclear deterrent' as a way of standing up, militarily as well as politically, to the two superpowers (the US and the USSR), of offsetting in a cost-efficient way its weakness in conventional weaponry and of ensuring its ranking in the world. China plays down its nuclear deterrent in the public discourse by emphasizing its purely defensive purpose and renouncing its use against non-nuclear countries.[77] Part of the rationale for its nuclear forces is Japan's military potential, the presence of US troops in Japan, and the future possibility of a Japan without the security treaty.[78] The US–Japan missile-defence plans have become an additional motivation for the expansion of China's nuclear deterrent. The Chinese pledge of no use against non-nuclear weapon states does not seem to apply to Japan.[79] When in the summer of 1998 the US and China reached an agreement to stop targeting each other's countries with nuclear missiles, a senior US official involved in the negotiation was quoted as saying that it did not cover US bases in Japan but only long-range missiles. This implies that China's medium-range DF21 ballistic missiles (180 km range) will continue targeting US bases in Japan.[80]

Rather than any immediate perception of threat, it was the delicate moment in global nuclear arms control, China's insensitivity towards Japan's anti-nuclear feelings, the growing realization of China's rise as a economic as well as a military power and the bickering over Japan's past in 1995 which led to a clash with China over its new series of tests. This occurred against the background of a nuclear moratorium by the other declared nuclear powers at the beginning of the 1990s, thus inviting criticism of China for going against the tide of banning nuclear testing altogether. In 1995 the Nuclear Non-Proliferation Treaty (NPT) was extended indefinitely and in September 1996 the Comprehensive Test Ban Treaty (CTBT) was accepted by the UN General Assembly. Despite these movements, China was seen to be improving its nuclear arsenal, miniaturizing its nuclear warheads, testing its medium-range missiles (M-9) in the sea around Taiwan and, according to US information, exporting nuclear weapon technology to Pakistan and Iran. The tests could therefore only reinforce the latent concern about a future 'Chinese threat'.

The timing of the resumption of nuclear testing on 15 May 1995 was particularly annoying for the Japanese. First of all, the tests were in contradiction to the new ODA guidelines of 1992, which call for the reconsideration of ODA in the case of production of weapons of mass destruction. But since then Japan had only expressed its regret when China tested its nuclear arsenal. This time, more importantly, the new series of tests occurred just as the NPT Extension Conference took place, in April/May 1995, to decide on the indefinite extension of the treaty. Japan therefore also protested against French nuclear tests and, in a rare diplomatic move, on July 20 1995 summoned the French ambassador to the prime minister's residence. In China's case it was particularly shocking for Japan that the Socialist prime minister, Murayama Tomoichi, had just visited China, from 2–5 May, and urged Beijing to refrain from testing.[81] Beijing continued with testing and on 17 August exploded another device. The date of this test was only two days after the fiftieth anniversary of the end of the Pacific War and shortly after the annual remembrance on 6 and 9 August 1945. As a result of mounting pressure from public opinion and politicians, on 29 August the Ministry of Foreign Affairs froze the major part of the grant aid for the fiscal year 1995 (except for ¥500 million for emergency humanitarian assistance and grassroots projects) and thereafter.[82] As Soeya Yoshihide points out, it was symbolic for the change in Japanese perception of China that this decision was made by a Socialist prime minister, because traditionally the so-called progressive forces and opinion leaders had been sympathetic to China's nuclear programme.[83] At the same time, however, the government declared that it continued to support China's economic modernization efforts.[84]

The suspension of grant aid for the fiscal year 1995 until March 1997 (¥7 billion) only affected a very small part of Japan's ODA to China, and there were therefore calls to freeze all loans.[85] Grant aid makes up a very small part of Japan's total aid to China – US$78 million, compared with US$1.4 billion of concessional loans for the fiscal year 1994.[86] Public opinion widely supported the suspension of ODA. In an opinion poll in 1995 only 7 per cent found it too harsh, whereas 69 per cent found it adequate and 18 per cent even found it too lenient.[87] Even the *Asahi Shimbun* supported some ODA-related retaliation after the first test and asked for the suspension of yen loans after the second test on 17 August.[88] The government felt, however, that the suspension of all yen loans, with its impact on China's five-year plan, would have been too strong a political signal and China would still go ahead with the testing.[89] This compares with a total suspension of aid to India and Pakistan after their nuclear tests in May

1998, although in both countries Japan is the biggest ODA donor, far ahead of the second-biggest donor.[90]

China conducted one more test in July 1996 and in the same month announced the decision to freeze nuclear testing, followed in September 1996 by an announcement that it would sign the CTBT. The Chinese side questioned Japan's moral right to protest because of the American nuclear umbrella and questioned whether Japan was not simply putting up a smokescreen for its own nuclear ambitions, calling it a 'quasi nuclear power'.[91] The PRC's Foreign Ministry spokesman, Chen Jian, used the 'history card' and suggested that 'the Japanese side ought to deeply self-examine its war crimes and conscientiously draw lessons from history' rather than make 'a big issue of China's nuclear testing.'[92] Japan resumed grant aid in March 1997 because in the meantime frictions had arisen again over Beijing's claim to the Senkaku Islands and China's opposition to Prime Minister Hashimoto's visit to the Yasukuni Shrine in August 1996.[93] In addition, the Hashimoto–Clinton Statement in April 1996 demanded some soothing of Beijing. One good outcome of the dispute was China agreeing to the first senior-level consultations on disarmament and non-proliferation of nuclear weapons, which took place on 25 July 1995.[94] Still, apart from the different context of the G-7 Summit decision to suspend ODA to China, this was the first time Japan had taken such retaliatory measures since 1972.[95] The US only temporarily suspended export credits to China as a result of China's test, and there was no concerted Western action.[96] Moreover, China's nuclear tests not only contributed to a less benign Japanese view of China, but also prepared the political ground in Japan for greater political support for strengthening the security alliance with the US and exploring TMD, both of which later became very contentious issues for Japan's relationship with China.

The Chinese nuclear tests led to greater attention being paid by the public and government to China's nuclear deterrent and its exports of nuclear technology and missiles.[97] Its strategic nuclear forces are still small, but they include between fifteen to twenty DF-4 (CSS-3), more than thirty-eight DF-3 (CSS-2) and around eight DF-21 (CSS-5), which can reach Japan.[98] Other missiles which could reach Japan are twelve CSS-N-3 (JL-1) missiles on China's one nuclear submarine (Xia SSBN) and about 150 short-range ballistic missiles DF-15 (CSS-6/M-9), with a range of 600 km.[99] China's strategic capability is composed of less than 200 nuclear warheads, of which only twenty to thirty may be operational at any given time.[100] The medium-range missiles would be those most likely used against Japan and the Japan-based US forces. According to Ogawa Shinichi, senior research fellow and deputy director of the Second Research Department at the National Institute for Defence Studies (NIDS), both China and North Korea can utilize their ballistic missiles as weapons of terror or as a means of intimidating US allies in East Asia to keep them from assisting US military operations in the Taiwan Strait or on the Korean Peninsula.[101] Reports about the development of North Korean short- and medium-range missiles, as well as Chinese missile tests in 1995/6 in the Taiwan Strait, have been crucial in creating an atmosphere which allowed the government to point to China's missile development, particularly after the North Korean side tested a missile on 31 August 1998 (Taepodong-1, with a range of about 2,000 km) which flew over Japan before plunging into the Pacific. In August 1999 the Gaimusho expressed its concern about the test launch of a new long-range missile to the Chinese embassy in Tokyo. The chief cabinet secretary, Nonaka Hiromu, voiced his regret about the test in view of global efforts towards non-proliferation and reduction of weapons of mass destruction.[102] The White Paper on defence in 2000 mentioned for the first time the capacity of China's medium-range missiles to reach Japan, and stated that the CSS-2 (Dongfeng 3A) was being gradually replaced by the more advanced CSS-5 (Dongfeng 21). It also mentioned that new short-range missiles were being deployed along the Taiwan Strait.[103]

Japan has also grown concerned about China's exports of equipment and technology related to weapons of mass destruction to North Korea and other sensitive countries in South Asia (Pakistan) and the Middle East (Iran, Libya, Syria).[104] The most direct concern is North Korea, which has been helped in the development of its missile force by China and which is exporting missile technologies directly as well as in cooperation with China.[105] The strongest reminder, apart from American efforts to rope Japan into stronger anti-proliferation policies, were the nuclear tests in India and Pakistan in May 1998. Many commentators in Japan linked Pakistan's ability to immediately follow up the Indian tests with their own to assistance from China.[106]

Territorial disputes

As if to impress on the Japanese the possible purpose of increasing defence expenditures and strengthening its nuclear arms, from the beginning of the 1990s China started to assert more strongly its territorial claims in the South China Sea and the East China Sea. This raised Japanese security concerns related to the safety of its sea lanes to the Middle East and Southeast Asia, the territorial dispute with China about the Senkaku/Diaoyu Islands, and its oil and fishing interests in the East China Sea.[107] Moreover, much of the focus of China's force modernization has been on the navy, which is still very underdeveloped except for its nuclear component.[108] According to an internal Chinese assessment, the Chinese navy will achieve parity with the Japanese navy by the year 2050.[109]

The protection of territorial integrity is at the heart of every national security policy, and territorial disputes therefore have the most far-reaching consequences for security relations. Also involved is national pride, which can play a decisive role in democratic as well as autocratic regimes. Due to the partial dependence of the Maritime Self-Defence Force (MSDF) on US military forces and their larger role in the protection of the Asia-Pacific sea lanes, the reliability of the Japan–US alliance also plays a considerable role. Finally, in the case of the territorial issues between Japan and China, given their proximity to as yet unquantifiable seabed-based energy reserves, raw material reserves and fishing interests, economic interests have gained increasing importance. In the case of oil and gas reserves, these interests are highlighted by the fact that major contemporary oil suppliers (mostly in the Middle East) are said to reach peak production by 2010–20, while Chinese energy needs are mounting.[110] In November 1993 China became a net oil importer, and, with its rapidly growing economy still mostly based on highly polluting coal, it is desperate to develop oil and gas fields.[111] From China being dependent on foreign supplies for just over 5 per cent of its oil needs in 1995, the corresponding figure in 2010 has been estimated to reach around 40 per cent.[112] According to Kent Calder, by 2010 Chinese oil imports could reach 3 million barrels per day, rising close to the current Japanese import levels, of around 4.5 million barrels per day, by 2015.[113] In 2001 China was said to be spending US$1.6 billion per month on oil imports, up to 8 per cent of its imports bill.[114] Oil made up 20 per cent of China's commercial energy consumption in 1996, and the International Energy Agency in Paris estimates that it will increase to 26 per cent by 2020, equalling a total of 8 million barrels a day. This amounts to about 400 million metric tons a year, more than the projected net imports in 2020 of Japan, South Korea, Australia and New Zealand combined.[115]

Senkaku Islands

The territorial dispute over the Senkaku Islands (called Diaoyudao by the PRC and Diaoyutai by the Republic of China, Taiwan) concerns eight uninhabited islands and barren rocks which have a land area of only 6.3 square km.[116] The islands are approximately 120 nautical miles northeast of Taiwan, 200 nautical miles east of the Chinese mainland and 200 nautical miles southeast of Okinawa.[117] In terms of the earliest historical records, the Chinese claims to the islands are very strong, but from 1884 until 1941 the Japanese side was the only one actively using and occupying them. Thereafter, the Chinese government under the Guomindang made no efforts to specifically claim the islands in the Cairo Declaration and the Potsdam Declaration, and no protests were made against the San Francisco Peace Treaty in 1951, which gave the US full administrative power over the area. Also, the government of the PRC did not protest or claim the islands until a UN survey was published in 1968. However, even Japanese publications were not consistent in including the Senkaku Islands.[118] Still, most non-Japanese and non-Chinese specialists give more credence to Japan's claim than to China's.[119]

The dispute surfaced with the publication of a seismic survey report under the auspices of the UN Economic Commission for Asia and the Far East (ECAFE) in 1968, which mentioned the possibility of huge oil and gas reserves in the area; this was confirmed by a Japanese report in 1969. Greg Austin mentions that Beijing stated its claim to the Senkaku Islands for the first time in 1970, after the Japanese government had protested to the government in Taiwan about its allocation of oil concessions in the East China Sea, including the area of the Senkaku Islands.[120] It is from 1970 onwards that the territorial dispute between Japan, on the one hand, and the PRC and ROC, on the other, became active. The dispute also affects decisions between Japan, China and Korea on the delimitation of the continental shelf and the EEZ of the whole area of the East China Sea.

Due to the improvement in relations between China and both Japan and the US since 1971, the territorial dispute was soon put to rest for most of the 1970s and 1980s. It flared up again with the promulgation of China's territorial law in 1992 and with the increase in Chinese survey ships around the Senkaku Islands in the 1990s. Both governments started to take a more assertive stance and incidents were triggered by nationalists on the Japanese as well as the Chinese side (mainly Chinese from Hong Kong and Taiwan).

In February 1992 the Chinese legislature passed the 'Law of the People's Republic of China on its Territorial Waters and their Contiguous Areas', which included not only the South China Sea, but also explicitly the Senkaku Islands. According to reports, it was the PLA which insisted, over the objections of the Chinese Ministry of Foreign Affairs, on explicitly referring to the Senkaku Islands.[121] The territorial law raised great concern with all China's maritime neighbours, including Japan, which protested against it officially.[122] In April of the same year a Chinese navy deputy commander was quoted in the Chinese press as saying that it was high time that China readjusted its maritime strategy and made more efforts to recover the oil and gas resources in the South China Sea, thus reinforcing the seriousness of Chinese motives and highlighting its energy problems.[123] But the Chinese top leadership was not interested in pushing the issue any further: when Jiang Zemin, then secretary-general of the CCP, visited Japan in April 1992 Prime Minister Miyazawa raised the issue of China's new territorial law, but Jiang referred back to a statement made in 1978 by Deng Xiaoping about leaving the issue for the future.[124] The 1992 Law complicated the preparation for the first Tenno visit to China, an event which both Japan and China hoped would pass off without incident. For this reason, as well as to calm the concerns of countries disputing territory with China in the South China Sea, the Chinese Foreign Ministry stated that the law did not represent a change in Chinese foreign policy and would not affect the joint development of contested territories.[125] Hashimoto Hiroshi, the head of the Gaimusho's Information and Cultural Affairs Bureau, demonstrated the Japanese side's interest in not letting the new law interfere with the Japanese–Chinese relationship when he explained that the Chinese legislation was 'merely a matter of China's tidying up its domestic legislation institutions' and 'the dispute would remain shelved as previously agreed'.[126]

Since then, however, the territorial dispute has attracted greater attention, fuelled by nationalistic zealots on both sides, by episodic reaffirmation of official territorial claims by the Japanese and Chinese governments, and by the rise of incursions of so-called Chinese 'research ships' as well as warships into the EEZ waters around the Senkaku Islands and Japan's EEZ in the East China Sea in general. Of the thirty-three Chinese intrusions into Japan's EEZ between 1996 and 1998, five were into the territorial waters around the Senkaku Islands.[127] In May 1999 the Defence White Paper stated that the presence of a fleet of

Chinese warships had been confirmed for the first time in waters around the Senkaku islands.[128] In 1999 the Japanese coastguard reported illegal activities by 1,548 fishing vessels from the PRC (1998: 1,547) and 197 (1998: 326) such vessels from Taiwan in the territorial waters around the Senkaku Islands.[129]

One of the flashpoints for conflict has been activities by right-wing organizations. In 1988 the Japanese government allowed one such organization to improve a non-governmental lighthouse facility on one of the Senkaku Islands, and in 1990 developments on this issue erupted in demonstrations in Taiwan and Hong Kong and led to attempts from these two places to enter the Senkaku Islands.[130] China was restrained in its reaction because of ongoing loan negotiations and its need to seek international rehabilitation in the aftermath of Tiananmen.[131]

Japan's declaration of an EEZ (a zone of 200 miles or circa 370 km around its territories) around the islands in June 1996 (taking effect on 20 July 1996) became another flashpoint for the dispute. Both countries differ on the entitlement of the Senkaku Islands to a continental shelf and EEZ.[132] The total area for the EEZ which may be claimed from the Senkaku Islands is about 20,500 square nautical miles. China claims that the islands are not entitled to a continental shelf or EEZ, whereas Japan asserts the opposite. Under article 121 of the UN Convention on the Law of the Sea (UNCLOS), 'rocks' are not entitled to an EEZ.[133] In June 1996 China and Taiwan protested Japan's declaration of a 200m EEZ around the Senkaku Islands.[134]

The declaration of an EEZ which surrounds the Senkaku Islands not only led to Chinese and Taiwanese protests, but Japanese rightists landed on one of the disputed islands to erect a lighthouse tower. These developments caused activists from Hong Kong and Taiwan to demonstrate and to attempt to land.[135] Japanese landings by right-wingers (e.g. members of Seinensha, and Nishimura Shingo, a Jiyuto member of the Lower House) to demonstrate for Japan's ownership have taken place sporadically since then.[136] In 1999 Futami Nobuaki, a member of Shinshinto and chairman of the Diet's Committee on National Security, supported an official visit by committee members to the islands, but the visit failed to materialize in the face of strong opposition from more moderate government leaders and the Gaimusho.[137] These developments reflected not only a greater Japanese assertiveness and coolness towards China in some Japanese quarters, but also the emphases of domestic politics in Hong Kong, China and Taiwan. The Japanese authorities could probably have prevented the rightists from landing on one of the privately owned islands (Kitakojima) because the owners had not given their consent to the landing.[138]

For the Chinese government, the encouragement of incidents involving Chinese activists in 1996 was also a means of protesting indirectly against the Hashimoto–Clinton Joint Declaration of April 1996 and the resulting Guidelines, as well as the Taiwan issue.[139] However, as in 1990, China carefully controlled the outburst in order not to jeopardize Japanese ODA. In return, Chinese officials even came under domestic attack for 'kowtowing to Japan'.[140] It has become known that the PLA was very dissatisfied with the Chinese Ministry of Foreign Affairs for downplaying the crisis in late 1996 and early 1997, and for vetoing the PLA's intention to protect activists from Hong Kong and Taiwan.[141]

Walking a tightrope

As we have seen, both countries are trying to keep the territorial dispute from further poisoning the bilateral relationship, but various circumstances on both sides keep it alive and occasionally enflame it. Both governments want to maintain their opposing claims and to accommodate the activities of non-governmental actors who are not totally under their control. In China's case, the differing interests of the PLA and the Ministry of Foreign Affairs have to be balanced. The Japanese government has to take into consideration public opinion at home as well as the implications of China's other territorial claims in the South China Sea, which are along Japan's sea and air lanes. China's government finds playing the nationalistic card at home useful, and sometimes necessary, to enhance its legitimacy.[142] The Chinese leadership sometimes uses the conflict to indicate its displeasure with American or Japanese policies. In addition to the above-mentioned use of the incidents in 1996 and 1997, media reports in May 1999 explained the sending of Chinese vessels into the vicinity of the disputed islands as sign of protest against the Japan–US guidelines and the accidental NATO bombing of the Chinese embassy in Belgrade.[143] But the ruling LDP also does not shy away from playing the nationalistic card to win elections, as it did at the end of September 1996 when it gave the campaign promise that the Senkaku Islands and Takeshima (under South Korean control and called Dokto in Korean) are Japanese territory.[144] From a Constructivist perspective, beyond aspects of international law and resources, the territorial conflict is, for Japan, part of an understanding of China which sees the giant neighbour threatening its identity in an increasing number of areas, whereas for China it is part of the historical discourse of regaining what should rightfully be returned to China in order to restore its former national status.

Japan's balancing act between reminding China of its position on the territorial issue (and this also applies to the yet to be agreed median line as the maritime border in the East China Sea, as discussed below) and keeping the bilateral temperature down is visible, for example, in the treatment of the issue in the Defence White Paper. While it has mentioned China's new territorial law and its inclusion of the Senkaku Islands since the 1992 edition, it is only since the 1997 edition that there is a mention of China conducting 'oceanological research' in the East China Sea beyond the median line between the two countries.[145] It was reported in 1994 that the Japanese Defence Agency seemed to be understating the number of Chinese aircraft violating Japanese airspace.[146] However, in 1995 it was reported that in autumn Air Self-Defence Forces (ASDF) fighter jets scrambled for the first time ever in response to Chinese jets intruding into Japanese airspace, and another report quoted the ASDF's intention to upgrade its F-4EJ fighters in the area with the more capable F-15.[147] In 1999, 15 per cent of the ASDF's sorties were due to Chinese aircraft, compared with 70 per cent to Russian aircraft. But there were far fewer scramble sorties altogether because of the declining activities of both countries (China and Russia).[148] The Chinese air force is also not yet able to deploy so far away from home bases. The only aircraft of concern to Japanese defence officials is China's Sukhov-27 bomber.[149] Asserting ownership without appearing provocative also partly explains the fact that the coastguard, rather than the MSDF, continues to be in charge of patrolling the area, despite the territorial dispute.[150] Japan has also not fortified the islands. At the same time, this 'business-as-usual' approach reinforces the government's claim that there is no territorial issue. On the other hand, in a conciliatory move the Japanese side informed Beijing that it would not allow any oil exploration in the territorial waters of the islands until an agreement had been achieved.[151]

Since 1972 the Chinese government has tried to avoid solving the problem in order to maintain its territorial claim without causing confrontation. When the Japanese government wanted to raise the Senkaku Islands issue in the 1970s the Chinese government refused to do so. When Prime Minister Tanaka Kakuei tried to raise the issue in 1972, Zhou Enlai declined to discuss it, dismissing the importance of the islands.[152] In 1975 the Chinese side made it known that the issue of Taiwan as well as of territorial ownership of the Senkaku islands was not to be discussed for the conclusion of the Peace and Friendship Treaty.[153] In 1978, when the treaty was finally concluded, both sides seemed to have accepted that solving the issue should be left to 'future generations'. That year Deng Xiaoping declared that the two sides had agreed to shelve the issue and leave it for future generations to solve, but there was no official Japanese confirmation of that alleged agreement. Deng repeated in 1983 that he wanted the issue to be decided 'at another time'.[154] When Prime Minister Uno Sosuke claimed in May 1989 that the territorial dispute had been settled because Japan enjoyed de facto control over the islands, the Chinese government rejected the statement, saying that the dispute was only shelved.[155] In 1992 Secretary-General Jiang Zemin referred back to Deng Xiaoping's 1978 statement when Prime Minister Miyazawa raised the issue of the 1992 National People's Congress Law, as we saw earlier. The Japanese government is now publicly denying that it ever tacitly agreed to shelve the issue and even denies the existence of a territorial issue, which is rather ingenious since it did not contradict the Deng 1978 and 1983 statements at the time.[156] Moreover, the above-mentioned statement by Press Secretary Hashimoto Hiroshi playing down the issue in 1992 showed that Japan had indeed agreed to shelve the issue. In 1990 the chief cabinet secretary, Sakamoto Misuji, also declared his agreement with Deng Xiaoping's 1978 statement to calm Chinese protests against Japanese right-wing activities on the Senkaku Islands.[157]

While postponing the solution of the territorial problem to the indefinite future by reiterating Deng's stance, the Chinese government also tried to insinuate that it holds the title to the islands. After yet another incident in April 1997, the Foreign Ministry spokesman Cui Tiankai stated that 'the Diaoyu Islands issue should be settled by negotiation on the basis of respecting facts when the time is ripe'.[158] Although this statement partly reflects Deng Xiaoping's 1978 remark, for many Japanese it assumes a rather ominous tone in the light of China's ongoing efforts to modernize its naval and air force. It is clearly a temporizing device since it is not logical to insist on negotiation if China's title to the islands is so clear. Moreover, some Chinese scholars predict that these islands will increase in importance in the long-term strategic competition between the two countries because of their potential natural resources and their strategic geographical location.[159]

US context

The territorial conflict over the Senkaku Islands has also given an insight into the vagaries of the Japan–US–China triangular relationship and the US's difficulty in simultaneously catering to the needs of the US–Japan alliance and maintaining a workable relationship with China. After the Second World War the US occupied Okinawa, and the Senkaku Islands were considered part of it, being used by the US military as a firing range. Funabashi asserts that during its occupation of Okinawa the US 'consistently maintained' that the territorial rights were Japan's and that the occupation meant only administrative rights.[160] The US position may not ultimately have a legal effect on the territorial claims of either side, but politically it reinforced the Japanese claim. This is particularly relevant for the period up to 1969, during which the PRC did not make any efforts to claim the islands. In a communiqué of 21 October 1971, however, the Department of State tried to facilitate the rapprochement with China by stating that the reversion of the administrative rights over Okinawa to Japan did not signify a bias towards any of the territorial claims of the parties involved, while at the same time confirming the applicability of the Japan–US security treaty to the islands.[161] This suddenly introduced separation between the administrative rights and sovereignty is therefore not very convincing. That the US wants to have it both ways is also demonstrated by the fact that its military continued to use some parts of the islands as a firing range and paid rent for this activity until 1979; that is, even after their reversion of Okinawa to Japan. The relevant rent agreement is still in force.[162]

Questions about the US position were also raised in 1996. When the Senkaku Islands dispute flared up again in October 1996, the spokesman of the US Department of State made a statement to the press which suddenly cast doubt on the applicability of the security treaty to the islands. These doubts were reinforced by a statement made by Ambassador Mondale in Tokyo. Later the US administration reverted to its contradictory position on separating administrative rights from sovereignty, which it has maintained since 1971.[163] This position of recognizing Japan's administrative but not its sovereignty rights is, incidentally, shared by Republicans and Democrats.[164]

It has been speculated that this contradictory US position emerged in 1971 against the background of the Cold War and the beginning of resumption of relations with China.[165] The initial Department of State statement in October

1996 is explained by Funabashi by the conflicting US aim at that time of simultaneously supporting the military alliance with Japan and improving US–Chinese relations. In 1996 the US administration was trying to repair American–Chinese relations in the aftermath of the 1995 visit of Taiwan's president Li Denghui to the US.[166] As we will see later in Chapter 4, this was yet another incident which gave many Japanese the impression that the Clinton administration was favouring China over Japan. Looking at the triangular dynamics involved, it indicates that the bilateral security treaty will for the foreseeable future most likely prevent any military confrontation over the Senkaku Islands, but in the meantime US political support for a solution in Japan's favour will stay very limited.[167] The US hopes that its military superiority will serve as a sufficient deterrent without risking more important interests towards China. Therefore, any new flare-up of tensions will highlight the rivalry between US–Chinese relations and US–Japanese relations. The Chinese side has warned the US not to intervene in the dispute since it considers it a bilateral issue between China and Japan only.

East China Sea

As we have seen, the Senkaku Islands issue is closely linked to the disputed continental shelf in the wider area of the East China Sea and one dispute blocks the solution of the other. The continental shelf in the East China Sea is 300,000 square km. China claims the whole shelf to the Okinawa Trough, including an unspecified portion of the Japan/South Korea Joint Development Zone. Japan claims the same shelf to a median line between its undisputed territory and that of China.[168]

Japan and South Korea had attempted to draft an area of joint development where their claims completely overlapped, but China objected to this in 1974. As a result, Japan deferred ratification of an agreement on the continental shelf demarcation with South Korea until June 1977.[169] A solution is made difficult since all East China Sea claimants (Japan, China, South Korea and Taiwan) cite different principles of international law to support their claims. Whereas Japan insists on the principle of an equidistant (median) line, China adheres to the natural prolongation theory. In 1996 Japan, South Korea and China declared a 200m EEZ. All three countries ratified the 1982 UNCLOS, but the convention does not help in all cases since it does not address historical claims, and its lack of clear definitions makes it difficult to judge how to apply its provisions on the EEZ and the continental shelf.[170] As Hiramatsu Shigeo states, there is no other way to clarify the continental shelf than by political negotiation.[171] However, in view of the fishing and mining interests involved, the stakes for Japan are considerable since its land territory is 380,000 square km (the sixty-first largest land area in the world), but the area of the EEZ amounts to 4.51 million square km (sixth largest EEZ area).[172]

Again, the Chinese side has been rather reluctant to engage in negotiations with Japan (but also with South Korea) on delimiting the sea borders under the new 1982 UNCLOS. The main reason is the fundamental difference between

China and its neighbours on the application of the Law of Sea. This situation led to tensions about rising incursions by Chinese vessels into disputed as well as undisputed areas of Japan's EEZ. Moreover, in the meantime China started actively to explore and even to produce oil and gas in the area adjacent to the median line. Hiramatsu Shigeo claims that the Japanese government, for its part, has also avoided a clarification of the territorial issue in order to protect the friendly relationship with China.[173] Under the 1982 UNCLOS, Japan has until 2006 (ten years after the convention took effect in 1996) to submit to the UN scientific research data including submarine landform and geology, geomagnetism and gravity in order to claim the continental shelf. China is pursuing this research much more actively than Japan, including within Japan's EEZ.[174]

The stalemate over the delimitation of the EEZ also negatively influenced the conclusion of a bilateral fishing agreement to replace the old one of August 1975.[175] The negotiations for the fishing agreement started in 1996 after both countries had ratified the UNCLOS, which raised the necessity of renewing the 1978 fishing agreement.[176] In November 1997 Prime Minister Hashimoto Ryutaro and Premier Li Peng signed a new fishing agreement, which came into effect only in June 2000.[177] The Senkaku Islands dispute was circumvented by excluding the area around the islands and leaving the existing fishing regime in place.[178] The agreement was held up by a disagreement over zoning, fishing operations and quota. Japan demanded that a more limited number of fishing vessels be admitted than China was willing to accept.[179] South Korea – which also encountered great difficulties in concluding a fishing agreement with China, let alone agreement on the EEZ – protested against this agreement and demanded trilateral talks because the designated area allegedly overlaps the EEZ that the ROC claims around its shores.[180] Under the pact, Japan and China agreed to establish a free fishing zone between 127 degrees 30 minutes east and 124 degrees 45 minutes east longitude, where boats from the two countries may catch fish without prior approval from their respective governments.

Incursions raising tensions

In the absence of an agreed sea border, incursions by Chinese oil exploration-related vessels, war ships and ocean research vessels into Japan's claimed EEZ around the Senkaku as well as inside Japan's EEZ elsewhere in the East China Sea have increased since 1995. It was the Japanese protest against China's resumption of nuclear testing in May 1995 which resulted in greater publicity being given to such incursions. During May–June 1995 Chinese survey ships cruised for eighteen days in the waters around the Senkaku Islands without respecting Japan's EEZ.[181] According to Japan's official interpretation of the UNCLOS, foreign research vessels can enter the EEZ of another country but they have to ask permission. Chinese ships refuse to do so, claiming that the sea area is Chinese territory, that it belongs to China's EEZ, or that the ship is engaged in legal activities.[182] The Chinese government thus used the absence of an agreed naval border to refute Japan's protests about the incursion of

Chinese ships into Japan's EEZ and territorial waters.[183] During the 7th Japan–China Security Dialogue meeting in June 2000, after the issue had aroused Japanese public opinion to a considerable extent, the Chinese side still dismissed Japanese complaints about the increasing movements of its warships as 'normal activities', but on the subject of its research vessels commented that it would pay attention to Japan's representations (*moshiire o jushi*).[184] However, Chinese incursions now even take place into Japan's EEZ, whose borders have never been an issue between the two countries. In 2000 the foreign minister, Kono Yohei, protested against the fact that the Chinese demanded that Japan should not raise the issue of incursions until the disputed borders were mutually agreed while reserving the right to continue these incursions.[185]

Whereas reports on Chinese incursions were initially prominently featured only by the more nationalistic media outlets such as the *Sankei Shimbun*, they are now also reported in the other media and have become the subject of Diet inter-pellations. Most of the incursions are by Chinese fishing vessels. The cases of so-called Chinese research vessels and lately also Chinese warships have attracted the greatest attention and raised bilateral tensions considerably.

The number of incursions into Japan's EEZ (including the territorial waters around the Senkaku) by Chinese research vessels increased from seven in 1995 to thirty-three in 1999 (see Table 2.2).[186] In summer 2000 the Maritime Safety Agency (MSA) reported that the activities of Chinese vessels had increased in the area between the median line and Japan's territorial waters, as well as in areas where the maritime borders between Japan and China are not disputed (e.g. south of Ishigaki Island or south of Danjo Island).[187] Since May 1999 Chinese warships have operated in the vicinity of Japanese territorial waters for the first time. The number of MSDF sightings of Chinese warships in waters around Japan (including passage through Japanese straits like the Tsuruga Strait) increased from two ships in 1998 to twenty-seven in 1999.[188] But since the Chinese ships operated in the Open Sea or in Japan's EEZ and passage there is in principle free, the MSA admitted that it was difficult to conclude that it was a problem relevant to international law. Moreover, there are no domestic Japanese laws on how to enforce the requirement of prior approval of foreign research

Table 2.2 Incursions of Chinese 'research vessels' into Japan's EEZ

1996	15
1997	4
1998	16
1999	33 [a]
2000	24

Source: *Chugoku kaiyo chosasen oyobi kaigun kantei no ugoki*, 8 August 2000 (paper submitted to the LDP by the MSA); and *East Asian Strategic Review 2001*, Tokyo: National Institute of Defense Studies 2001, 199–203

Note [a] 30 according to NIDS

vessels in Japan's EEZ, and the Japanese authorities have so far left it to warnings and protests through diplomatic channels. However, it argued that it was 'inappropriate for Japanese–Chinese trust and friendship'. The government simply insisted that it wanted to use diplomatic channels to address the problem and that it wanted to continue to study what more could be done within the existing legal framework.[189] The Chinese navy has now acquired tanker aircraft, which will enhance the operational radius of their air force. The distance of around 500km between China and the Senkaku Islands is about the same as the distance from Naha base, where ASDF fighters are deployed.[190]

The situation reached a climax in summer 2000 when the Foreign Affairs Committee of the LDP postponed a ¥17.2 billion loan package to China, making a release of the loan contingent on a satisfying clarification from the Chinese side during the forthcoming meeting of Foreign Minister Kono Yohei with his Chinese counterpart in Beijing at the end of August.[191] In the talks Foreign Minister Tang stated that the 'problem no longer existed' and that discussions should begin to establish a system of notification without prejudice to territorial claims.[192] As a result the LDP released the loan in September 2000 and the incursions and close movements of Chinese warships stopped for some time. In February 2001 both sides agreed on a system of prior notification for ships of both countries, but without a clear definition of the area to which it should apply.[193] Detailed maritime research by the Chinese navy in Japan's EEZ resumed in summer 2001, with and without prior notification, and the Japanese government was becoming more public in stating that these activities included exploration of natural resources, in violation of international treaties, and anti-submarine manoeuvres.[194]

The Kono–Tang talks in the wake of rising tensions also gave a new impetus to negotiations for the delimitation of naval borders. Japan and China had only started consultations on the delimitation of the EEZ and the continental shelves in August 1998, on the basis of an agreement made on the occasion of President Jiang's visit to Japan in November 1998. While one round took place in 1998, the next consultation, planned for 1999, did not materialize. Japan pressed China on this matter in 1999, without success for some time, but similar discussions took place in other fora.[195] During Prime Minister Obuchi's visit to China in July 1999, the Chinese foreign minister, Tang Jiaxuan, only expressed agreement that the planned talks for the EEZ should be realised soon. Finally, two rounds took place in 2000.[196] It is obvious that China is still not keen on finding a solution, in order to avoid the inevitable confrontation over the territorial claims of both sides, but the cost of this avoidance strategy is high in terms of Japan's growing perception of China as a long-term security threat and because it gives rise to new incidents.

Chinese oil and gas production

Apart from fishing and military interests, China's developing offshore oil industry accounts for a growing number of research vessel incursions. The simultaneous sharp rise in naval vessels has also been attributed to patrolling of the vicinity of these Chinese oil facilities.[197]

Probably in order to win time and circumvent the fundamental issue of territorial delimitation while still trying to benefit from Japan's technology, in 1978, 1990 and 1996 China proposed joint exploration of the continental shelf, but Japan demanded a settlement of the sea border first.[198] There is information that in 1980 the Japanese government proposed joint exploration to China provided that it would not prejudice territorial claims.[199] In the specific case of the Senkaku Islands, in October 1980 Deputy Premier Yao Yilin proposed joint oil development around the islands, which might also include the US.[200] In the same year Japanese–Chinese negotiations on joint development of the area, including the area around the islands, foundered after a series of meetings.[201] In October 1990 China suggested 'joint development' of the islands, but the report is not clear what exactly was meant by this.[202]

However, today not only is Japan refusing joint exploration as a solution to the conflict, but one can also assume that China no longer has an urgent technological need to rely on any kind of foreign involvement. China has been drilling for oil and gas in the East China Sea since the beginning of the 1980s, and has thus proved its willingness to go ahead on its own as well as its technological ability to do so.[203] In 1995 China launched test drilling in Japan's claimed EEZ about 570m away from the equidistant line; this was met by a protest from the Japanese government.[204] Hiramatsu Shigeo therefore warns that it will not be long before China crosses Japan's unilaterally established median line.[205] China National Offshore Oil Corporation (CNOOC) and Sinopec Star Petroleum Corporation (SSPC) operate several oil fields in the East China Sea. In June 2000 CNOOC announced that it wants to discover 600 billion cubic metres of natural gas reserves in the East China Sea between 2001 and 2005.[206] SSPC announced at the same time that it wants to spend US$2.9 billion in the East China Sea on oil and gas production and to have more than ninety wells by 2010. It wants to boost proven natural gas reserves in the region, from 40–50 billion cubic metres now to 150–300 billion cubic metres by 2003.[207] It is not clear whether these announcements have been followed up, since they also coincided with the flotation of these companies on the stock market. But they certainly reflected a continued strong Chinese interest in the oil and gas reserves of the area.

The major gas reserves are in the Chunxiao field and in the Xihu depression. The Pinghu oil and gas field in the Xihu depression (365km off the shore of China) is near the median line, the Chunxiao field only 5km from it. Pinghu is linked by one oil and one gas pipeline to Shanghai; the gas pipeline started to deliver 400,000 cubic metres of gas daily to Shanghai in 2000.[208] Another pipeline is planned from Chunxiao to the coastal city of Wenzhou.[209] In the past foreign oil companies drilled a total of fourteen dry holes in the East China Sea, but today only Chinese companies are involved in the area – except for the small Primeline Petroleum Corporation, which is a Canada-listed company with a Chinese majority shareholder.[210]

In contrast to Chinese energy activities, the Japanese government has refused to give permission for any activities by Japanese energy companies in the East China Sea in order to avoid confrontation with China. Four Japanese companies were refused licenses in the 1960s.[211] In 1981 Teikoku Oil sank a wildcat well off Miyakojima, an island about 120 miles southeast of the Senkaku Islands, but the results were not made public.[212] Most of the Chinese fields discovered in the East China Sea have, to date, been predominantly gas bearing and of medium size. Given the relatively limited gas reserve base of East China Sea fields, the distance from markets on the Japanese mainland and the current excess of liquified natural gas (LNG) supply capacity available in Asia, the incentive for Japanese investment in the East China Sea is currently not high.[213]

Hiramatsu Shigeo, however, argues that the Gaimusho has been rather lenient, to the detriment of Japan's interests.[214] This policy of Japanese restraint to protect Japanese–Chinese relations seems to go back to at least October 1980, when Japan's MITI minister declared that Japan would not develop oil fields around the Senkaku Islands if China did not participate.[215] Moreover, Japan's Export–Import Bank provided a substantial loan for the pipeline from the Pinghu field to Shanghai, as did the Asian Development Bank (ADB), where Japan's influence is very strong.[216]

As in the case of the Senkaku Islands, Japan cannot expect much US support in its conflict with China about the EEZ or territorial waters in the East China Sea. According to Foreign Minister Kono's Diet statement in May 2000, the intrusions into Japan's EEZ fall within the framework of the Japanese–American security treaty's Far Eastern clause, and this interpretation was shared by the US. In a later clarification he explained that the Senkaku Islands, as Japan's territory, fall within the framework of the security treaty's application, not just within the Far Eastern clause.[217] However, according to Article 4 of the security treaty, such a distinction is only made concerning 'consultations' for the implementation of the treaty. Article 5 speaks of meeting the common danger in case of armed attack against 'territories under the administration of Japan'. According to the Law of the Sea there is no specific difference between the type of administration a country exerts over its EEZ and its territories. In any case, the US does not pronounce itself on any territorial claims.

The South China Sea

The South China Sea is related to Japan's security because the safety of the country's major sea lanes of communication and air corridors are involved. The area is also important for natural resources and fishing. For China, the South China Sea is related not only to its territorial claim to the whole area, backed by strong nationalistic feelings, but also to securing its sea lanes, which are so far controlled by the US navy. The primary source of its oil imports is the Middle East, amounting to a share of 52.9 per cent in 1996, with the next biggest share coming from the Asia-Pacific, with 36.3 per cent.[218] In addition, the area is important for fishing and seabed resources.

Any conflict between China, on the one hand, and claimants and beneficiaries of the South China Sea, on the other, would have a negative impact on Japan's security environment and make compromise in the East China Sea even more difficult. In addition, China's handling of its claims to the South China Sea is an indicator of its willingness to use military force.[219] One of the more outspoken Japanese commentators, Professor Nishihara Masashi of the Defence Academy, addressed this linkage when he was quoted as saying that 'The way they [the Chinese] have behaved in the South China Sea may one day be applied to the Senkaku Islands. It's a creeping expansionism'.[220] The South China Sea is also relevant to Japan's security as it has been linked to piracy and, more recently, to illegal immigration.

Annually, over 40,000 ships pass through the South China Sea, which is considerably more than through the Suez Canal or the Panama Canal.[221] Also, around 70 per cent of Japan's oil imports, mostly from the Middle East, pass through the area. Other sea-bound imports of raw materials and exports of finished goods are also dependent on safe shipping through this maritime area, which directly links Japan with Southeast Asia, where Japan has established a network economy. Forty-two per cent of Japan's exports (by value) took the route through the South China Sea in the 1990s, as did 42 per cent of Japan's imports (by value).[222] The Chinese analyst Ji Guoxing estimates that Japan's and China's total trade via Southeast Asian sea lanes was US$260.4 billion and US$65.6 billion, 39 per cent and 27 per cent, respectively, of their total trade.[223] In 1994, 1,555 oil tankers used the South China Sea to reach Japan; 39 per cent of Japan's total trade and the equivalent of 6 per cent of Japan's total gross domestic product (GDP) passed through the South China Sea.[224] The development of the Chinese navy towards a blue-ocean navy is therefore of great importance to Japan. However, it has been pointed out that the Spratly Islands, in contrast to the also disputed Paracel Islands, do not straddle major shipping routes.[225]

Five nations (the PRC, the Philippines, Vietnam, Malaysia, Brunei and Indonesia) have claims to islands or maritime zones in some parts of the Paracel and/or Spratly Island chains, and outside powers like the US, South Korea and India are concerned as well. The claims do not just involve China, but also ASEAN countries among themselves. Japan does not support the territorial claims of any particular country.[226] Japan's official position is that in the San Francisco Peace Treaty it gave up its title to any of its previously occupied islands in the South China Sea but that the treaty did not stipulate to what country the islands should revert.

Since 1992, when China promulgated its new territorial law, the Japanese government has paid more attention to events in the South China Sea. The 1992 Defence Yearbook mentions that the delivery of SU-27 from Russia will expand the radius of activity of the Chinese Navy.[227] From the issue of 1993 the Yearbooks also mention political statements by Chinese leaders on the PLA's mission to defend China's territorial integrity. From 1993 on the Yearbook mentions China's construction of an airfield on Yongxing Island, the main island of the Paracel Islands.[228] Tensions rose in 1995 when the Philippines discovered that in 1994 China had constructed permanent structures on the Mischief Reef, claimed by the Philippines to be in its continental shelf, an action which also met with considerable criticism from ASEAN. Thereafter China's conversion of additional small buildings into concrete facilities in 1999 further raised tensions. These Chinese encroachments went hand in hand with promises to the ASEAN member states that it would abide by the Law of the Sea and abstain from the use of force. China's stance has therefore been characterized in the region as a 'talk and grab' strategy, which avoids open confrontation while pursuing a creeping invasion. China refuses to discuss the South China Sea with Japan because it is opposed to the involvement of all non-claimant countries.[229] For this reason Tokyo has not been invited to the annual Indonesian-initiated workshops on the South China Sea conflict. As a result it can only call for peaceful resolution of the territorial conflict and urge the maintenance of safe navigation.

Japan's minor participation in some energy developments in the South China Sea which are within the area claimed by China may have the potential to involve Japan directly in territorial disputes. One exploration is off the Vietnamese coast, operated by Japan–Vietnam Petroleum, in which Japanese companies have a share of 46.5 percent (involving the state-owned Japan National Oil Company, Nippon Mitsubishi Oil Corporation and Mitsubishi Corporation). It was set up to develop the Rang Dong field (Block 15–2), about 100km off the Vietnamese coast, within the Vietnamese EEZ but also just about within the zone claimed by China. The Company produced around 55,000 barrels of oil per day from the field in 1999.[230] Reserves were reported as 325 million barrels of oil and 300 billion cubic feet of gas. Clearly within the China-claimed zone is the major part of the Indonesian and Malaysian EEZs, which contain significant hydrocarbon reserves. Japanese companies are understood to have discussed participation in the huge Natuna D-Alpha gas field with the Indonesian state oil company, Pertamina. However, the technical problems of developing this field are likely to preclude gas production and no agreement with Japanese companies has been signed. In Malaysia, four areas that have been licensed by the Malaysian state oil company, Petronas, include Japanese participants, including Nippon Mitsubishi (operator of the SK-10 area in the South China Sea), Japan National Oil Company and Teikoku Oil. Fields included in the SK-8 and SK-10 areas in the South China Sea are currently under development to supply gas to the LNG plant at Bintuku, Sarawak, which produces LNG for shipment to Japan, Taiwan and South Korea. However, as far as is known China has not objected to any of the Japanese energy companies involved in South China Sea exploration and production.[231]

China's military modernization indicates that one of its goals is better control over the South China Sea. There are plans to establish rapid reaction forces, to reinforce the marine corps on Hainan and to deploy for this purpose ten heavy Russian transport aircraft (IL-76). China's main disadvantage is the lack of air cover for military engagements over 200km away from its coasts. So far China does not possess the military capability for long-term effective control of the whole South China Sea, but the continuous build-up of its blue-ocean navy capability, incidents due to territorial disputes and the confrontation over US observation flights in 2001 send alarming signals to all countries concerned.[232] The purpose of China's navy modernization programme seems to be less to achieve parity with the US than to raise the damage threshold for any country considering the use of force against China.

The US limits itself to declarations expressing the desire for a peaceful resolution of the various territorial disputes in the South China Sea and to demands for freedom of navigation in the region, while being militarily present with the 7th Fleet.[233] The former US navy colonel Evan A. Feigenbaum argues that US interest of military balancing would not be hurt by any recognition of China's legal claims.[234] The Chinese side realizes that the US has slightly changed its standoffish position since the Mischief incident in 1995, when it moved from 'passive neutrality' to 'active neutrality'. It has increased its access to ports in Southeast Asia and enhanced its military exercises with regional countries, which is perceived by China as building a 'united front' against China.[235]

Piracy

Japan's security interests in safe sea lanes of communications in the South China Sea are also threatened by piracy, which became a major issue there in the 1990s.[236] While the overwhelming majority of cases implicate citizens of other Southeast Asian states, notably Indonesia and Thailand, there was a stream of reports on cases in the mid-1990s, at times involving not only Chinese citizens and criminal syndicates based in China, but even Chinese military, coastguard or customs authorities.[237] Sometimes it was not clear whether these were simply criminal activities beyond the control of China's weakening central control or whether shootings and the impounding of vessels were intended to send a message to Japan and other claimants to territories in the South China Sea and East China Sea. The *Sankei Shimbun* reported in 1993 that since March 1991 Japanese fishing vessels sailing in international waters of the South China Sea frequently reported incidents in which unidentified but presumably Chinese ships fired warning shots at them, boarded them for inspections and tracked their movements.[238]

Initially, Chinese officials were not inclined to discuss the matter whenever Japanese diplomats brought this up, but in 1993 they changed their attitude. After seventeen of twenty piracy cases involved Russian ships in the East China Sea, Russia deployed naval ships to the areas in mid-1993 with orders to deal with any piracy.[239] In late June Japan and China began for the first time to discuss safe navigation in the South China Sea, and they agreed to cooperate in such areas as the handling of vessels found to be carrying contraband. The Chinese side also promised that official Chinese ships would exercise restraint before firing warning shots.[240]

However, after a decline in these incidents, piracy and robbery has increased again since 1997, partly reflecting the erosion of central and even regional power in China.[241] For the first time in 1994 the Japanese White Paper on

Defence mentioned the piracy issue in the section on Southeast Asia, but without indicating the nationality of the pirates.[242] The International Maritime Bureau (IMB) pointed out, however, that a network of a criminal syndicate headquartered in China was behind a spate of hijackings of ships at the end of the 1990s and that this network has expanded to each country in Southeast Asia. In the case of the hijack of the Japanese ship 'Tenyu' in 1998, the ship was found later on the Yangtze River, and Chinese authorities released the Indonesian pirates despite incriminating information from the IMB.[243] A new problem in this context is the rise of illegal Chinese emigration via the sea (see below).

The 1995–6 crisis in the Taiwan Strait

Arguably the greatest impact on Japan's shifting security perception of China derived from the latter's military exercises and missile tests around Taiwan in 1995–6.[244] These events were very close to Japan's own territory, they raised concern about China's willingness to use military force (and the US's willingness to reciprocate), they drew attention to China's missile force and proliferation of weapons of mass destruction, and they highlighted the role of the unresolved Taiwan issue in Japanese–Chinese relations. Since the resolution of reunification has become of the utmost importance to China's security policy and the leadership has staked a considerable part of its legitimacy on it, the issue will continue to demand great attention from Japan. According to several observers, the Taiwan Strait is the location where China is most likely to get involved in war.[245] Moreover, there are strong indications that China may use force despite US military superiority.[246] Finally, the Taiwan crisis of 1995–6 and developments since then have become a major motivation for the reinforcement of Japan's security arrangements with the US, but at the same time they have the potential to become a severe test of the Japanese–American alliance.

The military exercises and missile tests around Taiwan in 1995–6 have to be understood against the background of a deterioration in US–Chinese relations in the wake of the US allowing the Taiwanese president, Li Denghui, to attend a Cornell University alumni reunion in June 1995, followed later by Chinese pressure on Taiwan to influence the island's first presidential elections in March 1996.[247] The Clinton administration first resisted giving a visa to Li, but relented when faced with strong Congressional pressure and a positive attitude by President Clinton himself.[248] This American move touched a most sensitive issue in China's security policy at a time when the leadership feared that developments surrounding Taiwan would render the chances of reunification increasingly remote. The high point of the crisis was therefore reached around the time of the first direct presidential election in Taiwan, on 23 March 1996.

In order to show displeasure over the US move and to fend off accusations of not looking after China's desire for reunification, on 18 July 1995 the Chinese leadership announced a week-long series of military exercises, followed by a second round in August. These exercises saw the involvement of naval warships and warplanes, live firing, including the launching of missiles into the waters off Taiwan's coast. The Chinese military fired M-9 (Dongfeng-15) missiles into the East China Sea north of Taiwan. The US did not react to the missile tests. China held a third round of military exercises in November 1995, just before the Taiwanese parliamentary election. In December the US let the aircraft carrier Nimitz sail through the Taiwan Strait, ostensibly because of rerouting due to bad weather.

This did not deter the Chinese, and in February 1996 the PLA massed 150,000 troops along China's southeastern border for exercises and from 8 to 15 March fired DF-15 missiles even closer to Taiwan than the year before (30 miles off Gaoxiong in the south and Jilong in the north).[249] The third stage of the exercises was a landing exercise 30km from the Taiwan-controlled Matsu Islands, involving almost 400,000 troops.[250] In reaction the US deployed the largest group of ships in Southeast Asia since the end of the Vietnam War, including two aircraft carriers. It was decided, however, not to send the two carriers into the Taiwan Strait, and US Navy admiral Archie Clemins, commander-in-chief of the US Pacific Fleet, stated in 1999 that neither the USS Independence nor any other aircraft carrier were within 120 miles of Taiwan.[251] Tensions became very high and both sides tried to impress on the other their determination and resolve.[252] Secretary of Defence Perry was keen on sending a strong message to Beijing, with the dispatch to the area of two, rather than one, aircraft carriers in order to 'educate' the Chinese side about the US intention of staying a power in Asia.[253]

Japanese reactions

The culmination of the crisis with the missile tests in March 1996 attracted wide media attention in Japan, while officially the government tried to stay aloof and merely expressed their hope for a peaceful resolution of the confrontation. The missile tests drove home to the Japanese public how close the Taiwan conflict is to Japan and how any widening of it could affect the country's own security. The missile tests increased freight insurance and drove up air transport costs due to rerouting. Flights between Okinawa and Taibei were forced to make a detour.[254] One of the four missiles in March 1996 landed in the sea off the Taiwanese city of Hualian, about 60km from Japan's southern most island, Yonaguni (Prefecture of Okinawa), affecting its fishing industry. However, when the residents of Yonaguni asked for naval protection, Prime Minister Hashimoto ruled out sending the MSDF in order not to provoke China.[255] Moreover, the rising tensions in the Taiwan Strait motivated the Taiwanese navy to conduct more exercises in the same area.[256]

During the crisis, the Japanese government was concerned about the various implications, although on the outside it appeared calm.[257] Questions were raised within the Prime Minister's Office (PMO) about how to repatriate the 10,000 permanent Japanese residents and 10,000 Japanese tourists in Taiwan, what would happen to Japanese oil tankers passing through the Strait of Taiwan and how to react to possible US demands for military support. The Cabinet Research and Information Office and the Defence Agency did not exclude occupation by the PRC of at least one of the smaller Taiwan-held islands off the Chinese coast in order to force the Taiwanese government to hold its first democratic presidential elections under martial law. Around the March 1996 Taiwan elections, with the crisis at its high point, the SDF were continuously flying early-warning aircraft. On 6 March, when China announced its missiles tests, the Ministry of Foreign Affairs expressed the opinion that heightening tensions in the Taiwan Strait was not conducive to peace and stability in East Asia. It showed concern for sea traffic near the test area and asked for a peaceful resolution of the conflict.[258]

The crisis demonstrated again how much the Japanese government had to rely on US information. Whereas the Defence Agency received information about the deployment of the aircraft carrier Nimitz relatively early before the deployment, neither the Gaimusho nor the US embassy in Tokyo did. This prompted the Japanese government to launch a complaint with the US.[259] Later a hotline was set up between the secretary of state and Ambassador Mondale in Tokyo.[260] There were also virtually no Japan–US policy talks during the March 1996 crisis, let alone contingency consultations or exchanges of military information. Both sides agreed that the March crisis was not severe enough to invoke 'prior consultations' as contained in the bilateral security treaty.[261] It seems that the US did not want to run into any complications with Japanese public sensitivities about the application of the treaty.[262] One high official in the PMO involved in the management of the crisis revealed to Funabashi Yoichi that the government could not admit the seriousness of the situation because it might have triggered a Chinese attack on Taiwan or some similar dangerous situation.[263] The Japanese government also made clear that its position was more vulnerable than that of the US, and Prime Minister Hashimoto even expressed the hope that 'the US will exercise self-control'.[264]

There was concern in the Japanese government that the Taiwan crisis, having highlighted the strategic importance of Okinawa for US forward deployment in Asia, might wreck the compromise reached over the return of one US base in Okinawa, Futemna, and thus endanger once again public acceptance of the US military presence in Japan.[265] Zhang and Montaperto conclude from the absence of any Chinese diplomatic action against Japan and from the limited Chinese criticism of Japan that Japan's restraint was well appreciated.[266] However, Funabashi Yoichi quotes the foreign minister, Qian Qichen, who told his Japanese counterpart, Ikeda Yukihiko: 'Leaving aside the fuss made by the Americans, you're the only other country kicking up a fuss. China is shocked by that'.[267] China interpreted the deployment of the Yokosuka-based US aircraft carrier Independence to the Taiwan area as use of the Japanese–American security relationship to interfere in China's domestic affairs, 'tantamount to Japan hitching a ride on US tanks'.[268]

According to Funabashi Yoichi the US bases in Okinawa were not used beyond radar support.[269] Fukuyoshi Shoji, of Osaka Keizai Hoka University, mentions that the US stationed its missile tracking ship 'Observation Island' in Yokohama harbour during spring 1996.[270] Moreover, the MSDF supplied oil to US carrier group vessels.[271] Reports that the SDF was put on alert three (the highest being five) were, however, denied by the spokesman of the Gaimusho.[272]

The missile tests received a great deal of attention from the media, academia and politicians. Even a liberal paper like the *Asahi Shimbun* stated that the PRC exercises had demonstrated that the Chinese leadership had not shown reluctance about using military might to ensure its national unity, even though it also points out that the same is true of the US, which deployed its military resources.[273] Professor Soeya Yoshihide commented that the missile tests 'exposed the fundamental character of Chinese foreign policy at this time of transition – assertive projection of its long-term desires'.[274] Kayahara Ikuo, then a researcher at the National Institute for Defence Studies, argued that the military exercises gave the impression that China's threshold to use force was shown to be low and it raised a feeling of alarm (*keikaikan*) internationally.[275]

Statements, even by pro-China politicians, were very critical of the tests. The LDP's secretary-general, Kato Koichi, was quoted as saying that 'China's missile testing in international waters in the Taiwan Strait was behavior that cannot be tolerated'.[276] But he also ruled out any supporting role by the MSDF:

> But what if Japan had sent its Naval Self Defense Forces towards Taiwan in support of US force? This would have been strongly opposed by the two Koreas and China and greatly escalated a very delicate and dangerous situation. Once again, the unique role that the US plays in Asia-Pacific security was shown.[277]

Some parliamentarians asked for stronger protests than simply the one made by the director-general of the Asian Bureau of the Gaimusho to the Chinese embassy in Tokyo.[278] The March 1996 missile tests took place just when the LDP's Security Treaty Committee (*ampo chosakai*) was deliberating '[t]he new meaning of the Japan–US security system' (*Nichi-Bei ampotaisei no konnichi teki igi*). Since the tests were so close to Yonaguni, a major discussion was conducted during the meeting on 7 March 1996. Thereafter the chairman of the committee and the LDP's security specialist, Tamura Shigenobu, went to Foreign Minister Ikeda to demand an immediate cessation of tests, and on 19 March the committee sent its proposals to Prime Minister Hashimoto.[279] On 16 May 1995 the Committee on Foreign Affairs of the House of Councillors passed a unanimous resolution asking for a peaceful resolution of the China–Taiwan issue.[280]

But the Japanese government maintained its cautious approach throughout March 1996. No threats about cutting ODA were made. Another sign that it was downplaying events was the government's statements to the effect that the deployment of US forces from Japan in the crisis did not necessitate prior consultations as foreseen in the bilateral security treaty.[281] On 13 March a MOFA official went as far as explaining in the Upper House that US naval forces were conducting 'regular exercises'.[282] MOFA's press spokesman declared on 12 March that Japan was not expecting any military conflict to arise from the exercises and expressed its understanding in principle of China's right 'to carry out military exercises using the high seas, so long as those exercises will not hinder the usage of international seas by other countries'. He denied press speculation that the SDF in Okinawa had been put on alert.[283]

Taiwan's strategic importance

The Taiwan crisis in 1995–6 highlighted the role that the unresolved issue of Taiwan plays in Japanese–Chinese security relations and in the changing Japanese security perception of China. The issue has assumed even greater importance since the 1996 Hashimoto–Clinton Joint Declaration and the beginning of Japan's involvement in TMD (for these aspects, see Chapter 3). Reunification with Taiwan and the use of force if Taiwan declares independence has probably become, for China, the only issue which finds unanimous support among all sectors of government and the population.[284]

The most important official statement on the strategic importance of Taiwan for Japan can be found in the Sato–Nixon communiqué of November 1969. It is interesting to note that, while the Republic of Korea's (ROK) security was termed 'essential to Japan's own security', the reference to Taiwan only said that 'the maintenance of peace and security in the Taiwan area was also a most important factor for the security of Japan'.[285] In the Japanese Defence White Paper of 1979 and 1980 Japan is said to have great concerns about the area because it is close to Japan and forms part of an important sea lane. But this strategic interest is no longer mentioned in the following editions. In the 1992 edition, however, mention is made of the Taiwanese first 'Defence Report', which singles out the PRC as Taiwan's greatest security threat, followed by a short factual account of the island's armed forces.[286] Since then, the White Paper has merely repeated short summaries of Taiwan's armed forces and their modernization efforts, and there are other references to relations between Taibei and Beijing. The reason for this Japanese restraint is most likely that the Japanese government does not want to raise Chinese suspicions, and that it feels secure about its strategic interests being guaranteed by the security arrangements with the US.

With the more assertive stance taken since the end of the 1990s *vis-à-vis* China by Japan's politicians, the importance of a peaceful solution to the Taiwan issue is more clearly addressed. In summer 2000 Foreign Minister Kono declared in a rather frank speech at the Communist Party School in Beijing that 'peace and stability in the Taiwan Strait are critically important [*shikatsuteki ni juyo*] to the interests of Japan'.[287]

The expression 'critically important' is even stronger than the phrase used in the 1969 Sato–Nixon communiqué, although 'security' is replaced by the softer 'Japanese interests', which, however, is clearly the same. Although the government has been careful never directly to challenge China's right to use military force to reunify Taiwan with the mainland, it has always insisted on a peaceful approach.

There is not much of a public debate about Japan's strategic interests in Taiwan, notably about the key question of whether the status quo or reunification with the PRC is more favourable to these interests. Soeya argues that Japan's China and Taiwan policies do not have any strategic perspective and that they are merely reflections of Japan's alliance with the US.[288] He does not offer any suggestions for Japan's security interests in Taiwan. According to Nakai Yoshifumi, a researcher at the Institute of Developing Economies in Tokyo, the 'Japanese government treats the Taiwan issue as a minimally strategic concern'.[289] Political observers seem currently to be more focused on the implications of the application of the Japan–US security treaty to the Taiwan area, and the mode of change to the status of Taiwan. If this process is violent – and the Taiwan crisis in 1995–6 invoked such fears – it would destabilize Asia and raise concern about China's future behaviour to a new height, possibly leading to an arms race and new military alignments. If Taiwan passed to PRC control, the US military presence in the region would become even more important to Japan and increase US influence over Japan. For many Japanese, the treatment of Taiwan by the PRC is an indicator of the kind of international posture which the PRC is going to take.[290] Tanaka Akihiko also pointed out that if the PRC becomes militarily capable of simply taking over Taiwan this would raise concern because Okinawa is not very far from Taiwan. In addition, an arms race and strengthened military activities by the PRC and Taiwan would heighten the possibility of armed conflict.[291] If China was to take over Taiwan, peacefully or not, the island would become a major base for China's navy.[292] Soeya Yoshihide quotes a Gaimusho document of 1956 which expresses as the bottom line for Japan's interest that Taiwan 'will not become a military base of Communist China in any form'.[293] Military specialists may also consider that, so far, Chinese submarines have to operate in the shallow waters of the Taiwan Strait and the East China Sea. While they are easily detected there, it would be different after reunification because they could then operate in the much deeper waters east of Taiwan and better control the sea lanes to northeast Asia. PRC control over Taiwan would also mean control over the strait between the Philippines and Taiwan.

Tensions and even military intervention would also have a considerable effect on Japan's use of the important sea lanes east and west of Taiwan. President Li Denghui is quoted as having said that more than 500 foreign ships, including more than 200 from Japan, use the Taiwan Strait every day (only 114 ships on average use the Straits of Malacca).[294] More ships pass along Taiwan's east coast. It has also been argued that, as the third-largest information-technology hardware producer after the US and Japan, Taiwan has become so important to the world's digital economies, notably to Japan's production and supply chain within its Asian network economy, that any damage to factories and supply lines of Taiwanese companies would deal a strong blow to American and Japanese companies that rely on Taiwan for manufacturing and components.[295] In the medium term semiconductor supply would be insufficient because Taiwan has a share of 70 per cent in the supply of Japan.[296] The most serious effect of a long drawn-out US–China confrontation over Taiwan, even short of war, is, however, that it would cement China's views of a US-led world order (on which Japan so far wants to rely) and make its integration into the world community more difficult.[297] The Taiwanese government is naturally keen to impress on Japanese opinion leaders the strategic importance of the island since it is in its security interest. This is, for example, illustrated by the appointment of the retired admiral Chuang Ming-yao as the new head of Taiwan's Association of East Asian Relations, the main official body in charge of relations with Japan, after he had already served as its Tokyo representative from 1996 to 2000.[298] Mutual visits and conferences, often sponsored by the Taiwanese side, have increased in order to allow the exchange of information and promote Japanese security considerations of Taiwan.[299] Conservative strategists in Japan, concerned about China's assertive security policies, are now more willing to engage Taiwan.

PART 3: NON-TRADITIONAL SECURITY CONCERNS

Introduction

An analysis of the changing Japanese perception of China's security policy would not be complete without taking into account the impact of so-called non-traditional security concerns, in addition to that of the traditional ones already outlined. As suggested in the Introduction to this volume, an understanding of security as 'the protection and enhancement of values that the authoritative decisionmakers deem vital for the survival and well-being of a community' has to include non-traditional factors with an impact on survival, such as political, economic, societal and environmental factors. This generic definition is based on three criteria to warrant the security label in order not to dilute the concept of security: the value must be vital to survival; the threat to the value must be urgent; and the value must be determined by the authoritative decisionmakers.[300]

All the following non-traditional security concerns are directly or indirectly created by China's rapid economic development, to which Japan has contributed significantly through its trade, investment and ODA. China's economic development carries the seeds of self-destruction in terms of ecological unsustainability, political unsustainability (the creation of social imbalances and dislocations) and economic unsustainability (for example the collapse of the underlying economic model of export-led and FDI-driven development due to an international recession). These negative developments would affect Japan by way of transboundary pollution, illegal immigration, transboundary crime and economic losses. The transition phase in China's development, with all its difficulties (for example unemployment and underemployment) and generational impatience, has already led to illegal immigration into Japan, transboundary crime and pollution. But even the success of China's economic development generates increased international competition for scarce raw materials, food and energy resources on the international market. Finally, China's economic success would constitute a non-traditional security challenge to Japan because China's economic development, coupled with its demographic and geographic dimensions, will not fail to affect Japan's relative economic position and identity as the world's second-largest economic power.

Competition for access to natural resources

Competition for access to natural resources, energy and food is the result of China's continuing economic development. There is also a direct link with traditional security concerns: China's military modernization and, notably, its territorial claims have been put by Chinese strategists and political leaders into the context of China wanting to secure access to natural resources.[301] Shikata Toshiyuki, a former Ground Self-Defence Force (GSDF) officer and now professor at Teikyo University, assumes therefore that China will probably adopt a two-track policy of pursuing economic well-being and military strength.[302]

We have already seen how dependent China has become on oil, for which it needs either secure access lines (maritime or continental) or its own oil fields, including in the contested East China and South China Sea. Most of its oil and gas imports come from the Middle East and pass through sea lanes which are controlled by the US and its allies, including Japan. Even on the Eurasian continent, the US and Europe are trying to direct new oil and gas supplies to Europe and Turkey rather than promoting direct pipelines to China or to Iran or Afghanistan. Another aggravating factor is the competition for Middle East oil: not only is China's oil-import dependence on the Middle East increasing, but so is that of Japan (86 per cent of total oil imports in 2000) and other Asian countries.

The oil shocks of the 1970s enhanced Japan's consciousness of its vulnerability to foreign raw materials, energy and food. Since then it has developed very successful counter-strategies, although its increasing dependence on these resources is still a major subject in the public discourse. China is now dramatically increasing its reliance on oil, but it has no civilian oil stockpiling system for times of crisis. In Asia, only Japan and South Korea have such systems in place to cushion the impact of any oil-price hike or oil-supply shortages. This may contribute to China's taking a less confrontational attitude towards its territorial claim in the South China Sea for the time being.

It is obvious that China, with its huge population, will need an ever-increasing share of the world's food resources. Increasing wealth, in addition, leads to the consumption of more meat, which requires more grain supplies. Lester Brown's prediction in 1994 that China's food crisis would escalate to a worldwide food crisis dramatically highlighted this resource issue.[303] However, even specialists are divided on whether raw materials, energy and food resources will come to be in short supply or whether market forces will resolve the problem.[304] Free-market forces may theoretically solve these problems, but China is not yet a free market, and even in so-called free-market economies there is considerable state intervention when it comes to these goods. In addition, free-market forces may not solve a particular resource problem in time to prevent serious economic or even military clashes.

The environmental impact of China's economic growth

Closely related to the issue of access to natural resources is the impact of economic development on the environment, and these have therefore become the two main issues among non-traditional security challenges in the post-Cold War era.[305] Environmental degradation and transboundary pollution may aggravate or even act as catalyst in inter-state tensions (although the chains of causation are very complex) and reinforce those negative perceptions we encountered in the first part of this chapter. Recognizing a link between environmental damage and global security, the US National Intelligence Council (NIC), which is the umbrella over all US intelligence agencies, began to monitor these developments as closely as traditional threats to international security.[306] In an opinion poll in 1999, 62 per cent of the Japanese polled considered environmental degradation to be Asia's biggest problem for the twenty-first century, compared to 52 per cent of the Chinese respondents. This was followed for the Japanese respondents by concern about aging (44 per cent) and demographic increases.[307]

Environmental pollution in China has a particular saliency for the possible negative impact of even successful Chinese economic development on Japan.[308] A famous Japanese sinologist, Eto Shinkichi, even called for environmental issues to be given priority over all other matters pending between Japan and China.[309] According to official Chinese figures, 30 per cent of China's land area is already affected by acid rain and 18 per cent by desertification.[310] These problems provide further impetus to emigration, including to Japan.

Together with other economic and social problems, environmental problems could contribute to an explosive mix. In addition, transboundary air and sea pollution already affects the livelihood of Japan and the Korean Peninsula.[311] Pollution of the East China Sea originating from Chinese offshore oil production in that region potentially adds a further negative dimension to Japanese–Chinese territorial disputes. Although the impact of China's pollution is far greater and more immediate on China itself, the impact on Japan and other neighbouring countries should not be underestimated, particularly when seen in conjunction with the possible consequences for China's political stability and for other more traditional Japanese–Chinese security issues.

Crime and refugees

Illegal Chinese immigration into Japan and the rise of related crime is now a considerable problem for Japan. Both are developments which threaten not only Japan's internal security but also the country's identity of a homogeneous nation.

Both developments are also related to economic circumstances – that is, the attraction of Japan's economic strength, the wide gap between the two countries' economies and increasing unemployment due to the restructuring of China's state enterprises.[312]

Illegal Chinese immigration also conjures in Japan the fear of the consequences if China fails economically. It is obvious that the loosening of central and even regional control, combined with economic hardship and generational impatience, is contributing to illegal emigration and the regional expansion of criminal syndicates based in China. Amako Satoshi writes that if China's economy fails and the country disintegrates it is expected that this may lead to considerable refugee streams into China's immediate neighbouring countries. He also recalls that several thousands Chinese refugees landed in Okinawa and Kyushu after the massacre in Tiananmen in 1989.[313] The possibility of 100 million Chinese refugees destabilizing Asia is also mentioned in a book co-edited by the former prime minister Nakasone Yasuhiro.[314] As we will see in Chapter 3, on the revised guidelines of 1999, 'situations in areas surrounding Japan' also includes a scenario in which refugees come to Japan.[315]

As far-fetched as the refugee scenario may seem now, increasing Chinese illegal immigration to foreign countries, including Japan, piracy in the South China Sea, and the involvement of Chinese citizens in regional and domestic crime are seen as precursors of such disintegration, although these phenomena can also be interpreted as merely transitional and inherent in the process of modernizing China's political and economic system. According to the Japanese police and the MSA, about 90 per cent of people entering Japan illegally come from the PRC.[316] Until 1991 the number of Chinese nationals arrested for entering the country illegally remained in double figures, but it rose sharply, to 1,209, in 1997, falling again, to 824 in 1998. Between January and November 2000, 2,814 Chinese nationals were arrested, accounting for roughly half of all the arrests of foreigners. The number of Chinese being deported is increasing, and it exceeded 11,000 in 1999.[317] According to Justice Ministry statistics, 33,000 illegal Chinese immigrants have been confirmed in the country, the third-largest group, following illegal immigrants from the Republic of Korea and the Philippines.[318] According to National Police Agency (NPA) statistics, in 1999 45 per cent of all foreigners arrested were Chinese. Of that figure, about 35 per cent were residing illegally in Japan. Of 770 people apprehended in suspected human smuggling cases that year, 701 were Chinese citizens.[319] In 2000, 38 per cent of all prisoners of foreign nationality in Japanese prisons were Chinese.[320] The number of officially registered Chinese residents in Japan and their share among foreign residents has been constantly rising, from 40,000 (a share of 6.8 per cent) in 1950 to 252,164 (17 per cent) in 1997. Interestingly, the share of Chinese residents among foreign residents in Japan in 1890 was 56.6 per cent.[321]

In 2000, 54.2 per cent of crimes committed by foreign nationals were committed by Chinese, a 9 per cent increase on the previous year and the first time on record that the figure has topped 50 per cent.[322] In 1994 it was reported that the Japanese *yakuza* and organised criminal syndicates in Taiwan, Hong

Kong and China are helping illegal Chinese immigration into Japan.[323] There is considerable Chinese involvement in the smuggling of firearms and drugs into Japan. Hundreds of Chinese mobsters from more than ten of Shanghai's 300 gangs are now active in Japan. The real figures may be several times higher. In May 1998 the governments of both countries started talks on how to deal with this situation.[324] It is reported that almost 70 per cent of stimulants smuggled into Japan are produced in China's Fujian province. The trend marks a change from the 1980s, when most illegal drugs brought in came from Taiwan, and the 1970s, when the Republic of Korea was the main source.[325] The Japanese coast-guard reported that the largest amount of confiscated drugs in 1999, 48 per cent, came from China, followed by 34 per cent from North Korea.[326] The most recent crimes involving Chinese include 'cyber crimes'. In February 2000 the Japanese police reported that hackers behind a recent series of invasions of government-run websites gained access to the sites through computers located in China, the United States and Tokyo University.[327]

Although these developments are still minor, particularly if one compares illegal immigration into Japan with that into Western Europe, they have a very large impact on the perception of a relatively crime-free and isolationist society like Japan. They aggravate the negative perceptions created by China's military developments as analysed in the first part of this chapter. Since crime is much more widely reported in the media and touches the life, or at the least the imagination, of individual Japanese in a much more tangible way, one should not underestimate the impact of these developments on popular Japanese security perceptions.

Challenging Japan's identity as an economic power?

Japan's perception of the international environment and its identity in it as the world's second-largest economic power is strongly shaped by economic relations of power. The challenge to this by China's economic rise has therefore also to be considered in the context of an expanded security concept. Economic power influences not only Japan's foreign policies, but also its perception of the global hierarchy and its identity as a global civilian power in this hierarchy.[328] This status and identity are, of course, supported by the comprehensive alliance with the US.

The opening of China's economy to the outside from 1978 and the ensuing economic reforms, followed by spectacular economic growth and seen in conjunction with its demographic and geographic dimensions, cannot fail to have an impact on Japan's identity as the world's second-largest economic power. A sustained economic rise will assist China in becoming Japan's economic and political rival. With a population of about 1.3 billion, China is second only to Japan within East Asia in terms of GDP, while it comes very close to Japan in terms of its volume of foreign-currency reserves. China also comes second in trade within the East Asian region. Positive evaluations of the scale and progress of China's economic modernization were particularly provoked in Japan by the impact of World Bank Reports. In 1992 the International Monetary Fund (IMF)/World Bank estimated China's per capita GDP at a mere US$500 but its purchasing power parity (PPP) as being possibly around US$2000. It predicted that by the early twenty-first century China may surpass not just Japan but also the US, to become the largest economy in the world.[329] The World Bank announced that China's per capita GDP in 1996 (1994 figures) was US$2,500 on PPP, and in this way put China's economic strength much higher than the per capita GDP figures would do.[330] The reports came out at a time when China's economy – which had grown in 1989 and 1990 by 4.4 per cent and 4.1 per cent, respectively – suddenly surged, by 8.2 per cent in 1991 and by 13.4 per cent in 1992.[331] In 1999 Japan's GDP was US$4,079 billion, compared with only US$980 billion for China, but the latter's PPP had now reached US$4,112, surpassing Japan (with US$3,043) as the world's second-largest economy.[332]

China has been very careful with economic forecasts until recently, but in August 1997 an official Chinese institution, the Chinese Academy of Social Sciences (CASS) published one for the first time. According to that study, China's economy was to become the world's largest by 2030. By adopting the PPP measurement rather than the per capita GDP formula, it turned out that in 1996 China's GDP had reached one-quarter of the US's and half that of Japan. The forecast said, furthermore, that in 2010, given an average growth rate of 8–10 per cent, China would have surpassed Japan in terms of PPP-based GDP.[333] Not counting the uncertainties about Japan's economic future as of autumn 2001, Japan's GDP was estimated to decrease to US$4,091 billion in 2001 and US$$4,055 in 2003, compared with US$4,753 billion in 2000.[334] But even if one assumes that Japan's per capita GDP would rise by only 2 per cent annually (an overly optimistic assumption in view of Japan's current crisis) and China's by 16 per cent, it would take China until 2029 to reach that of Japan.[335]

To what extent do the Japanese consider China's rise as a challenge to their identity? Few mainstream observers of China directly address these questions. Takahara Akio estimates that Japan may feel threatened by China's economic rise because of its feeling of superiority *vis-à-vis* China in the economic sphere.[336] In its first long-range foreign-policy programme for the Asia-Pacific region, the ruling LDP merely predicted in 1997 that it was highly likely that China would overtake Japan economically by around the year 2010.[337] Concerns about China overtaking Japan because of certain economic advantages have been reinforced by Japan's economic problems, starting with its economic bubble bursting at the beginning of the 1990s.[338] Moreover, China's rise is directly linked to Japan's problems because of the widespread relocation of Japanese companies to China. An extreme reaction came, not surprisingly, from the right-wing governor of Tokyo, Ishihara Shintaro, who expressed in an interview his hope that China may disintegrate into several smaller states.[339] However, there is not yet any sense of urgency about China overtaking Japan. Mainstream China specialists point out the huge gap which still exists between China and other developed countries, and they emphasize the difficulties which still lie ahead despite past successes. However, the rise of China as an economic power and its link to Japan's economic woes reinforce the general perception of China as a multifaceted 'problem' for Japan, and I will come back to this point in Chapter 4 when considering the issue of Japanese–Chinese rivalry.

PART 4: INTERNATIONAL AND DOMESTIC CHANGES AND JAPAN'S CHINA DEBATE

International and domestic changes

The impact of the above developments has to be considered against the background of changes in the international strategic environment, in the Japanese–American alliance and in Japan's domestic politics.

In contrast to effects in the Atlantic world, the end of the Cold War in Asia was much less dramatic and, instead, with the sudden loss of the structuring as well as restraining forces of the East–West conflict gone, new uncertainties were felt in Japan. The most important sources of potential conflict in Asia – the division of China and the Korean Peninsula, but initially also the Cambodian conflict – were still there. The new era also opened the diplomatic game in ways which were difficult to foresee. Japan's room for diplomatic manoeuvre was enhanced, but this was not simply an opportunity to be seized or left; it was as much a challenge requiring a response for which Japan's parochial political system, used to the comfort of the US security guarantee as well as its diplomatic umbrella, was not prepared. China became less important for the US as a bulwark against Russia, but not for Japan as an immediate neighbour. To strengthen its strategic position China's leaders decided to improve their relationship with Russia, and the bilateral meeting in Beijing in December 1992 led to the conclusion of twenty-five agreements, culminating finally, in April 1996, in a 'strategic cooperation towards the 21st century'.[340] In August 1992 China and South Korea established diplomatic relations which potentially introduced a moderating influence on North Korea, but it was unclear whether this diplomatic enlargement would not on the contrary weaken China's influence on North Korea.

The end of the Cold War also created uncertainties relating to the viability and duration of the future US security commitment to the region, and the ups and downs of Sino-American relations began to affect Japanese–Chinese relations as well. According to Kokubun Ryosei the two political conditions that had supported Japanese–Chinese relations since 1972 were negatively affected by the end of the Cold War. One was the latent common objective of withstanding the Soviet Union, which disappeared with its demise. The other was full US support of the Japanese–Chinese friendly relationship, which now started to show signs of fluctuation.[341]

Two events in the immediate post-Cold War era, the 1991 Gulf War and the North Korean nuclear crisis in 1994, illustrated these post-Cold War uncertainties and profoundly influenced security relations with China. The first event exposed Japan's unpreparedness to contribute more to the maintenance of Western security and thus weakened US resolve to continue its security commitment to Japan in the same way as before. Although the country finally contributed US$13 billion to the war effort and the post-war rehabilitation programme, this support appeared belated and reluctant, and politically was not equivalent to the provision of soldiers by the other Western allies. Japan finally changed its laws so that the SDF could in future participate in UN PKO as long as these activities were limited to logistical tasks. This happened for the first time in 1992, when a SDF contingent was deployed in Cambodia.

The impact of Japan's reluctance to shoulder international burdens with greater military connotations was all the greater as it occurred against a background of a decline in the US military presence in Asia at the beginning of the 1990s. In the Philippines the US closed down Clark Air Force Base and the naval base at Subic Bay in the wake of the Philippine Senate's rejection of an extension of the bilateral base agreement – a move speeded up by the eruption of the Mount Pinatubo. The administration of George Bush Snr announced plans in 1990 and 1992 for substantial reductions in its forces in the Asia-Pacific region. These plans were only reversed in 1995 with the US Department of Defence report 'US Security Strategy for the East Asia-Pacific Region' (Nye Report), which committed the US to maintaining the existing force level of around 100,000 troops in East Asia (see Chapter 3). Another concern for Japan was the conclusion of SALT III (Strategic Arms Limitation Treaty) between the US and Russia in June 1992, which promised massive reductions in strategic nuclear weapons but which potentially raised a question mark over the future of the US nuclear umbrella, notably towards China.

The second event, a suspected North Korean nuclear-weapons programme at the beginning of the 1990s, had the greatest impact on Japan's perception of the post-Cold War world. This event and the handling of it by US and Japanese leaders created an atmosphere in which China's military developments looked more ominous.[342] The suspicion about North Korea's intentions fell on fertile ground in Japan because of the non-transparent character of the regime in Pyongyang and the general dislike for North Korea, which usually comes top in any poll measuring the 'most-disliked' country. Moreover, Japanese sensitivity towards nuclear weapons only enhanced the ill feelings towards North Korea.

In our context, the North Korean nuclear crisis from 1994 onwards is important in several respects. First, the crisis has served as a useful tool to engineer the strengthening of the Japanese–American security alliance, because it helped to find a new rationale for the Japanese–American security treaty after it had been solely fixated on the Soviet Union before the end of the Cold War. Second, the North Korean threat became a diplomatic code word in Japan for anxieties about China's growing military potential and future intentions, and the need to enhance the deterrence element of engagement towards China. Third, the North Korean nuclear crisis and the degree of China's support for Western measures to defuse it defined, to a certain extent, the state of US–Chinese and Japanese–Chinese relations.

The Chinese commitment to supporting Western measures to contain the suspected North Korean nuclear programme has been mixed, reflecting China's conflicting interests as a long-established ideological and military ally of North Korea and the function of the North as a buffer against US influence.[343] In addition, China has been concerned about losing influence over an ally which has looked with concern and distaste at China's ideological and economic changes. In September 1994 China withdrew from the Military Armistice Commission to please North Korea, although it still recognizes the Korean armistice agreement. China's limited willingness and ability to exert a moderating influence on North Korea became particularly clear in 1994 over the stand-off on North Korea's announced withdrawal from the Nuclear Non-Proliferation Treaty (NPT). The US finally managed to defuse the situation through the swap of two light–water reactors (LWR) for a North Korean freeze of its existing nuclear programme, but China refused to join the Korean Peninsula Energy Development Organization (KEDO), despite being offered the establishment of its headquarters in Beijing.[344] Since then, China's position on KEDO has been that it supports the project but feels it can be more helpful by not joining it.

In conclusion, Japan's perception of China's traditional and non-traditional challenges to its security interests were enhanced by global and regional developments which made these challenges appear even more ominous, while at the same time the security commitment of the US alliance partner to the whole region seemed to be weakening.

Domestically, generational change among politicians and greater Japanese assertiveness to the outside shaped Japan's perception of China's security challenges. China is now seen as part of the whole, not just as part of a bilateral relationship where differences are smoothed over by the incantation of *yuko* (friendship) and the adjective 'special'. The generational change was hastened by the LDP's fall from power after the party had continuously ruled the country since 1955. Due to a culmination of scandals and the fear of losing power, two groups in the LDP split off from the party in 1993 and supported a no-confidence motion, which led in June 1993 to the fall of the prime minister, Miyazawa Kiichi. The ensuing general election opened the way to a coalition government between a breakaway LDP faction and the Social Democratic Party of Japan (SDPJ). The succeeding coalition cabinets, since 1994 including again the LDP, brought the SDPJ – the hitherto perennial opposition party – into mainstream politics when it accepted the Japanese–American security treaty and the SDF. The power sharing led directly to its rapid decline, but the worldwide failure and disappearance of Communist states, as well as the revisionist policies of the surviving Communist regimes, notably that of the PRC, also reduced the electoral chances of the party. Thus China lost a major ally in its campaign against the security treaty and against increasing Japanese defence efforts. As we have seen in the context of Japan's protest against China's resumption of nuclear tests, it was under the Socialist Prime Minister Murayama that Tokyo took unprecedented retaliatory measures against China.

The new conservative leaders, notably Ozawa Ichiro, with his New Frontier Party, showed less inclination to exempt China's policies from criticism and exhibited a harsher attitude to China's security policy and its impact on Japan.

The demise of the SDPJ and the emergence of new conservative parties with younger leaders facilitated a more open security debate about the changes in the post-Cold War era. Notably, this affected the debate about China's security policies and military modernization, leading from an engagement policy with emphasis on political/economic enmeshment and deference to one in which the Realist aspects were increasingly emphasized. Inter-agency politics, interparty/electoral politics and intra-party/factional politics gained a much greater influence on Japan's China policy, considerably diminishing the so far uncontested control of the China hands in the Ministry of Foreign Affairs who had strived to keep relations with China in quiet and consistent waters.[345] Japan's cautious policy towards sanctions against China in the aftermath of the Tiananmen massacre was strongly supported by Japan's diplomats, although it also enjoyed support from the leading politicians at that time.[346] In this new critical atmosphere, the traditionally more accommodating 'China School' of the Gaimusho lost considerable power. Its members have become less influential among the other bureaux, and even within the Asian Bureau, to which the China Division belongs. This is also linked to a more general dissatisfaction with the Gaimusho in the wake of a widespread anti-bureaucracy mood. The Gaimusho had come under special criticism because of the alleged mishandling of foreign-policy issues like the Gulf War in 1991 and its aftermath, as well as its antiquated style.[347] In the 1990s the ministry came to be criticized by some quarters for being too fearful of offending China, only reporting domestic good news and being generally too innocent about China's intentions.[348] China's use of the 'history card' is now criticized as giving Beijing easy access to ODA.[349] The right-of-centre *Sankei Shimbun* has been particularly strong in its criticism of Chinese policies and of Japan's ODA policy.[350] Even among the China School diplomats there is growing dissatisfaction with China's 'big-power mentality' and its frequent 'advice on the history issue'.[351]

The fragmentation of the Japanese political scene since 1993 has given more influence to a growing number of more nationalistic and vocal politicians, who are to be found not only among the older politicians but also among the new generation.[352] The policy issues of the Nationalists go across the whole policy spectrum, ranging from support for Japan's candidature for a permanent UN Security Council seat to a more independent defence posture. Disenchanted with the traditional deferential tendencies towards China, concerned about China's rise to a great power, conscious of Japan's huge economic power (and at the same time its economic problems) and fed up with what they see as China's exploitation of Japan's colonial past, many Japanese politicians are reacting more forcefully to China and demand more reciprocity. This new mood in Japan's political world was expressed in November 1998 on the occasion of President Jiang Zemin's visit, when the LDP showed strong opposition to offering China a written apology as Tokyo had done shortly before to President

Kim Daejung of Korea. Piqued by this refusal, Jiang harped on the issue of Japan's past aggression against China during the entire visit, only reinforcing latent dissatisfaction with China. The election of the right-wing politician Ishihara Shintaro as governor of Tokyo in April 1999 may have had a great deal to do with the disaffection of Tokyo's voters with the traditional politicians, but it also brought with it many expressions of anti-PRC feelings by the new governor.

These domestic changes have not led to the disappearance of the deep divide in Japan between the so-called pacifist forces (including left-wingers and liberals, but also conservative forces which do not yet trust Japan's democratic institutions) and revisionists (including Realists, proponents of the Japan–US relationship and nationalists).[353] This divide, apart from considerations for other Asian countries, has been a strong barrier to knee-jerk reactions to China's policies along the Realist paradigm. However, we will see that the impact of China's challenges to Japan's security concerns (amplified by US demands for closer military cooperation) has significantly reduced Japan's inclination towards a restrained or even deferential China policy and strengthened a mood in which the revision of the Constitution and a more effective military cooperation with the US might be addressed more decisively.

The debate about the 'China threat' theory

Chinese writers assert that the Western 'China threat discussion' was launched by a Japanese academic, Murai Tomohide, a professor at Japan's Defence University, and then taken up by other Japanese and American writers for various reasons.[354] However, Murai's article was not influential in Japan at the time it appeared.[355] Yokoyama Hiroshi, a specialist in Chinese history, even argues that in some ways China has been seen as a 'threat' in Japan since the nineteenth century because of its failure to respond adequately to the West, its resulting weakness and then its resurrection under communism.[356]

It is, however, obvious that China's security policies, its greater international assertiveness and its economic growth have caused a shift in the writing of Japan's political commentators and China specialists to a greater and more critical focus on security issues between the two countries. Kojima Tomoyuki dates this shift towards discussing China as a big power and potential threat to around summer 1993.[357] The US shift from viewing Japan as the new threat after the demise of the Soviet Union to seeing China instead as the major threat has certainly contributed to this change in Japan.[358] The dearth of reliable information about China and a lack of transparency also tend to enhance negative perceptions. Watanabe Akio therefore calls China the region's most 'daunting challenge' because 'it is an enigma on so many fronts'.[359]

Public opinion

This change can be also observed in public opinion polls. The year 1996, with its Taiwan Strait confrontation, became a watershed in Japan's public opinion on

China when for the first time in the annual poll by the PMO the percentage of people responding 'I do not have friendly feelings towards China' (51.3 per cent) surpassed the percentage responding 'I have friendly feelings (45.0 per cent). According to an analysis by Osaki Yuji, the ratio began to shift decisively in 1989, after the Tiananmen incident, although it recovered temporarily in 1992 in the wake of the Emperor's visit to China.[360] In the 1997 PMO poll the negative ratio was slightly smaller, and it became slightly positive again in the 1998 poll, by about one percentage point. A poll by *Yomiuri* released in September 1999 confirms the sharp drop in the evaluation of bilateral relations on both sides: only 17 per cent of Chinese and 33 per cent of Japanese considered relations between Japan and the PRC to be good. Compared with a similar poll in 1988, the number of Chinese people who expressed a favourable opinion of bilateral relations dropped by 34 percentage points, while the number of Japanese who said they viewed relations favourably fell by 32 percentage points.[361]

In a poll by the *Yomiuri Shimbun* in late January 1997, 55.0 per cent considered North Korea likely to pose a threat, followed by China, with 39.1 per cent, and Russia, with 34.7 per cent.[362]. Asked in the same poll whether China will pose a threat to Japan in the future, 18 per cent responded that China will be a major threat, 45 per cent 'somewhat a threat' and 22 per cent 'not very much'.[363] According to a comparative poll by the liberal *Asahi Shimbun* in May 1998, only 9 per cent of Japanese felt a threat from China strongly (compared with 26 per cent of Americans), and 55 per cent felt it to a certain extent (51 per cent). A military threat was felt by 22 per cent of Japanese (27 per cent in the US), an economic threat by 20 per cent (25 per cent in the US), and 18 per cent felt threatened by the political system in China (19 per cent in the US).[364]

A multiple answer poll by *Yomiuri Shimbun* in 1999 seems to confirm that, while China's military expansion (31.1 per cent) and the Taiwan issue (27.3 per cent) scored highest among a list of concerns, most other high-ranking percentages concerned non-military issues such as China's increasing population/refugees (33.2 per cent) and the future of economic and political reform.[365] There is not yet any immediate feeling of threat, which seems also to be confirmed by a poll by the PMO in January 2000, where concerns related to China ranked only seventh (US–Chinese relations: 13.1 per cent) and eighth (Chinese–Russian relations: 11.7 per cent), after the Korean Peninsula (56.7 per cent), arms control and disarmament as related to weapons mass destruction and missiles (35.2 per cent), US–Russian relations (17.9 per cent), the situation of US forces around Japan (16.8 per cent), the Middle East (14.8 per cent) and Russian deployment of forces in the Northern Territories (13.7 per cent).[366]

Military threat perception in the literature

Mainstream authors express concern about China's military modernization, the rise in military expenditures, the issues of missiles (increase, export, testing), the development of an ocean-going navy (implications for China's territorial demands) and the general influence of the PLA on China's politics.[367] Nishihara Masashi pointed out that China was increasing its military power at a time when the US and Russia were cutting their armed forces and defence budgets.[368] Takahara Akio considers a serious arms race in East Asia as likely because of China wanting to compete with US hegemony in Asia.[369] Tanaka Akihiko wrote as early as 1994 that these developments appear to justify the hegemonistic power scenario of China's future.[370] Murai Tomohide considers that China's armed forces are no longer only for defence, but are now also able to be deployed to neighbouring countries. He thinks that, although China's military forces are not able to attack Japan, the countries in Southeast Asia would bend towards China if Beijing used military pressure.[371]

Some scholars focus on the importance of China's naval modernization, the territorial claims by China to the Senkaku Islands and South China Sea region, with their oil and gas resources, and the implications for Japan's security. Hiramatsu Shigeo comments that China's navy is still inferior to the American and even Japanese navy, but that even without resorting to military aggression China 'could deal a serious blow to Japan, Taiwan and South Korea simply by interdicting sea lanes'. He also warns that, by controlling the South China Sea and East China Sea, China could strengthen its influence over the countries in the region and later extend this influence to the Pacific and Indian Ocean. Writing in 1994, he pointed out the necessity of looking at the growing activities of the Chinese navy in the East China Sea.[372]

On the other hand, there is a clear perception among the experts that, despite rapid military modernization efforts, China's military is still no threat for the US and Japan.[373] Kayahara Ikuo and Amako Satoshi argue that, despite rapid military modernization, China is still a long way from being able to project power and to challenge the US in Asia.[374] Their concern is about the lack of transparency in China's military spending and the unclear political future of China. Amako calls it 'threat as an image' (*image to shite no kyoi*), which is based on the perception of China's intentions and potential threat.[375] Nakai Yoshifumi points to the misgivings in Japan as well as in the US concerning the Chinese political system and China's revisionist position towards its status as the two aspects of the 'China threat' perception.[376] Sakanaka Tomohisa warns of an overemphasis of China's military challenge by telling this author that China's military is outdated, the relationship of troops to population low, the training of the armed forces insufficient and China's industrial level low.[377] Kokubun Ryosei similarly points out that the proportion allotted annually to military expenditures had declined from around 15 per cent to around 10 per cent, compared with the figure for the 1980s.[378] In another book Kokubun also warns that the discussion of the China threat has something to do with the disappearance of a clear threat in the post-Cold War period, which threatens the vested interests of the military of every country.[379] Tanaka Akihiko concludes that China's external behaviour in the 1990s was reactive, cautious and centred on domestic politics. Still, he considers that the domestic changes in Taiwan could become a trigger for the use of military force because they challenge the status quo.[380] But he points out that China is not inherently evil (*juaku*) and it would be wrong to assume that once China is rich it would become evil.[381]

In this context one has to mention the strong US influence on Japanese security perceptions of China. In the first place, the Japan–US alliance introduces American opinions on China, and Chapter 3 will cover the practical implications of this. The productive and competitive think-tank culture of the US also exposes Japan to US evaluations of China. Finally, many of Japan's younger China specialists have been trained in the US, and their impact is particularly strongly felt among the Realist scholars. An important training ground has been the Research Institute for Peace and Security (RIPS) in Tokyo, which for many years has trained young Japanese scholars in security studies, financially supported for a long time by the Ford Foundation. But Japan's much closer proximity to China and the difference between Japanese and US military strength mediate this influence, apart from the impact of what Professor Royama, a known Japanese international relations specialist, once called Japan's 'unsophisticated pacifism'.[382]

Conclusions

This chapter has explained Japan's changing security perceptions of China as a result of emerging traditional and non-traditional security concerns against the background of uncertainties and shifts in Japan's security environment after 1989 and domestic changes. Traditional security threats, notably China's non-transparent military build-up, Chinese nuclear tests, the growing military connotations of the territorial dispute in the East China Sea (against the background of Chinese territorial assertiveness in the South China Sea) and disputes in the Taiwan area have particularly alarmed many Japanese China specialists, as well as the general public. Non-traditional security concerns ranging from China's challenge as a rising economic power to transboundary crime and illegal immigration into Japan have played an important role in reinforcing Japanese security concerns about China's security policies. It is difficult to quantify exactly the influence of the China experts quoted above on decision-making regarding China, but one can safely assume that the China policy changes to be analysed in the following chapters would not have been possible without this shift among the experts who so far had been rather 'understanding' of China's foreign and security policy. Under the influence of this perception shift and with the emergence of a new generation of politicians, public opinion towards China hardened, and the China School in the Foreign Ministry moved towards a greater assertion of Japanese security interests. Whereas the deterioration of Japanese security perceptions towards China was a new development of the 1990s, Chinese leaders and experts reverted to their previous distrust of Japanese intentions after the brief exception of the anti-hegemony struggle in the 1970s and 1980s. In the next chapters we will see how their perceptions were further affected by Japan's shift to a greater emphasis on the Realist elements of engagement in reaction to the developments analysed in this chapter.

3 Between power balancing and enmeshment policies

Since what China does is like the action of a yakuza, it does not help to confront it with the face of a gentleman. Faced with a yakuza we can only act in a yakuza way in return.

Professor Hiramatsu Shigeo, Kyorin University[1]

The prevalent way of thinking about international relations throughout the AsiaPacific region is in balance of power terms. Leaders in China, India, Russia, and other states talk of a multipolar world where major states represent centers of power, continually maneuvering to create balances. This is the world of Bismarck and 19th century Europe.

Admiral Dennis C. Blair, US Navy Commander in Chief of the US Pacific Command[2]

Introduction

Japan's engagement of China has been defined in the Introduction as a policy which consists of providing China with economic and political incentives to integrate into the regional/international political and economic system, hedged by military balancing through its own military force and the military alliance with the US. This chapter investigates engagement from a Realist, Liberal and Constructivist perspective. I conclude that the Realist component of engagement – power balancing and hedging – has gained greater prominence, which is most clearly expressed by the strengthening of the Japan–US military alliance in 1995–6. After a similar investigation in 1996, two American scholars, Benjamin Self (then at the Woodrow Wilson Center) and Michael Green (then at the Institute for Defense Analysis) called Japan's China policy 'a change from commercial liberalism to reluctant realism'.[3] I would like to argue that there has always been Realism but that it has only become less reluctant. In addition, we will see that the Japanese government is trying to develop further the other elements of the Liberal approach in order to pursue engagement more efficiently, but also to counterbalance the negative dynamics of engagement. To this belongs Japan's promotion of security dialogues at various bilateral and multilateral levels, which, from a Constructivist perspective, is the utilization of various communicative processes to influence China's security discourse and, hopefully, its future behaviour.

PART 1: MILITARY AND POLITICAL POWER BALANCING

The following analysis of Japan's military and political power balancing shows how the Realist elements of engagement have gradually gained greater prominence in reaction to China's assertive or even inimical security policies described in the previous chapter. Realist scholars in Japan are now openly supporting the hedging of the Liberal elements through Japan's military deterrent and a strengthening of the Japanese–American security alliance.[4] The China specialist Soeya Yoshihide even writes that the idea of containing China is gaining momentum, but only as an insurance against the failure of Japan's 'constructive engagement policy'. He offers one of the most comprehensive descriptions of Japan's engagement policy and its greater emphasis on the Realist elements:

1 'emphasis on stability within both China and the bilateral relationship' (through ODA, caution towards post-Tiananmen sanctions, etc.);
2 'long-term goal of integrating China into the regional and global web of interdependence (in economics) and attaining mutual restraint (in political and security domains)';
3 avoiding the pitfalls of the triangular Japan–China–US relationship (for example playing one off against the other);
4 an increasing weight on 'containing China' as an 'insurance against a failure in the constructive engagement policy';[5]

Conservative politicians now openly espouse military balancing against China. Ozawa Ichiro wrote in his 'Blueprint for Japan' that while cooperating with China for stabilization and development Japan must also prepare countermeasures for disorder.[6] In its first long-range foreign-policy recommendations for the Asia-Pacific region in November 1997, the LDP says that 'Japan must be candid with China, and must not hesitate to press for more open sharing of national defense information or to request peaceful negotiations when problems arise'.[7] The policy paper addresses clearly the hedging and power-balancing sides of engagement, saying that Japan must maintain a 'good measure of flexibility' in its policy towards China, make the Japan–US alliance 'a key dimension of our China policy' and 'maintain a close watch on the direction China is headed and be prepared to cope with a variety of contingencies'.[8]

Japan's military force structure and China

The changes in perception of China in the 1990s seem at first glance not to have had much impact on Japan's military force structure and expenditures. Military budget allocations after 1989 initially declined, and have only recently increased very slightly. However, structural changes are by their nature very slow and the importance of Japan's military force looks different if the progress of its integration into the Japanese–American alliance is considered. Moreover, even the most hard-line observer of China would agree that, given China's military backwardness and domestic constraints, it could not suddenly replace the Soviet Union when the latter gave way to a much weaker and more conciliatory Russia in 1990.

During the 1980s Japan had considerably expanded its military expenditures and armaments, driven by the perception of the Soviet threat and American demands for more burden sharing. With the end of the Cold War, but with a considerable time lag in comparison with Europe and the US, Japan's defence expenditures registered their first nominal decrease since the establishment of the SDF in 1954 only in 1998, to ¥4.929 trillion; and there was a further decline in 1999, to ¥4.920 trillion, before it picked up again slightly in 2000. The picture is different in dollar terms because of the changes in the yen–dollar exchange rate. The 1998 picture also saw a decrease in dollar terms, but not 1999 (an increase from $37.7 billion to $41.1 billion in dollar terms). This exchange-rate factor is very important because of Japan's massive arms imports from the US. However, reflecting the worsening economic situation in Japan, the rising costs for the relocation of US troops in Okinawa and the end of the Soviet military threat, in June 1997 the government reduced its 1996–2000 Five-Year Mid-Term Defence Programme from ¥25,150 billion to ¥24,230 billion, affecting frontline equipment and research and development.[9] In the original 1995 version of that programme the equipment procurement amount had already been cut by ¥4.28 trillion compared with its predecessor for the fiscal years 1991–5.[10] The new five-year procurement plan for 2001–5 totals ¥25,160 billion (US$209.6 billion at the exchange rate of ¥120 to the dollar), which is ¥930 billion, or 0.7 per cent over the previous revised plan.[11] Major equipment outlays include the acquisition of four aerial tankers, two 13,500 ton class helicopter-carrying warships (to replace the previous 5,000 ton class helicopter destroyers), and two additional Aegis destroyers.[12]

In terms of personnel, in 2000 Japan had around 237,000 people in active military service. The manpower of the army, with 148,500, compares with 113,950 for the British army, whereas the navy strength of the two countries is about the same, with 43,000.[13] Manpower numbers, however, do not directly translate into fighting power, for example if compared with the UK military, which has considerable combat experience. Japan's reserves are relatively low, with only around 50,000, and recruitment is difficult because of the more competitive civilian job market. In terms of hardware, the Japanese armed forces compare much better with its Northeast Asian counterparts, being constantly upgraded and modernized. The main equipment includes 1,070 main battle tanks, 16 submarines, some 55 principal surface combatants and 331 combat aircraft (plus 80 combat aircraft and some 80 P-3C in the navy). Since September 2000 the ASDF has started to take delivery of what will be a total of 130 multirole F-2 fighter-bombers outfitted with the latest in air-to-air and air-to-ground munitions, including the Maverick air-to-surface attack missile. This aircraft has a range of 620 miles and is an improved version of the US F-16 fighter.

Although numerically Japan looks much less impressive than China, the SDF compares very favourably with China because of the latter's obsolescent air and navy equipment and Japan's continuous force modernization, with the exception of China's nuclear force. Only China has nuclear-powered submarines (5); the ratio of diesel submarines is 57 to 16 in China's favour; for destroyer/frigates it is 60 to 55; and for amphibious shipping 59 to 9 in China's favour.[14]

There are few changes in the SDF's equipment or posture which can be traced to having been made or being planned partially or entirely in reaction to the Chinese military.[15] Jeffrey S. Wiltse concluded in 1997 that the 'reemergence of China in regional and international affairs has had almost no direct influence in the modernization process or the orientation of the Japanese defense forces'.[16] The Defence Agency officially denies that there has been any Japanese redeployment to counter Chinese moves.[17] But there have been several moves to enhance the defence posture in southwest Japan, which had been so far neglected. The *Nihon Keizai Shimbun* reported in 1995, however, that the Defence Agency had decided to deploy new F-15 air fighters to Okinawa and to enhance the mobility of the ground forces in Kyushu. The Defence Agency justified these plans with the Chinese deployment of SU-27.[18] The *Yomiuri Shimbun* quoted Defence Agency sources in February 2000, saying that plans adopted earlier for downsizing the Ground Self-Defence Force (GSDF) would be complemented by rearrangements in GSDF divisions so that the GSDF could shift its focus of operations from the defence of Hokkaido to the containment of potential threats to the Kanto and Kinki regions.[19] Later these changes were brought into connection with a possible attack by North Korea.[20] The decrease of the number of P-3C from 100 in 1998/9 to 80 now reflects the diminished Soviet/Russian naval deployment, which has not been offset by Chinese deployments. However, in response to an increasing Chinese presence in waters around Japan as well as North Korean incursions into Japanese and Korean waters, the SDF are planning to set up a patrol-helicopter unit to enhance maritime surveillance. A new unit was inaugurated in March 2002 as part of the Western Army, with around 660 personnel to patrol and defend the 2,522 islands around Kyushu and Okinawa.[21] For the same reason, the equipment of the Japanese coastguard is to be improved, and cooperation between it and the MSDF enhanced.[22] The MSDF is to take over or supplement some tasks of the coastguard like protection of EEZ/territorial waters.[23] At the beginning of the new century it has become clear that the immediate concern about the instability on the Korean Peninsula in conjunction with long-term concerns about China is behind a major drive to radically review the structure of the SDF. In August 2001 the Defence Agency was reported to be planning a substantial revision of the current 1995 National Defence Programme Outline (NDPO) by 2003, with a view to shifting the SDF's main deployment to Kyushu and Okinawa to deal with any possible crisis on the Korean Peninsula or in the Straits of Taiwan.[24]

The National Defence Programme Outline of 1995

Study plans by private and official bodies as well as official defence plans and allied security agreements provide more indications of the extent to which the changed Japanese perceptions of China's security policies influenced official defence policies and strategists in the 1990s. The National Defence Programme Outline of 1995 and the follow-up to the Hashimoto–Clinton Joint Statement of April 1996 have been the most important changes with China in mind.[25] Both are closely linked with the February 1995 US East Asian Strategy Report (EASR), known as the Nye Initiative.

As mentioned in the previous chapter, the strength of US commitment to Asia seemed to diminish in the immediate post-Cold War era. The administration of George Bush Snr published a report in April 1990, the East Asia Strategy Initiative (EASI), which proposed reducing US forces from East Asia by 14,000–15,000 personnel, i.e. 10–12 per cent over the following three years.[26] The Gulf War had not only strained Japan–US security relations, but also shown to Tokyo that the US had to rely increasingly on contributions from its allies. Economic disputes poisoned the Japan–US relationship at the beginning of the 1990s.

Under the chairmanship of the business leader Higuchi Hirotaro, Prime Minister Hosokawa Morihiro set up an advisory group in February 1994 which looked at Japan's post-Cold War security situation. Published in August 1994 under the Socialist Prime Minister Murayama Tomiichi, the report became an important step towards the 1995 review of the NDPO.[27] Although the report considered it unlikely that a state comparable to the former Soviet Union – one prepared to confront the US militarily and politically – would emerge in the near future, it contained two cautionary references to China.[28] It spoke of many Asian nations, 'including China', which now had 'political motives and economic foundations for improving military power', and referred to 'various problems that remain unresolved, such as those that exist across the Taiwan Strait, the status of Hong Kong, and the widening economic disparity between the inland and coastal regions'.[29] It also recommended that the SDF pay greater attention to new challenges to security, such as the safety of maritime traffic and territorial air space, which were partly inspired by China's involvement in piracy and territorial disputes. In addition, the report put considerable stress on multilateral security approaches; this was a response to the government's desire to contribute more substantially (that is, SDF personnel) to UN PKO as well as peacekeeping forces, but may also have been a nod towards pacifist domestic opinion.

The Higuchi Report prepared the way for the re-examination of the NDPO of October 1976. The deliberations for the revision of the NDPO in 1994–5 led to some considerable debate about China, but in the end direct references to China's security challenges were taken out. Kokubun Ryosei wrote that initially a text was proposed to the effect that '[a]gainst the background of the existence of great military potentials including nuclear weapons around Japan, it is necessary for the protection of our security', but it was dropped because of opposition from the Social Democratic Party.[30] Michael Green confirmed this by mentioning early drafts of the revised NDPO which focused on the threat emanating from China's military modernization, nuclear tests and expansionist policies in the South China Sea and the Senkaku Islands. However, these warnings, he added, resurfaced in the speech by Prime Minister Murayama to the SDF in October 1995 and in later editions of the Defence of Japan White Papers.[31] Christopher Hughes explains that for political and diplomatic reasons Japan could not officially have referred to a concern about China's security policy.[32] Tamura Shigenobu, a member of the LDP staff working on security issues, writes, however, that China's security challenge was very much on the mind of the LDP policy-makers, and this transpired also in their talks with US policy-makers.[33] Foreign Minister Kono Yohei, in an answer to a question about the redefinition of the security treaty before the Diet in October 1995, defended the alliance by stating that 'it is important that one does not forget about the China issue'.[34] However, the North Korean nuclear crisis in 1994 had brought to the forefront a much more imminent security challenge which could be used publicly by the government to strengthen national and alliance defence efforts. As a result, and in contrast to the Higuchi Report, which speaks of a variety of regional security concerns, the NDPO refers only to the Korean Peninsula.

The NDPO of November 1995 also put much more stress on defence cooperation with the US, mentioning the US thirteen times, compared with only twice in its predecessor in 1976. In contrast to the 1976 NDPO, the new one stated that Japan should seek US cooperation from the very beginning of a direct aggression against Japan. It spoke of the need to enhance the credibility of Japan–US defence cooperation and proposed to review the bilateral guidelines of this cooperation, which had been formulated in 1978.

The Nye Initiative: don't mention the C-word!

At the same time as the Japanese government was preparing the NDPO in close consultation with the US, the US administration was reviewing its post-Cold War East Asia strategy. During the second Clinton administration the US Department of Defence felt the need to counteract the impression in East Asia that the US would slowly but surely withdraw its troops from East Asia. In addition, it had also come to a more pessimistic appraisal of the new post-Cold War era. As a result of the East Asia Strategy Initiative in 1990 some 6,000 US troops had actually been withdrawn from Okinawa. Under Secretary of Defence Perry and Assistant Secretary of Defence Joseph Nye, in February 1995 the Department of Defence released the EASR, known as the Nye Report, which was meant to draw a line for such withdrawals, promising to keep 100,000 US troops in Asia.[35] This number had also been mentioned in the Pentagon's Bottom-Up Review of September 1993.[36]

For the US, the ensuing strengthening of security cooperation with Japan (as well as the re-equilibration of the bilateral relationship, which was suffering from severe economic frictions and the widespread feeling in the US that Japan had replaced the Soviet threat) was one of the most important steps by the US to reassert its willingness to stay in Asia, but not the only one. In July 1996 the US and Australia renewed their defence alliance (notably intelligence and joint exercises), which was called by Defence Secretary William Perry the 'southern anchor of the US strategy in the Asia Pacific region'; he referred to the US–Japan relationship as the 'northern anchor'.[37] Since 1999 the US has signed a Visiting Forces Agreement with the Philippines, initiated International Military Education and Training (IMET) programmes for Southeast Asian officers in the US, and become involved in an increasing array of regional multilateral exercises.[38]

At the same time, the Nye Initiative was a reaction to Japanese concerns about US commitment to Japan's and East Asia's security in the wake of the end of the Cold War, with its new but unclear security challenges. The US wanted now to adapt the security alliance to a post-Cold War world where China was a greater concern than the former Soviet Union, to draw the lessons from Japan's disappointing contribution (in terms of personnel at least) to the Allied Gulf War against Iraq, and to reduce Japan's temptation to tilt towards multilateral security alternatives (the latter concern had been raised by the emphasis of the Higuchi Report on multilateral security).[39] On both sides, concern about China's future path and role and how to gain the ally's support for deterring China from upsetting the current balance of power in Asia was a major motivation. Leaving Japan alone to balance China would set off an arms race and destabilize the region, and letting Japan bandwagon with China was also not desirable for the US.[40] A strengthened US–Japan relationship was meant to counter China's hope of 'playing a multipolar game'.[41] In some ways this was the revival of a previously pursued goal: after the revision of the Japan–US security treaty in 1960, the US saw that 'Japan offers the prospect of development as an increasingly important political, economic and, possibly, military counterweight to the rising power of Communist China'.[42]

For Japan's defence planners, the Nye Report brought relief as well as concerns, since the post-Cold War situation presented an illustration of their entrapment/abandonment dilemma *vis-à-vis* the US. Funabashi documents the concern of Japan's diplomats, expressed to Nye in the discussions leading to EASR, that the US might just play China off against Japan or later drop Japan. On the other hand, they were increasingly worried about China's military developments and territorial claims, a concern which in the end got the upper hand in 1995.[43]

China's future behaviour and how to engage China with Japan in order to prevent China playing the US and Japan off against each other were very much on Nye's mind.[44] With clear reference to China, Nye often expressed his concern about the instability which could result from the rise and fall of great powers.[45] The difficulty was how to formulate and implement a complex policy such as engagement, which also contains elements meant as hedging, deterrence and power balancing by the US and Japan, but which is seen by China as, at best, maintaining American hegemony in Asia (with the allegedly 'eternal' benefit of creating stability and keeping a check on Japan) and, at worst, keeping China down, containing it and foiling its aspiration for national reunification and taking back its 'due historical place' in Asia. The Clinton administration's basic foreign-policy stance of 'engagement and enlargement' also spelled out another element of engagement which was equally unpalatable in Chinese eyes – changing the Chinese regime through the propagation of democracy and human rights.

Nye rejected a policy of containment. He argued that containment of China discarded the chance that China would become a responsible great power in the region, it would be irreversible and, assuming China's enmity, would become a self-fulfilling prophecy.[46] He described the US strategy towards China based on engagement, mentioning 'a dialogue with China on a broad variety of fronts' and US promotion of Asia-Pacific Economic Cooperation (APEC) in the economic area.[47] However, Nye could not escape the problem that one crucial military component of the Realist part of engagement – military power balancing – relies on the same tool as containment: military superiority or, as Nye put it, preponderance, which relies on military power.[48] Funabashi describes how difficult it was for the EASR's authors to find the right language for what was carefully referred to as 'China's evolving role'. The American policy-makers were torn between the need to justify and redefine the Japan–US military alliance in the post-Cold War era and addressing China's role for the alliance and US strategy in general without sounding as if they were calling for China's containment. As Funabashi put it, 'It was just that, depending on place and time, Nye's strategy of "engaging" China could run perilously close to being "containment" '.[49] After all, the difference is only in the eye of the beholder.

Funabashi speaks of the Nye Initiative as being 'based on power politics to the very last', dealing with China and Japan as two emerging powers, but allying with Japan to balance China.[50] It was clear that the Department of Defence and the Clinton administration as a whole wanted Japan's help to balance against China and to impress on China, with the combined US–Japan diplomatic, economic and military might, the need for it to become a responsible international player and not a new hegemonic force. For diplomatic reasons and to avoid an 'entrapment' dilemma for the Japanese government *vis-à-vis* its domestic public, this could not be spelled out so openly.

The 1996 Joint Japan–US Declaration

The momentum created by the 1995 Nye Initiative and the November 1995 NDPO was to result in a Joint Declaration on the occasion of Clinton's planned Japan visit in November 1995 which was to give public expression to the strengthening of Japan–US security cooperation and to lead to more formalized arrangements. Due to the rape of an Okinawan girl by US servicemen in Okinawa, Clinton's visit took place only in April the following year. In Japan the Okinawa incident led to serious questioning of the military alliance and particularly the concentration of US bases on Okinawa, but the Taiwan Strait crisis in spring 1996 provided further strength to the argument about the need to balance China through greater unilateral and bilateral defence efforts.[51] In their discussions with the US side, the Japanese realised the important role of the 'Chinese problem' for the US policy-makers.[52] The importance of preserving peace in

East Asia, with reference to the Taiwan Strait confrontation, was mentioned publicly by Hashimoto as well as Clinton during the latter's visit to Tokyo.[53] However, the Joint Declaration avoided any reference to a security challenge from China, instead expressing the interest of Japan and the US in cooperating with China. However, the delay of the summit until after the March 1996 Taiwan crisis had put a much greater emphasis on the common concerns about China than both sides would have wanted. Moreover, Clinton's efforts to offset China's negative perception of the April 1996 declaration (and the visa to President Li Denghui in 1995) by courting China in a way which was seen as a sleight in Japan was to highlight the complexities of a coordinated China policy by Japan and the US.

The delay until April 1996 also had the result that the American side had to deal with a new prime minister, Hashimoto Ryutaro (January 1996 to July 1998), who was much more inclined to strengthen the security relationship than his predecessor from the Social Democratic Party, Murayama Tomiichi. In the Joint Declaration of 17 April 1996 it was proposed the promotion of 'greater policy coordination, including studies on bilateral cooperation in dealing with situations that may emerge in the areas surrounding Japan, and which will have an important influence on the peace and security of Japan'. Just prior to Clinton's visit, both sides had concluded an Acquisition and Cross-Servicing Agreement (ACSA) to clarify Japanese logistical support in peacetime but also in times of conflict in 'areas surrounding Japan'. The agreement had been suggested by the US back in May 1988 and was part of the discussion of the 1978 Guidelines for Japan–US Defence Cooperation. The North Korean crisis in 1994 and the uncertainties surrounding China had proved the insufficiencies of those guidelines and prompted the US to seek their revision.

The Japan–US preparation for the revision of the 1978 guidelines began after the April 1996 Joint Declaration. In June 1997 a mid-term report on the new guidelines was submitted by the government, with the final report following in September 1997. In April 1998 the Japanese government submitted a bill on the new guidelines (Bill Concerning Measures to Ensure the Peace and Security of Japan in Situations in Areas Surrounding Japan), as well as revisions to the SDF Law and to the ACSA, which were passed in May 1999 with minor amendments. The public debate on the new guidelines raised various concerns in Japan which are related to widespread reluctance to get further involved in defence efforts, and to the interpretation of Japan's constitutional restraints (for example, collective defence is not allowed under the government's – current – interpretation of the Constitution).[54] It has been hotly argued among security specialists whether the Joint Declaration constitutes a 'reconfirmation', a 'redefinition', a 'reinterpretation' or even a 'revision' of the security treaty. Those critical of the Joint Declaration and its follow-up, including China, call it a 'redefinition', others a 'reconfirmation'.[55] Joseph Nye later admitted that China was right in saying that the bilateral security treaty had been expanded towards a greater regional role because he wanted to make the treaty more mutually beneficial in order to reduce strains in the Japan–US economic and security relationship.[56]

Another hotly debated item was the ambiguous clause 'situations in areas surrounding Japan that will have an important influence upon Japan's peace and security', which is of particular importance in the context of the new direction in Japanese–Chinese security relations. As a result of the Diet debates the government had to add to this clause the phrase 'and if left as what it is, has a potential to develop into a direct armed attack against Japan'.[57]

The background to Japan–US cooperation on TMD

Before analysing the implications of the clause 'situations in areas surrounding Japan' for Japanese–Chinese security relations, we have also to deal with the joint Japan–US research into a missile defence system for the area around Japan, TMD, which cannot be fully understood without considering the impact of China's military policies.

The idea of TMD goes back to President Reagan's Strategic Defence Initiative (SDI), launched on 23 March 1983. In 1987 Japan exchanged with the US a Memorandum of Understanding on SDI which led in 1989, for example, to the production of the US Patriot system, which in its current figuration (PAC-2) is to intercept aircraft only.[58] The first Japanese TMD involvement was the participation of Japanese companies from December 1989 until May 1993 in the architecture study of an anti-missile defence system over the West Pacific (WESTPAC) which bridged SDI and TMD.[59] The final report in May 1994 recommended that the US and Japan develop and deploy missile defence systems against missiles from Russia, China and particularly North Korea, just after Japan had became alarmed about the North Korean test of the medium-range ballistic missile Nodong-1 (range of 1,300 km) in May 1993.[60] In December 1993 a Japan–US TMD Working Group was established. In 1994 the US presented four TMD options to Japan, requiring a budget ranging from US$4.5 billion to US$16.3 billion to be available by 2004–5.[61] In April 1995 the Defence Agency set up the Ballistic Missile Defence Research Office and in September 1998 both governments agreed at a Security Subcommittee meeting to proceed with joint TMD research. On 25 December 1998 Japan's National Security Council accepted TMD, which was formalized on 16 August 1999 by an agreement to conduct a five-year programme of joint technology research on the technical feasibility of the Navy Theatre-Wide Defence (NTWD) missile defense system (upper-tier system), which would be deployed on Aegis ships, of which Japan has four so far.[62] The Defence Agency has already decided to upgrade the Patriot system to PAC-3, which is a lower-tier ground-based TMD system.[63] In addition to the many political problems to be discussed hereafter – focusing on China – which may prevent Japan from moving to deployment, are also problems related to costs, technological feasibility, technical cooperation with the US and Japan's Constitution.[64]

Japan's motivation for joining the research phase of TMD is now more than just alliance politics and interest in specific technologies, which were predominant considerations for its involvement in SDI.[65] Ogawa Shinichi, senior research fellow and deputy director of the Second Research Department at the NIDS, argues that, since arms control, diplomacy, pre-emptive strikes and deterrence are insufficient to deal with the ballistic missile threat, Japan has started to consider TMD.[66] More than anything else, the North Korean missile test over Japan on 31 August 1998 (North Korea claims that it was a satellite launch) alarmed the Japanese public and politically facilitated the government's participation in TMD research. But there is no doubt that, although the missile threat from North Korea is in the foreground, China's ballistic missile proliferation has been playing an important part in moving Japan towards TMD, particularly since the Chinese tests around Taiwan in 1995/6. For diplomatic reasons, however, the North Korean developments have been highlighted by the Japanese and US governments. Moreover, we saw in Chapter 2 that China has been a major supporter of the North Korea missile programme.

The main reasons for the US to involve Japan in TMD are the protection of US forces in Japan and the hope for Japanese financial, if not technological, support.[67] TMD is also considered a necessary precursor to the planned National Missile Defense system (NMD), and TMD proponents argue that TMD will be ineffective without an effective homeland defence to prevent strategic blackmail by a regional opponent with intercontinental ballistic missile capability.[68] This clearly is also aimed at China and has implications for China's opposition to NMD as well as TMD. After the Taepodong-1 test on 31 August 1998 the US Congress passed legislation requiring the Secretary of Defence to conduct a study on the establishment and operation of a TMD system in the Asia-Pacific region to protect the US's 'key regional allies'.[69] Less often mentioned is the concern that a weakening of the US nuclear guarantee over Japan may ultimately prompt Japan to consider an autonomous nuclear deterrent despite the very large domestic and international obstacles to such a move.[70] Selig Harrison even argued that the US nuclear umbrella in itself will not be enough to prevent such a development if it is not accompanied by global nuclear arms control to curb China's nuclear deterrent.[71] Morton Halperin, before joining the Policy Planning Staff of the Department of State, argued that Japan might go nuclear if, for example, the US moves closer to China, withdraws from Asia or cannot resolve the contradiction between its nuclear deterrent policy and goal of global nuclear non-proliferation. The latter scenario could become a reality if a lack of progress in nuclear disarmament was to be coupled with an expansion of the Chinese nuclear capability. Another scenario would be the development of Korean nuclear capability.[72]

The Japanese–Chinese debate on Japan's new security policy

While there were few diplomatic inhibitions for the Japanese government to mention the relevance of the tensions on the Korean Peninsula to strengthening Japan–US defence cooperation, the situation was very different in the case of China.[73] In the interest of good Japan–China relations the government tried to

soothe Chinese concerns that the strengthening of Japan–US defence cooperation and joint TMD research were not aimed at containing China nor at
preventing PRC–Taiwan reunification. Moreover, the political opposition used
the negative Chinese reaction for its own agenda of curtailing a deeper Japanese
involvement in regional defence alongside the US.

Yet the Chinese side has been very critical of these new security policies and
has voiced strong objection to their implications for the reunification with
Taiwan and for Japan's greater regional security role.[74] It did not believe the
government line that the Joint Declaration and its follow-up did not constitute a
change to the Japan–US security treaty and did not target any specific country.
To make things worse, Japanese–Chinese relations were marred in the summer
of 1996 by the erection of a lighthouse tower on one of the Senkaku Islands by a
rightist group, by Prime Minister Hashimoto Ryutaro's visit to the Yasukuni
Shrine and by Chinese nuclear tests. The first two events further reinforced
Chinese suspicion and criticism of Japan veering to the right (and/or were used
to put pressure on Japan), whereas the latter could not fail to damage China's
image in Japan and facilitate the public's acceptance of Japan's stronger defence-
policy approach.

The inclusion of Taiwan in Japanese–US defence cooperation

The Chinese Japan specialist Wu Xinbo calls the Taiwan issue the most important in Japanese–Chinese relations, pointing out that many Chinese believe for
historical and pragmatic reasons that Japan does not want Taiwan's absorption
by the PRC and prefers the status quo.[75] China's most immediate concern has
been that the new measures to improve Japan–US security cooperation and
Japan's participation in TMD interfere in its relationship with Taiwan and make
reunification more difficult.[76] In reaction to the Japan–US Joint Declaration the
Chinese Foreign Ministry released a statement on 18 April 1996 which reiterated, in its first point, that the question of Taiwan was an internal Chinese affair
and that China would resist foreign interference.[77] Chinese suspicions were
linked to the geographical ambiguity of Japanese and American statements as to
the application of the Joint Declaration and the new guidelines, and also to the
possible implications of Japan's TMD participation to the reunification issue.
The concern is not only that Japan's logistical support will put the US in a
stronger position to intervene militarily in the Taiwan Strait, but also that this
possibility, as well as the possible involvement of Taiwan in TMD (made more
likely by Japan's TMD deployment), will encourage bolder Taiwanese resistance
to Beijing's Taiwan policies.[78]

The greatest conflict arose within Japan as well as between Japan and China
from the guidelines' ambiguity as to their geographical application. For China,
the main question has been whether the geographical area includes China, and
notably Taiwan. The Japanese government refused to give any geographical
meaning to the phrase 'in the area around Japan' (*shuhen*), claiming instead that it
was 'situational' and depended on the location of the threat affecting Japan. The

US fully shared this approach.[79] The government presented six types of examples of situations with an important influence on the peace and security of Japan, including domestic turmoil in a country with large refugee flows into Japan (which could obviously refer to the Korean Peninsula as well as China).[80] The first benefit of this ambiguous stance was that the possible scope of Japanese cooperation with the US could be expanded beyond the geographical limits of the so-called Far Eastern clause in Article 6 of the 1960 Japan–US security treaty.[81] Second, this element of strategic ambiguity further enhances the deterrence value of Japanese–US security cooperation. Or as Soeya puts it, the reaffirmed Japan–US alliance is 'primarily a tool to maintain general strategic stability over the Taiwan Strait'.[82] China saw proof of an extension of the geographical scope of Japan–US military cooperation in the fact that the Hashimoto–Clinton Joint Declaration mentioned a dozen times the 'Asia Pacific region', but not once the 'Far East'.[83] Takagi Seiichiro, then professor at the National Graduate Institute for Policy Studies, rebuffs such an interpretation since references to the Asia-Pacific came up in the 1970s and 1980s as a result of the growing economic integration of the region.[84]

The question of whether Taiwan is an object of Japan–US defence cooperation goes back to the Far Eastern clause of the revised Japan–US security treaty in 1960. In an official declaration on the scope of the Far East on 26 February 1960, Prime Minister Kishi Nobusuke defined it as broadly (but not exclusively) the areas north of the Philippines and surrounding Japan, including the areas under the control of South Korea and the ROC (Taiwan).[85] The 1969 Japan–US joint communiqué between Prime Minister Sato Eisaku and President Richard Nixon called the 'maintenance of peace and security in the Taiwan area … a most important factor for the security of Japan' (see Chapter 2). When Japan normalized relations with China in 1972, the foreign minister, Ohira Masayoshi, presented a 'unified government understanding' in the Diet which said that the 'Taiwan issue is basically an internal problem of China. The US–Japan security treaty should be implemented cautiously with consideration of the friendly relationship between Japan and China'.[86] During the normalization talks Prime Minister Zhou Enlai had asked for the nullification of the 1969 Japan–US agreement on Taiwan and for the non-application of the Japan–US security treaty to Taiwan, but the speedy conclusion of diplomatic relations took precedence over any written agreement on these two items. Prime Minister Tanaka Kakuei only responded that he understood, and after normalization declared in the Diet that nothing about these two items had changed.[87] The issue was raised again in 1978 with the conclusion of the bilateral Peace and Friendship Treaty. Foreign Minister Sonoda told the Diet in September 1978 that the 1969 Japan–US joint communiqué had lost its meaning. On another occasion he declared that the new treaty with China had made it unnecessary to consider Taiwan as a part of the 'Far East' covered by the Japan–US security treaty, but that the status of Taiwan as part of the Far East in its relation to the Japan–US security treaty was a question to be settled through consultation between Japan and the US.[88] But several days later, in December 1978, he backed down and explained that the Japanese government had not started consultations because of concerns about the possibility of the Soviet Union gaining influence in the Taiwan Strait if the Far East clause was changed. The US State Department had earlier declared that they saw no need for consultations on the Far East clause.[89] This Japanese reversal is worth remembering because the Chinese side did not forget about it and Foreign Minister Sonoda's first statement was recalled in 1997 by the Chinese vice-foreign minister.[90] In April 1998 the vice-foreign minister, Yanai Shunji, increased confusion when he tried to bridge the gap between the meaning of the Far East and *shuhen*, stating that the concept of 'situations surrounding Japan' is similar to the meaning of 'Far East' used in the 1960 revised security treaty.[91]

Interpretational somersaults on Taiwan's inclusion after 1996

Not only has the Japanese government been unwilling clearly to rule out the inclusion of China and Taiwan from the application of the new guidelines, but contradictory official statements after April 1996 have only reinforced the commonsense conclusion that Taiwan, as one of the most likely flashpoints, is included. There has also been no coherence between statements from the Japanese and US sides.[92] Moreover, the Japanese side did not do well in dispelling Beijing's suspicions when briefing China on the new guidelines. The US side was well aware of the need to handle China carefully with regard to the strengthening of Japan–US defence cooperation, and Joseph Nye was the first to brief China, in November 1995, before the planned and then cancelled visit by President Clinton.[93] The Japanese briefings in Tokyo and Beijing have been carried out, however, by officials of lower rank and have been conducted belatedly. Japan's most comprehensive background briefing took place only in March 1997 at the fourth round of Japan–China security talks.[94]

Joseph Nye told Funabashi Yoichi that the US side tried to convince the Chinese that the Joint Declaration was directed at contingencies on the Korean Peninsula and not China.[95] Only a page later, Funabashi quotes Akiyama Masahiro, the director of the Defence Agency's Defence Bureau, who said that he explained to the Chinese that neither China or Korea were the reason for the reaffirmation.[96] But that China was certainly on the mind of the US administration, as it was in the case of the Nye Report, is documented by a briefing of visiting Japanese politicians on US views of East Asian security in June 1997 by the deputy assistant secretary of defence Kurt Campbell. He mentioned five US security concerns:

- instability in North Korea;
- Sino-Russian rapprochement as a potential threat in the next fifteen years;
- the Chinese military build-up as a non-negligible development;
- unstable PRC–Taiwan relations;
- the growing military spending in Southeast Asia.[97]

While a Japanese diplomat was preparing the Chinese side for the imminent April 1996 declaration, US Secretary of State Perry declared at about the same time that the US–Japan alliance was also an insurance against the possible destabilization of the region by the PRC.[98]

There were also some statements of the obvious on the Japanese side: an article in the *Beijing Review* claimed that Foreign Minister Kono declared in a Diet interpellation on strengthening the Japan–US security treaty in 1995 that it was now necessary to consider the presence of China.[99] In March 1997, during the 4th Security Dialogue, Tanaka Hitoshi, deputy bureau director of the Gaimusho's North American Affairs Bureau, replied to insistent Chinese questions about what Japan would do if military tensions occurred in the Taiwan Strait: 'It depends on the case'.[100] According to a Taiwanese newspaper, Prime Minister Hashimoto declared in a private meeting in April 1997 that not only the Korean Peninsula and the Taiwan Strait but also the Spratly Islands would be included in the expanded Japan–US security cooperation. The following day the US Department of State denied this.[101] As a result, China reportedly included the Spratly Islands in an expression of concern to the Japanese government when criticizing the revised guidelines and their ambiguous geographic scope.[102]

The confusion in the Japanese government about the inclusion of Taiwan was heightened in July 1997 when Kato Koichi, then LDP secretary-general and known to be pro-China, told the Chinese government that the new guidelines had as their background changes on the Korean Peninsula. According to other reports he explicitly excluded Taiwan.[103] This prompted the chief cabinet secretary, Kajiyama Seiroku, a known pro-Taiwan LDP member and opponent of Kato, to say on a television programme in August 1997 that the peninsula was a problem, but that this should not mean that other regions were not also a problem. The area of Japan–US defence cooperation naturally included the Taiwan Strait. This was then supported by several statements from the government.[104]

In May 1998 Takano Toshiyuki, director-general of the Northern American Affairs Bureau, told a Diet committee that Japan's logistical support for US forces in regional emergencies would be limited to the Far East and its surrounding areas, as defined under the Japan–US security treaty. He was severely reprimanded for having given a geographical meaning to *shuhen* which included Taiwan and led to a rise in Chinese protests. In a clarification Yamazaki Taku, chairman of the LDP Policy Affairs Research Council, told the Chinese ambassador that developments concerning Taiwan would not constitute a regional emergency unless Beijing tried forcefully to reunify Taiwan with the PRC.[105] The Chinese side could hardly take this as a reassurance. The concern of the Chinese government about these developments was demonstrated during the acrimonious discussions about the wording of the November 1998 Joint Declaration: while most remember visiting President Jiang Zemin's demand for an apology for Japan's past deeds, the other demand concerned a clarification on Taiwan.

In 1999 Ozawa Ichiro, then leader of the Liberal Party, which was part of the coalition government, declared that Russia, the Korean Peninsula, China and Taiwan would naturally come within the scope of the new Japan–US defence cooperation guidelines.[106] Ozawa explained later to a high-ranking Chinese official that the revised guidelines should set an appropriate limit to Japan's help and prevent such support from getting out of hand (*zuru zuru kakudai suru koto ni hadome o kakeru*).[107]

In order to soothe vehement Chinese opposition to the revised guidelines, Prime Minister Obuchi made several conciliatory remarks, although he still did not explicitly exclude Taiwan from the application of the security treaty or lift Japan's ambiguity. In June 1999, at the G-8 Summit in Cologne, he reminded his colleagues that Northeast Asia was not amenable to the same kind of use of force as NATO used in Kosovo, implying that China should not worry that the US would use force against Taiwan or Tibet.[108] On the occasion of his visit to China in July 1999 he said to Prime Minister Zhu Rongji in Beijing that in applying the revised guidelines Japan would consider Japanese–Chinese friendly relations as one of its important national interests ('*Chugoku to no yuko kankei mo juyo na kokueki no hitotsu to shite jushi shite iku*') and that 'The law will be applied under our sovereign decision' ('*Horitsu no unyo wa waga kuni ya shutaiteki na handan no shita ni okonau*').[109] This was not really much of a change from the official Japanese position given by Foreign Minister Ohira Masayoshi in 1972 (quoted above). Moreover, Obuchi was also quoted in July 1999 as saying that he did not expect the use of force in the Taiwan Strait, thus basically telling the Chinese that it would all depend on them. As one high-level Defence Agency official told the author: 'There is no clause which says that Taiwan is *not* part of "shuhen" '.[110]

It is therefore not surprising that the Chinese don't seem to have any doubt about Taiwan's inclusion in the guidelines.[111] Moreover, they fear that a militarily stronger Japan is more likely to support US intervention in Taiwan.[112] It is not clear, however, to what extent the Chinese appreciate (or want to appreciate for tactical reasons) from Japanese interpretational somersaults that Taiwan's inclusion is contested even among conservative leaders. But Japan's consistent cultivated ambiguity about the legal status of Taiwan (see Chapter 1) and the increasingly warm relations between the island and Japan (see Chapter 4) can only further increase China's suspicion about Japan's 'true' intention on the Taiwan issue.

China's opposition to TMD

China's strident opposition to Japan's involvement in an upper-tier TMD (China is not opposed to Japan upgrading the Patriot system!) is also linked in the first place to its perceived impact on China's national reunification.[113] Beijing voiced its opposition to Japan's participation in TMD for the first time on the occasion of the 3rd Japanese–Chinese Security Dialogue in January 1996.[114] China is concerned that an Aegis-based Japanese NTWD system could easily be used for the defence of Taiwan by deploying these ships nearer to Taiwan and/or could make the acquisition of such a system by Taiwan more likely. From a technical point of view, Taiwan could easily be included in the currently researched NTWD system, because the defended footprints have a diameter of several hundred kilometres, to nearly 2,000 km.[115] Even if Taiwan is covered by TMD neither formally nor through direct deployment, the US can de facto cover it by a TMD located on US naval platforms.[116] Moreover, the administration of George W. Bush has made its commitment to the military defence of Taiwan much more explicit, and in July 2001 John Bolton, US under-secretary of state for arms control and international security, stated that Taiwan could be covered by a missile defence system.[117] Japan's concern about North Korean missiles is often presented by Chinese observers as an excuse to protect Taiwan from PRC missiles. In fact, in 1999 Taiwan's defence authorities asked the US to sell them Aegis ships, but even the Republican Bush administration turned this request down (at least for the time being), out of consideration for relations with China as well as for practical reasons.[118] President Li Denghui is quoted as having proposed in August 1999 that Taiwan should join a Japan–US TMD system.[119] Some Japanese have argued that a Japanese upper-tier TMD system might be useful to deter Chinese missile attacks or even to defend Taiwan in such a situation.[120]

Apart from the impact on Taiwan, China advances several more reasons for opposing Japan's TMD deployment, in particular, and TMD in general.[121] One concern is that it may be a step for Japan to acquire a more offensive missile capability, or even ultimately to go nuclear. TMD is compared to a shield behind which Japan may prepare a spear. The Chinese see Japan's TMD participation as a further strengthening of the Japan–US military alliance against China.[122] At least from a technical point of view, the Chinese side has a point. TMD is not a purely defensive system because:

- the components involved can be used as offensive potential;
- in theory, TMD can be used as a shield for offensive purposes;
- since it will necessitate cooperation with the US for reasons of technology/budget/alliance cohesion, let alone operational necessities, it can never just be separated from the different agenda of the US and its regional/global goals.

TMD would require a much greater real-time integration and cooperation with the US than ever before, with a considerable loss of independent Japanese decision-making.[123]

China also voices concerns that TMD would spark an arms race and unhinge the regional and global military balance. The Japanese government, however, believing in the deterrence value of TMD, argues that TMD would *prevent* an arms race.[124] The latter argument is, however, very controversially discussed among experts.[125] China is also concerned that TMD is only part of the US intention to build an NMD system which is to neutralize China's limited nuclear deterrent.[126] This concern was confirmed by the Bush administration in 2001 when it dropped 'national' from NMD to reflect concern by European allies about decoupling. Together with Russia, China warns that TMD and NMD would destroy the Anti-Ballistic Missile (ABM) Treaty. American experts recognize that a TMD system would raise ABM Treaty compliance issues and would also have an NMD capability for defending US allies in East Asia from North Korea.[127] The administration of George W. Bush has made it clear since 2001 that it is keen to drop the treaty altogether, and has proceeded along these lines.

The Chinese concern about the ABM Treaty is politically rebutted by Urayama Kori as being based more on a free-riding spirit than concern for that treaty, since China is a non-signatory of the treaty and has propelled the move towards TMD by its own missile developments.[128] Moreover, China is also criticized for invoking the logic of the ABM Treaty while pursuing its own missile defence projects.[129] While there are good technical, political and budgetary arguments against TMD, China's criticism also betrays an unwillingness to accept a Japanese right to consider protection against Beijing's growing nuclear missile deterrent.[130] In the eyes of the Chinese, as a country militarily allied with the US and under its nuclear umbrella, Japan is perceived as having no right to protect itself against China's smaller nuclear deterrent. China's 'delegitimization' of Japan's protest against China's nuclear deterrent came up as early as 1994, when Beijing refuted Japan's protest against continued Chinese nuclear tests by pointing to the US nuclear umbrella. Japan's claims to be a non-nuclear power are countered by the observation that Japan is a 'quasi' nuclear power because of its advanced nuclear and rocket technology and its possession of considerable plutonium stockpiles.[131] These observations are also reflected by some Western observers. Barry Buzan argues that Japan has a 'recessed deterrence'.[132] American representatives of the Realist School even predict that Japan will go nuclear in the future, which finds a ready echo with China's historical determinism.[133]

Political power balancing of China

A much less often noticed strengthening of the Realist aspects of Japan's engagement policy towards China is linked to Tokyo's more activist foreign policy. It basically consists of mirroring military deterrence and power balancing by building a front of as many countries as possible to politically deter China from being an 'irresponsible' country ('soft containment'), and thus to further encourage it to become a stakeholder in a global order based on Western-initiated international norms and regimes.[134] In what follows I will limit myself to East and Central Asia as the main areas for Japan's political power balancing against China. However, Japan's foreign policy towards its main partners, as well as multilateral fora like the G-8, also includes elements of political power balancing in the form of raising the subject of China, seeking understanding of Japan's China-relevant perceptions and policies, and promoting exchange of information on China.

One reason for the low visibility of Japan's power-balancing policy is probably that it has become submerged in the general perception of Japan asserting its foreign-policy interests in many areas more strongly and trying to play a more important role in Asian affairs. Another reason is Japan's low-key diplomatic style. The impetus for this greater foreign-policy activism goes back to the US (and other Western and Asian allies) urging Japan to share more international burdens, but also to Japan's greater self-confidence as the second-biggest economic world power and the towering economic giant of Asia which has gradually been translating this economic power into political power.[135] The following will show that many elements of this greater foreign-policy role are supported by various policy constituencies whose motives may include goals which have nothing to do with China (for example improving Japan's investment opportunities in Vietnam), let alone with power balancing. It is important to notice the growing role of the Defence Agency in developing relations with Asian countries which are relevant for power balancing against China. Although the Gaimusho is in charge of Japan's security policy and the relevant top posts in the Defence Agency are headed by diplomats on secondment, since the 1990s the agency has increased its contacts with and intelligence gathering about other countries, notably with regard to Asia. The 1995 Defence Programme Outline stated the intention of expanding relations and contacts with other countries beyond the US. In 1997 the Defence Agency established the International Planning Division (Kokusai Kikaku ka) within the Defence Bureau for this purpose.[136] Greater interest in PKO is also part of this opening as is interest in more bilateral defence dialogues.[137] The search for a greater international security profile in Asia also reflects the concern that Japan's voice will otherwise not be sufficiently heard in view of US involvement in regional security dialogues.[138] At the same time, these contacts enhance Japan's political enmeshment of China by putting pressure on Beijing's reluctant military leadership to be as willing as other Asian countries to facilitate military exchanges.

The policy tools of political power balancing and deterrence in Asia include wooing countries away from falling into the Chinese orbit (Burma); obviating the build-up of Chinese military power and intervention by strengthening neighbouring countries with domestic instabilities (Central Asia); supporting countries which are natural allies against China because they have grievances towards China (Vietnam); and encouraging Asian regionalism to induce China to become a responsible power supporting the status quo rather than face an adversarial Asian common front (ASEAN).

The area where Japan's foreign policy has become most assertive and activist is doubtless Asia, notably East Asia and Southeast Asia.[139] Japan's geographic location means that it is dependent on stability in the region, where it has been successful in creating an economic network which is very much centred on Japan in terms of trade, technology transfer, FDI and ODA. The key sub-regional organization is ASEAN, which straddles Japan's sea lanes of communication. The main security problem of this region – apart from economic and political instabilities like those in Indonesia and before that in Cambodia – is China's territorial claim to the whole of the South China Sea. Japan therefore has many interests in keeping ASEAN as politically coherent and economically prosperous as possible in order to counterbalance any destabilization which may originate from this problem. This effectively also means preventing Chinese hegemony while supporting the continuation of US regional predominance.[140] While some countries may to some degree resent US influence, they do not want instability or Chinese hegemony, which might cause Japan to regain a position more reminiscent of the period before 1945 than of its post-war economic predominance. If possible, the region wants both the US and Japan to balance China. As Lee Kuan-Yew put it: 'At present the balance is maintained by the US. In future it will be necessary that the US and Japan balance China. Together with the US, Japan will naturally be able to exert the role of balancing'.[141] This is closely related to the Asian interest in having the top economic world powers continue their strong economic involvement in Southeast Asia rather than shifting to China.

Japan's policy tools towards Asia are mostly economic and diplomatic because of Asian and domestic Japanese sensitivities relating to military power. Japan has played a major role in strengthening the political and economic resilience of the Southeast Asian countries, which was demonstrated again in the aftermath of the Asian economic crisis. Since the 1990s Tokyo has increasingly introduced bilateral security dialogues with its Southeast Asian partners, in addition to multilateral security dialogues mainly in the ARF. In addition, it has a dense web of military attachés at its regional embassies and it encourages Asian officers to study at its military educational facilities.

The obstacles for Japan's power balancing are the political, economic and cultural diversity of the region (including the sizable Chinese minorities in many of the region's countries), China's competition for leadership, the scope of the political and economic challenges from China, divergent and/or contradictory US policies towards the region, and Japan's inability to come to regionally more acceptable terms with its past. ASEAN may be the most advanced regional association outside of the European Union (EU), but it encounters considerable difficulties in creating a free-trade area, let alone shaping a security community. At home in Japan, the underdevelopment of strategic debate and strategic thinking puts severe restraints on pursuing a consistent and effective policy of power balancing, particularly at times when difficult policy choices have to be made.

Chinese–American policy differences, or US policies which make China and the other Asian countries rally against the US (for example the US emphasis on human rights) can further help China to prevent an Asian front forming against it. Any strong anti-China position immediately makes many Asian countries wince away from the US. This was illustrated when US Defence Secretary William Cohen declared on his visit to Hanoi in March 2001:

[O]ne of the very important and beneficial aspects of ASEAN is that you have collective interests, and those collective interests can in fact, if you act in concert, give considerable leverage in dealing with China in the future on a peaceful and cooperative basis.[142]

While many Southeast Asian leaders may secretly agree, they do not like to be put on the spot and to emphasize the anti-China slant of their regional integration efforts.

The following analysis of several bilateral relationships with Asian countries distils the China-relevant power balancing of Japan and illustrates the problems mentioned above.

Burma/Myanmar

A particularly interesting but also complex case is Japan's policy towards Burma/Myanmar. Despite its geographic and political distance from Japan, the death of 190,000 Japanese in Burma during the Pacific War and the involvement in Burma's independence struggle have created special links between the two countries.[143] The Japanese love affair with Burma continued after the war, leading to considerable Japanese 'quasi' reparations and later generous ODA programmes. The establishment of the martial law regime by the State Law and Order Restoration Council (SLORC) in September 1988 caused a cooling of relations and curtailing of aid. However, in contrast to its Western partners, notably the US, Japan has been much more accommodating to the new regime, arguing for maintaining a dialogue and some aid rather than comprehensive sanctions.[144] As a result Tokyo has been criticized by the US and Europe. In May 2001 US Secretary of State Colin Powell criticized Japan for providing aid for the construction of a hydroelectric plant in Burma.[145] While most motivations for this policy line are related to sentimental Orientalism, disapproval of imposing Western human rights ideals on a poor developing country, hope of playing a mediating role between Burma and the West and/or economic considerations, there are strategic considerations as well.[146] First of all, Burma is now member of ASEAN, which Japan strongly supports. Since Burma faces (like Cambodia) considerable difficulties of integration into the association for political and economic reasons, Japan has been keen to help this process in order to avoid a weakening of ASEAN.[147] Second, Burma's close links with China (reinforced by Western disapproval of its regime) are seen as a possible threat to Japan's sea lanes of communication through the Indian Ocean. There are reports of Burma having allowed China to set up listening posts in its territory for surveillance of ship traffic in the Indian Ocean.[148] There is the feeling that Japan has to work against a too-close Burmese–Chinese relationship in order to provide China with more incentives to be committed to the security of sea lanes; otherwise China could be tempted to open a land corridor to the Indian Ocean through Burma. The current Burmese regime is seen as the only possibility of stabilizing Burma politically and economically.[149] In view of Burma's past troubled relationship with China (support of Burmese insurgencies), some Japanese policy-makers and specialists consider there to be enough political will in Burma to avoid too close a relationship with China. Nagatomi Yuichiro, a former Ministry of Finance official now working for a Ministry of Finance (MOF) linked institution, explained to this author that Burma is a 'cordon sanitaire' against China.[150] The most immediate difficulty for Tokyo in pursuing this strategic calculus is US/European opposition to the Burmese regime and the fear of becoming isolated from its Western partners. Incidentally, Tokyo's lenient approach to Cambodia's governance problems has many similar motivations.

Vietnam

Japan has become more active in Vietnam because of its economic interests, and its desire to stabilize this most important but also very vulnerable new ASEAN member (since 1995) and to build up ASEAN against China.[151] However, Japan often had to accommodate different US policies towards Vietnam, although currently there are no longer any major divergences. Vietnam is particularly important in Japan's power balancing because of Vietnam's difficult history with its Chinese neighbour and its geographic/demographic dimensions. As a new member of ASEAN it has gained further importance: on the one hand, it has the potential to make a substantial contribution to ASEAN as an important bloc because of its size; on the other, it may weaken ASEAN's strength and cohesion because of its political and economic differences and backwardness. Since Vietnam became a member of ASEAN Tokyo has been very keen to stabilize it and to help with its integration into the association. The current weakness of Indonesia has made the stabilization of this big country even more important. Vietnam is Japan's fourth-largest aid recipient, after Thailand, China and Indonesia. For Vietnam, Japan is the biggest ODA donor since the resumption of ODA in 1992. In terms of cumulative investment, Japan is Vietnam's fourth-largest foreign investor. Tokyo's embassy in Hanoi counts among the top twenty Japanese embassies in the world.

The defence relationship has grown astonishingly fast. Since 1995 Japan has a military attaché in its embassy (GSDF). The Japanese director-general for defence visited Vietnam in 1997 and 2000, which is a rare development of contacts for a country with which no relations existed before. In 2000 both top defence officials agreed bilateral cooperation on maritime search-and-rescue operations for civilian ships in the South China Sea, which had been suggested by the Vietnamese defence minister.[152] In March 2001 Foreign Minister Kono Yohei proposed to his Vietnamese counterpart the holding of politico-military talks between the two sides composed of Foreign Ministry and defence officials.[153]

India

Japan's potentially most important Asian partner for power balancing outside ASEAN is India. The country had been neglected by Japan for most of the postwar period because of geographic/cultural distance, limited economic interest and their divergent positions in the East–West conflict.[154] India's opening towards the West after the end of the Cold War, politically as well as economically, made it a more interesting partner. Its crucial role for the maintenance of stability in the South Asian region, along Japan's sea lanes of communication through the Indian Ocean, but also its role in the UN (India and Japan support each other in striving for a permanent Security Council seat, although Japan refrains from stating this publicly because of India's nuclear policies) and in the non-aligned movement, make it an important political partner. But India's difficult relationship with China and its potential to keep a check on China in the future have been important incentives for both to discuss common strategic interests. This also becomes quite obvious when looking at the exchanges, which started to pick up after 1997 and which survived the crisis in the bilateral relationship after India's and Pakistan's explosion of nuclear devices in May 1998.[155] After the South Asian tests yet another motive for continuing an expansion of political dialogue with India was the concern that Indian nuclear-weapons developments might accelerate the build-up of China's nuclear arsenal.[156] After having initially imposed economic sanctions on India and Pakistan, Japan and the US relaxed them when the two new nuclear powers promised in 1999 to sign the CTBT in future and to abstain from further tests. Japan has made clear that it does not want to link the whole bilateral relationship to the CTBT issue.[157]After the terror attacks in New York on 11 September 2001, India became even more important to Japan (strongly encouraged by a pro-India shift in US diplomacy) and it dropped its sanctions against India (but also against Pakistan), which had been imposed after the nuclear tests.

High-level visits started in July 1997 when Foreign Minister Ikeda went to India. This was followed by three visits by Japanese defence officials. The first high-level defence talks were planned for May 1998 but temporarily fell victim to India's nuclear test. Reciprocal visits resumed, however, in 1999 with the former prime minister Hashimoto's visit to India in February 1999 and Foreign Minister Jaswant Singh's visit to Japan, followed in January 2000 by the visit by Defence Minister George Fernandes, the first ever by an Indian defence minister, which resulted in an agreement on regular defence talks.[158] When Prime Minister Mori visited India in August 2000, he agreed with his counterpart, Atal Bihari Vajpayee, to set up three Wise Men's panels, of which one is devoted to dialogue on security policy ('High-Level Security Forum'), starting in 2001.[159] Both sides agreed on a 'Global Partnership between Japan and India in the 21st Century', marking a strong difference to Mori's visit to Pakistan during the same South Asia tour. India is also included in Japan's Asian initiative to combat piracy after the Indian coastguard was helpful in arresting the pirates of the Alondra Rainbow. In November 2000 a patrol vessel of the Japanese coastguard visited India and Malaysia and implemented joint training to combat piracy. As part of Japan's logistical support to the US and British forces in the Indian Ocean after 11 September 2001, the SDF obtained oil in Mumbai (formerly Bombay).[160]

The strengthening of Japanese–Indian ties did not fail to attract negative comments from China, and Indian media interpretations on the need of the two countries to 'deal with China' together only reinforced Chinese suspicions.[161] Prime Minister Mori's visit was criticized by the Chinese media as an attempt to contain China.[162] The Japanese–Indian security relationship will not easily turn into very effective political power balancing, however, because of India's nuclear policy (and India's perception that Japan does not want to understand the China-related rationale for it), its missile testing (Japan, for example, strongly protested the Indian missile test in January 2001), the need for a certain balance towards Pakistan, and Japan's concern about Chinese sensitivities – which has become stronger since the administration of George W. Bush made a very public display of its pro-Indian line, particularly after the terror attacks on 11 September 2001.[163] It is understood in Japan that it may be useful for the regional balance to improve Japanese–Indian relations, and the campaign against terrorism since 2001 has given additional incentives, but it would be counterproductive for their relationship to be stressed too much.[164]

Russia and Central Asia

Japan's post-Cold War policy towards Russia and Central Asia is also partly motivated by power balancing against China.[165] In 1997 Prime Minister Hashimoto Ryutaro launched his 'Eurasia Diplomacy' as part of a new approach to post-Cold War Eurasia. Most of the policy was oriented towards Russia and China, and one brief part dealt also with the so-called Silk Road countries – that is, the five new Central Asian Republics (Kazakhstan, Uzbekistan, Turkmenistan, Kyrgyzstan and Tajikistan) and three new countries in the South Caucasus (Georgia, Armenia and Azerbaijan).[166]

The policy speech was Japan's belated response to the end of the Cold War and the eastward expansion of NATO since 1990, which is having a major lasting impact on Japan's strategic environment, notably concerning its relations with Russia and China. These developments had initially deprived Japan of any shaping influence on the emerging Eurasian security structure and sidelined it in the competition to gain access to considerable energy resources. The strong US/European support of Russia's political and economic rehabilitation and integration isolated Japan in the Western camp and demanded a new approach to its main Russia-related concern, the return of the so-called Northern Territories. The resulting economic and political engagement of Russia by Japan was also to countersteer the closer Sino-Russian relationship. With the July 2001 Treaty of Good Neighbourliness and Friendly Cooperation, the improvement in Moscow–Beijing relations achieved a new high point. Despite all the limitations of the scope of a Sino-Russian rapprochement and its questionable future, in the strategic as well as the economic sphere, there are many in Japan who are concerned about NATO expansion pushing both countries together into an uneasy alliance with negative implications for the Eurasian security environment.[167] The Russian–Chinese honeymoon may not last very long, but in the meantime it will strengthen China, particularly militarily, and give it a breathing space.[168] One of the most negative outcomes has been China's acquisition of advanced weapons from Russia. Criticizing the strengthening of America's alliances, China has directly linked NATO's expansion and the strengthening of the Japanese–American security alliance in April 1996 to its improving relationship with Russia.[169] This connection seemed to have received official US endorsement (later disavowed) by deputy assistant secretary of defence Kurt Campbell when he said that the new Japan–US guidelines were the Asian version of NATO's eastward expansion.[170]

Japanese–Russian relations have improved remarkably in all spheres since Japan started its 'smile offensive' towards Russia in 1997 under Prime Minister Hashimoto. Despite the primacy of the territorial conflict, Hashimoto also had power balancing against China in mind. He is quoted as saying, 'We must make Russia Japan's ally. We don't want China and India fighting for supremacy in Asia in the 21st century. That's why we need to keep Russia as a balancer'.[171] In the security area, Japanese–Russian military confidence-building measures and military visits have been most conspicuous, and they have a certain showcase effect on China, which has been very reluctant in responding to similar Japanese proposals (see further below).[172]

It is doubtful that Japan's new Russia policy will in the foreseeable future attain its foremost goal, the return of the Northern Territories. Nor has this new policy done much to prevent closer Sino-Russian ties. On the contrary, China and Russia are actively involved in expanding the function and membership of the Shanghai Five regime, which in 2001 was renamed the Shanghai Cooperation Organization (now including Russia, the PRC, Kazakhstan, Kyrgyzstan, Tajikistan and Uzbekistan).[173] Japan has become one of the top ODA donors in the Central Asian region, although its focus on yen loans in countries with weak governance may in the long-term weaken rather than strengthen them. In the more immediate future, stabilizing the new Central Asian republics and preventing spill-over effects from their problems may prevent China from having to use force against its own Muslim minority of Turkic minorities (notably an estimated 7 million Uighur, but also some Kazakh, Tajik and Kyrgyz) and against its Central Asian neighbours (Kazakhstan, Kyrgyzstan and Tajikistan), thus reducing the need for China to increase its military strength. The oppressed Turkic minorities in China's Northern border region have become discontent, and they have more than sympathies with their ethnic brethren (for example Uighur in Uzbekistan) to help them in their struggle against the government in Beijing; which could, however, become a pretext for Chinese intervention in Central Asia.[174]

In the long run a stabilized and Western-oriented Central Asia might provide 'soft containment' of China and help to integrate it into the region, while strengthening Japan's hand in the regional competition with China. For Realist strategists like Professor Sato Seizaburo, Japan's Silk Road diplomacy is a means of encircling China with buffer countries. He considered power politics to be the best way to reach China's leaders, with their nineteenth-century understanding of international relations.[175] Japan's support for China's secure access to oil and gas in Central Asia may not only reduce international market pressure in view of

China's increasing energy demands, but also relieve the need for China to become more assertive in the South China Sea and East China Sea, where the US navy may block Chinese shipping.[176]

Finally, in the context of Japan's Russia/Central Asia policy one has to mention Mongolia, where Japan has become the most important ODA donor. Japan's ODA accounts for around 25 per cent of Mongolia's annual budget. It was visited by Prime Minister Kaifu in 1991 and by Prime Minister Obuchi in 1999. The February 1995 visit of the Mongolian defence minister resulted in an agreement on a regular security dialogue. While Japan's disproportionate political and economic involvement in a nation of only about 2.4 million inhabitants also has to do with its attraction as a racially close people and Tokyo's desire to respond in non-military ways to Western demands for international burden sharing, the strategic considerations with regard to China are no secret.[177]

Korea

The Korean peninsula does not lend itself easily to Japanese political power balancing. The Democratic People's Republic of Korea (DPRK) is not amenable to any kind of front-building against the PRC. Kim Ilsung prompted the PRC leadership to espouse the theory of Japan's revival as a militarist country from 1970, until the Chinese party leadership later recognized it to be mistaken.[178] Because of their difficult bilateral relationship, Japan and the DPRK have not yet achieved established diplomatic relations, and even talks to that end have not made any progress. Since the PRC is North Korea's most important backer, the current leadership in Pyongyang is not likely to risk its relationship with Beijing by showing any sympathies for Japan, even after the future establishment of diplomatic relations. In principle, however, there is concern in Pyongyang about China gaining too much influence over the country, particularly in view of North Korea's growing economic and political dependence on China against the background of its failing economic and political system and China's model character for the reform of a Socialist system.

In the case of South Korea, there are also severe limits to Japan even giving the impression of trying to win Seoul over to power balancing against China. Seoul's priority is to reduce China's concerns about national reunification, to avoid any reinforcement of the Pyongyang–Beijing axis and, if possible, to get China's tacit, if not active, support for reducing tensions on the peninsula. South Korea is, moreover, anxious to keep all its powerful neighbours (including the US) in a balance which does not endanger its security or reduce its diplomatic and economic options. Finally, its relationship with Japan is still fraught with many problems, as was demonstrated by the cooling of relations in 2001 after a successful improvement, which had started in 1998. Still, China's growing regional importance provides an additional motive for a better relationship with Japan. South Korea cannot afford any isolation in the face of an increasingly powerful China. The planned Free-Trade Agreement between Japan and South Korea is very much inspired by the wish of both countries to enhance their bargaining power *vis-à-vis* China's economic power.[179] But security cooperation with Japan is a very delicate issue in view of Japan's past colonial history on the peninsula and China's sensitivities. South Korea shares the same military alliance partner with Japan but is very wary of any linking of the two alliances. Even the development of military exchanges has been advanced only very prudently, and it was suspended in 2001 when the history textbook dispute flared up yet again. The extent to which Chinese considerations are taken into account was demonstrated in August 1999 when Korea proposed to invite Chinese naval officers to observe a planned Japan–Korea joint training exercise in the East China Sea. Due to the MSDF's refusal, the Chinese were not invited.[180] Moreover, Seoul has declined to participate in TMD, not only because its concerns have to do with very different categories of North Korean weapons, but also because of China's opposition. Seoul has also no interest in Japan strengthening its military potential or its military cooperation with the US to such an extent that China is encouraged to become a hostile power in Northeast Asia. In view of these circumstances, and despite concerns about China's rising power being similar to Japan's, South Korea's role as a power balancer of China is limited to maintaining its military strength and hosting US forces, and this is directed in the first instance against North Korea. Other elements of Japan's engagement policy *vis-à-vis* China are, however, supported by Seoul's efforts to include China in moves to settle the division of the peninsula (for example China's participation in the now-stalled Four Party talks since 1996), and to support China's involvement in regional and sub-regional discussions and cooperation (ASEAN+3, ARF, etc.).

PART 2: POLITICAL AND ECONOMIC ENMESHMENT

A   Bilateral and multilateral security dialogues

Introduction

Engagement is most widely presented and discussed as political and, notably, economic engagement – or what I would prefer to call 'enmeshment', in order to differentiate the wider concept of engagement from the policies which aim at providing political and economic incentives for China to become a responsible world power which accepts international norms and regimes.

The tools of political enmeshment rely on involving China in ever closer dialogues and cooperation at bilateral, regional and multilateral levels. At the bilateral level, the aim is mainly to convey to China Japan's points of view and interests, and to create mutual confidence. At the multilateral level, confidence building is complemented by socialization – that is, communicating to China the norms of the international community, persuading it of the merits of adhering to them, and enmeshing it increasingly into the web of international commitments, responsibilities and benefits which accrue from them to make it a 'stakeholder'.

The incentives of political enmeshment for China are exchanging information and evaluations related to bilateral and international issues, gaining benefits on issues of national interest (for example reunification with Taiwan), establishing linkages to economic enmeshment with its material incentives, and accommodating its desire for regional and international recognition and leadership.

It is only to these enmeshment elements of engagement and their goals that the Japanese government refers in the official presentation of its China policy. In its basic policy for relations with China, the Ministry of Foreign Affairs merely states:

> It is important to call on China to become a constructive partner in the international community, so as to maintain stability and prosperity in the Asia Pacific region. In this regard, the following points should be stressed:
>
> a. Support for China's open and reform policy through such measures as economic cooperation and support of China's early accession to the WTO [World Trade Organization].
>
> b. Promotion of bilateral and multilateral dialogue and cooperation (high-level exchanges, Japan–China Security Dialogue, ASEAN Regional Forum, APEC among them).[181]

In 2000 the Ministry of Foreign Affairs's vice-minister, Kawashima Yutaka, explained the first point as developing 'a dense web of mutual interdependence and common interests' so that China could develop a 'deeper understanding that to be part of the international system is indispensable to its reform, open door policy and modernization'.[182]

In a recent report by a Gaimusho-initiated study, the aim of Japan's China policy is described as getting China to become a member of the international community (*kokusai shakai no ichiin*) and China's economy becoming part of the global economy (*sekai keizai to no ittaika*).[183]

In what follows I will focus on the issues and policy tools of political enmeshment, which is relevant for security in its expanded understanding, as explained in the Introduction. Before doing so, however, it is useful to illustrate the difficulty both sides experienced in even establishing a framework for political enmeshment in the security area – that is, in agreeing on how to qualify the bilateral relationship. China attaches great importance to such qualification in order to express some of the goals it hopes to achieve in a bilateral relationship and to differentiate between various bilateral relationships. Since China aims at a new world order in the post-Cold War era, consisting of a system of partnerships rather than traditional security alliances, it has given to several partnerships the epithet 'strategic' to express this desired shift away from strategic alliances of the past.[184] In the case of Chinese–Russian relations, we have seen that the relationship was qualified in 1996 as a 'strategic partnership of equality, mutual confidence and mutual coordination directed towards the 21st century'.[185] According to the Japanese China expert Kojima Tomoyuki, strategic partnerships are defined as having an influence which is long term, which not only affects the two countries but concerns the region and the world, and which consists not of a single aspect but of a variety of aspects, which include economic, security and other considerations.[186] In the case of the Japan–China relationship, Japan did not want to attach the adjective 'strategic' because it could be interpreted by suspicious neighbours as a regional hegemony or contradict the Japan–US military alliance.[187]

But up until 1998 the Japanese–Chinese relationship was not even officially called a partnership. Such a proposal was only made by the Japanese side in preparation for President Jiang Zemin's visit to Japan in November 1998.[188] On this occasion, both sides finally issued a Joint Declaration on Building a Partnership of Friendship and Cooperation for Peace and Development. Japan was the last major country in the 1990s with which Beijing concluded an agreement which qualified the relationship under China's new 'multipolar diplomacy' as a partnership of some kind. The delay was due to the various bilateral disputes and China's reluctance to give too much public recognition to Japan's importance. However, after the 1996 Japan–US Joint Declaration, China realised that continuing to exclude Japan from its 'partnerships' would only push it closer to the US. Although the term 'strategic' was omitted, there are indications that for China the relationship is a 'strategic' one, albeit not in the narrow military sense. Prime Minister Zhu Rongji declared in 2000, for example, that 'it is important to foster Japan–China relations from the strategic standpoint'.[189]

Bilateral security dialogue and military exchanges

The promotion and expansion of bilateral dialogue has been an essential part of the political enmeshment element of the Japanese government's engagement policy towards China since the resumption of diplomatic relations in 1972. As we saw in Chapter 1, Japan only reluctantly suspended political dialogue and the exchange of official visits with China as part of Western demands for sanctions after the Tiananmen massacre, and was actively pushing for ending these sanctions.

The establishment of security-related dialogues and exchanges between Japan and China was slow to begin after the establishment of diplomatic relations in 1972. At the urging of the Japanese government, the exchange of defence attachés started in 1974 (see Chapter 1). Since 1999 the Japanese embassy in Beijing has also had a Defense Agency official, and since the sending of a defence attaché from the MSDF in 2000 the embassy now has representatives from all three services.[190] The Chinese embassy in Tokyo has also four military representatives. But more important for mediating conflicts and exchanging security-relevant information and views are the exchanges of civilian and military officials working in various security-relevant areas in both governments.

The development of dialogues and exchanges in the security area occurs at the following levels:

- defence minister;
- vice-defence minister;
- top uniform level (for example chief of the General Staff);
- working level (political-military talks and military-to-military talks);
- functional (medical officers, intelligence officers, educational institutions);
- unit level (for example naval visits).

So far there have been no unit-level exchanges or military-to-military talks. The functional exchanges between educational institutions, to which China agreed in 1998, have not advanced much beyond visits by heads of these institutions. In 1999 China started a two-month course (Asia Pacific security into the 21st century) at its National Defence University and a uniformed Japanese from NIDS took part. The Chinese side itself only refers to it as a 'symposium'.[191] The Chinese military has participated in the annual Asia-Pacific Security Seminar on Confidence-Building Measures (for military officers), organised by NIDS since 1994, but did not attend in 1996 and 1997. They have also attended other international seminars and conferences organised by various other organs of the Defence Agency (for example the Asia-Pacific Forum of Defence Officials, organised since 1996).

Naval ship visits have been conspicuously absent from the bilateral exchanges. The failure by the Chinese side to follow through on its agreement to such visits in 1998 is all the more significant since China is maintaining an active naval-exchange programme with many other countries. During the 1990s China's navy sent ships to over twenty countries and hosted port calls from seventeen countries.[192] Japan and China agreed to ship visits for the first time on the occasion of the visit to Japan by Defence Minister Chi Hao Jian in February 1998, and this intention has been reiterated at every high-level meeting since then.[193] When it looked close to realization in 2001 the deterioration of the bilateral relationship after Li Denghui's Japan visit and the new textbook crisis pushed the project into the background once again. The first Chinese navy ships are now to visit Japan in 2002 on the occasion of the thirtieth anniversary of the establishment of diplomatic relations.

Given China's top-down government structure and the degree of instrumentalization of exchanges to influence other countries, the development of security dialogue and military exchanges has always been heavily dependent on the initiatives of the top leadership, with top-level visits making a start but also exposing the exchanges to the vagaries of the political climate. Until the 1980s security discussions were limited to the top leadership and the diplomatic services of both countries, or occurred on unofficial occasions. Apart from the aforementioned 1984 unofficial visit by the Chinese defence minister, Zhang Aiping, and the return visit in 1987 by his Japanese counterpart, Kurihara Yuko (see Chapter 1), China's chief of the General Staff, Yang Dezhi, visited Japan in 1986. Reflecting China's acceptance of Japan's defence efforts and its alliance with the US at the time, Zhang Aiping was very much in favour of more exchanges, but the Japanese side was reluctant to agree to these Chinese proposals and set limits.[194] Before defence exchanges could expand, notably between defence establishments, Japan suspended them in the wake of the Tiananmen massacre in 1989. In addition, relations cooled at the end of the 1980s because China had started to criticize Japan's defence policies again. As a result of these sanctions, it took Tokyo until May 1993 to propose the resumption of the bilateral security dialogue and the involvement of Beijing in regional security discussions to the Chinese foreign minister, Qian Qichen (see Table 3.1). Since then the bilateral security dialogue has become a means of gaining a better understanding of China's security policies as well as passing on Japanese concerns about some of China's security policies. The visit of Foreign Minister Muto Kabun to China in May 1993 was an opportunity to complain to Qian about repeated attacks on Japanese fishing boats in the East China Sea and also to raise the issue of Chinese nuclear testing.[195] When Foreign Minister Hata visited China in January 1994 he queried his interlocutors about the intentions behind the 15 per cent increase in the Chinese defence budget and urged China to abide by the guidelines of the Missile Technology Control Regime (MTCR).[196] On the occasion of Muto's visit, the establishment of a bilateral security forum to enhance the transparency of both countries' defence policies and to conduct dialogue on regional security issues was agreed. Qian Qichen declared respect for Japan's wish to take on an important global political role and reversed the earlier Chinese criticism of Japan's participation in PKO in Cambodia.[197] As a result, the first meeting of the bilateral security dialogue (headed by bureau chief officials of the Japanese and PRC foreign and defence ministries) took place on 20 December 1993 in Beijing. However, the Japanese side was not successful in receiving Chinese agreement to its proposal of including military personnel.[198] The agenda of the meeting included confidence building through enhanced transparency, proliferation of nuclear weapons and missiles, nuclear-weapons tests, regional security cooperation and UN PKO. Japanese hopes for a coordinated approach towards the North Korea did not materialize.[199] In January 1995 the second round of the security dialogue included civilian and military representatives for the first time.[200] The third round of the security dialogue, in January 1996, had the largest number of mili-

Table 3.1 The chronology of the security dialogue

	Date	Place
1a	December 1993	Beijing (only diplomats)
1b	March 1994	Beijing (only defence officials)
2	January 1995	Tokyo
3	January 1996	Beijing
4	March 1997	Tokyo
5	December 1997	Beijing
6	October 1999	Tokyo
7	June 2000	Beijing
8	April 2002	Tokyo

Source: Gaiko Forum, November 2000, p. 53; Yomiuiri Shimbun, 3 March 2002

tary representatives so far because the Chinese delegation head was the deputy chief of the General Staff, Xiong Guangkai. Defence exchanges picked up in the second half of the 1990s with a series of visits by leading defence officials from Japan (administrative vice-minister of defence, chairman of the Joint Chief of Staff and the president of the National Defence University), reciprocated by a visit of the chief of the General Staff to Japan. But it was obvious that Japan was made to appear as the side requesting more exchanges while China did not feel the same urgency.

After the Joint Declaration in April 1996, the Japanese side wanted to win the understanding of China while the latter sought all means to oppose the resulting enhancement of Japanese–American security ties because of its suspected anti-Chinese orientation. Initially, this meant that the Chinese government suspended exchanges.[201] The Defence Agency had started to see the expansion of military exchanges with all Asian countries as beneficial and used the promotion of the exchanges with other countries, notably with Russia, as a lever to prompt the Chinese military leadership to be more willing to engage.[202] Nishihara Masashi, now heading the Japanese Defence University, mentioned improved security links with Russia as a means of preventing China from using its increasingly close ties with Russia to put pressure on Japan.[203] Exchanges and security discussions between Japan and Russia have been held since 1996 at all levels. The first exchange visits of naval vessels took place in Vladivostok and Tokyo in July 1996 and June 1997, respectively, and they have been continued since then on a regular basis. Japanese–Russian naval ship visits since July 1998 have advanced to the level of joint disaster drills.[204]

A breakthrough in Japanese–Chinese exchanges seemed to have been achieved with the official visit to Tokyo by Defence Minister Chi Haotian in February 1998, the first official visit of a Chinese defence minister, which was reciprocated in May of the same year by the director-general of the Defence Agency, Kyuma Fumio. During Chi's visit, both sides agreed on the intensification of mutual exchanges in different fields and at different levels.[205] However, the momentum did not last long, and no further visits at the same level occurred as of summer 2001. Vice-ministerial exchanges (*Jimu jikan*) had last occurred in 1997, but they were suspended in May 1998 and resumed only in November 1999 with a visit by Vice Minister Ema to Beijing.[206] The 6th Japan–China Security Dialogue took place in October 1999 after a gap of one year and ten months.[207] The eighth meeting was delayed until April 2002 because of the renewed textbook crisis and the visit to the Yasukuni Shrine by Prime Minister Koizumi in 2001, which had derailed most bilateral meetings between the two countries.

Japan's goals for bilateral security dialogues and military exchanges may be summarized as follows:

1   Explanation of Japanese defence policies and reassurance of China about Japan's goals.

2 Protests against certain Chinese defence policies (nuclear tests, increases in defence expenditure, etc.).
3 Building confidence through the enhancement of the transparency of both sides' defence policies.
4 Improvement of communication by widening scope and number of channels;
5 Gaining Chinese support for stability on the Korean Peninsula and on other regional issues.

Explaining to the Chinese side and winning their consent to, or at least their tacit acceptance of, the intensification of Japanese–American military cooperation and its ensuing measures (notably revision of the guidelines and TMD) has been the central goal of bilateral dialogue and exchanges since 1996. The keen Japanese wish for these meetings gave the Chinese side the opportunity to use the scheduling of them (as well as opposition to Japan's wish for expansion and upgrading of these exchanges) to protest and to put pressure on Japan to reconsider its new defence policies. As Yang Bojiang writes: 'Sino-Japanese military relations cannot exceed their political and/or economic relations'.[208] Suspension or curtailing of exchanges is all the easier for the Chinese side since it can rely on government-controlled media to transmit its opinion to Japan and other countries. In contrast, Japan has been much more careful in venting its displeasure about Chinese defence policies publicly, and prefers confined diplomatic venues for this purpose, although this has somehow changed since September 1992, when Japanese politicians started to raise their concern publicly about alleged Chinese intentions to buy an aircraft carrier (see Chapter 2).

An overwhelming part of the dialogue and exchanges is basically aimed at confidence building. As we will see in greater detail in the context of multilateral security discussions, the Japanese/Western concept of confidence building is very different from that of China.[209] Within the bilateral context, confidence building for China ideally means Japanese agreement on the major security policies at stake, and this is a precondition for engaging in security dialogue and exchanges, or at least determines the level and scope of such dialogue. This is, of course, very different from the idea of confidence building as a step towards facilitating the solution of disputes and disagreements. As a result the Japanese–Chinese security dialogue has been hostage to the vagaries of the general political relationship and the agreement, or rather lack of it, on particular security policies. Just at a time of conflict of interest when the need for enhancing mutual understanding and reducing the political temperature is most needed, China reduces, or even suspends, political and security dialogues. The problematic nature of this approach is also recognised by some Chinese security experts.[210]

Urging greater Chinese transparency about its defence policies has been a major item on Japan's agenda since the beginning of the working-level security talks in 1993. Progress in this matter has been glacial because transparency within the Chinese government system, even outside the security sphere, is not very developed and is seen as a danger to the rule of the Communist Party. In the security area, transparency is seen as a danger to national security because it would diminish an important force-multiplier of a military so much behind Western forces and invite foreign interference. In short, the Chinese basically consider transparency to be inappropriate for a weaker country like theirs.[211] In addition, transparency in the form of access to information on the military strength of China's adversaries through visits to military installations can also serve as a deterrent by impressing on China its military weakness and the futility of using military force. This complaint has been made frequently by China towards the US.[212] Japanese demands for explanations concerning its rapid increases in defence expenditure are rebutted by pointing to the PRC's domestic economic growth, the need to modernize and the low increase rate in comparison with some advanced countries.[213]

Still, there has been some progress in China's military transparency, and although it cannot solely be ascribed to Japanese efforts because of concurrent multilateral and other bilateral dialogues, Tokyo has certainly been an important voice. Due to international pressure, China finally published a White Paper on Arms Control in 1995 and a White Paper on National Defence in 1998. It is significant that the Chinese side used the third Japan–PRC working-level security talks in January 1996 to announce the publication of the White Paper on Arms Control.[214]

The establishment of a telephone hotline for emergencies has a special symbolic value for confidence building as well as improving communications. A hotline was finally opened between the seats of both leaderships in October 2000, when Prime Minister Zhu Rongji visited Japan, after it had been proposed in November 1998 by Japan on the occasion of President Jiang Zimin's visit.[215]

The expansion of fora and agenda

The Japanese government has been trying to expand the fora and agenda of security-relevant subjects as it has done in other subject areas relevant to the bilateral relationship (for example regular human rights consultations since 1997). In addition, there has been a growing involvement by private institutions in enhancing the bilateral security dialogue.

Consultations related to the territorial issues between the two sides and the start, in July 1995, of the first senior-level consultation on arms control, disarmament and non-proliferation on Japan's initiative have already been mentioned in Chapter 2. After the end of China's nuclear tests, gaining China's support against nuclear proliferation and missiles (notably by North Korea) became the new centre of Japan's interest in the latter forum. On a more general level, Japan hopes to bring Beijing within international arms-control agreements in view of China's importance for the success of global and regional nuclear non-proliferation, arms control and disarmament. In the 1980s Japan was instrumental in encouraging China to sign the NPT.[216] Since 2000 Japan has also been leaning on China to ratify the CTBT in order to facilitate the treaty entering into force.

For China, on the other hand, the arms control forum has become very useful to oppose TMD and the militarization of space.[217]

In 1995 the Japanese government also started unofficially to explore China's interest in talks on PKO cooperation, probably encouraged by China's reversal of its initial criticism of Japan's participation in PKO in Cambodia.[218] At that time the Defence Agency suggested joint training for PKO.[219] Although PKO cooperation continues to be mentioned during political talks, no forum has yet been set up.[220] The subject has also raised interest outside government channels. During his visit to China in December 2000 Hatoyama Yukio, the leader of the Democratic Party of Japan (DPJ), proposed a Common Agenda which included PKO, next to environment and information technology.[221] Two Japanese think tanks have also separately proposed some kind of PKO cooperation with China.[222] However, China's general attitude towards PKO in general, let alone PKO cooperation with Japan, is still very reserved, particularly after the resurgence of PKO since the end of the 1990s. Moreover, China probably does not want to give any additional support for Japan enhancing its own PKO involvement.

Japan has also failed so far to conclude an agreement on preventing incidents at sea between the two navies. Such agreements had become an important confidence-building measure during the Cold War. Japan and Russia signed one in May 1993, and the subject has been on the Japanese–Chinese agenda since Defence Minister Chi Haotian's visit in 1998. However, China is not likely to agree to it until after the exchange of ship visits. Such an agreement will become more than just a confidence-building measure once the Chinese navy becomes more of a blue-ocean navy and encounters with the Japanese navy are more likely. A complicating factor for the conclusion of an agreement is probably the territorial dispute about the EEZ and the Senkaku Islands.

Mention has also to be made of Japan's removal of chemical weapons from Northern China which date from its war against China before 1945, because this constitutes an additional, albeit coincidental, forum for military exchanges. Under the 1997 Chemical Weapons Convention (CWC) Japan is obliged to remove chemical weapons which the Imperial Army abandoned after its retreat in 1945.[223] When Japan was first confronted with this obligation in 1992, during the negotiations for the Convention, it dragged its feet for internal bureaucratic, financial and technical reasons before actual removal operations started in 2000, based on a 1999 Memorandum of Understanding between Japan and China on the Destruction of Abandoned Chemical Weapons in China.[224] Only in November 1995, following the declassification of US government records on the issue, did the Japanese government finally admit the use of chemical weapons during its war against China. However, the removal of these abandoned weapons may be useful for Japan's engagement strategy since it brings a considerable number of Japanese and Chinese military personnel together until at least 2007 (this CWC-imposed deadline is likely not be met for technical reasons).

In response to Japan's public security concern with crime related to China (illegal entry, drugs and other organized crime), in 1999 both sides started a regular Japan–China Public Security Authorities Consultations meeting. The Japanese delegation in 2000 included officials from the National Police Agency, the Ministry of Justice, the Ministry of Finance, the Ministry of Health and Welfare, the Public Security Investigation Agency and the Maritime Safety Agency.[225] Other exchanges of law-enforcement institutions are now also taking place. Katzenstein and Okawara report on closer ties between Japanese and Chinese provincial police forces.[226] It has yet to be seen how effective these consultations will become. Japan is certainly still far behind South Korea, which in October 2000 signed a criminal extradition agreement with the PRC.[227]

Japan as China's second-class security partner?

In conclusion, one has to state that bilateral security dialogue and military exchanges are still underdeveloped, notably in comparison to those China has with other major countries in Asia and Europe, let alone with the US. The difference from the developments in the Japanese–Russian defence relationship is particularly striking. The need to remedy the situation is regularly recognized by Chinese leaders visiting Japan, but changes are still very slow and very much hostage to the vagaries of negative events in the bilateral relationship, as the stalement in 2001 yet again illustrated.[228] Simply expanding the number of fora is not enough if there is no will to talk. China's political instrumentalization of dialogue and exchanges is illustrated fittingly by its attitude to telephone diplomacy. The Chinese side takes a rather casual attitude, and one Japanese Foreign Ministry official was quoted as saying: 'When they don't want to talk to us, they say it is not customary in China to conduct telephone diplomacy. Yet, when they want to tell us something, they think nothing of ringing us up'.[229]

The reasons for this underdevelopment of security relations, however, go beyond China's political frontloading and instrumentalization. One other reason is the Chinese perception of Japan's international ranking as an independent actor. For most of the post-war period China has seen Japan as dependent in its foreign and security policy on the US, which has been the last arbiter in any conflict of interest.[230] In theory, China could consider both alliance partners as a tool to influence the other, but the perceived weakness and second-class status of Japan in the alliance means that China's leaders tend to see the US as the main interlocutor and lever. It will take China a long time to overcome its reluctance to treating Japan as an equal partner.[231] Kenneth W. Allen and Eric A. McVadon speak of the PLA's persistent negative attitude, which is based on the premise that the SDF should not be trusted and should not be treated as a normal national military organization.[232] In another publication McVadon writes about the hatred harboured against Japan by many PLA officers, which made them rebuff Japanese overtures towards military-to-military contacts.[233] These attitudes are all related to and reinforced by the growing regional Japan–China rivalry (see Chapter 4).

Finally, bilateral dialogue and military exchanges at government level are sometimes affected by bureaucratic and political structures. As one senior China specialist in the Gaimusho wrote to the author: 'Chinese policies toward Japan and vice versa do not have comprehensive, integrated approaches, but are divided into separate political, economic and security areas. Occasionally consultations or adjustments are taking place, but basically each area is pursued on its own'.[234] An example of insufficient domestic communication on the Chinese side was the conflict over the incursion of Chinese 'research vessels' into Japan's EEZ and territorial waters in 2000. During his visit to Japan in October 2000 Prime Minister Zhu Jongji claimed not to know about the Chinese navy's intrusions even though the issue was supposed to have been solved in summer of that year.[235] The incident showed that the Chinese Foreign Ministry and even the prime minister are sometimes not sufficiently informed about certain activities of the PLA. Whereas the Gaimusho is responsible for Japan's security policy and the Defence Agency is to execute it, the distance between the Chinese Ministry of Foreign Affairs (Waijiaobu) and the PLA is much greater. The PLA can act fairly independently from the rest of the government (albeit not from the CCP). Other factors like insufficient briefing of top political leaders may aggravate this problem.

Track II and Track III dialogues

The 1990s saw a rise in bilateral security dialogues at Track II (semi-official and academic) and Track III (private) levels in order to overcome the difficulties encountered by official dialogue channels (Track I). Private involvement in promoting security relations between Japan and China has been increasing, along with the increase in general private Japan–China contacts and exchanges.[236] One of the most influential and best-funded organizations is probably the Sasakawa Japan–China Friendship Fund (about US$2 million operating funds per year), which has established good relations with the Chinese military. The work most relevant to the bilateral security relationship is the funding of conferences on security issues, the Japan–China Security Research Exchange (including the invitation of retired high-ranking military officers to Japan) and university scholarships for Chinese security specialists to study the Japanese language.[237]

Track II activities would seem appropriate for the two countries because China has practically no private organizations involved in security issues, and even in Japan the private sector in this specific area is very small. However, there was a drop in interest after the Tiananmen incident, and the growing perception of China as a threat affected the enthusiasm on the Japanese side as well.[238] Falling interest has also been recorded at the non-governmental level, which is not concerned with political or security issues. As an example, since 1994 the formation of sister-city links has dropped off rapidly.[239]

Another circumstance affecting the efficacy of the Track II and private levels in the security area is the decline of the pro-China lobby in Japan. This is particularly noticeable in the LDP, with the death or fading away of major actors like Ito Masayoshi, Gotoda Masaharu and Takeshita Noboru. These leaders (and the bilateral private associations which they supported) had played a crucial role in the normalisation of diplomatic relations with China and smoothed the many conflicts which had regularly shaken the relationship since then.[240] The importance of such figures in times of Japanese–Chinese tensions was demonstrated most recently when Nonaka Hiromu, a former secretary-general of the LDP, was officially invited by the Chinese government in July 2001 to mediate the crisis over the revised textbooks and the planned visit of the Yasukuni Shrine by Prime Minister Koizumi. Nonaka apparently won the favour of China when he visited a memorial museum in Nanjing in 1998 in his capacity as LDP secretary-general.[241] Domestic turbulences in Japan have, however, continued to weaken such figures: Nonaka Hiromu is now outside the political mainstream and Kato Koichi lost his power base when he had to leave the Diet as a result of a corruption scandal in 2002. On the Chinese side, similar figures who had been instrumental in supporting the relationship have also disappeared. Moreover, Chinese researchers who are specialists in Japanese affairs have to be very careful not to appear as 'apologists' for Japan, and their role as go-betweens is therefore limited.

To enhance the non-governmental level of dialogue and exchanges between Japan, on the one hand, and China and Korea, on the other, Prime Minister Obuchi's Commission on Japan's Goals in the 21st Century suggested a process of 'neighbourly relations' (*rinko*) in January 2000.[242] The process would be based on Japan's full understanding of the histories, traditions, languages and cultures of the peoples of its neighbour countries. While the report received considerable attention (notably because of his recommendation about elevating the role of English in Japan), it has not been followed up and was soon forgotten among the disputes arising thereafter between Japan and China.

Multilateral security dialogue and exchanges

Multilateralism is understood in international relations as 'coordinating behavior among three or more states on the basis of generalized principles of conduct'.[243] For Japan, multilateralism has for a long time been a politically minor but rhetorically and financially (in terms of contribution) important feature of Japan's foreign and security policy tools even while its US-focused bilateralism has been preponderant. The Japan–US framework has been the strongest constraint to (Japan's desire not to move out of step with US policies) but also the strongest incentive for (US demands for Japanese burden sharing, Japan's diplomatic hedging) the vigour and direction of Japan's multilateral diplomacy, in addition to the country's economic interests and the outcome of the dichotomy between its pacifism and military alliance with the US.[244] Increasing the involvement in multilateralism and carefully enhancing the autonomy of diplomacy are effective ways of softening the consequences of the 'alliance game' of abandonment and entrapment.

Multilateralism reduces transaction costs, enhances transparency and predictability, and socializes countries around generally accepted norms of behaviour.[245] It has therefore become an important part of the political enmeshment of China by Western countries like Japan and the US, but also by its regional partners. To promote China's involvement in multilateralism Japan has been active on its own as well as in supporting similar endeavours by other countries. Even Japan's interest in participating in Asia–Europe Meeting (ASEM) was initially strongly motivated by its desire to bring China into yet another regional multilateral institution.[246] The attraction of multilateralism for China is a combination of economic benefit, prestige, peer pressure and competition with other powers. Not being part of an international or regional organisation can be such a liability politically that joining it may appear the lesser evil.

Multilateral approaches to security at regional level aim at the establishment of a cooperative security arrangement through dialogue, consultation, confidence-building measures, conflict prevention, conflict resolution and public security cooperation. There is no clear concept of an enemy country as in bilateral security arrangements; instead, the enemy is strategic instability and the possibility of conflict breaking out among the parties to the cooperative security arrangement.[247]

One of the main advantages of multilateral security discussions is the circumstance that the 'political baggage' which may burden the bilateral relationship (for example the history issue between Japan and China) becomes diluted in a multilateral framework. Compared with bilateral security dialogue and exchanges between Japan and China, the process of multilateral security approaches in many ways facilitates the addressing of sensitive security issues. A Japanese diplomat is quoted as saying about the ARF in this context: 'Japan wants to say nice things to China bilaterally and bad things multilaterally'.[248] Without doubt, multilateral dialogue and exchanges have a positive impact on bilateral contacts, and both are helped by Track II and Track III exchanges. The Pacific Economic Cooperation Council (PECC) prepared the way for and then provided input into APEC, and the same can be said about the role of ASEAN Institutes of Strategic and International Studies (ASEAN–ISIS) and the Council for Security and Cooperation in Asia-Pacific (CSCAP) for the ARF.[249] Multilateral security approaches can contain the same deterrence function as is in bilateral power balancing with other countries against China: Japan can build coalitions with other Asian states and use this to apply peer pressure on China.[250] China has therefore warned against using ARF as 'multilateral containment of China'.[251] Using the multilateral stage, Japan can also introduce proposals and ideas through other regional members and assuage Chinese concerns about Japanese regional leadership.

Multilateral security approaches are also encouraged by those who doubt that a balance-of-power policy in Asia will work, at least not on its own. Kosaka Masataka argued that the diversity and weaknesses of Asia's main players would prevent one country from establishing superiority, and that the competition and cooperation among them would prevent a system of power balancing which could solve the problems occurring in the international society.[252] Tennichi Takahiko warns that balance of power will not establish a common agenda in the region, nor would it necessarily operate in a period of power transition.[253]

A kind of first step in the direction of multilateral engagement of China occurred when Prime Minister Kaifu visited China in August 1991. He proposed deepening the bilateral dialogue on issues of importance to the whole international community like arms control, disarmament and the environment, and referred to this international society-relevant level of bilateral relations as 'Japanese–Chinese relations in the global community' (*'sekai no naka no Nitchu kankei'*).[254] One result of Kaifu's visit was China's accession to the NPT to improve its international standing in the wake of the Tiananmen massacre. In Chapter 1 we saw that Japan became relatively isolated in the Western camp in its eagerness to resume normal relations with China after the Tiananmen massacre, and the 1991 Kaifu visit to China became the most high-profile symbol of the Japanese position. In order to enhance Western acceptance of Japan's conciliatory policy and to do away with the special character of the Japanese–Chinese relationship, the government was keen to project 'Japan–China relations which contribute to the international community' by prompting China to become a responsible power.[255] But this was also a recognition of the fact that relations could not be further developed by merely relying on the bilateral level and that this could only be done by cooperating on a multilateral level.[256]

The expansion of norms first tried out in Europe during the Cold War, as well as domestic pressures, played an important role in assisting Southeast Asia's and Japan's conversion to multilateral security mechanisms after 1989.[257] The increase in regional security meetings in the 1990s at Track II and Track III levels helped Japan as well as China to adopt these new values to varying degrees. The previously mentioned Higuchi Report of August 1994 had reflected this shift by putting considerable stress on multilateral security approaches at the regional and global level. Multilateral security approaches were deemed appropriate in the new post-Cold War climate, which was characterized by strategic uncertainties and the absence of a clear-cut enemy. An important step toward greater Japanese support for cooperative security at the global level was made when Japan passed the International Peace Cooperation Law and participated for the first time in UN peacekeeping in Cambodia in 1992.

The main obstacle to Japan's embrace of multilateral security approaches in the region was the opposition of its American alliance partner to the concept until the end of 1992.[258] With the start of the Clinton administration in 1993, the US abandoned its opposition to regional security approaches, which it had harboured because of concern about losing its influence over regional security in Asia and about further weakening the Japanese willingness to enhance US–Japan security cooperation. The new US stance was expressed in the April 1996 Joint Declaration, in which both sides stated that they wanted 'to further develop multilateral regional security dialogues and cooperation mechanisms such as the ASEAN Regional Forum, and eventually, security dialogues regarding Northeast Asia'.[259] The statement was intended to convince China, but also other Asian countries, that Japan and the US were not only focusing on bilateral security approaches while providing US backing for Japan's strong support for regional security approaches. Multilateral security approaches therefore became important as reassurance measures for Japan's increasing military efforts. At the beginning of the ARF's discussion about confidence-building measures, Japan even tried to replace the expression by using the term 'mutual assurance measures'.[260] Regional security approaches have been useful in reconciling the disparate aspects of engagement policy towards China, but also in narrowing, in a much broader way, the gap between what Mike Mochizuki called the 'civilian internationalists' and the 'great power internationalists' in Japanese politics.[261]

Japan's aims in embracing multilateral dialogue and exchanges which are most relevant to its policy to China may thus be summarized in the following way:

*   reassurance of all its Asian neighbours about its security policies, particularly after the strengthening of Japan–US relations in 1996;
*   building confidence and creating transparency;
*   getting support from its Asian neighbours to prompt China to become a responsible regional partner, while hedging against Chinese non-compliance by preparing a front against China (notably concerning the peaceful solution of the Taiwan issue);
*   addressing the South China Sea issue and getting China's support for the peaceful resolution of other regional security issues (notably Korean division);
*   prevailing in the competition for regional influence with China.

The role of ARF

ARF has become the most important regional forum for security multilateralism in Asia where Japan can work towards the achievement of the above agenda. The Japanese government played an important part in the process which led to the ARF's creation in 1994. As early as September 1991 Foreign Minister Nakayama proposed that security issues should be on the agenda of the ASEAN Post-Ministerial Conference (ASEAN–PMC). But the Japanese initiative was very guarded and Nakayama did not consider including China and Russia.[262] Initially Japan planned to have groupings of concerned nations discuss problems like Cambodia or the South China Sea, or to simply use existing fora like APEC or the ASEAN–PMC. Until 1992 there were discussions in Japan as well as in other APEC countries about whether APEC should also deal with security issues.[263] The Thai prime minister, Anand Panyarachun, who opened the APEC meeting in Bangkok in September 1992, suggested in his opening speech that APEC could play a role in regional political and security coordination. No other member echoed this sentiment and the association agreed not to take on a political role.[264] Secretary of Defence William Perry was still suggesting the inclusion of security issues into the APEC agenda in 1995, but by then this was no longer an option because China did not want it, with Taiwan being an APEC member, and ASEAN was concerned about its leadership.

When ASEAN and its seven dialogue partners (Australia, the US, the EU, Canada, Japan, South Korea and New Zealand) finally decided in July 1993 to set up the ARF, China and Russia were observers, but they became members of ARF when it had its first meeting in Bangkok in 1994. The Japanese government had changed its position on the exclusion of China in spring 1993.[265] Even when the ARF was established the Japanese approach was very cautious, insisting on the supplementary role (to the existing Japan–US military alliance) of such institutionalised regional security dialogue and its function of reassurance rather than confidence building.[266] At the same time the Defence Agency became interested in regional security dialogue and officially recognised that dialogue among Asian nations was an important means of improving the security environment in Asia and reducing uncertainties.[267]

In recent years the ARF process has not made much progress because of the growing diversity of the group since the expansion of ASEAN's membership and the crisis in Indonesia, which had been the leading force. The ARF's programmatic intention of moving from confidence building via preventive diplomacy to conflict resolution is notably hindered by China's and Vietnam's reservations. At present, ARF discussions are limited to exploring the 'overlap' between confidence building and preventive diplomacy. Not least because of China's reluctance about cooperative security, progress is only moving 'at a pace comfortable to all participants', by consensus and 'on the basis of non-interference into one another's internal affairs', as the standard expressions describe it.[268] There seems to be a very pronounced deference by the ASEAN member states towards China. They consult closely with China before setting the agenda for the Senior Officials Meetings so as to keep China on board, which considerably weakens the ARF's ability to handle conflicts of interest.[269] Takagi Seiichiro, then professor at the National Graduate Institute for Policy Studies, called China's attitude towards ARF ambiguous: on the one hand China was praising ARF for its contribution; on the other it does not think that multilateral security cooperation should touch the fundamental areas of the defence system of individual nations.[270]

Despite all the shortcomings of ARF, China's different views on confidence-building measures and other regional issues, the inclusion of China into the ARF and ASEAN has drawn Beijing into regional security multilateralism more than its leadership was initially willing to accept.[271] This success has been paralleled at the global level by China becoming more and more involved in multilateral regimes.[272] Within the space of three years the Chinese went from being hostile to confidence-building measures, to voluntarily co-chairing the working group on confidence-building measures, to proposing their own.[273] While initially China refused any multilateral discussions about the South China Sea, it now accepts them as long as they do not touch on issues of sovereignty. Moreover, it has accepted that a resolution has to be based on international law. The pressure from the ARF for greater Chinese military transparency had a decisive influence on China's decision to issue two defence-related White Papers. Japan played an important role in China's hesitant steps towards greater Chinese military transparency by strongly pushing for it bilaterally as well as multilaterally.[274] Even if their content does not go much beyond what was publicly known already, it was the first step in the right direction.[275] China still puts an emphasis on declaratory measures (for example 'no first use') without inspections.[276] One should also consider that several ARF participants are also uncomfortable with a high degree of transparency, which is demanded by Western countries.[277]

ASEAN's desire for leadership in regional security talks has also led to the first trilateral summit meetings between Japan, China and the Republic of Korea. Since ASEAN and the ARF's agenda were initially focused on ASEAN issues, while some of the most urgent disputes concern Northeast Asia, ASEAN was risking diminished saliency as well as losing its leadership in regional security. For this reason as well as others, since 1997 ASEAN has been organising the 'ASEAN+3' forum on the occasion of the post-ministerial meetings. This forum aims to promote economic linkages and maintain a direct line of communication with Beijing, Tokyo and Seoul. At the Hanoi meeting of December 1998 they agreed to institutionalize the meeting and to include a security agenda. The new forum prompted Prime Minister Obuchi at the time to suggest a trilateral Japan–China–South Korea summit meeting, but he was rebuffed by the Chinese side. When Prime Minister Zhu Rongji agreed at short notice to a trilateral informal breakfast meeting during the Manila Summit of November 1999, Zhu initially insisted that this mini-summit should only discuss economic issues. China was obviously concerned about the relationship with North Korea and was more interested in a Free-Trade Agreement with ASEAN.[278] The three leaders met again trilaterally on the occasion of the ASEAN+3 summit in Singapore in 2000. They agreed to meet annually at the same occasion and agreed to designate 2002 as the official year of exchange between their citizens.[279] Korea expects from this trilateral forum help from China on North Korea, participation at the head table of Northeast Asian leaders, and balancing of its two big neighbours to enhance its own diplomatic position. Japan hopes to create yet another channel for communication with China and get support from Korea for the issues where both agree. Since Tokyo is excluded from the Four-Power talks on Korea, such a venue is also a means of increasing its say on the peninsula. China's interest is mostly economic and it would prefer to stick to an economic agenda but has by now accepted that regional security issues have to be discussed because of Japan's and Korea's strong desire to do so. But China's role will be limited because it is only represented by its prime minister, whereas the president has the final authority in Chinese foreign and security policy.

South China Sea

With the South China Sea being the greatest long-term security issue in the region and Japan not being able to bring it up in its bilateral security exchanges with China, Tokyo has sought to use regional security fora to deal with it. China, however, has been very reticent to include security issues in fora which are of direct relevance to it. This concerns not only the Taiwan issue (which the other ARF participants would like to raise) but also the South China Seas issue, in which most ASEAN members are directly involved. At the July 1993 ASEAN Foreign Ministers meeting, Qian Qichen stated that it (ARF) 'should not make decisions nor take common action on a certain country, a certain region or a certain question'.[280] China also opposes the involvement of states which are not geographically contingent to the South China Sea, which excludes not only the US but also Japan. China is wary of discussions even among regional claimants in order to avoid the internationalization of the conflict. It now allows the discussion of the South China Sea in general, but not its legal territorial aspects. High hopes had been put on efforts by ASEAN, the ARF and an ongoing series of informal Workshops since 1990 on the South China Sea.[281] However, these workshops have not got far, and ASEAN and China, and even the ASEAN members among themselves, have failed to narrow their differences on a proposed Code of Conduct.[282] While ASEAN wants specifically to include a halt to any occupation of islands and reefs, China insists on a much weaker wording which excludes any action that would 'complicate the situation'.[283]

One approach Japan has started to use in order to influence the issue of the South China Sea indirectly and to promote cooperative security approaches in a tangible way is the proposal of measures to improve maritime safety in the area. Nishihara Masashi suggested in 1995 the establishment of a UN naval and air peacekeeping force to monitor the movement of ships and aircraft in the South China Sea.[284] Sato Koichi, of Hoso University, proposed that Japan could work towards the establishment of something like the 1968 Malacca Strait Council.[285] The increase in piracy in the South China Sea in the last few years has prompted the Japanese to become active in this area. As a result of some well-publicized piracy cases the aircraft and vessels of the Japanese coastguard were deployed as far as Thailand (the *Alondra Rainbow* case) and India's Andaman Islands (the *Global Mars* case).[286] Subsequently, Prime Minister Obuchi proposed an anti-piracy conference at the Japan–ASEAN Summit held in Manila November 1999. In March 2000 Japan sponsored a 'Preparatory Meeting of the Coast Guard Agencies for the Regional Conference on Combating Piracy and Armed Robbery against Ships' in Singapore, followed later by the 'International Conference on All Maritime Related Concerns, Both Governmental and Private, on Combating Piracy and Armed Robbery Against Ships' and the 'Regional Conference on Combating Piracy and Armed Robbery Against Ships' in Tokyo (27–29 April 2000). The latter was attended by coastguard agencies from Brunei, Cambodia, China, Hong Kong, India, Indonesia, Japan, Laos, Malaysia, Myanmar, the Philippines, the Republic of Korea, Singapore, Thailand and Vietnam. At this conference, Japan proposed to 'explore the possibility of providing support for those Authorities which request technical assistance' to train personnel and provide relevant technology and equipment.[287] As we saw in Chapter 2, China has been, directly or indirectly, involved in piracy in the region. Incidentally, when in 2000 the coastguard considered the budgetary request for two jets capable of flying long distances because of the mounting cases of piracy against Japanese vessels in Southeast Asian waters, officials stated that the aircraft would also be tasked to keep a watch on Chinese research vessels in Japan's EEZ.[288]

China has, however, reacted rather reluctantly to the Japanese initiative. The main reason is most likely concern about any infringement of its sovereignty and any admission that its anti-piracy measures may not be sufficient. Another circumstance is China's opposition to Japan assuming a regional leadership role (see Chapter 4). During the anti-piracy meetings China opposed the presence of Japanese coastguard vessels beyond Japan's maritime borders.[289] China said it did not consider it necessary to hold joint exercises in waters related to China, as was suggested by Japan. China also strongly resisted Japan's proposal for joint exercises and patrols. 'We clearly don't need joint exercises with other countries,' said Li Ding, a senior border-security official from China's Public Security Ministry; 'We already have an assured ability to investigate piracy crimes ourselves.' China's suspicions were certainly not alleviated by India criticizing the Chinese stance.[290]

In the context of diffusing the South China Sea issue one may also mention US military Track II activities, in which Japan has always taken part, whereas Chinese participation is more recent. In the mid-1980s the US military in the Pacific Command started to socialize military and civilian defence officials from various Asian countries through regional seminars and conferences.[291] Since the beginning of the 1990s the US Navy in Newport has organized the Western Pacific Naval Symposium (WPNS), which is part of the International Sea Power Symposium. China took part in the WPNS for the first time in 1996, when it met in Tokyo. During the later years of the Clinton administration the US military became very active in promoting cooperative security and joint exercises in the field of disaster relief.[292] Although China has not yet taken part, it was represented by observers when the exercise called 'Pacific Reach 2000' (a multilateral submarine rescue exercise) was held in October 2000 with the US, Japan, South Korea and Singapore.[293] China warned Japan about the latter event 'that countries concerned in carrying out this kind of activities or military exercises should not do anything that may be detrimental to stability and peace in this part of the world'.[294] But in June 2001 China participated in the first Western Pacific Mine Countermeasures Exercise, which was sponsored by Singapore.[295]

Track II and Track III security discussions

The multilateral security dialogue in Asia crosses the borders of Track I (government-to-government), Track II and Track III. The borderlines between the first two are very diffuse: they often mean the participation of the same government officials in an official or private capacity, in addition to academics and specialists, and the funding of both may come directly or indirectly from the government.[296] The main governmental institution on the Japanese side for Track II is the Gaimusho-funded Japan Institute of International Affairs

(Kokusai Mondai Kenkyusho, JIIA), which is led by diplomats on secondment and staffed by private researchers. In contrast to the bilateral Track I level, Track II and Track III security discussions have been easier to establish and operate. There are now a number of fora which include Japan and China either within Asia-wide or trilateral (for example involving Japan, China and the US) fora.

Asia-wide, the most important Track II forum is CSCAP, established in June 1994, which supports the ARF through working groups formed to address issues identified in ARF statements. It brings together security specialists from academia and former as well as current defence officials.[297] Other major Track II organisations promoting regional security dialogue are the North Pacific Cooperative Security Dialogue (NPCSD) and the Northeast Asia Cooperation Dialogue (NEACD).[298]

The first Asia-wide Track II forum in which China has taken a major role is the Boao Asia Forum, established in 2000. It was initiated by the former Australian Prime Minister Hawke and the former Philippine President Ramos in 1998 to create an Asian version of the Davos World Economic Forum, but China became the main actor in organizing its first meeting in November 2000 in Boao on Hainan Island. The meeting was attended by delegations from twenty-five Asian countries to discuss issues concerning regional economic development and cooperation. From the Japanese side, Okamoto Yukio and Nakasone Yasuhiro, both known for their interest in security rather than economic issues, took part.[299] The Chinese side invited Prime Minister Koizumi Junichiro to a meeting of the forum in April 2002, on the occasion of the thirtieth anniversary of the establishment of Japanese–Chinese diplomatic relations.

Trilateral Track II and Track III discussions in various configurations have become particularly important because they may facilitate Japanese–Chinese encounters, they can offset trilateral configurations from which either Japan or China is excluded, they may prevent playing one against the other, and they can reduce the suspicion of other East Asian players about Japan–China contacts.

The latter applies particularly to the Republic of Korea, which has a historically ingrained concern about being squeezed by either China or Japan, or, in the worst case, by both at the same time. The most important is the Nitchukan no Sankyoku Forum (Japan–China–Korea Trilateral Forum), established in 1996, which is organized by JIIA on the Japanese side, the China Institute of International Studies (Zhongguo Guoji Wenti Yanjiusuo, CIIS), and the Institute of Foreign Affairs and National Security (IFANS) in Seoul.[300]

The main trilateral Track II and Track III conferences are between Japan, China and the US. In April 1996 the Japan Centre for International Exchange (JCIE) launched its 'Global ThinkNet' scheme, which in a way laid the foundation for such trilateral security discussions either at Track II or at Track III level. In December 1996 JCIE launched a trilateral workshop in Beijing in collaboration with the Institute of American Studies of the Chinese Academy of Social Sciences, and the Chinese Reform Forum on the Chinese side and the Carnegie Endowment for International Peace on the US side.[301] It was followed by several similar JCIE-sponsored conferences.[302] Trilateral Track III talks were also initiated by several private institutions, like RIPS, which invited the Beijing Institute of Strategic Studies and the Center for Strategic & International Studies in Washington.[303] Several substantive publications also resulted from a trilateral meeting organised by RIPS, Pacific Forum Hawaii (Center for Strategic and International Studies; CSIS) and Zhongguo Guoji Zhanlue Xuehui.[304]

At the same time, the Japanese government has also been pursuing the idea of a trilateral Track I forum. In the spring of 1997 it approached the US about holding a China–Japan–US summit on security in the Asia-Pacific. The US did not react to the suggestion but in August made a similar proposal to China.[305] It conveyed the proposal, through National Security Advisor Samuel Berger when he visited China in August 1997, as an issue on which the US wanted to reach agreement during President Jiang Zemin's visit to Washington in October that year.[306] The matter was discussed again at a summit between Prime Minister Ryutaro Hashimoto and US President Bill Clinton in Denver in mid-June 1997 on Hashimoto's initiative in order to prepare his meeting with Jiang in September 1997. Hashimoto proposed a meeting of defence ministers from Japan, the United States and China, a trilateral summit of the three countries and a Northeast Asian sub-regional security forum that would focus on the Korean Peninsula, based on current bilateral security dialogues.[307] The US seemed to have continued a cautious attitude towards the idea, saying it was too early to discuss such issues when the two governments had not yet reached an interim agreement on the new guidelines for bilateral defence cooperation.[308] This negative position was reversed in 1997. In September of the same year Foreign Minister Qian Qichen told visiting Japanese journalists that China could agree to hold a trilateral meeting if it was an informal meeting among academic circles.[309] At the November 1997 Li Peng–Hashimoto summit in Japan both leaders emphasized 'promoting tripartite relations'.[310] In July 1998 a preparatory trilateral conference in Beijing allowed the then president of the Japan Institute of International Affairs, Matsunaga Nobuo, to get China's agreement for a trilateral dialogue at Track II level. The first trilateral meeting then took place at Harvard University in January 1999; it was followed by another in Japan in September of the same year and two meetings in 2000. At the May 1999 summit between Prime Minister Obuchi and President Clinton, the latter expressed public support for trilateral efforts for the first time by expressing his hope that 'great things could be achieved in the Asia-Pacific region' if the three countries cooperated.[311]

The difficult birth of this trilateral Track II forum (and the failure to have it at Track I level as planned by Japan) symbolizes the treacherous dynamics of the trilateral Japan–US–China relationship. Interviews by this author with some participants prove the same with regard to its actual operation. The original hope of Japan was to make it more difficult for China to say one thing to the US and another to Japan.[312] In addition, Tokyo hoped to be more successful in soothing China's concerns about the intensification of

Japanese–US defence relations since 1995. But there was also concern about possible damage to the Japan–US relationship, and the Defence Agency considered it possible that the US would dominate such a forum if there was not first an improvement in Japan–China relations.[313] For China, the venture raised fears of Japan and the US ganging up on it and diminishing its ability to offset its weakness by playing one against the other. Turning down the proposal for the forum or reducing its level was seen as a means of showing displeasure with the 1996 Joint Declaration. Lu Zhongwei, vice-president of CIIS, clearly expressed that China thought the time not yet ripe for Japan–China–US dialogue because China was facing a two-against-one situation, particularly in the wake of the revised defence guidelines.[314] From the US perspective, we have seen the concern that a trilateral forum might reduce its leverage on Japan to follow through with the 1996 Joint Declaration. Moreover, it enhances the US diplomatic burden.[315]

The evaluation of security dialogues

In contrast to the bilateral level, regional security dialogues and exchanges at Track II and III levels have flourished and have come to play an important role in Japan's political enmeshment of China.

The relative ease of establishing Track II and Track III fora is due to the lower expectations and, in the case of the Japan–China security relationship in particular, the lower weight of the burdening baggage of the bilateral relationship. Moreover, Asian countries are more comfortable with dialogue fora: whereas the Atlantic believes in institution building, Asia has shown more interest in creating networks.[316] But, as Fukushima Akiko notes, Track II dialogues may be easy to create but it becomes difficult to maintain the initial momentum unless there is a certain *raison d'être*.[317]

The dialectic dynamics between the various Track levels are very useful for each of them. Without the consensus-building work of the Track II and Track III level meetings, the regional Track I institutions, which in the security field is the ARF, would not have been created as early, and this certainly had a positive influence on Japanese–Chinese bilateral exchanges. However, the trilateral activities at Track II and III or ARF have not yet led to a trilateral government-to-government forum.

On the other hand, the following observations of China's attitude have slowed progress on China's involvement in multilateralism in general, and raise the question of the efficacy of multilateral approaches in time of a crisis:[318]

1   China remains ambivalent, if not suspicious, of global regimes; it is concerned about any infringement of its sovereignty and territorial integrity, foreign influence.
2   China aims at maximization of rights and minimization of responsibilities and obligations.
3   It puts primacy on economic growth.

4   In the case of security multilateralism, China still demonstrates a greater tendency towards tactical learning (adaptation) rather than normative learning.

A further obstacle related specifically to the Japanese–Chinese relationship is the rivalry between the two countries (see Chapter 4). Based on China's cultural background and recent historical experience, Yuan Jing-Dong described the essence of Chinese attitudes towards multilateralism and regionalism as 'thinking unilaterally, pursuing issues bilaterally, and posturing multilaterally'.[319]

From Japan's perspective (a perspective shared by the other Asian countries to varying degrees), regional security approaches are only supplementary to national security approaches and, moreover, face many obstacles due to the diversity of the members. Multilateral dialogue and exchanges have 'worked' so far because there has not been a serious challenge by a major crisis – and thanks to military and political power balancing. The Indonesian political crisis and Timor have shown, however, that ASEAN, let alone ARF, has difficulty in jointly undertaking any major action or even finding a common position.

Have Japan's efforts (and that of other relevant countries) been successful in employing regional security approaches for the political enmeshment of China? Judging the issue as a process and as only part of a much more complex policy, the answer should be positive. China has been willing gradually to accept greater involvement in regional security cooperation, albeit with considerable reservation and ambiguity. China now feels a greater urge to defend its security policies and to reassure its Asian neighbours that it does not want to constitute a threat to them. The following quote from the Gaimusho's spokesman in March 1997 gives an official view of this development:

> I would like to draw your attention to the fact that Prime Minister Li Peng specifically said that development of China would not become a threat to any other country. This was the first time a Chinese leader explicitly talked about this. The Government of Japan does not make an official assessment to this part of the statement. However, it may indicate that the Chinese leaders are more sensitive about the reactions of China's neighbors on this subject. Therefore, we will continue dialogue with the Government of China on defense policy in order to realize more and more transparency in the defense policy of China in the future.[320]

The academic discussion about the success of this element of engagement evolves around whether the progress in China's attitude is just tactical or normative learning. I would like to follow Bates Gill's dismissal of such either/or dichotomy and speak of processes which occur interactively – that is, 'learning and adaptation', 'learning to adapt' and 'adapting to learn'.[321] The slowness of these processes cannot only be put at China's door but also at Japan's: as an advanced industrialized country with over 125 million inhabitants, one might expect greater intellectual and political input from Japan into regional cooperative security.[322] In addition, Japan's failure to come to terms with its historical legacy has not helped either.

B Economic enmeshment

Introduction

Economic enmeshment is based on the assumed pacifying and democratizing effects of increased economic interdependence. The use of economic policy tools for the prevention of potential security challenges by China is aptly described by the picture of two boxers locked in a close embrace which prevents either of them from generating the necessary force seriously to hurt the other.[323] The objective of this part is to give a brief overview of Japan's role in China's economic integration at the bilateral, regional and global level in terms of trade, investment and institutional anchoring. Against this background, we will ask in Chapter 4 how this integration affects the bilateral security relationship and to what extent it has created dependencies which could be beneficial for Japan to protect its security interests.

At the bilateral level, trade, FDI and ODA are the most important instruments for economic enmeshment. The multilateral level is concerned with supporting the activities of the former (for example creating rules for FDI) and making China adhere to international norms. There are many specific policies which straddle political and economic enmeshment but cannot be dealt with in detail here. One is the use of ODA aimed at helping China to build a more functional political system which supports economic enmeshment (for example assistance to build a judicial system which facilitates the dispute settlement needed for international economic activities) as well as political enmeshment (cooperation, confidence building). Another example is helping China with its environmental problems, which, apart from reducing problems of transboundary pollution reaching Japan and enhancing Japan's ecological security, supports economic enmeshment (making China's economic modernization sustainable) as well as political enmeshment (cooperation, confidence building, the creation of ecological interdependence).[324]

In Japan's public perception and official pronouncements, economic enmeshment figures as the most prominent policy tool in Japan's engagement strategy towards China. The main condition which facilitates this emphasis on the Liberal agenda of engagement is Japan's position as a 'global civilian power'. The prominence of economic enmeshment in Japan's policy towards China is also regionally welcome, since a more Realist emphasis is feared to give rise to political and military tensions. Historically, the civilian-power project owes much to the Japanese reflection on its war of aggression against China before 1945.

But economic enmeshment would not have been possible without China's economic opening since 1978, its emphasis on achieving economic security and 'comprehensive national power', and the importance given to economic relations with Japan. Moreover, the arrangement of renouncing war reparations in the expectation of major Japanese ODA flows to China has given Japan a particularly strong position in China's economic modernisation.

Economic enmeshment of China is widely supported by all major political orientations in Japan. Even specialists like Nishihara Masashi who emphasize the potential military challenge of China express support for this approach while at the same time urging that the power balancing element of engagement not be neglected.[325] Ozawa Ichiro says in his 'Blueprint for Japan' that 'Japan must do everything possible to foster China's stability and development'.[326] Business interests were a major influence in the preparation of the normalization of diplomatic relations in 1972. With the growing relocation of Japanese manufacturing to China and the importation of manufacturing goods from China, economic interests in Japan today go well beyond the trade sector, where they were established in the 1970s. Moreover, a majority of Japanese are convinced that the promotion of China's economic development will also promote democratization in that country. In a *Yomiuri Shimbun* poll in 1997, 57.1 per cent of the Japanese polled expressed the belief that economic development in China will promote democratization, compared with only 27.7 per cent in the US. Only 18.5 per cent of the Japanese said no to the proposition, but 51.7 per cent of the Americans did so.[327]

The Chinese side welcomes foreign economic interests since the decision in 1978 for an export- and FDI-led modernization of the economy. Within the concept of 'comprehensive national power', military power and economic power is given similar status in China's modernization. Moreover, China is espousing the idea of economic security being part of military security. China's National Defence White Paper in 1998 said:

> Economic security is becoming daily more important for state security. In international relations geopolitical, military security and ideological factors still play a role that cannot be ignored, but the role of economic factors is becoming more outstanding, along with growing economic contacts among nations ... more and more countries regard economic security as an important aspect of state security.[328]

Trade

Japan's economic interactions with China have only taken off on a grand scale since the normalization of diplomatic relations in 1972. Before 1972 the Cold War context and Japan's submission to the US's China containment policy did not allow trade and investment to occur on a significant scale despite the obvious complementarity of both economies (China: cheap labour, raw material, huge market; Japan: capital, technology, economic aid and export market). On the Japanese side, it was private business interests driving economic interactions, with the government trying to reconcile their scope with the parameters given by Japan's alliance with the US. From 1972 the government has been actively

Table 3.2 Japanese–Chinese trade (in US$ billion)

	Exports	Change (%)	Imports	Change (%)	Total	Trade balance
1988	9.475	+14.3	9.858	+33.2	19.334	−0.382
1989	8.515	−10.1	11.145	+13.1	19.661	−2.629
1990	6.129	−28.0	12.053	+8.1	18.183	−5.923
1991	8.593	+40.2	14.215	+17.9	22.808	−5.622
1992	11.949	+39.1	16.952	+19.3	28.901	−5.003
1993	17.273	+44.6	20.564	+21.3	37.837	−3.291
1994	18.681	+8.2	27.566	+34.0	46.247	−8.884
1995	21.930	+17.4	35.922	+30.3	57.853	−13.991
1996	21.891	−0.2	40.543	+12.9	62.435	−18.652
1997	21.781	−0.5	42.041	+3.7	63.823	−20.259
1998	20.098	−7.7	36.893	−12.3	56.991	−16.795

Source: *Gaiko Forum*, October 1999, p. 72

encouraging economic interactions, providing a facilitating framework (for example an investment protection agreement) and using governmental tools (notably ODA) in order to promote economic enmeshment as well as Japan's economic interests. Both governments have been actively promoting Japanese FDI into China, supporting if not initiating bodies like the Japan–China Trade Expansion Council (established in 1985) and the Japan–China Investment Promotion Organization (established in 1990). Although private economic interests became the driving motor of the phenomenal rise of Japanese–Chinese economic interaction after 1972, the facilitating role of government has been instrumental in encouraging companies to go into China despite stark contrasts between the two economic systems, the ups and downs of China's economic modernization policies, and bilateral political frictions.

In 1993 China became Japan's second most frequent destination for exports (see Table 3.2). Today China is Japan's second-largest trade partner, after the US, whereas for China, Japan is the largest. According to the Japan Export Trade Organization (JETRO), the total of Japan's import and export trade with China in 2000 came to US$85.8 billion, an increase of 29.5 per cent over the previous year, and for the first time topping the 10 per cent mark as a percentage of Japan's total trade figure. According to US figures, US–China two-way trade in 2000 was US$116.4 billion.[329] Since 1988 China has enjoyed an uninterrupted trade surplus with Japan, but only according to Japanese statistics.[330] In the period 1995–2000, this surplus increased from US$11.6 billion to US$25.3 billion.[331]

Investment

The role of Japanese investment in China's economic success and in creating interdependence between the two countries is impressive, and trade and investment have become closely linked due to Japanese relocation of manufacturing to China. Overall, however, trade has developed in a more positive way than investment in terms of absolute and relative amounts as well as in comparison with Japan's other Asian FDI recipients.[332]

Since 1992 Japanese investment in China has exceeded US$1 billion every year. But US investment outstripped Japan's investment in 1993 by 60 per cent. Japanese investment increased more after the increase of the yen in 1993.[333] This development was helped by rising production costs in Japan and the need to reduce direct exports from Japan to the US.

According to Japanese figures, the total Japanese investment in China at the end of 1998 amounted to 18,000 cases, with a value of US$33 billion. Until 1996 China came first in Asia as the destination for Japanese investment; in 1997 it came second after Indonesia; in 1998 third, with 16.3 per cent, after Thailand, with 21.0 per cent, and Indonesia, with 16.5 per cent.[334] The Asian economic crisis in 1997 affected China considerably, because it led to a decline in Japan's importance as a provider of FDI and a market for Chinese products. Japan's FDI declined from 258 cases in FY 1997 to 112 in FY 1998. According to Chinese figures for the calendar (rather than the fiscal) year of the two years, the number of cases on a contract basis fell only from 1,402 to 1,198.[335] Since 2000 there seems to be an increase again.[336]

The scale of Japan's FDI is more important than the above bilateral figures would suggest. Bilateral trade and investment are only part of a geographically and economically much larger picture, which is related to the manufacturing network Japanese companies have established in the whole of East Asia and in which China has been firmly integrated.[337] Although FDI figures put Japan behind Hong Kong and Taiwan, the figures for the latter two cannot entirely be divorced from Japanese FDI sources. Much of Hong Kong's investment actually originates in other countries, including to a substantial degree Japan. Japanese banks play a major role in Hong Kong. Taiwanese investment in China comes to an equally large extent from Japanese sources. If we take this into consideration, Japanese investment in China is probably higher than US investment in China. As a result, Japanese companies are directly as well as indirectly acting as providers of capital, technology, market and general production/trade faciliators (through trading companies).

ODA

ODA is the policy tool of economic enmeshment which is most directly related to the government's China policy, notably also in the security area. It is also the most important material policy instrument to enhance trade and FDI. This intention to draw Beijing closer to the West by encouraging Deng Xiaoping's policies of economic reform and opening the country was expressed by Prime Minister Ohira when he decided in December 1979 to extend the first yen loan to China.[338]

Facilitated by its economic success and capital surplus, Japan achieved the position as China's top or second-highest aid donor.[339] China is one of the world's largest recipient of economic aid, and total net official flows (including official development assistance and other official flows) amounted to US$56 billion during 1981–98. Multilateral institutions, of which Japan is often the second-largest contributor, accounted for the largest share in this period, with US$24 billion. Japan was the largest bilateral source of official flows during this period, with US$18 billion (to Indonesia, US$21 billion; Thailand US$14 billion). Around 90 per cent of Japan's ODA to China consists of loans. In 1999 Japan provided US$1.23 billion in ODA to China. Except for the two years 1990 and 1991, Japan provided more than half of China's bilateral ODA between 1979 and 1998. China's biggest ODA donors in 1998 were Japan, Germany, the UK, Canada and France, in that order. Japan's aid accounts for more than one-third of overall (bilateral and multilateral) ODA to China and it occupies over 30 per cent of state investments done through the national budget. Japanese banks accounted for one-third to one-quarter of the foreign-bank lending to China in the mid- to late 1990s, but the Japanese share fell markedly after 1997.[340]

Multilateral economic involvement

Multilateral economic organizations play an important part in economic enmeshment in various ways, most importantly by transforming the country's preferences to conform with those adopted by the other member states and to promote further integration.[341] Espousing the assumptions and goals of these organizations, Japan was supportive of China's involvement throughout the 1990s. China has become a member of a number of global and regional organizations. In 1985 China decided to participate in PECC, and joined the group at the Vancouver meeting in November 1986. It joined APEC in November 1991, along with Taiwan and Hong Kong, thus marking a further step towards overcoming its international isolation after the Tiananmen crackdown. At the time of writing this book, China had still not joined WTO, although it joined its predecessor organisation the General Agreement on Tariffs and Trade (GATT) as early as 1982 as an observer and applied for full membership in 1986. Japan has been actively supporting China's WTO membership and it signed the required bilateral agreement with China in July 1999, whereas the US did so only in November 1999. Although the Japanese move is presented as sending a political signal to the US about speeding up China's WTO membership, Japan is not seen as a facilitator or go-between for China–WTO relations. However, Japan seems to be arguing for making it easier for China.[342]

As in the case of China's enmeshment in regional security, its participation in economic multilateralism and regionalism is coloured by considerable reluctance and minimal input. In the case of the WTO, it is, moreover, questionable whether China is politically able and/or willing to play by the rules because of the expected onerous costs to the Chinese economy, at least at the beginning. Takagi Seiichiro characterized China's involvement in Asia-Pacific economic cooperation in the following way, which also applies in many ways to what was said above regarding its involvement in regional security cooperation:

1   The Chinese approach is basically reactive and passive.
2   It is based more on damage limitation than making a positive contribution to multilateralism.
3   China wants to proceed in an incrementalist way.
4   China's involvement seem to be related to the 'greater dynamics, such as regional or global developments'.[343]

An additional feature is the possibility of Japanese–Chinese rivalry colouring the creation and shaping of international regimes. In 1997 China – but also the US, albeit for different reasons – opposed Japan's proposed creation of a US$100 billion Asian Monetary Fund to help the regional economies after the economic crisis.[344] Later China changed its attitude in the face of widespread Asian support for the idea. On the positive side, multilateral economic institutions have so far been successful in prompting China to adhere to the rules, although China has always bargained hard to protect its national interests.[345]

Japan and China's export- and FDI-led strategy

Japan's economic enmeshment of China has contributed significantly to Beijing's economic success and to the degree of bilateral and multilateral enmeshment. Since 1980 China's real GDP has grown more than 7 per cent annually in all but three years (1981, 1989 and 1990).[346] Although the rate of China's economic growth has slowed down since 1996, China still has an annual growth rate of around 7 per cent, and is expected to keep the rate at from 6 to 7 percent during the first decade of the twenty-first century.[347] While this may seem high to the mature industrialized countries, particularly to Japan with its very low growth rate, for China it is the minimum rate which is required to absorb new arrivals on the job market. A growth rate under 8 per cent may even lead to an increase in the size of non-performing loans in the troubled financial sector.[348] China's export expanded almost twenty-fold in the period 1978–99, and its import almost fifteen-fold. In 1999 China ranked as the ninth-largest export nation and tenth-largest import nation in the world. It is now the seventh-largest trading nation and increased its share of world trade to 3.9 per cent in 2000. Total foreign trade grew by 31.5 per cent, to reach US$474 billion in 2000.[349] As a result, China's foreign trade:GDP ratio rose from 11.4 per cent in 1979 to 38.1 per cent in 1992, and reached 40 per cent in 1994.[350] The growing integration of China into the world economy is also illustrated by the role of FDI: joint ventures and other forms of ownership with foreign participation now account for over 50 per cent of China's trade.[351] According to some economic indicators (for example the GDP:trade ratio or the role of FDI in the domestic economy), China is even more integrated into the world economy than Japan.[352] China has attracted the third-largest amount of foreign investment in the world, behind only the US and Britain (overtaking Britain in 2000), rising from US$41 billion in 2000 to US$46.8 billion in 2001.[353] In Chapter 4 we will try to evaluate the implications of this economic achievement for Japan's security interest.

Conclusions

The 1990s saw a strengthening of the military but also of the political power-balancing elements of Japan's engagement towards Japan. Not all the momentum came from China's growing security challenges: the strengthening of the Japan–US security relationship and notably TMD were also inspired by North Korea, but China's shadow loomed always in the background. Moreover, referring publicly to China was not considered diplomatic and conducive to the overall strategy of engagement. Japan's greater diplomatic assertiveness was the general background for the efforts of power balancing through building up security relations with Asian countries. At the same time, Japan enhanced considerably the political and economic enmeshment elements as a complement to the Realist elements of engagement. Japan's efforts at bilateral and multilateral security dialogues at Track I, II and III levels met with certain, albeit slow, success in involving China more closely in bilateral and multilateral security fora, which gave Japan, China and any other fora members the opportunity to explain their positions and gain greater understanding of the other sides' perceptions and reactions. Japan has certainly played a useful role in China becoming less reluctant towards involvement in multilateral fora. The instruments of economic enmeshment have not only contributed to China's economic development (as well as to Japan's commercial benefit) but also integrated China to a great extent into the regional and global economy. Have these various elements in Japan's engagement policy made the Japanese–Chinese security relationship more stable and offset the negative developments of the 1990s? To answer this question I want to evaluate in more detail the various dynamics resulting from Japan's engagement and question some of the assumptions behind engagement.

4 The dynamics of engagement

There is nothing ... that adequately prepares us for the mixture of respect, disdain, emulation, and rivalry that has characterized the relationship between China and Japan for many centuries.[1]

Introduction

Bearing in mind that Japan is only one of the countries pursuing engagement towards China, albeit the most important one after the US, this chapter looks at the positive and negative dynamics arising from the different policy tools of Japan's engagement. First of all I want to look at the general debate about the assumptions underlying political and economic enmeshment. Economic enmeshment can address many problems and prevent China from opting for security policies which would be inimical to Japan's security interests, but the vagaries of economic development, even when successful, do not point to any predetermined positive or negative outcome. One of the ambivalent dynamics arising from political and economic enmeshment is the impact on Japanese–Chinese rivalry and competition. It has been referred to several times in the preceding chapters and deserves a comprehensive analysis as a shaping factor as well as a consequence of engagement. Since the US is one of the most important variables for Japan's security relations with China, I want to examine more closely the dynamics inherent in the triangular framework for the pursuit of engagement. Finally, we have to look at the gradual abandonment of Japanese deference and restraint towards China because of the recognition of its negative dynamics in the face of growing rivalry and competition in the bilateral relationship.

Open issues of political and economic enmeshment

The general debate between the Realist and Liberal schools of international relations about the conceptual soundness of engagement of China is still raging, because China has become neither an aggressive expansionist power nor a capitalist liberal democracy which has renounced the use of force, for example for solving the Taiwan issue.[2] China's future as a peaceful and compliant member of the international community is still uncertain, with many obstacles on the road being acknowledged by both schools. The Realists emphasize the likelihood of a negative outcome because of their Realist assumptions, but they cannot prove it. They point to China's growing military power, its increasing assertiveness and its willingness at least to threaten to solve the Taiwan issue by non-peaceful means. The German sinologist Kay Möller, referring to the limitations of China's opening policy and the very serious structural, domestic and foreign policy problems, considers a peaceful evolution the least likely outcome.[3] Since no one considers fully fledged containment politically feasible as an alternative to engagement, Realists can only recommend a mix of policy tools which is more or less weighted towards military and political power balancing and hedging. However, this leaves them vulnerable to the accusation of inviting the very outcome they warn about.

Liberalists can refer to some encouraging tendencies in China towards becoming a more democratic and capitalist country, but they still cannot claim that these tendencies are irreversible, that the feared transition period will be mastered successfully; nor can they establish a clear causality between a given engagement policy and the outcome, exclude the (later) hijacking of economic strength for non-peaceful purposes or guarantee the political and ecological sustainability of economic development.[4] Paul A. Papayoanou and Scott L. Kastner cautiously conclude that the goals of economic enmeshment have been achieved, but warn that core issues of national sovereignty and the uncertainty about future political scenarios may reduce the role of economic interests.[5] As we saw in Chapter 2, China's economic modernization has already caused serious social and ecological disruptions, with as yet unknown consequences for China's political stability and the political sustainability of the course of current reform. Since the economic reform process creates positive as well as negative dynamics, it cannot be considered to be on 'autopilot'.[6] There is concern that China's economic growth path – export- and FDI-led development – may create the same conditions which devastated parts of Southeast Asia in 1997.[7] Moreover, China's economic modernization creates non-traditional security concerns including transboundary pollution, illegal immigration and competition for scarce resources on the international market. The growing opening of China to international market forces has weakened central government control, which may reduce the temptation of using military means to solve security issues, but it can also prevent the government from effectively limiting such unwelcome developments.

We saw in Chapter 3 that China's response to political and economic multilateralism is still hesitant, ambiguous and minimal. The question is why China, as a major and self-confident power, should accept rules which were written by Western-oriented governments before it joined and which may incur economic and/or political costs. But even if China joins, can the relevant institutions maintain their character in view of China's political and economic size and its revisionist agenda? The problem is whether the expected gains in advancing the goals of engagement by admitting China to a multilateral institution will not outweigh the costs to that institution in terms of its efficiency and coherence. This problem has been very prominently raised in the last years in the context of China's membership of the WTO or ARF.

But, despite these reservations, Liberals are positive about developments in China. While traditional Realism is still the dominant feature in the PRC's foreign-policy outlook and content, PRC analysts have begun using concepts such as interdependence, geonomics, global norms and international community as China's open-door policy and its economic interdependence with the outside world have developed. This can be particularly well observed in China's growing regional outreach to Asia, where it has to respond to concern about China's territorial demands and military modernization. It has become 'an increasingly invested stakeholder in international security and economic systems'.[8] Thomas J. Christensen considers that China's 'realpolitik quest to restore its place among internationally recognized great powers might actually be the most important force pushing China into international institutions and agreements'.[9]

The problem for the Liberals is the difficulty of tracing causality in individual cases of policy because engagement is channelled through domestic perceptions and domestic structures which may hinder or impede a given policy.[10] Eliciting cooperative foreign policies rather than conflictual policies depends on how much influence internationalist economic interests can wield in the non-democratic state.[11] Certain engagement policies are accepted, thanks to a coalition of Chinese policy-maker constituencies, despite different assumptions and intentions on individual policies (for example the economic opening of China). Finally, causality can not be attributed to just one engagement partner. The US and Japan are the most important ones, but the EU and other Western countries play a crucial role as well and may be more important in certain sectors than the US and Japan.

The interdependence of China and the international economy is growing. But the increase in this interdependence is not the same in all sectors, the leverage given to China's engagement partners is partial and ambiguous, and at the same time it also creates trade conflicts and it enhances rivalry. While there is no consensus that greater involvement in the international economy leads to a more peaceful stance, one can at least say that economic interdependence and integration are increasingly limiting the room for governmental behaviour which is far outside international norms. China's *Realpolitik* approach in the security sphere is increasingly constrained by international commitments, status relationships, power balances and foreign values. China's economy is enmeshed to such a high degree into the world economy that it could not extract itself without suffering severe domestic problems, because its fast-growing standard of living and the legitimacy of its leadership are based on it.

China's economic success: good or bad?

This favourable tendency confirming the Liberal approach to engagement is also acknowledged by Japanese Realists. Tanaka Akihiko argues that engagement has turned China into a status-quo power (*genjo ichi seiryoku*).[12] According to a critical China specialist in the Ministry of Foreign Affairs, the economic reform process has put China on an economic track towards free capital markets which seems to be irreversible.[13]

At the same time, many Japanese observers see challenges for Japan in the case of China's success or failure.[14] Yokoyama Hiroshi even expressed concern that if China failed Beijing would blame Japan because of its involvement through FDI and ODA.[15] The conclusions of Japanese experts on whether China's economic success is good for Japan's security depend very much on the vantage point of the observer. Security specialists, who are more likely to be Realists, tend to stress the possibility that China's economic and political development might either go wrong or have negative implications for Japan's security and other interests. Economists like to point out the huge tasks and challenges of China's economic development.

It seems that Japanese China-watchers are more sceptical about China's economic development and future, or are at least giving greater credence than Western China experts to the possibility that China may disintegrate internally or become unable to handle the fallout resulting from failed social and economic policies.[16] The mixed experience by business in China since the country's opening in 1978 has created an atmosphere which now allows a more sober evaluation.[17] Professor Tanaka Akihiko even wrote 'We cannot dismiss the possibility that China will fall into the same sort of confusion as Indonesia experienced in 1998'.[18] Many others describe the various dangers and shortcomings of China's economic development.[19]

One indication of concern in Japan's bureaucracy about the sustainability of China's economic development is the ongoing review of ODA policy towards China, which has been so instrumental in this development.[20] A 1999 Japan International Cooperation Agency (JICA) study of Japan's ODA to China mentions, among other unstable factors, macroeconomic growth, lack of reform in state-owned enterprises, expansion of poverty and regional disparities and environmental degradation.[21] The security implications are implied rather than spelled out.

Although China survived the Asian economic crisis of 1997 rather well, and even played a positive role in its containment, that experience and China's economic slowdown (which started even earlier) have had a sobering effect on many China-watchers and made them see China's development in a more critical light, although the majority does not anticipate its collapse. There also is a feeling in Japan that China bears some responsibility for the outbreak of the crisis because of the earlier devaluation of the Renminbi.[22] This feeling is in contrast to many Western opinions, which instead praised China for not devaluing the Renminbi after the outbreak of the 1997 Asian crisis.

This more critical assessment of China's economic problems has certainly been one of the most important factors in considering negatively the linkage between economic growth and military security, but there is also a greater awareness in Japan of the implications for 'human security' of failed economic and social development in developing countries, which was particularly highlighted by Russia's problems.[23] Notably, defence analysts are, not surprisingly, more inclined to combine the conclusion that China's economic growth will encourage China to become a threat with the warning that current economic growth creates systemic problems.[24] Even economic success may undermine the current political system of China because of the growing discrepancy between the political and economic systems, leading to economic collapse or to the establishment of a more aggressive political regime.[25] While China's entry into the WTO is generally seen as likely to exert a positive influence on China's economy and global integration, a Defence Agency official pointed out to the author that it will devastate China's agriculture, with unpredictable consequences.[26]

The August 1994 Higuchi Report on Japan's defence mentioned China's difficulties transforming itself into a market economy and the 'widening economic disparity between the inland and coastal regions'.[27] Analysts in the Defence Agency are concerned about the threat to China's domestic stability emanating from the economic slowdown, pointing, for example, to localized riots in the countryside.[28] In 2000 alone there were said to be around 10,000 cases of local rioting reported in the Chinese press, and one can assume that there were many more that went unreported.[29] Lieutenant-Colonel Kato Hisanori of the GSDF mentions that, due to China's military modernization and its strategic aims (including the option of liberating Taiwan by force and protecting its territorial interests in the South China Sea), as well as the inherent negative dynamics in China's economic development, new threats different from those during the Cold War era may arise. In particular, he includes threats arising from the proliferation of weapons, especially weapons of mass destruction, from massive movements of refugees, and from causes other than political or economic problems (that is, environmental damage).[30]

Finally, there is the debate on the extent to which Japan's contribution to Chinese economic growth helps China to develop its military capability. From a Realist perspective this help is considerable and casts doubt on the validity of the Liberal approach to engagement. From a Liberal perspective there is the hope that, in the end (I would like to add: but will it happen in time?), the spread of economic interdependence and welfare will diminish any aggressive intentions which might be nourished by a strengthened defence potential and military industry as the inevitable consequence of economic enmeshment. Japanese ODA, investment and technology transfer certainly help China's armament industry directly or indirectly.[31] One difficulty in assessing this is the fact that Japan is not the only advanced industrialized country active in China. Even after the US stopped non-lethal arms transfers to China after 1989, weapons technology reached China directly or indirectly.[32] Japan has even been more careful than the US in transferring high technology to avoid a commercial boomerang effect. Another difficulty in assessing the impact of economic interactions with Japan is the scarcity of empirical data. Trade and investment flows with threshold countries inevitably provide at least dual-use technology and equipment (for example measuring instruments) which can be used for military production.[33] Often the greatest obstacle to such leakage is the high boundary between civilian and military production. In China, however, this problem may be offset to some extent by the high involvement of military production sites in civilian production. In 1998 the Chinese press reported that between 1,200 and 1,300 converted military factories had absorbed about US$4.5 billion in foreign investment by the end of 1997 and that this investment was particularly welcome in the shipbuilding, automobile, computer and other high-technology sectors.[34] It is also obvious that Japanese and other FDI frees the state to invest scarce resources in military production rather than in civilian sectors.

The tenuous link between interdependence and leverage

In Chapter 3 we saw the extent to which Japanese and Chinese economic fortunes have become dependent on each other. The assumption of the Liberal School is that interdependence reduces friction, helps to make the newcomer a peaceful stakeholder in the world community, and gives leverage to the country which engages on the strength of its economic power. Does the Japanese experience bear this out?

Economic interdependence is a very ambiguous concept in the actual world of economic interactions. Although the economic dependence of China on Japan appears to be higher than the other way round because of the direction of FDI and ODA flows, other indicators indicate a growing Japanese dependence on China. China, as Japan's second-largest trade partner, cannot easily be replaced by another country. The importance of China for Japan is even more visible in terms of Japanese dependence on China for Japan's relocated manufacturing industry, particularly in view of Japan's reluctance to graduate from certain manufacturing sectors. China, as a growing regional and intra-regional gravitation power, is increasingly becoming a competing economy in manufacturing sectors and even in research, where Japan has so far enjoyed superiority, forcing it to constantly adapt, relocate and restructure even if it will be very difficult for China to catch up with Japan's high technological advance as long as Japan's economy does not go into irreversible decline.[35]

This has an impact on what Denny Roy referred to as the deterrence value of interdependence.[36] Japan's leverage over China accruing from its position as China's economic partner is obviously reduced by the growing equality of mutual dependence and vulnerability. Moreover, there is no clear Japanese hierarchy of issues which could be singled out for 'penalties' against a 'misbehaving' China, and many of these issues are influenced by US positions. The same dilemma applies to the US–China relationship. Paul A. Papayoanou and Scott L. Kastner express the concern that economic ties may constrain US ability to balance China if core issues of national sovereignty (Taiwan) and unfavourable future political scenarios reduce the effectiveness of engagement.[37] Are human rights important enough to trigger penalties, and what kind of penalties should then apply, or is this threshold only reached with the 'unprovoked' invasion of Taiwan? In the case of human rights, there is no consensus on whether improvement in China can be speeded up by pressure now (but with what tools?) or whether it is better to further engage China and wait for long-term success.

There is empirical evidence for ODA giving Japan some leverage. The Japanese government did not just rely on the assumptions of the democratic peace theory, but has been trying to use ODA to influence China's security policy. The Japanese government under Prime Minister Ohira Masayoshi enunciated in 1979 ODA principles targeted specifically at China, stipulating, among other things, that no military assistance would be provided.[38] This was, first of all, a consequence of Japan's ban on arms export, but it was also meant as a signal to China that Tokyo did not want to strengthen China's military potential, not even as part of China's anti-hegemony campaign against the common Soviet adversary.[39] In the general ODA guidelines of 1992 Japanese ODA was made contingent on the security policy of the recipient. In 2000 Miyamoto Yuji, then minister at the Japanese embassy in Beijing, wrote that '[s]ecurity considerations in Japan's ODA to China are natural'.[40] In practice, however, the Japanese government has not strictly insisted on China adhering to the 1992 guidelines. Nevertheless, Japan twice suspended its ODA to China to protest against Chinese policies. As we saw in Chapter 1, however, Japan was merely following the US lead in 1989, when it temporarily suspended ODA, and was working hard behind the scenes to convince the US to reinstate it. Only the suspension of the grant portion of its aid to China and the delayed disbursement of the loan portion after China's nuclear tests in May and August 1995 was initiated by Japan (see Chapter 2). But China's subsequent moratorium on nuclear tests cannot simply be attributed to pressure from Japan.

Still, since around 1994 Japan has used its ODA position to reduce the heat of bilateral conflicts, sometimes successfully, as well as to protest at the highest levels against Chinese security policies.[41] Japanese insistence on greater Chinese military transparency has certainly contributed to the publication of Chinese White Papers, even if it has not slowed down China's military modernization. We saw in Chapter 2 how the Chinese government carefully controlled the public outcry in 1996 on the occasion of the Senkaku Islands dispute, even to the point of becoming vulnerable to domestic criticism about caving in to Japanese pressure. This is also confirmed by Chinese experts. Jin Xide, a researcher at CASS, mentions that Japan's ODA programme has been a success in that it has suppressed to some extent trouble originating from issues related to Japan's past and the Japanese–US security treaty.[42] An indirect official acknowledgment of Japanese pressure was given by Zhu Rongji in Tokyo in 2000, when he said that Japan should not use its economic assistance as a diplomatic card to draw concessions from China.[43] In May 2000 Chinese Foreign Minister Tang was quoted, on the subject of Japan's plan to review ODA to China because of Beijing's steep increase in military spending, as saying: 'This issue should not be discussed in a political context'.[44]

These official linkages of ODA with Chinese security policies increased because widespread dissatisfaction with such policies had led to an increase in critical comments on ODA in many Japanese quarters.[45] In August–September 2000 the LDP delayed its consent to low interest loans to China because of the unresolved issue of incursions by Chinese research vessels.[46] The irony is, however, that as a result of demands for cuts in ODA to China and other developments, the ability of the government to use ODA as a major tool to influence China may soon decline.

Japan's ODA budget declined in FY 2001–2 by 3 per cent, and for FY 2002–3 cuts of 10 per cent were decided.[47] With regard to China, ODA has recently come under fire because there are increasingly critical comments that aid is often wasted, that China does not stick to its conditions, that aid should go to areas where there is real need, including the environment, that China is not grateful, that China is itself an ODA donor, that China does not acknowledge the aid domestically, and that China spends too much on the military. Moreover, there is a feeling that Japan is losing its ODA leverage on China because of China's successful economic modernization.[48]

As a result of these various concerns about ODA, Japan is reducing its yen loans for infrastructure projects in China's coastal provinces, is giving more attention to inland provinces and plans to concentrate on poverty reduction and environmental projects. Loans pledged in FY 2001 dropped by 25 per cent on the previous year, to ¥161 billion, the biggest drop since ODA to the country began in 1979.[49] The Gaimusho and politicians with foreign-policy knowledge are fighting a further decline in ODA in general and to China in particular, arguing openly that 'it serves a crucial diplomatic function as Japan doesn't have military forces'.[50] In 2000 Japan stopped giving China a lump sum for each five-year economic plan, and from 2001 ODA is negotiated on a year-by-year basis, as has always been mandatory for all other Japanese aid recipients.[51] This may give Japan more frequent opportunities to exert leverage over China, but the reduction in the size of individual stakes may work against Japan's leverage. Japan's decrease in its ODA to China should be offset by the fact that other Western countries have also been reducing their overall ODA (with a lower share of China's ODA compared to Japan). However, if the experience in 2001 is anything to go by, the annual negotiation rounds will also lead to annual frictions with China when the next ODA plan is being negotiated, particularly if the negotiating round becomes affected by other disputes.[52] At the same time, China is becoming less dependent on ODA and more interested in investment because of the progress of economic development.[53] The relative weight of yen loans has declined and, instead, private investment is becoming increasingly important.[54]

Rivalry and competition

The positive dynamics of economic and political enmeshment are further qualified by the increasingly apparent economic and political rivalry and competition between Japan and China. Engagement partly mitigates or offsets this rivalry, but it also partly reinforces or even creates it. Takagi Seiichiro argued as early as 1994 that a considerable part of the 'China threat' discussion has become a discussion about Japan–China rivalry and a fight for hegemony in South East Asia.[55] Even a Chinese scholar like Wu Xinbo referred to 'competitive coexistence'.[56] Denny Roy concludes that 'serious political tensions between China and Japan are certain, and military conflict is likely, if China's economic power continues to grow rapidly relative to Japan's'.[57] Is the goal of economic enmeshment – that is, China's economic development – therefore counterproductive to Japan's security interests because it engenders tensions and rivalry? What about the relationship between political-strategic rivalry and political enmeshment? In order to explain these dynamics we have to look at economic as well as political/military elements of engagement and how they interact.

Economic rivalry

Some elements of economic rivalry have already been mentioned in the context of China's economic success challenging core values of non-traditional security like national identity, the acquisition and/or protection of rank or competition for natural resources (Chapter 2). Here we want to look at concrete frictions arising from the economic relationship rather than the ideational challenges or future challenges about access to natural resources.

First, we have to ask how seriously China's economic development is considered a threat to Japan's economy. In an opinion poll of the general public by the *Yomiuri Shimbun* in 1997, 74 per cent responded that China's economic power will pose a great or some threat, and in another poll in 1995, 37 per cent thought that China will have more economic power than Japan and become Asia's biggest economic power.[58] In 1995 a Nikkei–Dow Jones poll found that 16 per cent of Japanese already regarded China as the strongest economic power in the world, compared to 5 per cent of Americans. In the future, 66 per cent of Japanese saw China as the strongest economic power, compared to only 17 per cent of Americans.[59] Nakanishi Terumasa, then professor for international relations at Shizuoka Prefectural University, stated in 1994 that the 'China issue' was also a question of Japan's 'economic survival', although he did not refer to China as an immediate challenge.[60]

There are several indicators that point to relatively low Japanese concern about the (at least immediate) impact of China's economic development:

1   The prevailing preponderance of the US as an economic partner for Japan in public opinion: public opinion polls in Japan still indicate that, in terms of economic relations, the US will be more important for Japan in the future – 40 per cent (both in 1998 and 1997), whereas only 31 per cent and 36 per cent (1998 and 1997, respectively) thought that China will be more important, with 23 per cent and 19 per cent (1998 and 1997, respectively) considering both equally important.[61]

2   The perceived gap between the two economies: a recent report reviewing Japan's ODA to China points out that although China's GDP increased by 3.8 times between 1979 and 1998 the gap between Japan and China in

terms of per capita GNP rose, from 34:1 (US$8,730:260) in 1979 to 43:1 (US$32,350:750).[62] In 1997 Japan had a share of 72.4 per cent of the total GDP of East Asia, compared with 8.3 per cent for China. The per capita income of Japan was higher than that of China by the factor 53.3.[63] Nakai Yoshifumi points out that, while China's economy may at some time in the twenty-first century become the world's largest economy, this is based on considerable assumptions, like coping with limitations on a global scale of limited raw materials, food problems, population and environment, and above all the assumption that China would pursue the transformation of its economy into a liberal market economy. However, at present China's GDP is only one-ninth that of Japan and one-thirteenth that of the US.[64]

3   Japanese business is not reducing its involvement in China. Instead, Japanese–Chinese economic relations have witnessed a tremendous expansion since 1978, and Japan's economic woes are fuelling an increase of industrial relocation to China and cooperation with China. While business is often accused of being the slave of short-termism, this does not apply so much to how Japanese business is generally judged. Japanese–Chinese economic relations have developed so well because of the underlying complementarity of the two countries' economies.[65] The involvement of Japanese business in China is shaped by the perceived business environment in China (including the political climate) and the consideration of risks against future prospects.[66] In the latter calculation there are certainly flowing considerations of how sales or investment may affect the competitive status of Japanese business to avoid a so-called boomerang effect. This is one of the reasons why Japanese FDI into China has been less than that of the US, or is less spectacular than Japan's ODA to China. But, in general, either the strong economic relationship does not reflect an urgent concern that it would be counterproductive for Japan in terms of competition or it reflects the confidence (or perceived necessity) of Japanese business that it can stay ahead of China. However, the strong involvement of Japanese business in China reflects evaluations of opportunities and the business climate for foreigners rather than considered opinions of the long-term soundness of China's economic development. While profits are not high, sales are rising and there is widespread optimism about the Chinese market.

Despite this low level of immediate Japanese concern about China as a (potential) economic rival, and the rise of cooperation between Japanese and Chinese enterprises at an increasingly equal level, we also witness more economic tensions between the two countries, which is due to competition and rivalry. Growing Chinese exports to Japan threaten politically sensitive economic sectors (agriculture, small business) in Japan and have led to an increasing number of trade conflicts. In the past the Japanese government retreated from planned protectionist measures, for example to curb surging Chinese imports of textile and apparel in 1995. However, against the background of recession in Japan and domestic pressure on the ruling conservative parties, Japan imposed punitive tariffs on certain Chinese agricultural imports in April 2001 and China retaliated with tariffs on some Japanese imports.[67] In addition, Japan has become much more vocal about what it considers obstacles put up by China against Japan. These frictions are likely to increase, particularly during the transitional period after China joins the WTO.

Japanese businesses active in China have become increasingly critical of the difficulties they encounter in China which are linked to the country's economic and political problems, while at the same time considering China a crucial market. But these negative observations and complaints from business reinforce the negative perception of China's economy and the bilateral relationship in general.[68] The collapse of the Guangdong International Trust and Investment Corporation (GITIC) in 1999 had a very negative effect on the perception of China's economic health.[69] Japan was particularly hit by it because its banking sector is the greatest creditor of this institution. In January 2000 a Chinese court ordered a debt-collection freeze for a number of Chinese non-banks, effectively making it impossible for creditors to get their money back. Chinese non-banks owe foreign banks a total of around US$8 billion, half of which is said to be owed to Japanese banks.[70] In addition to the China-generated problems from which all foreign companies suffer (non-transparent regulatory framework, arbitrary tax system, etc.), Japanese companies have recently been targeted by Chinese court cases.[71] At the same time, some of the problems Japanese FDI encounters are due to the greater reliance on the Japanese banking sector (compared with the US) or to the low indigenization of Japanese transplants.[72] Paralleling the Japanese government's greater willingness to protest about China's security policies, it is now also raising these economic issues more publicly with the Chinese government at all levels.[73]

According to a German economist, economic conflicts (for example over market access, anti-dumping charges, investment licenses, etc.) arise as a consequence of the close economic relationship, Japan's delay in restructuring its economy and differences over the distribution of gains, but are not indicators of a fundamentally flawed relationship.[74] However, they are also the consequences of competition and rivalry between countries which have very different political-economic systems and which are at different levels of economic development. At least some features of the trade conflict (for example market access, anti-dumping charges, but also the concurrent increase in enterprise-to-enterprise cooperation at increasingly equal level) are very reminiscent of those between Japan and the US or Europe in the 1970s and 1980s.

The Japanese–Chinese economic rivalry also has a regional dimension. The ASEAN countries want Japan to share their concern about China becoming the dominant regional economic power which attracts most FDI, particularly after China's entry into the WTO.[75] Japan is receptive to this concern, not only for economic reasons (it can not be in Japan's interest that most of its FDI goes into China), but also for political-strategic reasons.

This increasingly conflict-prone economic rivalry and competition is worrying, in our context, for the following reasons. In conjunction with other issues, these economic conflicts and rivalry can have an aggravating effect on the overall relationship at a sensitive moment. This was illustrated in 2001 by the simultaneous occurrence of Japan's imposition of extra duty on Chinese agricultural products to protect its own agriculture, the Li Denghui visit to Japan, acrimonious ODA negotiations and the visit to the Yasukuni Shrine by Prime Minister Koizumi.

This sense of competition and rivalry is also present on the Chinese side, where it adds to the existing distrust and dislike of Japan. It is nurtured by hurt pride that the former aggressor is economically more successful and that China is so dependent on it as an economic partner and model. China never accepted (at least in its political rhetoric) the 'flying geese' model of Japan and Japan's regional economic leadership strategy, but in practice China follows Japan's export-led model.[76] Recently, the Chinese public has also become agitated about suspicions that Chinese customers are treated as second rate by Japanese companies.[77] When China is not satisfied with Japan's economic activities, one hears that Tokyo wants to prevent China's growth and keep it down. The following quote by Xu Zhixian illustrates this point:

> It has deliberately substituted environmental protection for infrastructure projects in its focus of economic assistance to China and add political conditions to the assistance to prevent rapid Chinese economic growth.[78]

These economic conflicts and rivalry decrease the conflict-reducing and confidence-building function of economic enmeshment. Rather than helping to offset the tensions arising from the political-strategic rivalry, they may further reinforce them. The partial failure of confidence building is particularly noteworthy in Japan's ODA.[79] The Chinese public hardly knows about the role of Japanese ODA in China's economic development because the leadership has so far kept this information away from it. The leadership itself views Japanese ODA as Japan's moral obligation after China waived reparations in 1972. At the time, it was meant to strengthen China's position in Japan, but when China opened itself to the outside after 1978 the gesture was turned into a tacit understanding to get ODA.[80] This Chinese shift allowed Japan to use ODA as its major tool to influence China, but today its confidence-building potential has been somewhat reduced because it leaves Japan vulnerable to Chinese accusations of not giving enough aid.[81] Proper Chinese recognition is also prevented because Chinese pride has become involved: Chinese officialdom likes to refer to ODA as a 'joint economic programme' (*he zuo*) or the 'introduction of foreign capital', and this is partly abetted by the Japanese for ODA in general, '*keizai kyoryoku*' (economic cooperation), which implies the cooperation of two economic equals.[82]

Political-strategic rivalry

Japanese–Chinese political-strategic rivalry can be observed at bilateral, regional and multilateral level, partly reinforced by economic rivalry and competition. It is nourished by China's contrasting goal of a 'multilateral world', its suspicion of Japan on its own as well as in tandem with the US, and by certain engagement policies. The significant improvement of Japan–Taiwan relations in the 1990s is one important factor for the increase in Chinese distrust of Japan's true intentions in the region in general.

This rivalry is now openly recognized by many Japanese experts. The China specialist Mori Kazuko agrees with some US experts that 'political rivalry' (*kyoso*) will increase. Miyamoto Nobuo, of Nomura Research Council, asserts that 'Japan and China will not be able to extricate themselves from a relationship of political and strategic competition for the next 50–100 years'.[83] This political-strategic rivalry is also mentioned by non-Japanese China specialists. Gerald Segal detected signs of strategic rivalry as early as 1993.[84] David Shambaugh speaks of a strategic rivalry which is now in its incubation.[85] Gurtov and Hwang unambiguously say that Japan is China's principal rival for regional leadership.[86] It is not only a rivalry between Japan and China, but one which involves all major powers in the region. Japan's close alliance with the US, and its interest in keeping the US involved in and committed to Asian security, clashes directly with China's hope for a 'multilateral world'.

This rivalry is on both sides also culturally bound and reinforced. The known sinologist Eto Shinkichi speaks of Japan's 'periphery minority complex', which is expressed by a love–hate syndrome: 'When the Japanese feel that China is weak and incompetent, they accentuate the hate side of this love–hate complex by becoming arrogant. When the Japanese feel that China is stronger, they emphasize the love aspect, becoming rather servile'. [87]

On the Chinese side, it is a superiority complex deriving from their civilization and cultural pre-eminence before Japan opened itself to the West in the nineteenth century.[88] This superiority complex is not softened, but rather reinforced, by China's concurrent inferiority complex, which results from its failure during a substantial part of the last 150 years to develop economically and maintain its sovereignty.

Competition over Taiwan

In this context, one has also to look at Japan's approach to and relationship with Taiwan, which has some elements of competition for security, economic benefits and the hearts of the Taiwanese. The terms of the establishment of diplomatic relations in 1972 had allowed Japanese ambiguity over Taiwan's legal status (Chapter 1). The strengthening of Japanese–American security cooperation since 1995–6 had created a rather transparent ambiguity over the inclusion of Taiwan in this cooperation (Chapter 3). Chinese distrust about Japan's Taiwan policies was further aggravated in the 1990s by a growing relationship between Japan and Taiwan, which is also seriously affecting the efficacy of Tokyo's engagement. These Japanese policies were adopted to address US interests in Taiwan, but also to protect Japanese economic and security interests in the Taiwan area.

Before 1972, relations between Japan and Taiwan were carried by trade and the links between Japan's conservative ruling party and the Guomindang, but not so much by people-to-people contacts. This explains to some extent the enthusiasm of the Japanese people for normalizing relations with the PRC in 1972.[89] Since then, however, the Japanese feeling of affinity with (reciprocated by many Taiwanese, including the young) and concern for Taiwan has been enhanced by Taiwan's democratisation, which started in 1988, the concurrent loss of the PRC's democratic credentials after Tiananmen in 1989, Taiwan's economic success, the 1995/6 Taiwan crisis, and the astute handling of Japan by former President Li.[90] Taiwan has also benefited from the growing Japanese security concerns raised by Chinese political and military actions. Trade between Japan and Taiwan increased from US$1.4 billion in 1972 to US$28 billion in 1992, and reached US$41 billion in 1999. Between 1987 and 1992, Japan's trade with Taiwan was higher than with the PRC.[91] In 1998 Japan's trade with China amounted to 8.6 per cent of its total trade, compared with 6.9 per cent for Taiwan.[92] Japan's FDI in Taiwan was US$278 million in 1994.[93] The figures are considerable if one takes into account the difference in scale between Taiwan and the PRC. Moreover, they cannot convey a complete picture because of Japan's regional production network, as mentioned before. The number of Japanese visitors to Taiwan reached a height of 920,000 in 1996, decreasing to 830,000 in 1999; while the number of Taiwanese visitors to Japan has increased from 48,000 in 1972 to 840,000 in 1999.[94] Although political ties have weakened, there still exists an active Diet-member network through the Nikka Giin Kondankai (around 300 members, mostly LDP) and the Nikka Kondankai (around forty members, mostly from the Minshuto), the latter being established only in May 2000 by Minshuto.[95] However, the election of Chen Shuibian as president in March 2000 has led to a generational change and weakened the long-established channel between the Guomindang and the LDP. Cultural and academic ties have continued since 1972 but suffer from administrative and political obstacles due to the absence of diplomatic ties and political pressure from the PRC.[96]

At the same time, Japanese media attention towards Taiwan has dramatically increased. This is to some extent facilitated by the presence of all Japanese media in Taibei since 1999 when the PRC ended its ban on *Sankei Shimbun* having a bureau in Beijing and stopped imposing sanctions on Japanese media establishing representations in Taiwan. In addition, former President Li used his excellent knowledge of the Japanese language and his many contacts in Japan, dating back to his time at Kyoto University, to promote sympathy for Taiwan. Although the Japanese government did not allow him to visit Japan as president (he was not allowed to take up a Japanese invitation in 1994 for the Asian Games in Hiroshima), his book on Taiwan received wide attention in Japan, including a launch party with prominent figures in Japan's public life in July 1999.[97] After his retirement, Beijing put pressure on Tokyo not to allow him to accept a Japanese invitation, but in 2001 the Koizumi government allowed him a visit for medical purposes, which contributed to a worsening of Japan–PRC relations. Earlier, President Chen Shuibian had managed somewhat to undercut China's opposition to his visit to Japan as president by sending his wife and family to Japan in July 2000.[98] Several Taiwanese cabinet members visited Japan in the 1990s.[99] After his election as governor of Tokyo, Ishihara Shintaro, a known right-wing politician of the LDP, irked China's with his pro-Taiwan statements and activities, which were criticized by Beijing.[100] In this new climate, Diet-members are less inhibited from having contact with Taiwan. In October 2000 one prominent LDP member and former education minister, Hatoyama Kunio, went so far as to support Japan's recognition of Taiwan as a state and as a member of the UN.[101] Japan's reaction to Taiwan's earthquake in 1999 symbolized the new affinity for Taiwan. Japan was the first country to deliver aid to the earthquake-stricken area, and many Japanese volunteers went to Taiwan.[102] At the time Director-General Norota, of the Defence Agency, even considered the delivery of aid by the SDF as the MSDF had just provided similar goods to Turkey after the earthquake near Istanbul.[103]

Regional competition

The regional level is another arena for Japanese–Chinese rivalry. Regional competition with China involves Japan not only on the side of the US, but also on the side of other Asian countries like ASEAN and India, as we saw in the context of Japan's power balancing.

Compared to other Asians, Chinese are the most hostile to a Japanese leadership role in Asia. In an opinion poll with business executives and academics in the Asia-Pacific region (eleven countries, including Taiwan and Hong Kong), it turned out that 70.2 per cent in all the eleven Asian countries agreed to a leading Japanese role, but only 16.2 per cent did so in China and 43.2 per cent in South Korea.[104] When Prime Minister Kaifu situated Japanese–Chinese relations in a wider context in 1992 (*sekai no naka no Nihon*), this was perceived with suspicion in China as a Japanese attempt to establish itself as a big political power.[105] Rex Li argues that Tokyo's Asia strategy causes the greatest concern in China.[106] According to Kokubun Ryosei, what upset China so much about the 1996 reaffirmation of US–Japan security relations was Beijing's concern over the prospects for a higher political profile for Tokyo in the region.[107] David Shambaugh reports on a consensus view at a symposium for leading party and PLA representatives on the emerging international order and potential threats to China in the coming years, that Japan would become China's major rival and enemy, a view held by 60 per cent of the participants. By way of comparison, Russia and the US were given this epithet only by 10 per cent and 25 per cent, respectively. What makes Japan ranking so high is its economic success, the distrust originating from its negative historical legacy, Japan's geographic contiguity, its growing political assertiveness and regional/global role, and Japan's allegedly 'unclear' future policy.[108]

China's hostility to a Japanese leading role is also demonstrated by Beijing's willingness and ability to undermine Japan's regional ambitions. It partly explains Beijing's ambiguous attitude towards Japan's support for becoming engaged in regional multilateral fora like ARF, its outright opposition to Japan's proposal for regional anti-piracy cooperation, and its initial opposition to Japan's proposal for an Asian Monetary Fund (see Chapter 3). China is also opposed to the inclusion of Japan in any new Track I multilateral security group in Asia.[109] Prime Minister Hashimoto Ryutaro's visits to the US and Australia in 1997 were interpreted as joining the 'northern anchor' and the 'southern anchor' to pin down China.[110] Chinese scholars admit that their government's reluctance to respond to Japanese proposals on confidence-building measures or to get involved in trilateral or quadrilateral talks at Track I and Track II level is meant to prevent Japan from playing an expanded regional security role, legitimizing such a role or putting itself on par with others as a fully fledged power.[111] In 1998 China opposed a US proposal to invite Japan to a conference of nuclear powers in Geneva to work out a strategy after the nuclear tests by India and Pakistan.[112] Apart from weakening US supremacy, this policy of keeping Japan in a position of strategic subordination and preventing it from joining the ranks of 'normal' nations helps China to realize its ambitions of regional leadership.

Chinese experts accuse Japan of trying to contain China and to keep it down, using the 'China threat' argument.[113] One means of China counteracting this is to impress on Japan that its regional leadership ambitions are dependent on Beijing's approval and are heavily compromised by Japan's inability to own up to its historical legacy before 1945. From China's perspective, Japan cannot seek an expanded regional role and will not be qualified to play a larger role in maintaining peace and stability in the region as long as it cannot satisfy its neighbours on its past.[114] The 'history card' has here a motivational as well as an operational function. China is even quoted as arguing to other Asian partners that Japan cannot be a regional leader because it is not Asian, on the grounds that it stations US troops, conveniently ignoring the fact that other Asian countries like South Korea do the same.[115]

As a result of China's various sensitivities, and its stance against a Japanese leadership role in particular, most regional leaders are very ambivalent about policies which may have an impact on China. Dennis Roy noted ASEAN's double standard in 1994: 'A Chinese military buildup, while not welcomed, is acceptable; a Japanese defense buildup is not. ... China thus faces far weaker political constraints against building a superpower-sized military capability – an important prerequisite of hegemony – than Japan'.[116] When Japan discussed the revision of the Japan–US guidelines for military cooperation in 1997, there were many voices coming from ASEAN which warned about negative consequences for Sino-Japanese relations, including from Singapore. Singapore's prime minister, Goh Chok Tong, warned of 'grave consequences for Sino-Japanese relations if Japan did not exclude Taiwan from areas which might require it to provide logistical and non-combatant support for the US'.[117]

Global-level competition

The same rivalry and opposition can be observed at the international level. According to China, if Japan wants to become a big political power it will need

China's cooperation and support, and this requirement is used as a card to obtain a China-friendly Japanese foreign and security policy.[118] According to Yang Bojiang, in China's view Japan seeks the status of a political power by sending forces overseas, and China is therefore very skeptical about Japan's personnel contributions to PKO.[119] Beijing does not oppose Japan's quest for a permanent seat on the UN Security Council openly, but its attitude towards Security Council reform in general is lukewarm and it has refused Tokyo's repeated request for support of its bid.[120] Chinese experts assert that without China's support Japan cannot achieve a permanent seat on the Security Council, linking the lack of support to Japan's 'excessive reliance on the US'.[121]

One example of China's opposition to being engaged by Japan in multilateral organizations was the failed attempt by former Prime Minister Obuchi to invite China to the G-8 Summit in Okinawa in 2000. The issue deserves some attention because it is indicative of the bilateral rivalry and of China's ambivalent attitude towards multilateralism.

Japan's global leadership would have received a boost from Japan being instrumental in getting China in the forum, although subsequently its influence would have become relativized by China. However, China joining the G-8 would mean a much greater socialization of China than UN Security Council membership can provide, and Japan, as a G-8 member, could have used support of Chinese G-8 membership to get favours from China in other areas, including support for its Security Council ambitions. Japan's failure to include China as a guest, let alone as a new G-8 member, at the Okinawa Summit was due to China's refusal to accept Tokyo's invitation as well as to opposition from Japan's G-8 partners. Members were far from having found a consensus on enlarging their circle by including a country which was still politically and economically so far removed from them.

Japanese considerations of bringing China closer to the G-8 process go back to the beginning of the 1990s.[122] The highest-level attempt to get China into the G-8 process started in October 1997, when Prime Minister Hashimoto proposed China's invitation to the 2000 Okinawa Summit to President Clinton, who rejected it.[123] But in the end Japan's efforts were thwarted by China itself. One can only speculate about China's reasons, but they probably included concern about losing its credentials in the Third World if it was admitted into the rich man's club. The G-8 was also out of favour with China because it had supported the bombing of Yugoslavia in the spring of 1999. In China's eyes the G-8 is without international recognition and also elitist. A Chinese researcher in Beijing described the Okinawa venue as 'very delicate', obviously in view of the likelihood that Chinese participation would be interpreted as Chinese acquiescence to US bases in Japan and to the security treaty in general.[124] There may also be some historical resonances in view of China's historical suzerainty over Okinawa, which was broken by Japan during the Meiji period, as well as the territorial issue around the Senkaku Islands. But a very important political consideration was certainly the fact that the invitation came from Japan, whose regional or international leadership China does not want to recognize because of its own leadership aspirations. Moreover, in view of its own economic weakness, the de facto inferior role of Russia in the G-8 due to the considerable difference in its economic strength compared with the rest of the group does not look appealing to a country which is as conscious of prestige as China.[125] The participation of China also raises problems within the Chinese leadership concerning who would have to represent China, President Jiang Zemin or Prime Minister Zhu Rongji.[126]

Despite all the disclaimers about not intending to become a superpower or a hegemon, it is clear that China wants to become a great power (*da guo*).[127] Gurtov and Hwang dismiss Beijing's duplicity, writing that China 'wants to be treated as a great power, practices international relations like one, and has many assets of one'.[128] Amako Satoshi observes that China expressing the wish to make foreign intervention impossible means that it wants power commensurate with the world's superpower, the US. He quotes President Jiang Zemin as saying that China wants to be a big country that can exert influence on the world.[129] Moreover, not becoming a global superpower despite its phenomenal economic rise would contradict the validity of China's historical determinism towards Japan, in relation to whom it claims that big economic powers inevitably become big military powers. Ironically these repeated Chinese denials that it intends to become a superpower seem to be part of the Japanese–Chinese strategic rivalry, since Japan similarly claims that it does not want to become a big military power despite already being one.[130]

Triangular dynamics: challenges arising from the US context

The most important factor shaping Japan's engagement, particularly its Realist elements, is the Japan–US relationship. Japan cannot address the security dimension of its relationship with China on its own, because the US, with its ambitions and capabilities in the Asia-Pacific and its comprehensive relationship with Japan, has a decisive impact in promoting conditions for a peaceful outcome of China's rise. In the strengthening of Japanese–US security cooperation since 1995, we have already seen some of the dynamics of this US context, notably illustrations of Japan's entrapment/abandonment dilemma. Here I want to examine other implications of the US context within the Japanese–US, US–Chinese and Japanese–Chinese relationships. As part of this I want to look at the dynamics resulting from differences between Japan–China and US–China relations and how they impact on Japan's engagement. The question for Japan is ultimately how to respond to the dynamics resulting from these three relationships, which is crucial not only for managing the Japanese–Chinese security relationship, but in the end also for the survival of the Japan–US alliance.

Japan–US asymmetries and engagement

Japan–US asymmetries in power, security interests and political systems have certain implications for the conduct and coordination of engagement towards

China. They provide China with opportunities partially to offset its disadvantage as the outsider in the Japan–US–China triangular competition. One Japan–US asymmetry concerns subtle differences in the perception of China as a security challenge. Given the power asymmetries of the Japan–US–China triangle, one would suspect that Japan is more concerned about China as a security threat than the US. The reality is much more complicated. US analysts generally evaluate the issue of China as a military threat from an American perspective, discussing the point of time in the future when China could challenge US military supremacy in Asia or even constitute a direct threat to the US homeland. Relying mostly on a naval presence for maintaining its military position, and given the circumstance that China is particularly backward in this arms category, China's challenge looks relatively comfortable despite alarmist US media and public opinion polls, and despite China's ability to make sustaining US supremacy more costly and/or difficult (Taiwan!) in the meantime.[131] The US does not face China as a geographical neighbour, which can disrupt Japan's peace in many more ways than sending nuclear missiles. This relaxed American attitude is probably too complacent because it does not sufficiently take into consideration the practical implications of different evaluations by America's alliance partners, on which the naval presence in Asia is partially based. The US may consider the Chinese navy still far away from becoming a blue-ocean navy, but for Japanese policy-makers China's predominantly coastal navy is rather close to Japanese waters, as we have seen in the context of the disputes over the Senkaku Islands and the EEZ.[132]

In fact, as a civilian power which is primarily focused on economic interests – employing economic tools to protect these interests and playing down military means while feeling confident about the US security umbrella – there is a greater immediate concern in the public in Japan about the various implications of China's economic growth and how to employ economic enmeshment to deal with China's challenges than in the US. As a military superpower with a population highly sensitive to military strength and its relative changes, public opinion polls show greater security concerns in the US about China: in 1998, 77 per cent of Americans felt China was a threat to US national security, while only 64 per cent of Japanese believe China posed a threat to their nation's security.[133] The following quote of an official in the Ministry of Foreign Affairs is very revealing about this Japanese emphasis on economic enmeshment, as well as of the widespread misperception in Japan of the true complex nature of Japan's engagement:

> There are differences in approach between the US and Japan with regard to China policy. When we talk about 'engagement', the Japanese emphasis is closer to the true [*sic!*] meaning of engagement. If China misbehaves, then we have no option but containment, but we would like to keep it discreet.[134]

A further Japan–US difference lies in the expected scope of influence on China. Despite the strong belief in the Liberal elements of engagement, there is a difference between Japan and the US about the possibility of changing China, for reasons of practical politics as well as differences in power resources. The Japanese government is less interested in changing China's domestic politics than in exerting influence on its conduct of foreign policy. There is a lesser expectation that Western approaches to political and economic governance are all applicable to China, at least in the short and medium term. The focus on economic means to influence rather than change China also contributes to another Japan–US difference. As Sato Hideo points out:

> [T]he more leaders are inclined to believe in the ultimately salutary effect of economic development on political stability and international convergence, the more they are willing to take a long-term perspective and gradualist approach on different Chinese behaviours and violations of international norms and be more accommodative. This seems to be the case with Japan and less so with the US.[135]

Johnstone mentions in this context that Japan tends to pay more attention to its long-term aims with China than the US, which is guided more by issues like trade or human rights.[136]

The greater US expectation of changing China, backed by its comprehensive power, also creates differences in the use of economic enmeshment. Due to issues ranging from security and human rights to trade imbalances, even normal economic interactions between the US and China like trade and investment are often hostage to domestic US politics and sometimes increase rather than soothe tensions. Moreover, the US cannot employ bilateral development aid, which is the most important policy tool for Japan's engagement strategy towards China. The US cannot extend bilateral ODA to China because of its domestic laws banning such assistance to a Communist country.[137] In the past this has invited US accusations of Japan using unfair means to promote its economic interests in China against the general background of rising Japan–US competition in the China market.[138] Japan–US conflict occurred, for example, in 1979 when there were some US complaints about Japan's minimum interest rate for its China loan programme, although Japan successfully withstood US pressure.[139] Christopher Johnstone doubts whether Japan's ODA provides it with much commercial advantage because of inefficiencies and political conditions.[140] However, Japan–US tensions may rise in future, with the Chinese market becoming more contested between the two.

US multilateral aid is also curtailed because of Congressional opposition to China's human rights record and to any programme involving birth-control assistance.[141] This may not only weaken China's efforts to cope with its enormous economic, demographic and environmental problems, but also reduce the West's effort to integrate China into multilateralism. It also encourages those Chinese hardliners who believe that US policy is ultimately aimed at keeping China down and contained, and that Japan is a willing partner in this endeavour.

Different emphases on certain regional security issues may also challenge Japan's engagement. The main issue is certainly Taiwan, which is the most sensitive bilateral problem China has with both countries. Although Japan and the US both seem to accept China's position that Taiwan is part of China, to oppose Taiwan declaring independence and to insist on a peaceful resolution of the issue, the commitment to power balancing or even sanctions if China does not comply with the principle of the non-use of force shows some differences between Tokyo and Washington. These differences between Japan and the US are also recognised by Kurt Campbell, who was in charge of the Pentagon's Asia policy during most of the Clinton administration.[142] We saw in Chapter 3 that the Japanese government has ultimately decided that the value of strategic ambiguity is higher than transparency, which has been one of the justifications towards the outside for the new guidelines. But from this one cannot assume that Japan would indeed support US intervention in the Taiwan Strait.[143] The guidelines do not include an explicit guarantee by Japan to help the US in an emergency; nor do they guarantee any particular level of support which might be given. Professor Nakanishi Hiroshi, of Kyoto University, argues that this ambiguity not only helps Japan towards China, but also allows it some bargaining power towards the US.[144] Japanese domestic support for a Taiwan not dominated by the PRC or even declaring independence is totally different from the situation in the US. An outright and unprovoked attack on Taiwan by the PRC would be more likely to trigger US intervention than a PRC attack as the result of a Taiwanese move towards openly proclaimed independence. Such an attack would be more likely to see a certain degree of Japanese cooperation with US forces. But the Japanese side would always have to weigh its limited security (and domestic) interests around Taiwan and long-term security interests in a good relationship with the PRC against any wider implications for the Japan–US alliance. The military alliance with the US would suffer great, if not irreparable, damage if Japan refused to allow US troops based in Japan (including the Yokosuka-based US aircraft carrier) to be deployed if it would not provide logistical and other support as envisaged under the revised guidelines. However, there are considerable differences between Japan and the US on the necessity to counter the use of Chinese force. A senior civilian official at the Defence Agency therefore told the author that Japan and the US never agree on Taiwan and the Chinese side should decide themselves.[145]

Despite the recent warming of Japan–Taiwan relations, there is no Japanese willingness to sacrifice national security to protect Taiwan against the mainland. Nakai Yoshifumi points out that Japan's reaction to Taiwan's democratization was rather cautious compared with the US's warm embrace because for Tokyo it 'destroyed the congenial spirit of cross-strait communication'.[146] He also sees Japan–US divergences about China's allegations that conspirators are behind moves for Taiwanese independence (that is, Japanese ones), the role of Japan outside its territory (that is, Japanese territorial ambitions for Taiwan) and the deployment of TMD in Taiwan.[147] Japan refused to repeat President Clinton's publicly stated 'Three Nos' of June 1998 in Shanghai when President Jiang

Zemin visited Japan in November 1998.[148] Under the Taiwan Relations Act the US is obliged to support Taiwan's security against China, and it continues to provide weapons and military advice to the island, thus maintaining a fluctuating level of tensions with China. Japan fully shares the US policy of insisting on a peaceful and democratic settlement of Chinese reunification, but is concerned about possible US attempts to enhance Taiwan's international status.[149] There is the feeling in the Defence Agency that the US may underestimate the willingness of Taiwan to compromise with Beijing.[150] Concern about the US's image as a reliable partner, which seems so often to obsess Washington, in this case weighs much less in Japan than entrapment into the American use of force over events in Taiwan.

Another issue where the congruence of Japanese and US interests has to be carefully watched is the Korean Peninsula. Whatever tool the US chooses to use in addressing the tensions in that theatre, Japan will always be concerned about China's reaction to it, as much as it shares US concerns about North Korean missiles, nuclear proliferation and destabilizing actions. As in the case of Taiwan, Japan's post-war pacifism will also have an impact on any decision to support the use of US military force. At the moment, the Japan–South Korea–US consultations on how to meet the North Korean challenge have led to an unprecedented degree of coordination, but this may change if military action is required, or if it impacts on the position of China in Northeast Asia. The US will remember that it made a list of 1,059 logistics requests in anticipation of US military actions to deal with North Korea's suspected nuclear-weapons programme, but that Japan's government hesitated and was not even willing to impose an embargo on financial transfers from Japan to North Korea.[151] Although the strengthening of Japan–US military cooperation has brought changes to deal more positively with such requests (for example revision of the guidelines and ACSA), it is not clear what the Japanese government might be willing to do in the case of a new crisis on the Korean Peninsula.

Future developments on the Korean Peninsula may also give rise to differences between Japan and the US. The tensions created by North Korea have served Japan and the US well in adjusting the security alliance to the post-Cold War era. But Japanese–Chinese relations will suffer if the North Korean threat goes after reunification and the US insists on continuing to station troops in South Korea. China will perceive such a development as a confirmation that the main function of the Japan–US alliance is, as it always assumed, the prevention of Chinese reunification and of containing China in a more direct way. Japanese Realists, however, seek 'a united Korea that is friendly to Tokyo and Washington, that is economically viable and politically open, and that will allow token US presence to remain'.[152]

Finally, there are differences in policy-making and political style which complicate Japan's China policy. Pursuing engagement, and even more so coordinating this policy with the US, is affected by inconsistencies and changes in US foreign and security policy in general, including towards China, not only between different administrations but even within the period of the same administration. The unpredictability of US China policy is also increased by the very success of economic enmeshment, which has made both Japan and the US competitors in the Chinese market. Cossa and Skanderup argue that US–Japan economic-policy coordination towards China has been shown to be a pipedream because of different approaches.[153] In the American debate among analysts and policy-makers not only is the emphasis and the robustness with which some rather than other goals and elements of engagement are to be pursued unclear and constantly shifting, but the debate itself is also subject to domestic politics which often have more to do with scoring points against the executive than with protecting American national interests on a long-term basis, let alone the interests of close allies. Edward Luttwak cynically recommends an incoherent China policy, arguing that it would maintain the acceptability of US predominance with its allies.[154] The increasingly pronounced inclination towards unilateralism in US foreign policy can only further aggravate the unpredictability of its China policy.[155]

Aware of its lesser power, greater geographical closeness to China and concern about entrapment, reinforced by a general inclination to be less assertive and confrontational, the Japanese government is much more restrained in any open criticism of China and often even shows a more deferential attitude towards China than the US. Whereas Japan officially abstains from referring to the concept of engagement, the US has no such qualms (see above). The difference in using the name of the same policy may appear to be merely a semantic and public relations issue but, given the implications of Japan as a civilian power, the much greater importance for Japan of China as a direct and powerful neighbour and its restraint in admitting power balancing, the difference may reinforce an attitude in Japan which in the case of a military crisis could add to a split between Japan and the US on the use of force against any Chinese aggression, for example in the Taiwan Strait. At the same time, the restraint of the Japanese government in expressing its security concerns about China may prompt the American side to feel that Japan is not that concerned about China, or at least strengthen those in the US who themselves consider China not (yet) much of a military challenge from an American perspective.

Japan in the triangular vortex

Japan and most other Asian countries know that good US relations with China are essential for stability in the region as well as for good relations between themselves and China, but at the same time these gains may be offset by the negative implications of a US–China relationship which is too cosy. In a very simplistic way, one may say that bad US–China relations make Japan more important as a security partner for the US, but at the same time this heightens the danger of becoming entrapped in military power balancing against its most important neighbour, without a guarantee that the US will not change course later or even fail in a confrontation with China. US–China relations which go beyond a certain degree of cosiness (which would be hard to specify beforehand) raise the spectre of Japan's abandonment by the US in the face of regional Chinese hegemony, or at least US–China deals to the detriment of Japanese interests. In the meantime these entrapment/abandonment fears give China's leaders opportunities to play one off against the other. Both scenarios implicitly assume China's aggressiveness.

Since 1971, when Kissinger went to Beijing to prepare the normalization of US–China relations without prior consultation with Japan, Japanese experts have been obsessed by the fear of yet another kind of Nixon shock and the US agreeing with China to keep a check on Japan's growing influence in Asia. In 1999 newly declassified US documents disclosed that in 1972 President Nixon and Prime Minister Zhou Enlai discussed Chinese concerns about Japan increasing its influence in Taiwan and other Asian countries as a result of US withdrawal from some parts of Asia (see Chapter 1). Japan was, at the time, concerned about the US making deals with China which might be detrimental to Tokyo's security interests.[156] Another idea cherished by some US policymakers and experts is the use of China to counterbalance Japan's rise or to keep both Asian powers in check. In the past the most prominent proponents of the view of China as a counterweight to Japan were Nixon and Kissinger.[157] In a press conference in 1990 President Bush seemed to suggest that the US needed China as a counterweight to the growing power of Japan.[158] Although the majority of US experts are now more concerned about Japan not playing enough of a regional role, there is even today a lingering ambiguity in some US quarters about Japan's power, let alone Japan as an independent big military power – as was demonstrated as recently as in June 1999 when a memorandum prepared by the US National Intelligence Council cautioned that Japan is 'pursuing greater autonomy or independence'.[159] Tennichi Takahiko therefore aptly summarizes the dilemma of Japan's foreign policy under the Japanese–American security treaty: 'Independent diplomacy by Japan might accelerate US efforts to implement its balancing strategy, while subordinate diplomacy might lead to another "Nixon shock"'.[160] While the conservative leadership of Japan, at least, has accepted the Japan containment element of the Japan–US security alliance (former Foreign Minister Shiina Etsusaburo jokingly referred to the US in the 1960s as Japan's watchdog or '*go banken*'), there is no willingness to let China become an assistant watchdog.[161] Kan Naoto, for example, commented on President Jiang Zemin's stopover in Honolulu (where he pointedly visited the war memorial of Japan's attack against Pearl Harbour) on a visit to the US in 1998, saying that the US and China should not contain Japan.[162] Such Japanese concerns are at least indirectly fed by reports about US government officials who have tried to reconcile the Chinese government to the strengthening of the US–Japan military alliance since 1995 by referring to the Japan-containment element of a strengthened alliance.[163]

More concrete are those Japanese concerns about the US moving closer to China and at the same time away from the Japan–US alliance as the cornerstone of the US commitment to Asia. Such concerns about US–China relations were incited in the 1990s by certain moves and statements of the second Clinton administration. In October 1996 a senior administration official (assumed to be then National Security Advisor Anthony Lake) reportedly stated: 'I see China more as a natural partner than Japan'.[164] Japanese concern was also raised when in 1996 conflicting US statements were initially issued about whether or not the security treaty applies to the Senkaku Islands (see Chapter 2). US media comments in 1998 suggested that China could replace Japan as Washington's partner of choice in Asia.[165] Since President Jiang's visit to the US in October 1997, the two sides have spoken of their mutual desire 'to build towards a cooperative, strategic partnership for the 21st century'. In May 1999 Secretary Madeleine Albright spoke of a 'strategic dialogue' having begun half a decade before.[166] Some Japanese, as well as Americans, critical of the pro-China inclinations of the Clinton administration feel that the US was increasingly viewing Japan through Chinese lenses, and that there was a kind of US–Chinese bipolarity or virtual bipolarity.[167]

Most critical Japanese comments were instigated when President Clinton visited China in June 1998 without stopping over in Japan. According to some reports this was due to Chinese pressure. Nor did the President mention in China the US–Japan security treaty and its stabilizing function for Asian security.[168] During the visit the US seemed also to 'gang up' on Japan by joining with China in criticizing Japan's alleged inactivity towards the Asian economic crisis or refloating its own economy.[169] The negative impression in Japan was also reinforced by alleged Chinese contributions to Clinton's presidential re-election campaign against a background of close relations between the Democratic Party and the Chinese leadership. Other circumstances which sometimes raise concern in Japan are the level of military contacts between China and the US, which during certain recent periods have ranged from military exchanges to sales of American weapons to China.[170] Even after Tiananmen there were reports about US military technology reaching China directly or indirectly.[171] An internal US Department of Defence document called 'Game Plan for 1999 US–Sino Defense Exchanges' outlined more than eighty activities by the US and PRC militaries planned for 1999; the plans were interrupted by the accidental bombing of the Chinese embassy in Belgrade.[172]

While the Japanese media was full of speculations about 'Japan passing' or even 'Japan nothing' in the wake of Clinton's diplomatic snub to Tokyo in 1998, the Ministry of Foreign Affairs was trying hard to play down the matter. The Gaimusho spokesman referred to the various summit meetings between the leaders of the three countries in 1998 and presented Clinton's China visit as part of the strengthening trilateral dialogue.[173] Sakanaka Tomohisa, then director of the Research Institute for Peace and Security, said that when Clinton and PRC President Jiang Zemin agreed to stop targeting missiles at each other, all of Asia benefited. At the same time he was certain that the US cannot stand in Asia without the cooperation and presence of Japan.[174] But even a pro-American China expert like Soeya Yoshihide wondered about the long-term effectiveness of such Japanese restraint as the Gaimusho was showing.[175]

Not least because of these events in 1998, public opinion in both countries is divided about the importance of the other country in relation to China, and even about the ultimate objective of the Japan–US security treaty. According to a 1998 poll, more than 60 per cent of the Japanese believe the United States is more important to Japan than China, whereas only 47 per cent of Americans say US–Japan relations are more crucial than US–China ties. The survey indicates that 16 per cent of Japanese believe the relationship with China to be more important than that with the United States. But 37 per cent of Americans polled view relations with China as more important than those with Japan.[176] Two years later, the importance of China has grown further on both the Japanese and the US side, but even more on the US's. Asked which country among the US, Japan and the PRC will be more politically important in the future, 49 per cent of Japanese respondents said they feel the US will be more important, while about 31 per cent chose the PRC; 49 per cent of Americans said they feel the PRC will be more politically important in the future, while 43 per cent favoured Japan. Only in the economic field did 50 per cent of American respondents feel Japan will be more important, while 43 per cent chose the PRC.[177] A poll of the general US public and of US opinion-makers commissioned by the Ministry of Foreign Affairs about the importance of Japan, China and Russia today predictably comes up with a more favourable figure for Japan (see Table 4.1).

Apart from the special circumstances in 1998 there are several other factors that account for the rising US rating of China's importance and for the perceived rapprochement between the US and China. There is, first of all, a long American fascination with China, which has been reinforced by China's recent rise to become a superpower in the future on the basis of its geography, demography and economic potential. In addition, China is already now a nuclear power with 3 million men under arms, permanent membership on the UN Security Council, and association with a series of issues which raise regional and international security concerns and which often can only be addressed with China's cooperation. In contrast to these factors, Japan is smaller in terms of demography and geography, it has not managed to translate its

Table 4.1 A poll on the following question: Thinking of all Asian countries, which country in this region is the most important partner of the US?

	1999 (%)	*2000 (%)*
General public:		
Japan	51	53
China	21	22
Russia	8	6
Opinion leaders:		
Japan	75	72
China	19	20
Russia	2	3

Source: http://www.mofa.go.jp/region/n-america/us/survey/survey2000html

economic power into commensurate political and military power (thanks to the US!), and the recent Asian economic crisis has cast serious doubt about its future economic potential and its ability to exert economic leadership in Asia. Its potential for political leadership continues to be hampered by the legacy of the past.[178] In a way the US can take Japan for granted as a loyal ally, whereas more attention must be paid to China, as the country which challenges the US regional and global preponderance in a much more tangible and credible way, while at the same time it has become an indispensable partner on regional and global issues.

Japan's continuing economic problems since the beginning of the 1990s have created the impression that the country is in decline and therefore not that important for future US calculations.[179] Not only did the 1997 Asian crisis affect China much less than most other Asian countries, but China's abstention from devaluating the Yuan gave it a 'hero' image in some quarters in the US.[180] In addition, economic enmeshment of China by the US has created strong US economic interests, which have time and again provided sufficient momentum to overcome serious political differences but which have also led to what has been criticized as 'a new moral equivalence among trading states'.[181]

The regular downturns in US–China relations (for example after the 1989 Tiananmen-related sanctions or after the 1995 granting of a US visa to President Li Denghui and the April 1996 Hashimoto–Clinton Joint Declaration) also create a momentum of apparent US appeasement: after a downturn the US administration feels it has to be more generous to China in order to repair relations with a country which it considers so important for its national interest. This was certainly the case in the second Clinton administration, and it found expression in the pro-China moves in 1998 mentioned above.[182] Some US experts even blame China's skilful manipulation of the US for neither Tokyo nor Washington having followed up aggressively on the momentum created by the 1996 Joint Declaration because of concerns over Beijing's hostile reaction to the reinvigoration of the bilateral security relationship.[183] Zhang and Montaperto even speculate that China's warning may have prevented the US and Japan from forming an explicit and permanent anti-China alliance.[184] It is interesting to observe that at the autumn 1997 US–China Summit in Washington more than seventy specific agreements covering a wide range of bilateral issues were produced, including policies involving third countries (for example nuclear proliferation in South Asia, the Asian financial crisis). This compares with thirty-three projects at the Obuchi–Jiang Summit in Tokyo in November 1998.[185]

China is not only skilfully exploiting these US circumstances, but considers the US as its most important counterpart. The reasons are economic, military and political. China perceives the US as the country which is on more of an equal footing with itself than Japan, or at least China wishes that to become the case. Confident about their growing political, economic and military strength, many Chinese seem to have the impression that US–China relations will surpass the importance of US–Japan relations, or that they have already done so.[186] In the meantime, China also encourages those in Japan who consider Japanese–Chinese relations to be as important as Japanese–US relations.[187] At the same time, China is not averse to giving Japan the impression of wanting to gang up with Tokyo against Washington if a good opportunity presents itself. It has shown considerable understanding for Japan's earlier frustration over US complaints about trade disputes with Japan. Funabashi refers to some Chinese attempts to appeal to Japan's nationalism because of US bases on its territory.[188]

In view of the analysis of China's policies so far, including that in previous chapters, China's triangular tactics may be summarized in the following way:

- to 'befriend the distant states as well as associate with the near one';[189]
- to exploit the differences between Japan and the US to gain points and to weaken the Japan–US alliance;[190]
- to exploit the weaknesses of the Japanese position (entrapment/abandonment dilemma, Japan's historical legacy, Japan's economic difficulties while China is growing fast);[191]
- to emphasize the importance of China for Japan to legitimize its regional and global ambitions (for example its quest for a permanent seat on the UN Security Council);[192]
- to maintain a US-first diplomacy despite a series of bilateral disputes over Taiwan, human rights, Chinese trade surpluses, espionage scandals, etc., but never to allow either relationship (China–US; China–Japan) to deteriorate too much;
- to reinforce the US inclination towards 'bipolarity' and try to replace Japan as the more important Asian partner of the US;
- to reinforce US suspicion about Japan's 'true' intentions for the future and cultivate the hope of those Americans who consider China to be useful as a counterweight to Japan;[193]
- to delegitimize Japan's security concerns about China.

China's decreasing acceptance of the Japan–US alliance

China's shifting position on the Japan–US alliance and the concurrent delegitimization of Japan's security concerns deserve some further analysis because they are so fundamental to the viability of Japan's engagement towards China. We saw in Chapter 3 that the Taiwan issue, in both the revised guidelines and Japan's TMD participation, has been the most public issue in China's criticism. This is reflected in a marked decrease in the acceptance of the new Japanese–US security relationship and Japan's increased regional role. While the Chinese statements to be presented in what follows were obviously aimed at preventing the full development of a closer Japan–US military alliance, they have also led to a greater Japanese–Chinese confrontation over the future of the Japan–US alliance.

With the start of the Japanese work on the revision of the guidelines shortly after the Hashimoto–Clinton Joint Declaration, the tone of China's criticism became harsher.[194] Zhao Jieqi, the deputy director of the Institute of Japanese Studies (Chinese Academy of Social Sciences), alleges that the 'nature and function' of the bilateral security treaty would be changed from 'coping with threats' to 'containing regional conflicts' and it would become a kind of Asian NATO under US guidance.[195] This concern is also linked to Chinese concern raised by NATO's eastward expansion.[196] Moreover, the role of Japan in the alliance would change from defending its own territory (the concept of defensive defence) to providing logistic support to a much wider area and a greater number of contingencies.[197] Zhao Jieqi therefore concludes that Japan's role is changing from being a 'shield' to that of becoming an 'auxiliary spear' of the US.[198]

Japan was also accused of helping the US to maintain its domination of the world and run against the post-Cold War tendency towards a multipolar world.[199] On the basis of this interpretation of the 1996 Joint Declaration and the ensuing legislation to implement the new guidelines, China has been accusing Japan and the US of continuing the Cold War in Asia and containing China by extending the security treaty beyond the scope of the two countries to target third countries, that is China.[200] Going against the 'tide of history' in an age of growing multipolarity and multilateralism, the Japan–US security treaty is referred to as a relic of the Cold War.[201] In the declaration of the Chinese Foreign Ministry of 18 April 1996, just after the Hashimoto–Clinton Joint Declaration, the Chinese side warns that the Japan–US security treaty should not go beyond the bilateral framework, otherwise it would cause trouble in the region.[202] One of the generic statements used by the Chinese side to express its concern was the stated hope that the Japan–US security treaty would not become 'inconsistent' with the 'sound development of relations between Japan and China'.[203] The Chinese criticism skilfully played the dynamics of triangular relations by focusing on Japan rather than the US. While Wang Jisi asserts that the major Chinese target is still the US as the militarily stronger one, the Japanese side perceived the criticism as being more directed against them than against the US. Some speculated that this was due to China valuing Chinese–American relations more highly, while others interpreted it as China's tactic to drive a wedge between Japan and the US and to weaken Japan's willingness to enact the new guidelines.[204] Michael Yahuda of the London School of Politics and Economics (LSE) suspects that it is a general Chinese tactic because Southeast Asians have also observed that Chinese pressure about American alliances is directed towards them rather than the US.[205] In the case of the application of the guidelines to Taiwan, it is sometimes argued that the Chinese side has stronger emotional and practical reasons to oppose Japan rather than the US.[206] The cultivated official Japanese ambiguity about the legal status of Taiwan (see Chapter 1) is seen by some Chinese as of greater concern than the US position, which is much clearer because of the existence of the Taiwan Relations Act and official statements.[207]

In 1999 the Chinese press used an official Japanese statement on the possibility of a pre-emptive attack to warn further against any move by Japan to become more offensively oriented. In March 1999 Norota Hosei, then director of the Defence Agency, declared in a Diet interpellation that the Japanese Constitution allowed Japan to attack other countries first in the case of an imminent and unlawful attack.[208] This interpretation of the Constitution by the government is not new. Norota's remark was made in the context of the missile threat from North Korea. The China Daily reported that the South Korean minister of national defence, Chun Yong-taek, warned against such a strike without prior consultation with Seoul and the *Renmin Ribao* criticized Norota.[209] In the summer of the same year it became known that after the Nodong launch in 1993 the ASDF had studied the possibility of an attack, assuming that it would be done without US support.[210]

But the Chinese reactions after the Hashimoto–Clinton Joint Declaration also show a growing inability or willingness, at least among China's leaders and officials, to understand Japanese security concerns within the Japan–US–China triangular context.[211]

Thomas Christensen writes that the Chinese tend not to recognize that particular Chinese actions or weapons developments may influence Japanese defence policies. Instead, such concerns are dismissed as 'excuses' by Japan's hawks to justify the country's military build-up.[212] Looking, for example, at China's argument against Japan's involvement in TMD – that Japan is allied with a nuclear power – it is obvious that Japan as a separate state is not given the legitimacy of having its own security concerns. A Japanese diplomat told the author that China cannot understand Japan's concern, understand various viewpoints, or put itself into the position of another country.[213]

Japan's record of aggression, and/or its allegedly unrepentant attitude towards this legacy, is also used to delegitimize Japanese security concerns towards China. Sha Zukang, director of the Bureau for Arms Control and Disarmament in the Chinese Foreign Ministry, in July 2000 dismissed Japanese concerns about Chinese missiles as unjustified by pointing out that Japan had killed 30 million Chinese.[214] Michael Yahuda of the LSE therefore remarked:

> China's concern to elicit an appropriate apology for wartime aggression and atrocities does not absolve its leaders from recognizing that Japan may have legitimate security needs. Unfortunately there is no sign of any such acknowledgment.[215]

China's difficulty in understanding Japanese concerns about China's security policies is also cultivated by the constant propaganda that China has only benevolent intentions and is still so backward that no Chinese security policy can possibly be considered as offensive by other countries. The media and official declarations incant that China will never be a superpower, never seek hegemony, and will always be a force for peace and stability. Basically there is the self-satisfied feeling that China was badly done to in the past and therefore cannot do bad forever thereafter. Japan was one of the main culprits and is now allied to the US, which wants to maintain its predominance in Asia by keeping China down.

As a result, China's previous – albeit grudging and ambivalent – support for the Japan–US security treaty has considerably eroded. Chinese academics and decision-makers are unwilling to accept that Japan is allowed by the US to play a bigger security role in Asia.[216] They suspect that this increased role may ultimately allow, or necessarily lead, Japan to free itself from US control and embark on a new military role in East Asia. The Japan–US alliance is now seen less as a cap on the bottle than an eggshell for the development of a strong military power.[217] In 1997 Chinese officials started openly to express the view that the continuation of the US presence in Asia would not help regional stability.[218] Questions are being asked among Chinese specialists about whether security treaties can really exist without a declared enemy, particularly in the post-Cold War era.[219]

Japanese deference and restraint

Finally, we have to reconsider the value of Japan's restraint or deference for its engagement policy towards China. Japan's restraint in exercising its considerable power in conflicts of interest with China is a strikingly prominent feature of Japan's engagement policy which is difficult to explain purely in terms of Realism or Liberalism. In the previous chapters we have seen several examples of Japan reacting to China in a way which may be called deference or restraint although it had the upper hand in terms of power and/or resisting would not have involved much political cost. While there is already a strategic Japanese–Chinese rivalry, Japan seems often to be waging this rivalry in a very restrained way, whereas China maximizes its relatively inferior power resources. But, despite these power asymmetries in Japan's favour, deference has been particularly obvious and enduring. Of course, any economically, politically or militarily strong state encounters limits to its ability to deploy economic, political or military power. The amount of power necessary to achieve the intended goal may surpass the available power resource, or there may be insufficient domestic support (for example competing demands, fear of counterproductive results, low level of interest, etc.). However, there are cases in Japan's China policy which are beyond obvious or straightforward calculations of resources and interests and which are better explained from a Constructivist perspective.

To start with, the Japanese government officially declines to refer to its China policy as 'engagement' (*kanyo*), and instead refers to the normative goals of its China policy and to the Liberal-institutional policy tools to achieve them.[220] This is all the more interesting as the US administration under Clinton always referred to 'engagement' and one would normally expect Japan to do the same. Obviously, the closest Japan–US cooperation is in the area of military power balancing, which is exactly the area which Japan would not like to emphasize publicly. The close association of engagement with US policy, notably under the Clinton administration, would only reinforce China's tendency to consider Japan not as an independent actor but as an integral part of US China policy. The association of engagement with military power and thus the Japanese–American security alliance might evoke China's latent concerns about Japanese militarism and US hegemony, eclipsing the intentions of the Liberal elements of engagement. The abstention from using the term 'engagement' is even adhered to in joint Japan–US statements which refer to China, such as the Hashimoto–Clinton Joint Declaration of April 1997. The declaration simply expresses the expectation that China will perform a constructive role (*kensetsuteki yakuwari o hatasu*) in international and regional politics. In the previously mentioned LDP's first draft for a long-range foreign policy, 'Japan's Strategy towards the Asia-Pacific Region' in 1997, the word 'engagement' appears only in the English translation, whereas the Japanese text speaks of cooperation (*kyoryoku*).[221]

There is a long list of other examples of deference and restraint shown in official (but also private) contacts with China[222]. The Ministry of Foreign Affairs, with its China expertise, has been the most responsive to Chinese sensitivities among the government agencies. This ranges from using geographical names acceptable to China, to 'taking into consideration relations with China' when refusing non-profit organization (NPO) status to Falungong's representatives in Tokyo or not allowing the Dalai Lama to visit Japan.[223] In the security field we have seen above how much 'understanding' Japan showed for China's concern after the NATO bombing in Serbia and Kosovo in 1999. In the territorial conflict about the Senkaku Islands, the Japanese government has refused oil-exploration licenses to Japanese companies in Japan's EEZ.

As we saw in Chapter 1, there are many sources for deference apart from the history legacy which are either China-specific (for example cultural affinity, cultural debt, war guilt) or not (for example a general tendency of conflict avoidance), and which often reinforce each other (war guilt, pacifism, sympathy of the Japanese Left for Chinese Communism). Again, China has been very astute in exploiting these features for its benefit.[224] As a specialist of Chinese history, Yokoyama Hiroshi also refers to China's demand for 'kowtow diplomacy' (*dogeza gaiko*) from Japan, which reinforces Japan's deferential inclinations.[225] Finally, Japan, as an Northeast Asian society, is deeply influenced by the notion of hierarchy, and China was traditionally the leading political and cultural state.[226]

As a result of China's assertive diplomacy and security policy, an increasing number of Japanese opinion leaders, diplomats and politicians are questioning whether Japan's deference is (still) appropriate. The question is not raised necessarily for reasons of nationalism and Japan's increased self-confidence – although that plays a role to some degree – but because it is seen as ultimately ineffective in managing relations with China, inviting misunderstandings and provoking China to put more pressure on Japan. Thomas Christensen even warns that accommodating behaviour towards China (which he observes with the Clinton administration) can provoke Chinese 'hypernationalism'.[227] There is a realization that conflicts can no longer be solved by avoiding clarity and not making clear Japan's interest.[228] Ozawa Ichiro recommends in one of his five guidelines for Japan's diplomacy that his country makes clear its diplomatic aims and strategy for the twenty-first century with regard to China.[229] In Chapter 2 I mentioned the generational change among politicians which resulted in a much more critical attitude towards China. Moreover, the rising widespread concern about China in Japan has shown that the traditional accommodative, cautious or even deferential attitude in the face of China's assertive security policy has bred so much resentment in Japan that a negative backlash has been caused which generates pressure for a radical shift. This resentment has been vented sometimes with unexpected force: for example, an LDP panel delayed consent to a loan to China in August 2000, and Finance Minister Shiokawa Masajuro burst out in July 2001 with the opinion that Japanese aid should be used more effectively and that huge amounts of aid should not be granted to countries that possess nuclear arms and are building up their military capabilities. A senior member of the LDP Foreign Affairs Department with personal connections to China was quoted as saying that the delay of the loan in August 2000 was an 'epoch-making event: 'It is no longer acceptable to adopt diplomatic approaches that curry favour with China just for the sake of keeping friendly ties.'[230] The Ministry of Foreign Affairs has come under particular criticism, with even the China-friendly Nonaka Hiromu saying that '[t]he ministry has yet to get rid itself of the diplomacy of humiliation'.[231]

There is also the wish to have a 'normal' relationship with China, which was, for example, expressed by the LDP Dietman Hayashi Yoshiro, chairman of the Japan–China Dietmen's Friendship League, who said in 1999 that there would be no equality if China is always right and that the bilateral relationship could only be a normal one if both tell each other what must be said.[232]

Even China's leaders realize the backlash from pushing Japan too hard into a corner (notably over the past), particularly after the visit of President Jiang Zemin to Japan in November 1998. Thereafter, China became more conciliatory. The Chinese realize that causing official Japan to hold back on stating its opinion also distorts their own insights into the domestic forces which shape Japanese attitudes towards China.

Moreover, Japanese deference risks reinforcing Chinese distrust of Japan. In view of China's own Realist approach to international relations, Japanese deference only enhances their suspicions of Japan, which are in any case aroused because of their historical determinism (economic superpowers becoming military superpowers; Japan is bound to become a militarist power again because of its flawed attitude towards its past). If Japan shows so much deference despite its great economic and military power, it may be hiding something or playing for time until the US allows it to become a militarist power again.

In conclusion, deference is one of the main features of Japan's China policy; it initially had a positive effect on Japanese–Chinese relations in general and on the security relationship in particular by smoothing off the Realist edges of engagement, but it has become a negative factor against the background of China's developments since the 1990s.

Conclusions

We have seen that the general debate about the merits of engagement between the Realists and the Liberals is still open, and that both sides can provide good reasons for being right in the absence of a final outcome where China has become either an aggressive or a well-integrated power. Analysing the negative dynamics arising from the complex nature of engagement, notably within the Japan–US and the triangular frameworks, we have seen many counterproductive results of engagement which endanger the very tools and objectives of the various elements of engagement. The growing competition and rivalry between Japan and China is partly an outcome of engagement policies, and partly arises independently of them. Particularly worrying for Japan's Realist engagement policies is China's gradual distancing from its previous implicit and sometimes even explicit acceptance of the Japanese–US security alliance as the 'lesser' evil. The analysis of this array of dynamics evolving from the interactions among Japan's engagement policies, China's policies and the regional/international environment does not, however, lead to any conclusions on whether engagement in future is misguided or impossible.

Conclusions

> If Japan and China cooperate, they can support half the Heavens.[1]
>
> Deng Xiaoping

> I am more pessimistic about the future of US–China relations than I have been for several decades.[2]
>
> William Perry, former US Secretary of Defence, in 2001

The 1990s and the beginning of the twenty-first century have witnessed a marked deterioration in Japanese perceptions of China because of the latter's security policies and other developments negatively affecting Japan's security interests. This deterioration has been reinforced and facilitated by domestic changes in Japan and rising uncertainties in the international environment. As a result, Japan started to voice its dissatisfaction with China's military modernization, rising military budget, non-transparency of military modernization, nuclear weapons tests and China's greater assertive territorial claims. Facilitated by worrying developments on the Korean Peninsula and the need to adapt the Japan–US security alliance to the post-Cold War era, towards the middle of the 1990s the Japanese government started to put greater emphasis on military power balancing of China when it revised its National Defence Programme Outline in 1995, and since 1996 it has taken measures to strengthen the alliance with the US. In addition, it started to support multilateral security approaches in Asia, embarked on political power balancing in Asia and used its economic aid in a more focused way to influence China's policies towards Japan.

To analyse these Japanese reactions in an appropriate framework I have referred to an understanding of engagement which reflects more realistically its true complex nature: economic and political enmeshment (providing China with economic and political incentives to integrate into the regional/international political and economic system) and political and military power balancing (political front-building, SDF and the Japan–US security alliance). The latter is meant to support the former by deterring China from going against internationally recognized norms (for example the use of force), and at the same time is to provide an insurance in case of the failure of economic and political enmeshment. By conceptualizing engagement thus, from a Realist, Liberalist and

Constructivist perspective it is possible to appreciate the existence of coercion and force, which is so often ignored in analysing and evaluating engagement. Given the political system of the major powers which profess to engage China, engagement is simply not possible without China having to take account of the presence of their military deterrent. Through its own military force, as well as by supporting US forces in and around the country, Japan has maintained a deterrent which has also always had a deterrent function against China. One can therefore reject the assertion that Japan has accepted 'all the assumptions of realism but applied them purely in the economic realm'.[3] This comprehensive understanding of engagement, and taking into consideration the historical determinism and Realist thinking of China's leaders and foreign and security experts, allows us to take better account of China's perception of engagement, which is essential to gauging the efficacy of this policy. In addition, by using Realist, Liberal and Constructivist approaches I discussed critically the assumptions of the various elements of engagement and dissected the diverse dynamics created by this policy.

On the basis of this analysis, is it possible to judge Japan's engagement policy a success in ensuring its security interests *vis-à-vis* China? Is this policy sustainable? What are the costs?

A first caveat is that Japan's engagement policy cannot be considered in isolation because other major powers are pursuing similar policies, and the US is the most important among them. The US is not only pursuing a very similar engagement policy, but it is also an enabling as well as conditioning factor for Japan's own policy. So far, engagement has been successful because peace has been preserved between Japan and China, the domestic stability of China has been maintained, and China has become integrated into the global economy to an extent which in some respects is more far-reaching than has Japan, and this seems not to be reversible without very high costs being incurred by the Chinese political and economic system. However, while engagement can be credited – to some unquantifiable extent – with having prompted China to move in the intended direction and has been helpful in setting a welcome process in motion, none of the major security issues described in Chapter 2 (except for the moratorium on nuclear tests) has been solved: China's military modernization is still benefiting from annual budgetary increases of over 10 per cent, the transparency of its security policy has hardly improved despite token gestures by China, the territorial disputes still exist, China's naval incursions into Japan's EEZ continue despite a promise of prior notification, and China has still not renounced the use of force to solve the Taiwan issue and the territorial claims in the South China Sea. Concerning non-traditional security challenges there is also no change, although a dialogue and even some cooperation have started on transboundary pollution and crime. Moreover, due to China's growing economy these non-traditional security challenges are bound to increase. It is therefore still possible that in the future some elements of engagement may be considered responsible if China diverts significantly from accepted norms of international behaviour.

The same differentiation between starting a desired process and achieving success has to be made when evaluating political enmeshment: the bilateral relationship between Japan and China has become much more substantial; the economic relationship has achieved wide-ranging interdependence, which dampens political disputes; there are now more fora between the two countries at Track I, II and III levels, etc. But trust has not yet been established for old as well as new reasons: Japan's historical legacy (in combination with China's historical determinism and instrumentalization of the 'history card') and Chinese vehement opposition to the strengthened Japan–US military alliance, as well as rising strategic rivalry. China is only a reluctant and reserved participant in multilateralism. But this does not mean that the process cannot be successful, only that more effort may be needed on all sides.

Particular attention has therefore to be paid to the centrifugal dynamics which the process of engagement is engendering due to its complexity, inherent contradictions, ambiguities and triangular aspects. The major source of negative dynamics derives from trying to equilibrate military and political power balancing, and economic enticement/confidence building and restraint *vis-à-vis* a Chinese leadership which is still steeped in Realist thinking and historic determinism, and has major revisionist goals in terms of its international status and the integrity of its national territory. The danger always exists that engagement reinforces (at least for tactical purposes) the conviction that international relations is a zero-sum game and requires greater Chinese economic and military power.

Another major source of negative dynamics threatening to undermine engagement (but at the same time the source of hope for a peaceful and prosperous China) is China's rapid economic growth as a developing country of tremendous demographic and geographic dimensions. According to Realism, but also empirical evidence, China's economic growth is allowing China to modernize its military potential and to pursue its revisionist goals with greater vigour. The international environment (notably US positions, supported or not by Japan) and the achievement of balanced political and economic development in China (on which Japan has a considerable impact) will decide in the end whether Liberalism and the 'democratic peace theory' is right, or whether Realism is.

China's economic growth potentially carries the seeds of its own destruction in terms of ecological unsustainability, political unsustainability (the creation of social imbalances and dislocation) and economic unsustainability (for example the collapse of the underlying economic model of export-led and FDI-driven development due to an international recession). Some of these negative dynamics are partially already in existence and affect Japan to some extent by way of transboundary pollution, illegal immigration, transboundary crime and economic losses. But while Japanese experts do not rule out China's economic failure and perceive such an outcome as very serious for Japan's security and welfare, they are also concerned about China's economic success challenging its identity as a civilian power and as the world's second-biggest economy.

Both the Realist and the Liberal elements of engagement contribute to yet another negative dynamic, which is the increasing strategic/political and economic rivalry between Japan and China. Military and political power balancing, notably the strengthening of Japan–US military cooperation, with its perceived impact on Taiwan, will reinforce China's military and political assertiveness and Realist thinking. For the Chinese leadership the Taiwan issue has become so sensitive that it cannot afford to be seen to be soft on it.[4] While the increasing integration of China into regional and global institutions can be partly attributed to Japan's political enmeshment policies, we have also seen that it leads to competition and rivalry in the UN (for example, China opposes Japan's quest for a permanent UN Security Council seat), as well as to China working against cooperative security proposals within regional fora. Increasing trade frictions are relevant in our context, since they can contribute to a general atmosphere which may facilitate the violent eruption of security disputes. Closer economic relations and the growth of mutual interdependence are bound to lead to frictions, particularly between countries with different political-economic systems, different levels of economic development and different sized economies. Moreover, given China's size, but also Japan's current economic difficulties, which are leading to ODA cuts and Japan's lesser importance as an economic partner for China (if not possibly to a regional economic meltdown), Beijing's economic success will increasingly reduce Tokyo's ability to influence its giant neighbour politically.

While Japan's restraint and deference towards China have for a long time been a means of soothing the contradictions of engagement, reducing conflicts of interests and offsetting the strength of Beijing's 'history card', they are now increasingly perceived as outdated, ineffective and even as becoming counterproductive. The restraint and deference shown by Japan's leaders in the face of China's assertive security policy have bred resentment in Japan, and a negative backlash has been caused which generates pressure for radical shifts. Moreover, Japanese deference has bred Chinese distrust of Japan's true intentions because of China's own Realist approach to international relations. The resulting drive in Japan to have a 'normal' relationship with China by communicating more clearly and openly would be a positive outcome of this negative dynamic (but not necessarily always and/or in the immediate future). China seems to understand the negative dynamics of Japanese restraint and deference, and may refrain from further fomenting this negative backlash.

Finally, the comprehensive relationship with the US creates some negative dynamics. We have seen that the different mix of engagement policy tools, different perceptions of China and other asymmetries sometimes generate centrifugal dynamics which not only impact negatively on Tokyo's engagement, but ultimately also on the future shape and even survival of the Japan–US military alliance. The crucial issue is Taiwan, but a military move by China in the disputed EEZ of the East China Sea or even against the Senkaku Islands could become a severe test of the military alliance. Apart from the Taiwan issue, it is Japan–US TMD cooperation which vividly illustrates the negative dynamics of the strengthened alliance.

The triangular Japan–US–China framework is, moreover, creating centrifugal dynamics which Japan finds it difficult to deal with, while China, despite its disadvantaged position as the 'outsider', skilfully plays on them.

In sum, when considering the sustainability and costs of Japan's engagement one has to weigh the strength of the positive process towards China becoming a stakeholder in regional and global peace and stability, and adopting the norms of democratic countries, against the strength of the negative dynamics generated by even the successes of engagement, let alone by its complexities and ambiguities.

Challenges

There are therefore several interrelated challenges to the sustainability of engagement. The most important challenge is the unresolved issue of Taiwan, which may reach a dangerous point in the near future because of strengthened US support for Taiwan under the Bush administration, which encourages a growing momentum in Taiwan towards independence, while China is facing a change in leadership in 2002 and sees its options to achieve national reunification running out. Since the integration of Hong Kong into the PRC and the new developments in the PRC–Taiwan relationship, Chinese determination and willingness to use force if needed seems to have become a greater possibility for many Japanese. Japan would prefer the status quo, but the issue is whether this is realistic in the light of the changes in Taiwan started under former President Li Denghui to assert the island's independence.[5] Tanaka Akihiko points out that China is a status-quo power, but that the domestic developments in Taiwan are increasingly challenging China. These developments, rather than the military balance, are for him the issue which may trigger China's use of force.[6] There are speculations in Japan that the domestic timetable of Chinese leadership elections, the ongoing military preparations, China's accession to the WTO (engaging the Western world in China to an extent that sanctions in the case of a military solution to reunification become difficult to support), and even China's attempts to improve relations with Japan after 1998 are all preparations to solve the Taiwan issue by force if peaceful means fail.[7]

Closely related is the growing US unilateralism, which is certain to encourage Chinese leaders and foreign-policy experts in their belief that might is right and that China therefore has to continue to enhance its military capabilities. Betts and Christensen remind us of frequent US interventions in its own hemisphere, which most Americans consider 'legitimate, defensive, altruistic and humane', and warn that 'if China acts with the same degree of caution and responsibility in its region in this century as the United States did in its neighbourhood in the past century, Asia is in for big trouble'.[8] Casting doubt on the 'democratic peace' theory, Paul Wolfowitz mentions the US as one example of a democracy 'behaving with bellicose aggressiveness', and warns about a more democratic China reflecting popular nationalist pressures.[9] In addition to serving as a negative model for great-power behaviour, US unilateralism is weakening multilateralism at a critical time when political and economic enmeshment policies are trying to involve China in global and regional regimes.[10] One of the most important issues is the fate of the Anti-Ballistic Missile (ABM) Treaty, which is linked to China's core security interests: Taiwan and the survival of its nuclear deterrent. But even without US unilateralism, rising tensions in the US–Chinese relationship since 2001 and the Bush administration weakening international regimes, we face a major challenge to economic multilateralism since China finally joined the WTO in 2001. In addition, multilateralism is the only way to make the US accept the ultimately inevitable abandonment of its determination to be the dominant Asian power. As long as the US does not accept this abandonment, there can be no way of accommodating China as a new regional power and of avoiding some of the negative dynamics of engagement.

Finally, there is the sheer complexity and ambiguity of engagement, which is difficult for one country to manage but in effect requires various degrees of cooperation and cooperation with other countries. Even within Japan, engagement has to cater to the explicit and implicit goals of a rather disparate group of overlapping policy constituencies. To name just a few: one that wants security for Japan, one that wants to maintain the Japan–US comprehensive relationship, one that wants to maintain Japan's military establishment in the post-Cold War era, and one that wants to benefit commercially from the economic aspects of engagement.

At this critical juncture, Japan finds itself politically, economically and socially weakened. With its consumer-oriented and rapidly aging society, Japan's vigour and adaptability will be increasingly challenged by China, which has a much larger population strata of young and dynamic people who also find it easier than their Japanese counterparts to become internationally effective. Okamoto Yukio laments that China's young people, educated in the US and Europe in the post-Cultural Revolution era, are quite capable of coming up with new ideas, whereas Japan is now beginning to fall behind in terms of its ability to take on new challenges.[11] Japan's decade-old economic crisis has finally started to bite seriously, absorbing the attention of the whole political system and diminishing Japan's ability to employ its most powerful and US-independent policy tool – that is, economic enmeshment. The realignment of the political power configuration which started in 1993 is not yet concluded and still absorbs an inordinate amount of Japan's politicians' time, reinforcing rather than reducing the parochial nature of Japanese foreign and security policy. At such a time it is even more difficult for the political leadership to gather the strength and courage to deal positively with one of the greatest millstones and exploitable vulnerabilities of Japan's foreign and security policy towards China, the historical legacy. In addition, the bureaucracy, which traditionally ran the political day-to-day work rather autonomously, has also been weakened by frequent political changes and corruption scandals. The China School in the Gaimusho is forced to adopt a firmer position towards China to maintain its credibility, and it is not inconceivable that China's policies and attitude towards Japan may turn the China School against China in the same way as happened with the Soviet Union and the Gaimusho's old Soviet School. The Gaimusho overall is weakened by scandals and by the bruising experience with the former foreign minister Tanaka Makiko, who turned out to be more divisive than she was reform oriented. This and the reduction in ODA (administered to a large part by the Gaimusho) effectively removes the major force in Japanese foreign and security policy to stem the tide of increasingly relying on military and political power balancing. These developments also reduce Japan's ability to assume a long-term perspective in pursuing engagement, while the short-term effects of economic reform are likely to increase social unrest and political repression. Japan's long-term perspective would be particularly needed if China's WTO membership, as often predicted, leads to serious sectoral and social problems in the short term.

Scenarios

I suggest four possible scenarios for the future of Japanese–Chinese relations :

- Japan managing to skilfully equilibrate the diverse elements of engagement;
- Japan accepting China's predominance in Asia and making itself accepted by scaling down the military alliance with the US (bandwagoning);
- Japan further integrating itself into the Japan–US military alliance and strengthening political and military power balancing against China;
- Japan developing its own autonomous military power and trying to assume a posture of neutrality and a role as mediator among the powers in Northeast Asia.

Which of these four scenarios is more likely depends mainly on the development of China–US relations and China's ability to promote balanced political and economic development. However, the last scenario seems to be the least likely: first, given Japan's nature as a post-industrial consumer society, its lack of political leadership, its historical legacy, its enmeshment in international interdependencies (economically, politically, culturally), its deepening economic crisis and its record of aligning with the strongest power during the last 150 years, there does not seem to be much room for it to become a neutral and autonomous military power which would be accepted by either China or the US. The idea of Japan as a mediator or bridge between East and West has always had some residual resonance in Japan, and it has also been proposed by some Japanese.[12] There have been a few Japanese attempts at actively mediating conflict between the US and China, but without success.[13] Tennichi Takahiko dismisses the idea of Japan as a mediator because Japan is merely a messenger between China and the US in the absence of it being able to articulate an agenda, having a universally applicable culture, etc.[14] Japan lost a great deal of time in establishing an impressive longstanding record of ability and sincerity (for example in coming to terms with its past) while its economic power was at its peak and that of China much lower. There is therefore now not much likelihood of China accepting such a Japanese role: while China may welcome any Japanese move which could weaken the US or US–Japan relations, it would be reluctant to give Japan the opportunity to expand its regional or global role by playing a mediating role between Beijing and Washington.

The first scenario is the most optimistic. Twomey assumes such an outcome and speaks of Japan's 'circumscribed balancing defined by a propensity to avoid strong countervailing alliances, to ignore an opponent's growth in peripheral geographic areas and issue areas, and to avoid offensive strategies'.[15] However, he does not appreciate sufficiently the implicit need to make very difficult decisions concerning the negative dynamics and challenges described above, which would require strong and wise Japanese political leadership, a situation which is not evident at the moment. Such a scenario would depend even more on China managing to find the right balance between its political and economic development, on Western engagement policy being calibrated in the right way, on China moderating its nationalism and revisionism, on the successful handling of possible instabilities in the region by all concerned parties, and on the US being willing to cede considerable political, military and economic power to China. Despite the enormous assumptions underlying it, this outcome cannot be totally excluded, even if there may be many difficulties and conflicts in the interim. The strongest force behind it is China's growing involvement in the world economy and the increasing number of stakeholders in China's middle class, as well as business sectors outside China (notably in the US). If the Taiwan issue could be resolved in an way that is acceptable to China as well as the US, the chances of this scenario would increase significantly. But as Aaron Friedberg warns, one cannot place too much faith in the collective human capacity to learn correctly from history.[16]

The second scenario, bandwagoning, has considerable plausibility on the assumption that US importance for Japan weakens (either because of US withdrawal from its security commitments, economic decline, or even linking up with China in bipolarity), that China's political and economic rise continues, and that the rest of Asia gradually accepts China's hegemony. As Pyle observed, Japan has historically tended to ally itself with the strong ascendant dominant power and adjusted its policies to this power.[17]

The first possibility, US withdrawal from its security commitments, could occur as the result of a catalytic event (for example the failure of US military intervention in the Taiwan Strait, or US frustration with Japan over not sufficiently supporting such an intervention or one on the Korean Peninsula). Another reason may be imperial fatigue: China's current military potential has already started to make US predominance in Asia more difficult and costly, and this development is bound to continue if the US simply wants to maintain the current power status quo. The current campaign against terrorism in the wake of the terrorist attacks in the US absorbs many political, economic and military resources, and China can be a very useful ally in view of its own problems with Muslim irredentism. It would be foolish for the US to compare China with the former Soviet Union, and to argue therefore that the West only has to be tough and risk an arms race on the assumption that China will in the end fail like the Soviet Union. China's economic foundation is much stronger and more promising despite all the risks. Moreover, 1.3 billion Chinese failing is an even more daunting prospect than 285 million Soviets failing.

The possibility of the East and Southeast Asian states bandwagoning with China seems to be supported by the prediction of many observers, even if such warnings are often only intended to encourage the US to exert countervailing pressure to prevent such a development. Samuel Huntington expects China to become the regional hegemon, with Asian states knowing how to adapt to it without sacrificing too much national independence. According to him, the Asian states have to choose between 'power balanced at the price of conflict' and 'peace secured at the price of hegemony'.[18] Denny Roy speaks of the prevalence of appeasement by the Southeast Asian states because they assume that nothing can be done or strong policies only would make China angry.[19] Murai Tomohide thinks that the countries in Southeast Asia would bend towards China if Beijing used military pressure.[20]

There is also some reserved and conditional acceptance of bandwagoning with China among the Japanese. Tennichi Takahiko considers it acceptable for Japan to consider a Pax Sinica if China becomes a democratic country and pursues free trade while the US loses its power.[21] Inoguchi Takashi does not exclude the possibility that the US may leave regional security in Asia to a democratic China, and that Japan would then have no reason not to follow its historical inclination to join the regionally preponderant state.[22]

The most likely scenario for the time being is the third one, which is encouraged and supported by concern about developments in China and in US–Chinese relations, as well as by Japanese political and economic weaknesses. It would depend on the successful management of the most dangerous negative dynamics arising from engagement. But this scenario is not likely to last long, either because China's successful economic and political development makes Japan's reliance on US protection and on US regional hegemony unnecessary or unacceptable to China or even to Japan (a democratic China is likely to be as nationalistic as the US today), or because Japan feels forced into bandwagoning with China due to a rise in intolerable military tensions between the US and China.

Policy recommendations

Nothing is historically predetermined and any prediction is impossible in view of the inability to quantify the various dynamics precisely and to simulate their interplay at a given moment in the future. There are ways for Japan to make positive contributions to promote the more peaceful scenarios. The responsibility of the bilateral security relationship lies, of course not only with Japan, but also with China and the US, but Japan should choose those areas where it has the greatest means and can have the greatest impact.

First, Japan should strive to prevent Japanese–Chinese economic rivalry from poisoning an already difficult bilateral relationship. Trade disputes are a natural but only a transitional and partial phenomenon, as we have also witnessed between Japan and the US, as well as Japan and Europe in the 1970s and 1980s. At the same time, we now see an increasing number of various kinds of Japanese–Chinese enterprise cooperation which make the bilateral economic relationship more equal and interdependent. Japan will have to ask itself whether its economic well-being is at risk because policies pursued to achieve China's economic development may harm the regional and global economic framework, or whether China's economic development will lead to Japan having to defend more strongly – or even abandon – its present economic power status and concede an increasing number of commercial sectors to China. For the former, Japan may find (even if not a perfect and notably timely) recourse in the international trade regime (for example WTO's dispute-settlement system). Beijing will ultimately realise that contravening international economic norms and standards is against its own long-term interests. Losing its status to China may hurt Japan's national identity as the world's second-biggest capitalist economy, but it is a development which Japan just has to accept as an inescapable historical development, and one which it has inflicted on others before. It should see this challenge as a means and an additional motivation to restructure its economy and its social organization. Chinese immigration should be directed in such a way that it enhances mutual understanding while helping Japan to restructure and revitalize its economy. It would be better for Japan and China to consider economic competition as a means of developing their own individual strengths and becoming stronger in the process overall, though not necessarily in each economic sector, rather than view this competition as a zero-sum game. Finally, cooperation with the European Union would strengthen Japan's efforts to integrate China in a more binding way into international economic (but also political) organizations and arrangements.

Second, Japan should try more seriously to diffuse the territorial dispute over the Senkaku Islands and the EEZ in the East China Sea, and to prevent it from becoming a flashpoint or a convenient tool for China to exert pressure on Japan. Simply continuing the game of each side not recognizing the EEZ border of the other side is no longer helpful, and Japanese companies are losing out. Tokyo should propose joint exploration of the energy resources in the area and shelve the sovereignty issue, so that Chinese as well as Japanese oil and gas companies benefit from the contested area, and such cooperation could help with confidence building. Such a proposal should be made as early as possible, before Chinese companies no longer have any interest in Japanese exploration and pipeline technology. Once joint exploration and production have begun, the territorial issue will be less urgent and both governments will be more able to reduce the influence of their respective nationalists.

Third, Japan has to recognize more squarely its past aggression against Asia, particularly against China and Korea. This is not about demanding continuous apologies, but in the first instance about avoiding actions – like official government visits to the Yasukuni Shrine and allowing revisionist textbooks – which give the impression that Japan does not admit its responsibility for having caused tremendous harm to many Asians. Without such honesty, Japan will not gain full credibility and trust from its Asian neighbours, and this will allow China to continue to play the 'history card' in order to divert attention from its unfriendly security policies and will prevent the trust-building function of political and economic enmeshment.

Fourth, Japan has to communicate more openly and clearly with China, and encourage the latter to do the same by its own example as well as by exhortation. For this to be possible, all Japanese players will first have to understand, prioritize and discuss among themselves and with other concerned countries what Japan's security interests are and what repercussions they have at the bilateral, regional and global levels. The Japanese have to help themselves and their Chinese counterparts to understand that in an ever closer relationship between two very different countries differences of interest are natural and legitimate, but that they cannot be aggregated by silence, deference, emotional outbursts, incantations of general principles or accusations about past aggression. Deeper and more meaningful exchanges (at all levels, official as well as private) are, however, only a first step towards addressing differences of interest, mutual ignorance and misunderstandings.

Finally, Japan has to recognize that, due to the mounting negative dynamics arising from the Japan–US security alliance, it cannot simply continue to strengthen military cooperation with the US. Apart from the resulting strains on Japan's domestic security consensus and the costs to its national sovereignty (particularly in the case of TMD cooperation, but also in maintaining the current strength of US forces in Okinawa), deepening Japan–US security cooperation will increasingly appear as containment of China, which cannot help to integrate China into the concert of East Asian powers. Just 'explaining' to China the inoffensive intentions of the new guidelines and their non-geographic meaning is not convincing and contradicts Japan's insistence on Chinese transparency in its security policy.[23]

In the case of TMD, the Japanese will have to decide soon whether they want to deploy or not, or whether China has been sufficiently restrained by regional arms-control measures.[24] TMD may offer incentives to discuss a range of arms-control and confidence-building measures to which China may react positively, particularly if China's main concern about Taiwan could be ruled out by Japan and the US.[25] Japan should clarify what the purpose of TMD will be after the North Korean missile threat has gone, and what the connectivity between TMD and US plans for NMD are.[26] TMD is only part of the increasingly confrontational China policy (other examples are weakening the ambiguity about the US defending Taiwan or publicly calling China a strategic competitor) under the new Bush administration and Japan will have to work harder on its military ally to stem this tide in its own interest. Japan has to explain to the US that it cannot tolerate the same degree of confrontation with China which the US can afford as a distant and solitary superpower.

The most important task for Japan is to help to open up the rigid bilateral alliance system in Northeast Asia. Funabashi Yoichi commented that '[I]n the post-Cold War years, the biggest challenge for alliances is whether or not they can get Russia and China into the international community as full members'.[27] In view of the inevitable challenge to the current security architecture after the reunification of the Korean Peninsula, Mochizuki and O'Hanlon argue that Japan will not be comfortable with an alliance designed primarily to deter China once the Korea problem is solved.[28] The alternative is for Japan to clearly and meaningfully discuss these problems with the US through an enhanced and much broader security dialogue, to use regional cooperative security approaches in order to integrate China into the work of maintaining regional stability, and to prompt the US to be more positively involved in helping China to cope with its serious economic and ecological problems. A precondition for this is US willingness to gradually abandon its desire to be the predominant force in Asia and to broaden rather than limit its array of policy tools, notably in the multilateral arena. The best hope for Japan is a growing American involvement in regional cooperative security efforts as a constructive participant who is different because it has more to contribute than the others, not because it is an offputting hegemon.

Japan has therefore to work towards a regional security system which includes China from the start and which takes care of some core Chinese security interests towards Japan as well as towards the region as a whole.[29] There is interest in China in such a regional security system (even in one proposed by the US!), as the following remarkable quote of the Chinese vice-premier, Qian Qichen, seems to show:

> China attaches great importance to the positive role played by the United States in resolving regional problems. China hopes that the United States establishes a new basic concept of security centring on mutual confidence, mutual interests, equality and cooperation to maintain regional peace and stability.[30]

Such a security system would eventually have to take over important functions of the two Northeast Asian security alliances which the US has with Japan and Korea (for example the 'cap in the bottle' function). It would also have to allow the establishment of a post-Korean reunification security arrangement. However, Japan, Korea and the US cannot simply merge the two alliances. A first step might be the creation of an East Asian equivalent of 'Partnership for Peace', as has been developed in Western Europe.[31] Former Secretary of Defence William Perry supports such a system:

> I don't think we can create in East Asia a regional security organisation like NATO, but we can hope for a setup like Europe's 'Partnership for Peace'. As Secretary of Defense I wanted to establish such a setup in Asia , but it ended in failure [*fushubi ni owatta*] … China's participation in any such setup is indispensable.[32]

There have been several Japanese proposals in these directions, but more radical approaches are needed. Sato Hideo suggests the establishment of a

Pacific security community to help maintain a 'healthy tension between Realist and Liberal approaches in the China policies of Tokyo and Washington'.[33] Hashimoto Kohei, a security specialist at the PHP Research Institute, suggested an Asian security framework which would, for example, address China's concerns about energy supply and the security of sea lanes of communication (SLOC).[34] Michishita Narushige proposed separate consultative and cooperative security links between China and the Japan–US alliance and China and the South Korea–US alliance, similar to the NATO–Russia Permanent Joint Council.[35] Nakasone Yasuhiro spoke of the need to have next to the Japan–US security system an Asian security dialogue organization that includes China.[36] The leader of the Democratic Party, Hatoyama Yukio, proposed an Asia-Pacific multilateral security system.[37]

For Japan to play a constructive role in integrating China into the regional security environment and thus to protect its security interest, such ideas would have to be pursued more vigorously and imaginatively. The foundations of the various elements of engagement towards China and their impact on all involved players are constantly shifting and therefore demand adaptation if engagement is not to degenerate into containment with mere decorative enmeshment policies. Only by involving China in the construction of a new regional security architecture can the whole region leave the world of Bismarck and nineteenth-century Europe!

Notes

Introduction

1 Morton I. Abramowitz, Funabashi Yoichi and Wang Jisi, *China–Japan–US: Managing the Trilateral Relationship*, Tokyo: Japan Center for International Exchange, 1998, p. 55.

2 Alastair Iain Johnston and Robert S. Ross, *Engaging China. The Management of an Emerging Power*, London: Routledge, 1999, p. xii.

3 For a critical review and rethinking of security, see Muthiah Alagappa (ed.), *Asian Security Practice. Material and Ideational Influences*, Stanford: Stanford University Press,1998, ch. 1. See also Keith Krause, 'Broadening the Agenda of Security Studies: Politics and Methods', *Mershon International Studies Review*, no. 40, 1996, pp. 229–54.

4 For a discussion of core values of national survival, see Muthiah Alagappa, op. cit., p. 39.

5 For Japan's concept, see John Chapman, Reinhard Drifte and Ian Gow, *Japan's Quest for Comprehensive Security: Defence, Diplomacy & Dependence*, London/New York: Frances Pinter/ St Martin's Press, 1983.

6 Muthiah Alagappa, op. cit., p. 689.

7 For a discussion of these two approaches, see Eric Heginbotham and Richard J. Samuels. 'Mercantile Realism and Japanese Foreign Policy', *International Security*, vol. 22, no. 4, spring, 1998, pp.. 172–3.

8 James Shinn (ed.),*Weaving the Net. Conditional Engagement with China*, New York: Council on Foreign Relations Press, 1996, p. 4. See also Peter Van Ness, 'Alternative US Strategies with Respect to China and the Implications for Vietnam', *Contemporary Southeast Asian Studies*, vol. 20, no. 2, August 1998, p. 159; Zalmay Khalilzad, *Congage China*, Santa Monica: Rand Corporation, 1999.

9 Dibb, Friedberg and Betts cited in Muthiah Alagappa, op. cit., p. 5.

10 Johnston and Ross, op. cit., pp. xiv–xv.

11 Johnston and Ross, op. cit., pp. 14–15.

12 For a list of ten goals of 'conditional' engagement, see James Shinn, op. cit., p. 4.

13 Thomas Berger, 'Set for Stability? Prospects for Conflict and Cooperation', *East Asia Review of International Studies*, vol. 26, no. 3, July 2000, pp. 405–28.

14 On Japan's pacifism, see Peter J. Katzenstein, *Cultural Norms and National Security*, Ithaca, NY: Cornell University Press, 1996; and Thomas U. Berger, *Cultures of Antimilitarism. National Security in Germany and Japan*, Baltimore, MD: The Johns Hopkins University Press, 1998.

15 Hiroshi Yokoyama, *Chugoku o muda ni shita eiyu tachi*, Tokyo: Kodansha, 1999, pp. 250–3.

16 See also Aaron L. Friedberg, 'Will Europe's Past be Asia's Future?', *Survival*, vol. 42, no. 3, summer 2000, p. 148.

17 Takuma Takahashi, 'Economic Interdependence and Security', in Mike M. Mochizuki (ed.), *Toward a True Alliance. Restructuring US–Japan Security Relations*, Washington, DC: Brookings Institution Press, 1997, p. 119.

18 Joanne Gowa therefore argues that 'free trade can disrupt the pre-existing balance of power among the contracting states' (Joanne Gowa, 'Rational Hegemons, Excludable Goods, and Small Groups: An Epitaph for Hegemonic Stability Theory', *World Politics*, vol. 41, no. 3, April 1989, p. 323).

19 Glenn H. Snyder, 'Alliance Theory: A Neorealist First Cut', *Journal of International Affairs*, vol. 44, no. 1, 1990, pp. 103–24.

20 For the game theory of Rapoport, see Gu Xue Wu, *ASIEN*, October 2000 p. 8.

21 *Ibid.*, p. 7.

22 The impossibility of an equal relationship among the three countries is, for example, recognized by the former diplomat Kunihiro Michihiko, who thinks only stabilization is possible (Kunihiro Michihiko, 'Nichi-Bei-Chu sankoku kankei wa torakku 2 kara', *Gaiko Forum*, November 2000, p. 52).

23 Hideo Sato, 'Japan's China Perceptions and its Policies in the Alliance with the United States', *Journal of International Political Economy*, vol. 2, no. 1, March 1998, pp. 1–2.

24 See, for example, Takagi Seiichiro's critical comments on triangular thinking in 'The Japan, China, US Triangle and East Asian Security. Symposium Report', *Japan Echo*, vol. 26, no. 3, June 1999, p. 20.

1 Japanese–Chinese relations under Cold War conditions

1 For an explanation of this dichotomy, see Reinhard Drifte, *Japan's Foreign Policy for the 21st Century. From Economic Power to What Power?*, Basingstoke: Macmillan, 1998, pp. 25–6.

2 *Foreign Relations of the United States 1951*, vol. 6, part 1, Washington, DC: US Government Printing Office, 1971, pp. 827–8. For further details on Yoshida's thinking on China, see Reinhard Drifte, *The Security Factor in Japan's Foreign Policy, 1945–1952*, Ripe, Sussex: Saltire House Publications, 1983, p. 128.

3 Reinhard Drifte, *The Security Factor in Japan's Foreign Policy*, op. cit.

4 *Ibid.*, p. 129.

5 For a well balanced discussion of various dimensions of the Nanjing massacre, see Dajing Yang, 'Convergence or Divergence? Recent Historical Writing on the Rape of Nanjing', *The American Historical Review*, vol. 104, no. 3 June 1999, pp. 842–65.

6 For a list of denials of Japan's acts of aggression in Asia between 1986 and 1995, see Mayumi Itoh, *Globalization of Japan. Japanese Sakoku Mentality and US Efforts to Open Japan*, New York: St Martin's Press, 1998, p. 73.

7 For a comparison between Japan and Germany on dealing with the past, see Ian Buruma, *Wages of Guilt*, London: Jonathan Cape, 1994.

8 A very illustrative example is the circumstances surrounding the apology adopted on the fiftieth anniversary of the war by the House of Representatives.

9 Kaneko Hidetoshi, 'Tenno hochu no butai ura', *Ajia Jiho*, July 1992, pp. 2–3.

10 For a critical analysis of this issue, see Yokoyama Hiroshi. *Chugoku o muda ni shita eiyu tachi*, Tokyo: Kodansha 1999, pp. 242–50.

11 On the tactical aspect, see Kokubun Ryosei (ed.), *Nihon, Amerika, Chugoku: Kyocho e no shinario*, Tokyo: TBS Britannica, 1997, p. 30.

12 See, for example, Osaki Yuji, 'Arata no Nitchu kankei no kochiku', in Kokubun Ryosei (ed.), *Nihon, Amerika, Chugoku: Kyocho e no shinario*, op. cit., p. 211.

13 Caroline Rose, *Interpreting History in Sino-Japanese Relations*, London: Routledge, 1998.

14 Tanaka Akihiko, *Nitchu kankei, 1945–1990*, Tokyo: Tokyo Daigaku Shuppankai, 1991, p. 166.

15 On Japan's pacifism, see Peter J. Katzenstein, *Cultural Norms and National Security*, Ithaca, NY: Cornell University Press, 1996; and Thomas U. Berger, *Cultures of Antimilitarism. National Security in Germany and Japan*, Baltimore, MD: Johns Hopkins University Press, 1998.

16 Wu Xinbo, 'The Security Dimension of Sino-Japanese Relations', *Asian Survey*, vol. 40, no. 2, 2000, p. 307.

17 Hideo Sato, 'Japan's China Perceptions and its Policies in the Alliance with the United States', *Journal of International Political Economy*, vol. 2, no. 1, March 1998, p. 17.

18 Michael Green and Mike Mochizuki, *The US–Japan Security Alliance in the 21st Century*, Washington, DC: Council on Foreign Relations, July 1998, p. 27. Available at http://www.foreignrelations.org/studies/transcripts/usjapan.html.

19 This information is based on an interview with Sadoshima Shiro, director of the China Division, 14 April 1999.

20 Reinhard Drifte, *The Security Factor in Japan's Foreign Policy*, p. 130.

21 Saitoh, Shiro. *Japan at the Summit. Japan's Role in the Western Alliance and Asian Pacific Co-operation*, London: Routledge, 1990, p. 21.

22 Christopher Howe (ed.), *China and Japan. History, Trends, and Prospects*, Oxford: Clarendon Press, 1996, p. 48.

23 For a Chinese perspective on this alignment, see Jianwei Wang and Xinbo Wu, *Against Us or With Us? The Chinese Perspective of America's Alliances with Japan and Korea*, Stanford, CA: Asia/Pacific Research Center, Stanford University, May 1998. Available at http://www.stanford.edu/group/APARC/publications/papers/Wangfu.pdf.

24 Released US documents disclosed, however, that the Lyndon B. Johnson administration feared that Japan might go nuclear because of China's nuclear test (see Sam Jameson, 'Combating the Nuclear Taboo in Japan', *IIPS News*, vol. 10, no. 4, fall 1999, pp. 4–5). The prime minister, Sato Eisaku, used the Chinese nuclear deterrent as a means of winning the US nuclear guarantee, stating that Japan would have the right to acquire nuclear weapons if China had them (*Japan Times*, 25 May 1998).

25 John Welfield, *An Empire in Eclipse. Japan in the Postwar American Alliance System*, London: Athlone Press, 1988, pp. 190–1, 196, 199.

26 Shiro Saitoh, op. cit., p. 16.

27 *Ibid.*, p. 46

28 Caroline Rose, *Interpreting History in Sino-Japanese Relations*, p. 48.

29 Newly released documents show, however, that Japan even then followed a 'dualistic diplomacy' (*niju gaiko*) (Ijiri Hidenori, 'Nitchutai kankei e no shin shikaku', *Chugoku21*, vol. 10, no. 1, 2001, pp. 63–4.

30 Soeya Yoshihide, 'Taiwan in Japan's Security Considerations', *China Quarterly*, no. 165, March 2001, p. 136.

31 Ogata, Sadako, *The Business Community and Japanese Foreign Policy: Normalization of Relations with the People's Republic of China*, in Robert A. Scalapino (ed.), *The Foreign Policy of Modern Japan*, Berkeley, CA: University of California Press, 1977, pp. 175–203. For a general account, see Soeya Yoshihide, *Nihon no gaiko to Chugoku, 1945–1972*, Tokyo: Keio Gijuku Daigaku Shuppankai, 1997.

32 Press Conference, 16 October 1998 (website of the Japanese Ministry of Foreign Affairs).

33 On China's suspicion about Japan's territorial ambitions in Taiwan today, see Nakai Yoshifumi, *Policy Coordination on Taiwan*, in Nishihara Masashi (ed.), *The Japan–US Alliance. New Challenges for the 21st Century*, New York: Japan Center for International Exchange, 2000, p. 88.

34 Interview with Tanaka Akihiko, 28 March 2001.

35 For an exhaustive analysis of these unofficial contacts, see Phil Dean, *Japan–Taiwan Relations, 1972–1992: Virtual Diplomacy and the Separation of Politics and Economics*, University of Newcastle-Upon-Tyne 1997, PhD thesis, p. 112.

36 The 1998 edition of *Defense of Japan* even put inverted commas around the title of Li Denghui (p. 47).

37 Amako Satoshi, 'Nihon kara mita Taiwan mondai to tenkanki no Nittai kankei', *Kokusai Mondai*, no. 488, November 2000, p. 54.

38 *Japan Times*, 24 April 1999; James Mann, *About Face. A History of America's Curious Relationship with China from Nixon to Clinton*, New York: Alfred A. Knopf, 1999, pp. 43, 89.

39 Frank Ching, 'Economic Dimensions of Tripartite Relations', in Susan C. Maybaumwisniewski and Mary A. Sommerville (eds), *Blue Horizon. United States–Japan–PRC Tripartite Relations*, Washington, DC: National Defense University, 1997, p. 180; Qingxin Ken Wang, 'Recent Japanese Economic Diplomacy in China', *Asian Survey*, vol. XXXIII, no. 6, June 1993, p. 629.

40 Qingxin Ken Wang, "Recent Japanese Economic Diplomacy in China', p. 628.

41 Christopher Howe (ed.), *China and Japan. History, Trends, and Prospects*, Oxford: Clarendon Press, 1996, p. 62.

42 Victor D. Cha, *Alignment Despite Antagonism. The US–Korea–Japan Security Triangle*, Stanford, CA: Stanford University Press, 1999, p. 105.

43 For the strong Chinese support of Japan's territorial interests against the Soviet Union, see Wang Jianwei and Wu Xinbo, *Against Us or With Us?*, op. cit., pp. 17–18.

44 *Asahi Evening News*, 27 June 1973; *Yomiuri Shimbun*, 9 March 1975.

45 Michael Pillsbury, *China Debates the Future Security Environment*, Washington, DC: Institute for National Strategic Studies, National Defense University, 2000, p. 113.

46 Quoted in Wang Jianwei and Wu Xinbo, *Against Us or With Us?*, p. 20.

47 Okabe Tatsumi, 'Nitchu kankei no kako to shorai', *Gaiko Forum*, February 2001, p. 15.

48 *Yomiuri Shimbun*, 10 November 1982; quoted in Nakai Yoshifumi, 'Chugoku no 'kyoi' to Nitchu, Nichi Bei kankei', in Amako Satoshi (ed.), *Chugoku wa kyoi ka*, Tokyo: Keiso Shobo, 1997, p. 112.

49 Okabe Tatsumi, 'Nitchu kankei no kako to shorai', op. cit., p. 20.

50 Wang Jianwei and Wu Xinbo, *Against Us or With Us?*, p. 16.

51 Quoted in Tanaka Akihiko, *Nitchu kankei, 1945–1990*, p. 135.

52 Wang Jianwei and Wu Xinbo, *Against Us or With Us?*, p. 27.

53 Quoted in Tanaka Akihiko, *Nitchu kankei, 1945–1990*, pp. 127–8; See also Wang Jianwei and Wu Xinbo, *Against Us or With Us?*, p. 15.

54 Wang Jianwei and Wu Xinbo, *Against Us or With Us?*, p. 21.

55 Takagi Seiichiro, 'In Search of a Sustainable Equal Partnership: Japan–China Relations in the Post-Cold-War Era', *Japan Review of International Affairs*, vol. 13, no. 1, spring 1999, p. 22.

56 Tanaka Akihiko, *Nitchu kankei, 1945–1990*, p. 132.

57 U. Alexis Johnson, George R. Packard and Alfred D. Wilhem, *China Policy for the Next Decade. Report of the Atlantic Council's Committee on China Policy*, Boston, MA: Oelschlager, Gunn & Hain, 1984, pp. 92–3.

58 For details, see William T. Tow, 'Sino-Japanese Security Cooperation: Evolution and Prospects', *Pacific Affairs*, vol. 56, no. 1, spring 1983, pp. 51–83.

59 Interview with Japan's first defence attaché, Yoshihara Mizuho, *Japan Times*, 17 September 1974.

60 *Daily Yomiuri*, 9 December 1984; *Jane's Defence Weekly*, 23 February 1985.

61 *Japan Economic Journal*, 25 April 1987.

62 Wang Jianwei and Wu Xinbo, *Against Us or With Us?*, p. 23.

63 Takagi Seiichiro, 'The Chinese Approach to Multilateral Security Cooperation in the Asia-Pacific Region', *Ajia Taiheiyo sekai to Chugoku. Kaihatsu no naka no ningen*, Series Chugoku Ryoiki Kenkyu no. 10, p. 25.

64 For the economic issues, see Laura Newby, *Sino-Japanese Relations. China's Perspective*, London: Routledge, 1988, ch. 2.

65 For a detailed analysis, see Caroline Rose, *Interpreting History in Sino-Japanese Relations*, ch. 5.

66 *Ibid.*, p. 143.

67 For an account of the *kokaryo* issue, see Tanaka Akihiko, *Nitchu kankei, 1945–1990*, pp. 155–8.

68 See Reinhard Drifte, *Japan's Foreign Policy*, London: Royal Institute of International Affairs/Routledge, 1990, p. 29. For a Japanese account see Nakanishi Hiroshi, *Sogo anzen hosho senryaku no saikosei*, in Kokubun Ryosei (ed.), *Nihon, Amerika, Chugoku: Kyocho e no shinario*, pp. 85–134.

69 Xinhua News Agency, in *FBIS* 27 August 1985; quoted in Harry Harding, *China and Northeast Asia. The Political Dimension*, Lanham: University Press of America, 1988, p. 29.

70 Harry Harding, *China and Northeast Asia. The Political Dimension*, p. 54.

71 Hanns Maull, 'Germany and Japan: The New Civilian Powers', *Foreign Affairs*, vol. 69, no. 5, 1990, pp. 91–106, text here from pp. 92–3; Yoichi Funabashi (ed.), *Japan's International Agenda*, New York: New York University Press, 1994.

72 Richard Rosecrance, *Rise of the Trading State*, New York: Basic Books, 1986.

73 Hanns Maull, *Germany and Japan*, pp. 92–3.

74 For more details about this process, see Reinhard Drifte, *Japan's Foreign Policy for the 21st Century*.

75 For the functionality of ODA to cover over these disputes, see Nakai Yoshifumi, *Chugoku no 'kyoi' to Nitchu, Nichi Bei kankei*, p. 112.

76 For the difference, see Wakisaka Noriyuki, *Nichi Bei no tai Chu keizai kyoryuoku*, in Kokubun, Ryosei (ed.), *Nihon, Amerika, Chugoku: Kyocho e no shinario*, p. 239.

77 Takagi Seiichiro, 'In Search of a Sustainable Equal Partnership', p. 23.

78 Harry Harding, *China and Northeast Asia. The Political Dimension*, p. 54.

79 For an excellent account of official Japanese reactions, see Tanaka Akihiko, *Nitchu kankei, 1945–1990*, pp. 172–6. See also Sohma Katsumi, *The Process of Foreign Policymaking in Japan: The Case of its Relations with China*, Boston, MA: PhD thesis, Boston University, 1999, p. 171.

80 Christopher Howe (ed.), *China and Japan. History, Trends, and Prospects*, p. 77. On the weak moral position, see Research Institute for Peace and Security (ed.), *Asian Security 1990–91*, London, 1990, p. 117.

81 Tanaka Akihiko, *Nitchu kankei, 1945–1990*, 1991, p. 174.

82 Akio Watanabe, *Japan's Position on Human Rights in Asia*, in S. Javed Maswood (ed.), *Japan and East Asian Regionalism*, London: Routledge, 2000, p. 81.

83 James Mann, *About Face*, p. 196.

84 Tanaka Akihiko, *Nitchu kankei, 1945–1990*, pp. 174–5.

85 For Japanese sanctions, see Allen S. Whiting and Jianfei Xin, 'Sino-Japanese Relations: Pragmatism and Passion', *World Policy Journal*, winter 1990–1, p. 108.

86 *Asian Security 1990–91*, op. cit., p. 117. Dennis Yasutomo, *The New Multilateralism in Japan's Foreign Policy*, Basingstoke, 1995, pp. 72–3; Kojima Tomoyuki, *Gendai Chugoku no seiji. Sono riron to jissen*, Tokyo: Keio University Press, 2000, pp. 362–3; Akio Watanabe, *Japan's Position on Human Rights in Asia*, op. cit., pp. 82–3.

87 Dennis Yasutomo, *The New Multilateralism in Japan's Foreign Policy*, op. cit., p. 74.

88 Takagi Seiichiro, 'In Search of a Sustainable Equal Partnership', op. cit., p. 23. See also Tanaka Akihiko, *Nitchu kankei, 1945–1990*, op. cit., p. 178.

89 Saori N. Katada, 'Why Did Japan Suspend Foreign Aid to China? Japan's Foreign Aid Decision-making and Sources of Aid Sanction', *Social Science Japan Journal*, vol. 4, no. 1, April 2001, p. 45.

90 Dennis Yasutomo, *The New Multilateralism in Japan's Foreign Policy*, op. cit., p. 73.

91 Katsumi Sohma, *The Process of Foreign Policymaking in Japan*, op. cit., p. 201.

92 Kojima Tomoyuki, *Gendai Chugoku no seiji. Sono riron to jissen*, op. cit., p. 363.

93 For an excellent account of the preparations for this visit, see Yoshibumi Wakamiya, *The Postwar Conservative View of Asia*, Tokyo: LTCB International Library Foundation, 1999, pp. 268–91.
94 Allen S. Whiting and Jianfei Xin, 'Sino-Japanese Relations', op. cit., p. 109.
95 Takagi Seiichiro, 'In Search of a Sustainable Equal Partnership', op. cit., p. 25.
96 For a detailed account of the Scowcroft mission, see James Mann, op. cit., pp. 205–9.
97 Andrew J. Nathan and Robert S. Ross, *The Great Wall and the Empty Fortress. China's Search for Security*, New York: W.W. Norton, 1997, p. 72.
98 Nakai Yoshifumi, *Chugoku no 'kyoi' to Nitchu, Nichi Bei kankei*, op. cit., p. 118.
99 Nakai Yoshifumi, *Chugoku no 'kyoi' to Nitchu, Nichi Bei kankei*, op. cit., p. 118; Tanaka Akihiko, *Nitchu kankei, 1945–1990*, op. cit., pp. 176–7.
100 Allen S. Whiting and Jianfei Xin, 'Sino-Japanese Relations', op. cit., pp. 111–13.
101 Takagi Seiichiro, 'In Search of a Sustainable Equal Partnership', op. cit., p. 23; Tanaka Akihiko, *Nitchu kankei, 1945–1990*, op. cit., pp. 178–80; Kojima Tomoyuki, *Gendai Chugoku no seiji. Sono riron to jissen*, op. cit., p. 363; Saori N. Katada, 'Why Did Japan Suspend Foreign Aid to China?', op. cit., p. 46.
102 Tanaka Akihiko, *Nitchu kankei, 1945–1990*, pp. 177–8.
103 Scarlett Cornelissen and Ian Taylor, 'The Political Economy of China and Japan's Relationship with Africa: A Comparative Perspective', *Pacific Review*, vol. 13, no. 4, 2000, p. 617.
104 Kojima Tomoyuki, *Gendai Chugoku no seiji. Sono riron to jissen*, op. cit., p. 362.

2 The rise of traditional and non-traditional security concerns

1 Quoted in Ezra F. Vogel, *Living with China: US–China Relations in the 21st century*, London: W.W. Norton: London 1997, p. 94.
2 A senior Chinese government adviser, quoted in the *Washington Post*, 18 October 2001.
3 For a thorough presentation of Chinese views on multipolarity, see Michael Pillsbury, *China Debates the Future Security Environment*, Washington, DC: Institute for National Strategic Studies, National Defense University, 2000, ch. 1.
4 *China Daily*, 28 October 1996. See also Takagi Seiichiro, 'Reisengo no kokusai kenryoku kozo to Chugoku no taigai senryaku', *Kokusai Mondai*, no. 454, January 1998, pp. 2–14.
5 Robert S. Ross, 'The Geography of Peace. East Asia in the 21st Century', *International Security*, vol. 23, no. 4, spring 1999, p. 81.
6 *Japan Times*, 11 March 1992.
7 For some Chinese sources on this point, see Rex Li, 'Unipolar Aspirations in a Multipolar Reality: China's Perceptions of US Ambitions and Capabilities in the Post-Cold War World', *Pacifica Review*, vol. 11, no. 2, June 1999, p. 134.
8 Zhou Jihua, 'Japanese Foreign Policy: The Direction of the Post-Cold War Adjustment', *Foreign Affairs Journal*, no. 25, September 1992, pp. 36–7.
9 Gaye Christoffersen, 'China and the Asia-Pacific. Need for a Grand Strategy', *Asian Survey*, vol. XXXVI, no. 11, November 1996, p. 1,074.
10 Takagi Seiichiro, 'Reisengo no kokusai kenryoku kozo to Chugoku no taigai senryaku', *Kokusai Mondai*, no. 454, January 1998, p. 4. See also Takagi Seiichiro, 'China's Approach to the Emerging International Order: Policy Implications for the Asia-Pacific Region', in *The Prospects of Security Cooperation in Asia*, JIIA Paper no. 7, 1993, p. 123.
11 *China's National Defense*, Beijing: Information Office of the State Council of the People's Republic of China, July 1998. On the evaluation of the US by China, see Rex Li, 'Unipolar Aspirations in a Multipolar Reality', op. cit., pp. 115–49.

12 Xu Heming, *The Redefinition of the US–Japan Security Alliance and Its Implications for China*, Washington, DC: Sigur Center for Asian Studies, George Washington University, 1998, p. 20. For similar statements by China's leaders, see Chu Shulong, *China and the US–Japan and US–Korea Alliances in a Changing Northeast Asia*, Stanford, CA: Asia/Pacific Research Center, Stanford University, June 1999, available at http://www.stanford.edu/group/APAR/publications/papers/Chu2.pdf, p. 6–7.

13 David Armstrong, 'Chinese Perspectives on the New World Order', *Journal of East Asian Affairs*, vol. VIII, no. 2, summer/fall 1994, p. 465.

14 See, for example, Wu Xinbo, *China: Security Practice of a Modernizing and Ascending Power*, in Muthiah Alagappa (ed.), *Asian Security Practice. Material and Ideational Influences*, Stanford, CA: Stanford University Press, 1998, p. 116.

15 For a thorough discussion, see Suisheng Zhao, 'Chinese Nationalism and its International Orientations', *Political Science Quarterly*, vol. 115, no. 1, 2000, pp. 1–33. See also James Miles, 'Chinese Nationalism, US Policy and Asian Security', *Survival*, vol. 42, no. 4, winter 2000–1, pp. 51–72.

16 See, for example, Banning Garrett and Bonnie Glaser, 'Chinese Perspectives on Nuclear Arms Control', *International Security*, vol. 20, winter 1995/6, p. 76.

17 Quoted by Andrew Marshall, director of the Office of Net Assessment, Department of Defense, in the *Washington Times*, 22 October 1999.

18 Michael Yahuda, 'Future Uncertain', *China Quarterly*, no. 159, September 1999, p. 653.

19 Chinese paper at the ARF Inter-Sessional Support Group on Confidence-Building Measures, Tokyo 18–19 January 1996.

20 Muthiah Alagappa, 'Systemic Change, Security, and Governance in the Asia Pacific', in Chan Heng Chee (ed.), *The New Asia-Pacific Order*, Singapore: Institute of Southeast Asian Studies, 1997, pp. 70–2.

21 For a review of this, see Robert S. Ross, *Managing a Changing Relationship: China's Japan Policy in the 1990s*, Carlisle: Strategic Studies Institute, 1996, p. 4, available at http://carlisle-www.army.mil/usassi//ssipubs/pubs96/manag/manag.pdf.

22 Thomas J. Christensen, 'China, the US–Japan Alliance, and the Security Dilemma in East Asia', *International Security*, vol. 23, no. 4, spring 1999, pp. 55–7.

23 Chu Shulong, *China and the US–Japan and US–Korea Alliances in a Changing Northeast Asia*, op. cit., p. 16.

24 *Comparative Connections*, January 2000 vol. 1, no. 3, 4th quarter 1999, p. 61, available at http://www.csis.org/pacfor/ccejournal.html.

25 For a Chinese discussion of China's negative views of Japan, see Cui Shihuang, 'Chugokujin no anbibarensu na Nihon kan', *Gaiko Forum*, October 1999, pp. 43–7.

26 Yoichi Funabashi, *Alliance Adrift*, Washington, DC: Council on Foreign Relations, 1999, p. 412, quoting *China Youth Daily*, 15 February 1997.

27 *Yomiuri Shimbun*, 1 October 1999.

28 Shaun Breslin, *Beyond Bilateralism? The Local, the Regional and the Global in Sino-Japanese Economic Relations*, paper presented at the conference Japan and China: Economic Relations in Transition, pp. 18–19, January 2001, Tokyo.

29 Thomas J. Christensen, 'China, the US–Japan Alliance, and the Security Dilemma in East Asia', op. cit., pp. 55–7.

30 *Japan Times*, 3 June 1994.

31 *Yomiuri Shimbun*, 5 September 1997.

32 Interview with a senior member of the SDF, 2 November 1999.

33 *Sankei Shimbun*, 4 November 2000.

34 Andrew J. Nathan and Robert S. Ross, *The Great Wall and the Empty Fortress. China's Search for Security*, New York: W.W. Norton, 1997, p. 5.

35 David Shambaugh, 'The Insecurity of Security: The PLA's Evolving Doctrine and Threat Perceptions Towards 2000', *Journal of Northeast Asian Studies*, spring 1994, pp. 8, 10.

36 Wu Xinbo, 'The Security Dimension of Sino-Japanese Relations', *Asian Survey*, vol. 40, no. 2, 2000, p. 301.

37 Michael Pillsbury, *China Debates the Future Security Environment*, op. cit., p. 153.

38 Thomas J. Christensen, *Pride, Pressure, and Politics*, in Yong Deng and Fei-Ling Wang (eds), *In the Eyes of the Dragon. China views the World*, Boston, MA/Lanham: Rownan & Littlefied Publishers, 1999, p. 243.

39 Thomas J. Christensen, 'China, the US–Japan Alliance, and the Security Dilemma in East Asia', op. cit., p. 52.

40 Allen S. Whiting and Jianfei Xin, 'Sino-Japanese Relations: Pragmatism and Passion', *World Policy Journal*, winter 1990–1, pp. 124–5. On the general difficulties of evaluating Japanese defence, see Reinhard Drifte, *Japan's Foreign Policy for the 21st Century. From Economic Power to What Power?*, Basingstoke: Macmillan, 1998, pp. 75–83.

41 David Shambaugh, 'The Insecurity of Security', op. cit., p. 15.

42 Richard A. Bitzinger and Bates Gill, *Gearing Up for High-Tech Warfare? Chinese and Taiwanese Defense Modernization and Implications for Military Confrontation Across the Taiwan Strait, 1995–2005*, Washington, DC: Center for Strategic and Budgetary Assessment, February 1996.

43 For China's thinking on the Revolution in Military Affairs, see You Ji, 'The Revolution in Military Affairs and the Evolution of China's Strategic Thinking', *Contemporary Southeast Asia*, vol. 21, no. 3, December 1999, pp. 344–64.

44 Charles Morrison (ed.), *Asia Pacific Security Outlook*, Tokyo: Japan Center for International Exchange, 1998, p. 47.

45 For a good presentation of China's strategy, see June Teufel Dreyer, 'State of the Field Report: Research on the Chinese Military', *Accessasia Review*, summer 1997, available at http:// www.accessasia.org/products/aareview/Vol1No1/Article1.html.

46 Richard A. Bitzinger and Bates Gill, *Gearing Up for High-Tech Warfare?*, op. cit., p. 10. See also Chapter IV of Yoshifumi Nakai (ed.), *China's Roadmap as Seen in the 15th Party Congress*, Tokyo: Institute of Developing Economies, March 1998.

47 Chu Shulong, *China and the US–Japan and US–Korea Alliances in a Changing Northeast Asia*, op. cit., p. 9.

48 Yoshifumi Nakai (ed.), *China's Roadmap as seen in the 15th Party Congress*, op. cit., p. 32.

49 *International Herald Tribune*, 7 March 2001.

50 *Comparative Connections*, vol. 3, no. 1, 1st quarter 2001, April 2001, p. 99, available at http://www.csis.org/pacfor/ccejournal.html.

51 For a discussion of these details, see Richard A. Bitzinger and Bates Gill, *Gearing Up for High-Tech Warfare?*, op. cit., p. 15.

52 *East Asian Strategic Review 1996–1997*, Tokyo: National Institute for Defense Studies, 1996, p. 109.

53 Kokubun Ryosei, 'Nichi-Bei-Chu kankei no genjo to tenbo', *Toa*, no. 402, December 2000, p. 37.

54 *Washington Post*, 20 July 2001.

55 *East Asian Strategic Review 2000*, op. cit., p. 223; *East Asian Strategic Review 1998–1999*, Tokyo: National Institute for Defense Studies, 1999, p. 141.

56 Frank Umbach, *Die chinesischen Streitkräfte auf dem Weg zu einer militärischen Supermacht?*, in Susanne Luther and Peter Opitz (eds), *Chinas Rolle in der Weltpolitik*, Munich: Hanns Seidel Stiftung 2000, pp. 70–1.

57 For an excellent discussion of the impact of China's military development on the US, see Richard K. Betts and Thomas J. Christensen, 'China: Getting the Questions Right', *The National Interest*, winter 2000/1, pp. 17–29.

58 Kayahara Ikuo, *Chugoku no gunjiryoku to kokubo seisaku no shinten*, in Amako Satoshi (ed.), *Chugoku wa kyoi ka*, Tokyo: Keiso Shobo, 1997, pp. 61–3.

59 Takahara Akio, '"Chugoku kyoiron" o umu Chuka sekai no kakuju to atsureki', *Gaiko Forum*, May 1994, p. 48.

60 Hisahiro Kanayama, *The Marketization of China and Japan and Japan's Response: Prospects for the Future*, Tokyo: IIPS, November 1993, pp. 27–9.
61 Yoshifumi Nakai (ed.), *China's Roadmap as Seen in the 15th Party Congress*, op. cit., p. 32.
62 Takahara Akio, ' "Chugoku kyoiron" o umu Chuka sekai no kakuju to atsureki', op. cit., pp. 51–2.
63 *Japan Times*, 28 March 1991.
64 Hideo Sato, 'Japan's China Perceptions and its Policies in the Alliance with the United States', *Journal of International Political Economy*, vol. 2, no. 1, March 1998, p. 7. The non-transparent character of defence expenditures was put ahead of concern about human rights when negotiating the fourth Japanese loan package (1992–3) (Zhao, Quansheng, *Interpreting Chinese Foreign Policy: The Micro–Macro Linkage Approach*, Oxford: Oxford University Press, 1996, p. 169).
65 *Japan Times*, 8 September 1992.
66 Reinhard Drifte, *Japan's Foreign Policy for the 21st Century*, op. cit., p. 59.
67 *The Modality of the Security and Defense Capability of Japan. The Outlook for the 21st Century*, Tokyo: Advisory Group on Defense Issues, 12 August 1994, p. 5. A copy of the Japanese and English version of the report was received from Professor Watanabe Akio, a member of the group.
68 Interview with senior Defence Agency official, 6 May 1999.
69 *Defense of Japan 1990*, Tokyo: Defence Agency, 1990, p. 57; *Defense of Japan 1991*, Tokyo: Defence Agency, 1991, p. 43; *Boei Hakusho Heisei 4 nen Ban*, Tokyo: Defence Agency, 1992, p. 68; *Defense of Japan 1993*, Tokyo: Defence Agency, 1993, p. 51; *Defense of Japan 1994*, Tokyo: Defence Agency, 1994, p. 51.
70 *Nihon no Boei*, Tokyo: Defence Agency 1995, p. 72.
71 *Defense of Japan*, Tokyo: Defence Agency, 1998, p. 51.
72 *Defense of Japan 1996*, Tokyo: Defence Agency 1996, p. 45; *Defense of Japan 1997*, Tokyo: Defence Agency 1997, p. 51; *Nihon no Boei Heisei 12 nen Ban*, Tokyo: Defence Agency, 2000, p. 50. This warning was also picked up by the *China Daily*, 21 October 1996.
73 *Nihon no Boei Heisei 12 nen Ban*, op. cit., p. 53.
74 *Asahi Shimbun*, 7 July 2001.
75 Wenran Jiang, *Competing as Potential Superpowers: Japan's China Policy 1978–1998*, Carleton University, PhD thesis, 1999, p. 258. However, the test in October led to a temporary suspension of Japanese–Chinese negotiations on the fourth yen loan package (1996–8). See Saori N. Katada, 'Why Did Japan Suspend Foreign Aid to China? Japan's Foreign Aid Decision-making and Sources of Aid Sanction', *Social Science Japan Journal*, vol. 4, no. 1, April 2001, p. 46, fn. 22.
76 See Reinhard Drifte, *Japan's Rise to International Responsibilities: The Case of Arms Control*, London: Athlone Press, 1990, ch. 1.
77 For a thorough discussion of China's nuclear policy, see Shimin Chen, 'La Dissuasion nucléaire et les rapports sino-japonais', *Revue Etudes Internationales*, vol. XXVIII, no. 4, December 1997, pp. 685–707.
78 Asano Ryo, *Chugoku no taigai seisaku*, in Amako Satoshi (ed.), *Chugoku wa kyoi ka*, Tokyo: Keiso Shobo, 1997, p. 75.
79 Kori Urayama, 'Chinese Perspectives on Theater Missile Defense: Policy Implications for Japan', *Asian Survey*, vol. XL, no. 4, July/August 2000, pp. 602, 608.
80 *Asahi Shimbun*, 14 July 1998.
81 This account is largely based on Kokubun Ryosei, *Reisengo no anzenhosho to Nitchu kankei*, in Okabe Tatsumi, Takagi Seichiro and Kokubun Ryosei (eds), *Nichi-Bei-Chu. Anzen hosho kyoryoku o mezashite*, Tokyo: Keiso Shobo, 1999, p. 24.
82 Osaki Yuji, *Arata no Nitchu kankei no kochiku*, in Kokubun Ryosei (ed.), *Nihon, Amerika, Chugoku: Kyocho e no shinario*, Tokyo: TBS Britannica, 1997, p. 107; *ODA Annual Report 1999*, Tokyo: Ministry of Foreign Affairs, 2000, p. 72.

83 Soeya, Yoshihide, *Japan. Normative Constraints Versus Structural Imperatives*, in Muthiah Alagappa (ed.), *Asian Security Practice. Material and Ideational Influences*, Stanford, CA: Stanford University Press, 1998, p. 205.

84 Wakisaka Noriyuki, *Nichi Bei no tai Chu Keizai kyoryuoku*, in Kokubun Ryosei (ed.), *Nihon, Amerika, Chugoku: Kyocho e no shinario*, Tokyo: TBS Britannica, 1997, p. 227.

85 For an official account of the freezing of grant aid and the exceptions for disaster and emergency relief, the polio elimination programme and grant aid for grassroots projects, see *ODA Annual Report 1997*, Tokyo: Ministry of Foreign Affairs, February 1998, p. 72.

86 Saori N. Katada, 'Why Did Japan Suspend Foreign Aid to China?', op. cit., pp. 46–7.

87 Poll conducted by *Yomiuri Shimbun*, reproduced on the website of the Roper Center: http://www.ropercenter.uconn.edu/JPOLL/.

88 Kokubun Ryosei, *Reisengo no anzenhosho to Nitchu kankei*, op. cit., p. 24.

89 Kokubun Ryosei, *Reisengo no anzenhosho to Nitchu kankei*, op. cit., p. 25; *Asahi Shimbun*, 3 and 10 June 1996. This was also supported by the business community: Saori N. Katada, 'Why Did Japan Suspend Foreign Aid to China?', op. cit., p. 47.

90 For a criticism of this difference, see *Asahi Shimbun*, 10 November 1998.

91 Wang Jianwei, 'Confidence-building Measures and China–Japan Relations', in Benjamin L. Self and Yuki Tatsumi (eds.), *Confidence-Building Measures and Security Issues in Northeast Asia*, Washington, DC: Henry L. Stimson Center, Report, no. 33, February 1999, p. 80; Takagi Seiichiro, 'Ajia Taiheiyo ni okeru anzenhosho jokyo no shinten' in Okabe Tatsumi, Takagi Seichiro and Kokubun Ryosei (eds.), *Nichi-Bei-Chu. Anzen hosho kyoryoku o mezashite*, Tokyo: Keiso Shobo, 1999, p. 79.

92 *Washington Times*, 30 August 1995. See also similar strident remarks by China's ambassador to Japan and other Chinese leaders in Wakisaka Noriyuki, *Nichi Bei no tai Chu Keizai kyoryuoku*, op. cit., p. 229.

93 The March 1997 date is given in *ODA Annual Report 1999*, op. cit., p. 194.

94 *East Asian Strategic Review 1996–1997*, op. cit., p. 268.

95 Kokubun Ryosei, *Reisengo no anzenhosho to Nitchu kankei*, op. cit., p. 25.

96 William J. Long, 'Nonproliferation as a Goal of Japanese Foreign Assistance', *Asian Survey*, vol. 39, no. 2, March–April 1999, p. 335, fn. 335.

97 Michael J. Green and Benjamin L. Self, 'Japan's Changing China Policy: From Commercial Liberalism to Reluctant Realism', *Survival*, vol. 38, no. 2, summer 1996, p. 44, fn. 30. For a general evaluation of China's missile deterrent, see Larry M. Wortzel, (ed.), *The Chinese Armed Forces in the 21st Century*, Carlisle: Strategic Studies Institute, US Army War College, December 1999.

98 For a list of Chinese ballistic missiles, see http://www.cns.miis.edu/cns/projects/eanp/pubs/chinanuc/bmsl.htm.

99 Figures based on *The Military Balance 1999–2000*, London: IISS 1999. Figures are much higher in Dean A. Wilkening, *Ballistic-missile Defence and strategic Stability*, London: IISS, Adelphi Paper 334, 2000, p. 76.

100 *East Asian Strategic Review 1996–1997*, op. cit., p. 109.

101 Shinichi Ogawa, *TMD and Northeast Asian Security*, 28 September 2000 (text distributed on the Nautilus website on 19 October 2000), available at http://nautilus.org/nukepolicy/TMD-Conference/index.html.

102 *Japan Times*, 4 August 1999. The Chinese test of a Dongfeng 31 (CSS-X-9) is also mentioned in *Nihon no Boei Heisei 12 nen Ban*, op. cit., p. 53.

103 *Nihon no Boei Heisei 12 nen Ban*, op. cit., p. 53.

104 For a recent update on these exports by the CIA, see *New York Times*, 9 August 2000. See also J. Mohan Malik, 'China and the Nuclear Non-proliferation Regime', *Contemporary Southeast Asia*, vol. 22, no. 3, December 2000, p. 457.

105 For recent reports about such exports, see *Washington Times*, 6 January 2000. For North Korean exports, see Lee Jung-Hoon and Cho Il-Hyun, 'The NK missiles: A

Military Threat or a Survival Kit?', *The Korean Journal of Defense Analysis*, vol. VII, no. 1, summer 2000, pp. 131–54. See also Kori Urayama, 'Chinese Perspectives on Theater Missile Defense', p. 612.

106 Quoted in Aoki, Shuzo, 'A New Nuclear Arms Race?', *Japan Echo*, October 1998, p. 26.

107 The following will not deal with Taiwan's territorial demands in the same area. For Taiwan's legal claims, see Hiramatsu Shigeo, 'Kakudai suru Chugoku no Higashi Shinakai shinshutsu', *Toa*, no. 382, April 1999, pp. 21–3.

108 For a thorough discussion of China's naval force, see Greg Austin, *China's Ocean Frontier: International Law, Military Force and National Development*, Sydney: Allen & Unwin, 1998, pp. 273–96.

109 Greg Austin, *China's Ocean Frontier*, op. cit., p. 288–9.

110 Norman Selley, *Changing Oil*, London: Royal Institute of International Affairs, Briefing Paper New Series, no. 10, January 2000.

111 On China's oil needs and territorial issues, see Greg Austin, *China's Ocean Frontier*, op. cit., ch. 9.

112 Paul. B. Stares (ed.), *Rethinking Energy Security in East Asia*, Tokyo: Japan Center for International Exchange, 2000, p. 25.

113 Kent E. Calder, 'Japan's Energy Angst and the Caspian Great Game', *NBR Analysis*, vol. 12, no. 1, 2001., p. 3, available at http://www.nbr.org/publications/analysis/vol12no1/essay.html.

114 *Financial Times*, 8–9 September 2001.

115 *International Herald Tribune*, 15 November 2000.

116 For a map of the boundaries of the US Administration in Nansei Islands 1952–72, see Greg Austin, *China's Ocean Frontier*, op. cit., p. xxiv.

117 For a description of the islands, see Unryu Suganuma, *Sovereign Rights and Territorial Space in Sino-Japanese Relations: Irredentism and the Diaoyu/Senkaku Islands*, Honolulu: Association for Asian Studies and University of Hawaii Press, 2000, p. 12. See also Greg Austin, *China's Ocean Frontier*, op. cit., p. 162.

118 Unryu Suganuma, *Sovereign Rights and Territorial Space in Sino-Japanese Relations*, op. cit., ch. 4. For a good international law analysis, see Yoshiro Matsui, 'International Law of Territorial Acquisition and the Dispute Over the Senkaku (Diaoyu) Islands', *Japanese Annual of International Law*, no. 40, 1997, pp. 1–31; William B. Heflin, 'Diaoyu/Senkaku Islands Dispute: Japan and China, Oceans Apart', *Asian-Pacific Law & Policy Journal*, vol. 1, issue 2, June 2000, available at http://www.hawaii.edu/aplpj; Dan Dzurek, 'The Senkaku/Diaoyutai Islands Dispute', 18 October 1996, available at http://www-ibru.dur.ac.uk/senkaku.html. For the official Japanese position, see *The Basic View on the Sovereignty over the Senkaku Islands*, available at http://mofa.go.jp/index.html.

119 Greg Austin, *China's Ocean Frontier*, op. cit., ch. 6.

120 *Ibid.*, p. 173.

121 *Ibid.*, p. 313.

122 Unryu Suganuma, *Sovereign Rights and Territorial Space in Sino-Japanese Relations*, op. cit., pp. 142–4.

123 *International Herald Tribune*, 19 June 1992.

124 Wolf Mendl, *Japan's Asia Policy*, London: Routledge, 1995, p. 82.

125 Ma Baolin, 'Legislation Doesn't Mean Policy Change', *Beijing Review*, 30 March 1992, pp. 10–11.

126 Yoshibumi Wakamiya, *The Postwar Conservative View of Asia*, Tokyo: LTCB International Library Foundation, 1999, p. 284.

127 Hiramatsu Shigeo, 'Kakudai suru Chugoku no Higashi Shinakai shinshutsu', op. cit., p. 18.

128 *Defense of Japan 1999*, Tokyo: Defence Agency, 1999, p. 38.

129 *Kaijo Hoan no Genkyo 2000*, Tokyo: Kaijo Hoancho, 2000, p. 47.

130 Unryu Suganuma, *Sovereign Rights and Territorial Space in Sino-Japanese Relations*, op. cit., p. 139.
131 Erica Strecker Downs and Phillip C. Saunders, 'Legitimacy and the Limits of Nationalism', *International Security*, vol. 23, no. 3, winter 1998, p. 124.
132 *East Asian Strategic Review 2000*, op. cit., p. 106.
133 Alan Dupont, *The Environment and Security in Pacific Asia*, London: IISS, Adelphi Paper 319, p. 35.
134 Mark J. Valencia, 'The East China Sea: Claims, Issues and Solutions', unpublished manuscript, East–West Center, April 1999, p. 44. For a description of the 1996 incident and related documents of the PRC and ROC, see Urano Tatsuo, *Di er zi Bao Diao yundong (Senkaku shoto jiken), ni kansuru Chugoku gawa shiryo*, Tokyo: Nihon Daigaku Hogaku Kiyo, vol. 41, 1 March 2000.
135 On the complex anti-Japan motivations and activities of Chinese from Hong Kong, see Arai Hifumi, 'Senkaku shoto mondai to Hong Kong Nationalism', *Kokusai Mondai*, no. 445, April 1997, pp. 38–50.
136 For a good summary of the 1996–7 incidents, see Research Institute for Peace and Security (ed.), *Asian Security 1997–98*, London: Brassey's, 1997, pp. 19–25. For an analysis of the involvement of Japanese right-wingers, see Phil Deans, 'Contending Nationalisms and the Diaoyutai/Sentaku Dispute', *Security Dialogue*, vol. 31, no. 1, March 2000, pp. 124–6.
137 *Asahi Evening News*, 14 August 1999; *Yomiuri Shimbun*, 8 August 1999.
138 *Japan Times*, 16 October 1996.
139 For a comprehensive analysis of China's motives, see Erica Strecker Downs and Phillip C. Saunders, 'Legitimacy and the Limits of Nationalism', op. cit., pp. 114–46.
140 Yoichi Funabashi, *Alliance Adrift*, op. cit., p. 407. See also Phil Deans, 'Contending Nationalisms and the Diaoyutai/Sentaku Dispute', op. cit., p. 124.
141 Andrew Scobell, 'Show of Force: Chinese Soldiers, Statesmen, and the 1995–1996 Taiwan Strait Crisis', *Political Science Quarterly*, vol. 115, no. 2, 2000, p. 239.
142 One example for this tit-for-tat game is a protest of the Chinese UN ambassador Qin Huasun to UN Secretary–General Kofi Annan on a UN report on the Law of the Sea which described the islands as under Japan's effective control. This protest, in turn, provoked a response from Japan's UN ambassador Owada Hisashi, providing the official Japanese position (Reuters, 24 February 1997 from the UN).
143 *South China Morning Post*, 19 May 1999.
144 Yoichi Funabashi, *Alliance Adrift*, op. cit., p. 408.
145 *Defense of Japan 1997*, Tokyo: Defence Agency, 1997, p. 50.
146 *Korea Times*, 18 April 1994.
147 On the scramble activity, see *Sankei Shimbun*, 22 August 1995, quoted in Michael J. Green and Benjamin L. Self, 'Japan's Changing China Policy', op. cit., p. 37. On the upgrading, see June Teufel Dreyer, *China's Military Strategy Regarding Japan*, in James R. Lilley and David Shambaugh (eds.), *China's Military Faces the Future*, New York: M.E. Sharpe, 1999, p. 328.
148 Figures provided by the Defence Agency to the author.
149 Interview with uniformed and civilian officials in the Defence Agency, 16 May 2000.
150 Yoichi Funabashi, *Alliance Adrift*, op. cit., p. 413–14. See also the Press Conference by the Press Secretary of the Ministry of Foreign Affairs on 8 October 1996, available at http://mofa.go.jp/index.html.
151 Kay Möller, *Sicherheitspartner Peking? Die Beteiligung der Volksrepublic China an Vertrauens- und Sicherheitsbildenden Maßnahmen seit Ende des Kalten Krieges*, Baden-Baden: Nomos Verlagsgesellschaft, 1998, p. 117.
152 John Welfield, *An Empire in Eclipse. Japan in the Postwar American Alliance System*, London: Athlone Press, 1988, p. 319.
153 *Asahi Shimbun*, 14 November 1975.

154 Unryu Suganuma, *Sovereign Rights and Territorial Space in Sino-Japanese Relations*, op. cit., p. 138.
155 Unryu Suganuma, *Sovereign Rights and Territorial Space in Sino-Japanese Relations*, op. cit., p. 139.
156 For a denial of ever having shelved the issue, see, for example, the report on talks between Prime Minister Hashimoto and Vice-Foreign Minister Tang Jiaxuan in October 1996 in *Yomiuri Shimbun*, 30 October 1996. For a denial of the very existence of a territorial issue, see, for example, the statement by the Press Secretary of the Ministry of Foreign Affairs in the Press Conference on 19 July 1996, available at http://mofa.go.jp/index.html.
157 Unryu Suganuma, *Sovereign Rights and Territorial Space in Sino-Japanese Relations*, op. cit., p. 140.
158 *Wen Hui Ribao*, 30 April 1997.
159 Wang Jianwei, *Confidence-building Measures and China–Japan Relations*, p. 79.
160 This point is supported in Jean-Marc F. Blanchard, 'The US Role in the Sino-Japanese Dispute Over the Diaoyu (Senkaku) Islands 1945–1971', *China Quarterly*, no. 161, March 2000, pp. 95–123. See also footnote 66 in Greg Austin, *China's Ocean Frontier*, op. cit., pp. 173–4.
161 Yoichi Funabashi, *Alliance Adrift*, op. cit., pp. 404–5.
162 *Sankei Shimbun*, 21 September 1996. See also Kay Möller, *Sicherheitspartner Peking?*, op. cit., p. 117.
163 Yoichi Funabashi, *Alliance Adrift*, op. cit., pp. 401–7. The US Congressional Service, in its studies of 1974 and 1996, came to the same conclusion (Kay Möller, *Sicherheitspartner Peking?*, op. cit., p. 117).
164 Richard L. Armitage *et al.*, *The United States and Japan: Advancing Toward a Mature Partnership*, Washington, DC: National Defense University, Institute for National Security Studies, 11 October 2000, available at http://www.ndu.edu/ndu/SFJAPAN.pdf, p. 5. In the Report it says: 'The US should reaffirm its commitment to the defense of Japan and those areas under the administrative control of Japan, including the Senkaku Islands'.
165 Jean-Marc F. Blanchard, 'The US role in the Sino-Japanese Dispute Over the Diaoyu (Senkaku) Islands 1945–1971', op. cit., p. 30. Yoichi Funabashi, *Alliance Adrift*, op. cit., p. 405.
166 Yoichi Funabashi, *Alliance Adrift*, op. cit., p. 406.
167 An intriguing situation could occur if it is correct that a descendant of the alleged Chinese private owner now lives in the US as an American citizen and holds the ownership document given to her ancestor in 1893 by the Empress Dowager (*Far Eastern Economic Review*, 3 October 1996).
168 Mark J. Valencia, 'The East China Sea: Claims, Issues and Solutions', op. cit., p. 13.
169 Greg Austin, *China's Ocean Frontier*, op. cit., pp. 51, 196–7. See also Chapter 8 in Robert L. Friedheim *et al.*, *Japan and the new Ocean Regime*, Boulder, CO: Westview Press, 1984.
170 Unryu Suganuma, *Sovereign Rights and Territorial Space in Sino-Japanese Relations*, op. cit., p. 33; Greg Austin, *China's Ocean Frontier*, op. cit., p. 57.
171 Hiramatsu Shigeo, 'Kakudai suru Chugoku no Higashi Shinakai shinshutsu', op. cit., p. 10.
172 Hiramatsu Shigeo, 'Kappatsuka suru Chugoku kaiyo chosasen no doko to sono mokuteki', *Gekkan Jiyuminshu*, August 1999, p. 46. In *Umi no baiburu*, he claims that Japan's EEZ (including Senkaku Islands and Takeshima Island) would be the seventh largest in the world if one excludes Russia. Kokusai Keizai Seisaku Chosakai (ed.), *Umi no baiburu 2000, vol. 2*, Tokyo: Kokusai Keizai Chosakai, March 2000, p. 275.
173 Hiramatsu Shigeo, 'Kakudai suru Chugoku no Higashi Shinakai shinshutsu', op. cit., p. 20. This was confirmed by a senior official in the Ministry of Foreign Affairs,

who admitted to this author that Japan and China will never be able to agree on the sea border and that for the sake of good relations the only way is to handle the problem diplomatically (2 February 2001).

174 *Sankei Shimbun*, 8 May 2000.

175 Due to the territorial dispute over Takeshima/Dokto Japan experienced similar problems with a new Japan–South Korea fishery agreement, but it was finally concluded in October 1998. The Dokto territorial issue was set aside and the island is simply included in the joint fishing area (Pak Chi Young, 'Resettlement of the Fisheries Order in Northeast Asia Resulting from the New Fisheries Agreements Among Korea, Japan and China', *Korea Observer*, vol. XXX, no. 4, winter 1999, p. 598).

176 Press Conference of the Ministry of Foreign Affairs, 10 September 1996, available at http://mofa.go.jp/index.html. See also Greg Austin, *China's Ocean Frontier*, op. cit., pp. 196–7.

177 *Daily Yomiuri On-Line*, 28 February 2000. For details of the new agreement, see Pak Chi Young, 'Resettlement of the Fisheries Order in Northeast Asia', op. cit., pp. 612–16.

178 See also the creation in September 1997 of a Japan–China joint control zone in the central part of the East China Sea, with the zone stopping some distance to the north of the Senkaku Islands (Greg Austin, *China's Ocean Frontier*, op. cit., p. 205).

179 *Asahi Shimbun*, 1 December 1999.

180 *AP-Dow Jones News Service*, 8 September 1997. South Korea's seven-year-long negotiation with China on a fishery agreement came to an end in August 2000, and came into force at the beginning of 2001.

181 Kokubun Ryosei, *Reisengo no anzenhosho to Nitchu kankei*, op. cit., p. 25.

182 *Kaijo Hoan Hakusho 1999*, Tokyo: Kaijo Hoancho, 1999, p. 11.

183 *Asahi Shimbun*, 10 July 1999. See also the quote by Wang Yi, the assistant minister of foreign affairs in *East Asian Strategic Review 2000*, op. cit., p. 106.

184 *Sankei Shimbun*, 20 June 2000.

185 MOFA statement on the meeting between Foreign Minister Kono and Foreign Minister Tang on the occasion of the Post-Ministerial Conference of the Association of Southeast Asian Nations in Thailand, 29 July 2000, available at http://mofa.go.jp/index.html.

186 *Kaijo Hoan no Genkyo 2000*,, op. cit., p. 49. For a comprehensive account of these research vessels up to 1998, see Hiramatsu Shigeo, 'Kakudai suru Chugoku no Higashi Shinakai shinshutsu', op. cit., pp. 12–23. For a list of incursions by Chinese research vessels and their exact activities, see Hiramatsu Shigeo, 'Kappatsuka suru Chugoku kaiyo chosasen', p. 49.

187 *Chugoku kaiyo chosasen oyobi kaigun kantei no ugoki*, 8 August 2000 (paper submitted to the LDP by the MSA).

188 *Nihon no Boei Heisei 12 nen Ban*, op. cit., p. 56. For a detailed map of these activities, see *East Asian Strategic Review 2001*, Tokyo: National Institute of Defense Studies 2001, p. 201.

189 *Chugoku kaiyo chosasen oyobi kaigun kantei no ugoki*, op. cit.

190 The Defence White Paper 2000 carries a photo of a Chinese tanker aircraft flying with two fighters (*Nihon no Boei Heisei 12 nen Ban*, op. cit., p. 53). According to the *IISS Military Balance 2000–2001*, China has six HY-6 tanker aircraft (*IISS Military Balance 2000–2001*, London: IISS, 2001, p. 197).

191 *Sankei Shimbun*, 9 August 2000.

192 Japan–China Foreign Ministers Meeting, 28 August 2000, China and Mongolia Division, Asian Affairs Bureau, Ministry of Foreign Affairs, available at http://mofa.go.jp/index.html.

193 *Sankei Shimbun*, 10 February 2001.

194 *Daily Yomiuri On-Line*, 26 July 2001; *Comparative Connections*, April/May/June, vol. 3, no. 2, 2001, p. 100; *Japan Times*, 8 September 2001.
195 Interview with a senior official of the Ministry of Foreign Affairs, Tokyo, 8 October 1999.
196 Interview with Yokoi Yutaka, director of the China Department, 2 February 2001.
197 *Sankei Shimbun*, 17 June 2000.
198 Deng Xiaoping included this proposal in his statement in 1978. See June Teufel Dreyer, *China's Military Strategy Regarding Japan*, op. cit., p. 325. Press Conference by the Press Secretary of the Ministry of Foreign Affairs, 15 October 1996. See also *Far Eastern Economic Review*, 3 October 1996; Unryu Suganuma, *Sovereign Rights and Territorial Space in Sino-Japanese Relations*, op. cit., pp. 141–2. Hiramatsu Shigeo mentions a Chinese proposal to a Japanese company in 1995 (Hiramatsu Shigeo, 'Kakudai suru Chugoku no Higashi Shinakai shinshutsu', op. cit., p. 11). For a Chinese proposal in 1990, see *International Herald Tribune*, 1 November 1990.
199 Greg Austin, *China's Ocean Frontier*, op. cit., p. 204, fn. 118.
200 *Asahi Evening News*, 11 October 1980.
201 *Far Eastern Economic Review*, 1 November 1980, p. 19.
202 *International Herald Tribune*, 1 November 1990.
203 For a brief mention on China announcing in 1981 and 1982 its intention to start exploration immediately adjacent to the Japan–Korea Joint Development Zone, see Greg Austin, *China's Ocean Frontier*, op. cit., p. 198.
204 *Sankei Shimbun*, 2 February 2000. Mark Valencia, of the University of Hawaii, even mentions that China has drilled wells more than 40 nautical miles beyond the median line (Mark J. Valencia, 'Northeast Asian: Navigating Neptune's Neighborhood', in Benjamin L. Self and Yuki Tatsumi (eds.), *Confidence-Building Measures and Security Issues in Northeast Asia*, op. cit., p. 7). For Chinese oil exploration on Japan's side of the median line, see also Hiramatsu Shigeo, 'Koko made kita Chugoku no Higashi Shina kai yuden kaihatsu', *Toa*, June 2000, no. 396, pp. 18–30.
205 Hiramatsu Shigeo, 'Kappatsuka suru Chugoku kaiyo chosasen', op. cit., p. 46.
206 *Dow Jones*, Singapore, 18 July 2000.
207 Xinhua News Agency, 5 July 2000. A more recent report confirms Chinese intentions to expand exploration and production considerably (*Petroleum Review*, November 2001, pp. 34–5).
208 Xinhua News Agency, 24 June 2000.
209 *Sankei Shimbun*, 17 June 2000.
210 *Dow Jones*, 30 May 2000. Interview with the consultancy Wood Mackenzie, Edinburgh, 25 February 2002.
211 Communication from Miyamoto Akira, Osaka Gas Co., 25 July 2000. See also Hiramatsu Shigeo, 'Kakudai suru Chugoku no Higashi Shinakai shinshutsu', op. cit., p. 20; and *Japan Times*, 8 September 2001.
212 *International Herald Tribune*, 16 March 1982.
213 Interview with the consultancy Wood Mackenzie, Edinburgh, 25 February 2002.
214 Hiramatsu Shigeo, 'Kakudai suru Chugoku no Higashi Shinakai shinshutsu', op. cit., pp. 11, 20.
215 Greg Austin, *China's Ocean Frontier*, op. cit., p. 204, fn. 118.
216 Hiramatsu Shigeo, 'Kakudai suru Chugoku no Higashi Shinakai shinshutsu', op. cit., p. 9.
217 Foreign Minister Kono, questioned by Takemi Keizo at the Foreign Relations and Defence Committee of the Upper House, 18 May 2000 (provided to the author by the Research Committee on International Affairs, Upper House). Article 4 (Far Eastern clause) of the 1960 security treaty reads: 'The Parties will consult together from time to time regarding the implementation of this Treaty ... whenever the security of Japan or international peace and security in the Far East is threatened'.
218 Paul. B. Stares (ed.), *Rethinking Energy Security in East Asia*, op. cit., p. 47.

219 For an account of Chinese use of force in the South China Sea in 1974 (clash with Vietnam over islands in the Paracels) and in 1988 (clash with Vietnam over islands in the Spratlys), see Mel Gurtov and Hwang Byong-Moo, *China's Security. The New Roles of the Military*, Boulder, CO: Lynne Rienner, 1998, pp. 260–4.
220 *Far Eastern Economic Review*, 14 April 1995.
221 Dirk Nabers, 'Japanische Außenpolitik. Teil 1: Verteidigungspolitik', *Japan Aktuell*, February 2001, p. 68.
222 Peter J. Woolley, *Japan's Navy. Politics and Paradox 1971–2000*, Boulder, CO: Lynne Rienner, 2000, p. 11.
223 Quoted in Scott Snyder *et al.*, 'Confidence Building Measures in the South China Sea', *Issues & Insights*, no. 2, 1 August 2001, p. 4.
224 Greg Austin, *China's Ocean Frontier*, op. cit., p. 270.
225 Ang Cheng Guan, 'The South China Sea Dispute Revisited', *Australian Journal of International Affairs*, vol. 54, no. 2, 2000, p. 212.
226 Lam Peng Er, 'Japan and the Spratlys Dispute', *Asian Survey*, vol. XXXVI, no. 10, October 1996, p. 996.
227 *Heisei 4 nen Ban*, op. cit., p. 67.
228 *Japan 1993*, op. cit., p. 50; *Defense of Japan 1994*, Tokyo: Defence Agency, 1994, p. 51; *Nihon no Boei 1995*, op. cit., p. 72; *Defense of Japan 1997*, op. cit., p. 50. See also Hiramatsu Shigeo, 'China's Advances in the South China Sea: Strategies and Objectives', *Asia-Pacific Review*, vol. 8, no. 1, 2001, p. 48.
229 Lam Peng Er, 'Japan and the Spratlys Dispute', op. cit., pp. 997, 1,006.
230 Figure from United States Energy Information Administration, available at http://www.eia.doe.gov/emeu/cabs/schinatabl.html.
231 Interview with the consultancy Wood Mackenzie, Edinburgh, 25 February 2002.
232 Frank Umbach, *Die chinesischen Streitkräfte auf dem Weg zu einer militärischen Supermacht?*, in Susanne Luther and Peter J. Opitz (eds.), *Chinas Rolle in der Weltpolitik*, Munich: Hanns Seidel Stiftung, 2000, pp. 73–9.
233 For an overview of the US position during the 1990s, see Guan Ang Cheng, 'The South China Sea Dispute Revisited', op. cit., pp. 207–9.
234 Evan A. Feigenbaum, 'China's Military Posture and the New Economic Geopolitics', *Survival*, vol. 41, no. 2, summer 1999, p. 79.
235 Wu Xinbo, 'US Security Policy in Asia', *Contemporary Southeast Asia*, vol. 22, no. 3, December 2000, p. 486.
236 *Independent*, 6 May 1993; *International Herald Tribune*, 11 January 1994, 17 March 1994.
237 Neil Renwick and Jason Abbott, 'Piratical Violence and Maritime Security in Southeast Asia', *Security Dialogue*, vol. 30, no. 2, pp. 186–7.
238 *Sankei Shimbun*, 10 February 1993; Peter J. Woolley, *Japan's Navy. Politics and Paradox 1971–2000*, op. cit., p. 113.
239 Mark J. Valencia, *Northeast Asia: Transnational Navigational Issues and Possible Cooperative Responses*, in Stephen Meyrick *et al.*, *Maritime Shipping in Northeast Asia: Law of the Sea, Sea Lanes, and Security*, Berkeley, CA: University of California, Institute on Global Conflict and Cooperation, Policy Paper 33, 1998, p. 6, available at http://www-igcc.ucsd.edu/.
240 Seiichiro Takagi, 'China as an "Economic Superpower"': Its Foreign Relations in 1993', *Japan Review of International Affairs*, vol. 8, no. 2, spring 1994, pp. 109–10.
241 *Japan Times*, 21 January 1998, reporting on the Annual Report of the International Maritime Bureau. See also *Asian Wall Street Journal*, 6 June 1996.
242 *Defense of Japan 1994*, op. cit., p. 54.
243 Kawamura, Sumihiko, *Combating Piracy and Armed Robbery at Sea*, conference paper on Regional Cooperation against Piracy and Armed Robbery, Bangkok, 24–25 March 2001, available at http://www.glocomnet.or.jp/okazaki-inst.piracy2001/pira2001.

kawamura.html. On Chinese involvement, see also *Newsweek* (Japanese edition), 7 July 1999.

244 For a discussion of the genesis of the crisis, see Andrew Scobell, 'Show of Force', op. cit. For a Japanese account, see Yoshifumi Nakai, *Policy Coordination on Taiwan*, in Masashi Nishihara (ed.), *The Japan–US Alliance. New Challenges for the 21st Century*, New York: Japan Center for International Exchange, 2000, pp. 71–102.

245 Andrew Scobell, 'Show of Force', op. cit., p. 228; Akihiko Tanaka, 'Dynamic Stability. Cooperative Strategies for Averting Crisis in East Asia', *Harvard International Review*, summer 1999, p. 73.

246 Thomas J. Christensen, 'Posing Problems Without Catching Up: China's Rise and Challenges for US Security Policy', *International Security*, vol. 25, no. 4, spring 2001, pp. 5–40.

247 For a representative cross-section of Japanese academic descriptions, see *Dai 136 kai Kokkai. Sangiin Gaimuiinkai Kaigiroku dai juichi go*, Tokyo: House of Councillors, Foreign Affairs Committee, 16 May 1996.

248 For an excellent account of the events, see James Mann, *About Face. A History of America's Curious Relationship with China from Nixon to Clinton*, New York: Alfred A. Knopf, 1999, ch. 17. See also Bernice Lee, *The Security Implications of the New Taiwan*, London: IISS, Adelphi Paper 331, 1999. For a wider evaluation, see Mel Gurtov and Hwang Byong-Moo, *China's Security. The New Roles of the Military*, op. cit., pp. 266–82.

249 The DF-15/M-9 has a range of 370-plus miles, carrying a 1,100-pound warhead, and is assumed to have an accuracy around 300 metres circular error probable (CEP) (Larry M. Wortzel, (ed.), *The Chinese Armed Forces in the 21st Century*, op. cit., p. 198).

250 For details of these exercises, see Yoichi Funabashi, *Alliance Adrift*, op. cit., pp. 355–6. For a semi-official military and political evaluation of the March 1996 exercises, see *East Asian Strategic Review 1996–1997*, op. cit., pp. 121–30.

251 James Mann, *About Face*, op. cit., p. 337; *Pacific Stars and Stripes*, 21 August 1999.

252 Tensions were apparently much higher on the American side than was known at the time (*Washington Post*, 21 June 1998).

253 James Mann, *About Face*, op. cit., pp. 336–7; Yoichi Funabashi, *Alliance Adrift*, op. cit., p. 368.

254 Press Conference by the Press Secretary, 8 March 1996, 12 March 1996.

255 Yoichi Funabashi, *Alliance Adrift*, op. cit., p. 394.

256 *Ibid.*, pp. 351–2. Until December 1995 the Taiwanese side had always given Japan prior notification of their plans for firing exercises, but had stopped to do so since then (Press Conference by the Press Secretary, 7 March 1997). The Taiwanese navy had been regularly conducting exercises in the sea off Yonaguni since 1994 (*Tokyo Shimbun*, 15 March 1996).

257 For a good analysis of some of the reasons for the government's attitude, see Nakai Yoshifumi, *Policy Coordination on Taiwan*, op. cit., pp. 76–80.

258 Quoted in Ming Zhang and Ronald N. Montaperto, *A Triad of Another Kind. The United States, China, and Japan*, New York: St Martin's Press, 1999, p. 97.

259 According to Nakai Yoshifumi, Funabashi Yoichi may exaggerate the Japanese concern about consultations (Nakai Yoshifumi, 'Comments on Your Draft', e-mail, 3 October 2001).

260 Yoichi Funabashi, *Alliance Adrift*, op. cit., p. 391.

261 *Ibid.*, p. 396.

262 *Ibid.*, pp. 397–8.

263 *Ibid.*, p. 401.

264 Ming Zhang and Ronald N. Montaperto, *A Triad of Another Kind*, op. cit., p. 88.

265 Yoshifumi Nakai, 'Turbulence Threatens', *The World Today*, vol. 55, no. 11, November 1999, p. 18.

266 Ming Zhang and Ronald N. Montaperto, *A Triad of Another Kind*, op. cit., p. 99.
267 Yoichi Funabashi, *Alliance Adrift*, op. cit., p. 423. This is also confirmed by Tetsuya Shimauchi, *Tensions in the Taiwan Strait and the Security of the Asia-Pacific Region*, Tokyo: Institute for International Policy Studies, IIPS Policy Paper 166E, February 1997, p. 17.
268 Yoichi Funabashi, *Alliance Adrift*, op. cit., p. 421.
269 *Ibid.*, pp. 386–91.
270 Fukuyoshi Shoji, 'Chugoku no gunjiryoku to Nichi Bei ampo zaiteigi', *Higashi Ajia Kenkyu*, no. 15, 1997, pp. 56–7.
271 Thomas A. Drohan, *The US–Japan Defense Guidelines: Toward an Equivalent Alliance*, Tokyo: Institute for International Policy Studies, Occasional Paper, November 1999, p. 9.
272 Press Conference by the Press Secretary, 12 March 1996.
273 *Asahi Shimbun*, 4 April 1996.
274 Yoshihide Soeya, *Japan's Dual Identity and the US–Japan Alliance*, paper for the Asia/Pacific Research Center, Stanford University, May 1998, p. 23, available at http://www.stanford.edu/group/APARC/publications/papers/Soeya.pdf.
275 Kayahara Ikuo, *Chugoku no gunjiryoku to kokubo seisaku no shinten*, op. cit., p. 59.
276 *Far Eastern Economic Review*, 15 August 1996.
277 *Ibid.*
278 Yoichi Funabashi, *Alliance Adrift*, op. cit., p. 394.
279 Tamura Shigenobu. *Nichi-Bei ampo to kyokuto yuji*, Tokyo: Nansosha, 1997, p. 184. Interview with Tamura Shigenobu, 5 October 1999.
280 Tetsuya Shimauchi, *Tensions in the Taiwan Strait*, op. cit., p. 17.
281 Greg Austin, *China's Ocean Frontier*, op. cit., p. 396.
282 Nakai, Yoshifumi, 'Turbulence Threatens', op. cit., p. 17.
283 Press Conference by the Press Secretary, 12 March 1996.
284 For this wide consensus, see Thomas J. Christensen, 'Chinese Realpolitik', *Foreign Affairs*, September 1996, pp. 46–7. For an official statement by the PRC on the importance of reunification, see *China's National Defense*, op. cit. The document specifically states 'The Chinese government seeks to achieve the reunification of the country by peaceful means, but will not commit itself not to resort to force'.
285 Victor D. Cha, *Alignment Despite Antagonism. The US–Korea–Japan Security Triangle*, Stanford, CA: Stanford University Press, 1999, p. 77. However, the communiqué does not refer to Taiwan (whereas it refers to the Republic of Korea) but to the 'Taiwan area', which indicates Japan's legal ambiguity about Taiwan.
286 *Heisei 4 nen Ban*, op. cit., pp. 70–1.
287 Address by the minister for foreign affairs, Yohei Kono, during his visit to the People's Republic of China, 30 August 2000 ('Seeking a True Partnership of Friendship and Cooperation', available at http://mofa.go.jp/index.html).
288 Yoshihide Soeya, 'Taiwan in Japan's Security Considerations', *China Quarterly*, no. 165, March 2001, pp. 130–46.
289 Yoshifumi Nakai, *US–Japan Relations in Asia: The Common Agenda on the Taiwan Issue*, 1999, p. 5, available at http://www.nichibei.org/je/nakai.html. See also Amako Satoshi, 'Nihon kara mita Taiwan mondai to tenkanki no Nittai kankei', *Kokusai Mondai*, no. 488, November 2000, p. 55.
290 See, for example, Kato Koichi, in *Far Eastern Economic Revew*, 15 August 1996.
291 *Dai 136 kai Kokkai*, op. cit., p. 51.
292 For some of these concerns, see *Japan Times*, 4 January 1996.
293 Yoshihide Soeya, 'Taiwan in Japan's Security Considerations', op. cit., p. 137.
294 Kien-hong Peter Yu, 'The Choppy Taiwan Strait: Changing Political and Military Issues', *Korean Journal of Defense Analysis*, vol. XI, no. 1, summer 1999, p. 61.
295 *International Herald Tribune*, 29 September 2000.

296 PHP Sogo Kenkyusho (ed.), *Taiwan yuji no shimyureshon. Kannenteki amporon kara gutaiteki kodo ron e no tenkan*, Tokyo: PHP Sogo Kenkyusho, 2000, p. 4.

297 Evan A. Feigenbaum, 'China's Challenge to Pax Americana', *Washington Quarterly*, vol. 24, no. 3, summer 2001, pp. 31–43.

298 *Japan Times*, 10 August 2001.

299 One of the main Japanese private think tanks, the Global Forum of Japan, organized a security-related conference with Taiwanese representatives (*Japan Times*, 14 July 2001).

300 Alagappa, Muthiah (ed.), *Asian Security Practice. Material and Ideational Influences*, Stanford, CA: Stanford University Press, 1998, pp. 689–91.

301 A Chinese navy deputy commander was quoted in the Chinese press as saying that it is high time that China readjusted its maritime strategy and made more efforts to recover the oil and gas resources in the South China Sea (*International Herald Tribune*, 19 June 1992). At the 14th Party Congress in 1992, Jiang Zemin defined the role of the military as 'the protection of the State's sovereignty, territory, waters, and maritime interests' (quoted in Yoshifumi Nakai (ed.), *China's Roadmap as Seen in the 15th Party Congress*, op. cit., p. 32).

302 Toshiyuki Shikata, *Japan's Security Strategy: Meeting the Needs of a new Era*, Tokyo: Institute for International Policy Studies, Policy Paper 145E, November 1995, p. 9.

303 Lester R. Brown *et al.* (eds), *Who Will Feed China, A Worldwatch Institute Report*, Washington, DC: Worldwatch Institute, 1994, available at http://www.worldwatch.org/. See also Liming Wang and John Davis, *China's Grain Economy. The Challenge of Feeding More Than a Billion*, Aldershot: Ashgate, 2000; and Alan Dupont, *The Environment and Security in Pacific Asia*, op. cit., pp. 44–7.

304 For this debate, see the 'Introduction', in Paul B. Stares (ed.), *Rethinking Energy Security in East Asia*, op. cit., pp. 19–41.

305 For a good example of this expansion of the security concept, see Jessica T. Mathew, 'Redefining Security', *Foreign Affairs*, vol. 68, no. 2, spring 1989, pp. 162–77. On the justification of the environment as a security issue, see Keith Krause, 'Broadening the Agenda of Security Studies: Politics and Methods', *Mershon International Studies Review*, no. 40, 1996, pp. 229–54.

306 Lester R. Brown and Brian Halweil, 'China's Water Shortage Could Shake World Food Security', *World Watch Magazine*, July–August 1998, available at http://www.worldwatch.org/.

307 *Asahi Shimbun*, 24 October 1999.

308 Yamamoto Shigenobu, *Higashi Ajia no keizai hatten to kankyo kyoroku*, in Okabe Tatsumi, Takagi Seichiro and Kokubun Ryosei (eds.), *Nichi-Bei-Chu. Anzen hosho kyoryoku o mezashite*, Tokyo: Keiso Shobo, 1999, pp. 216–62.

309 Shinkichi Eto, 'China and Sino-Japanese Relations in the Coming Decades', *Japan Review of International Affairs*, vol. 10, no. 1, winter 1996, p. 29. For further details, see Tozaki Hajime, *Chugoku ni okeru kankyo mondai Nihon senryakuteki taio*, in Amako Satoshi (ed.), *Chugoku wa kyoi ka*, Tokyo: Keiso Shobo, 1997, pp. 317–39.

310 Gaimusho, *21 seki ni muketa tai Chu keizai kyoryoku no arikata ni kansuru kondankai*, December 2000, p. 5, available at http://www.mofa.go.jp/mofaj/gaiko/oda/seisaku/seisaku_1/sei_1_13_1.html.

311 Ralph A. Cossa and Jane Skanderup, *U.S.-Japan–China Relations: Can Three Part Harmony Be Sustained?*, Honolulu: Pacific Forum CSIS, September 1998, available at http://csis.org/pacfor/pubs.html, p. 24. For the scale of acid rain in East Asia, see Akimoto Hajime, 'Higashi Ajia no sanseiu e no torikumi', *Gaiko Forum*, October 2000, pp. 42–6. Page 60 contains a table on SO_2 levels in Japan, China and the Korean Peninsula.

312 Iguchi Yasushi, *Gaikokujin rodosha shinjidai*, Tokyo: Chikuma Shobo, 2001, p. 62.

313 Amako Satoshi (ed.), *Chugoku wa kyoi ka*, Tokyo: Keiso Shobo, 1997, p. 9, ch. 7. See also Hideo Sato, 'Japan's China Perceptions', op. cit., p. 11.

314 Nakasone Yasuhiro, Sato Seizaburo, Murakami Yasusuke and Nishibe Susumu, *Kyodo Kenkyu 'Reisen igo'*, Tokyo: Bungei Shunju, 1992, p. 281. The idea that the outflow of refugees poses a 'grave threat' to Japan in the case of economic/political failure is also shared by Toshiyuki Shikata, *Japan's Security Strategy*, op. cit., p. 9.

315 *East Asian Strategic Review 2000*, Tokyo: National Institute for Defense Studies, 2000, p. 129.

316 *Kaijo Hoan Hakusho 1999*, op. cit., p. 17.

317 *Asahi Shimbun*, 24 February 2001. See also *Sentaku*, May 1999.

318 *Keisatsu Hakusho Heisei 12*, Tokyo: Finance Ministry Printing Office, 2000, p. 246.

319 *Asahi Shimbun*, 26 August 2000.

320 *Asahi Shimbun*, 17 November 2001.

321 Chunghsun Yu (ed.), *Ethnic Chinese. Their Economy, Politics and Culture*, Tokyo: Japan Times, 2000, pp. 147–9.

322 *Mainichi Daily News*, 23 March 2001.

323 *Far Eastern Economic Review*, 4 August 1994.

324 *Daily Yomiuri*, 20 June 1999; *Asahi Shimbun*, 24 June 1999.

325 *Asahi Shimbun*, 4 May 1998. For a brief mention of the role of the Chinese, see H. Richard Friman, 'Gaijinhanzai: Immigrants and Drugs in Contemporary Japan', *Asian Survey*, vol. XXXVI, no. 10, October 1996, p. 965.

326 *Kaijo Hoan no Genkyo 2000*, op. cit., p. 9.

327 Yamada Hideki, ' "Saiba kogeki senryaku" no kaihatsu o hajimeta Jinmin Kaihogun ni Nihon wa ippo okure o toru', *Sapio*, 22 March 2000.

328 See Reinhard Drifte, *Japan's Foreign Policy for the 21st Century*, op. cit., ch. 1.

329 Tanaka Akihiko, *Chugoku to taito*, in Ito, Kenichi (ed.), *21 seki Nihon no daisenryaku. Shimaguni kara kaiyo kokka e*, Tokyo: Nihon Kokusai Foramu Fuoresuto Shuppan, 2000, p. 205. For 1999 the IMF estimated China's per capita GDP at US$782.4 (exchange rate based).

330 Samuel S. Kim, 'China as a Great Power', *Current History*, September 1997, p. 247.

331 Tanaka Akihiko, *Wado poritikusu. Gurobarizeshon no naka no Nihon gaiko*, Tokyo: Chikuma Shobo, 2000, p. 111.

332 World Bank Report, 2000.

333 *Financial Times*, 7 August 1997.

334 *Financial Times*, Japan Supplement, 25 September 2001.

335 Ito Takatoshi, ' "Suitai" no shimureshun to "fukatsu" e no shinario', *Gaiko Forum*, May 2001, p. 20.

336 Akio Takahara, 'The Present and Future of Japan–China Relations', *Gaiko Forum* (English edition), summer 2000, p. 49.

337 *Japan's Strategy Towards the Asia-Pacific Region*, Liberal Democratic Party, 28 November 1997 (Japanese version, *Nihon no Ajia Taiheiyo senryaku, henka e no chosen*), p. 24.

338 Denny Roy, 'China's Threat to East Asian Security', *International Security*, vol. 19, no. 1, summer 1994, pp. 117–18.

339 *Der Spiegel*, 15/2000, p. 20.

340 Kenneth W. Allen and Eric A. McVadon, *China's Foreign Military Relations*, Washington, DC: Henry L. Stimson Center, October 1999, p. 60.

341 Kokubun Ryosei, *Reisengo no anzenhosho to Nitchu kankei*, op. cit., p. 21.

342 For an excellent account of the North Korean nuclear programme, see Leon V. Sigal, *Disarming Strangers. Nuclear Diplomacy with North Korea*, Princeton, NJ: Princeton University Press, 1998.

343 On China's contribution to diffusing the conflict, see Shimin Chen, 'La Dissuasion nucléaire et les rapports sino-japonais', op. cit., pp. 702–6.

344 *Asahi Evening News*, 18 February 1995; *Washington Post*, 16 April 1995.

345 Michael J. Green and Benjamin L. Self, 'Japan's Changing China Policy', op. cit., pp. 39, 45–7.

346 Wakisaka Noriyuki, *Nichi Bei no tai Chu Keizai kyoryuoku*, op. cit., p. 238.

347 On the Gulf War, see Reinhard Drifte, *Japan's Foreign Policy for the 21st Century*, op. cit., p. 22.

348 See, for example, Suzuki Masayuki and Takubo Tadae, 'Beijing "Nihon taishikan" dogeza gaiko no ichibu shiju', *Shokun!*, January 1997, pp. 38–49.

349 Hasegawa Hiroshi, 'Gaimu kanryo no nationalism', *AERA*, 31 May 1999, p. 18.

350 Komori Yoshihisa, 'Machigai darake no Chugoku enjo', *Chuo Koron*, March 2000, pp. 94–109. For a sympathetic review of such criticism by a diplomat at the Japanese embassy, see Miyamoto Yuji, 'Tai Chu keizai enjo o do suru ka', *Gaiko Forum*, no. 144, August 2000, pp. 78–83.

351 *Sentaku*, April 1999; *Asahi Shimbun*, 10 April 1999.

352 For a discussion of recent nationalism in Japan (as well as in China), see Caroline Rose, ' "Patriotism is Not Taboo": Nationalism in China and Japan and Implications for Sino-Japanese Relations', *Japan Forum*, vol. 12, no. 2, 2000.

353 On this divide, see Reinhard Drifte, *Japan's Foreign Policy for the 21st Century*, op. cit., pp. 25–8.

354 For a summary of these reasons and the Japanese authorship of the 'China threat' discussion, see Takahara Akio, ' "Chugoku kyoiron" o umu Chuka sekai no kakuju to atsureki', op. cit., pp. 49–50; Murai, Tomohide, 'Shin Chugoku "kyoi" ron', *Shokun*, May 1990, pp. 186–97. For a Chinese reference to Murai's article, see Wang Zhongren, ' "China Threat' Theory Groundless', *Beijing Review*, 14–20 July 1997, pp. 7–8.

355 Interview with Tanaka Akihiko, 28 March 2001. This was confirmed by Nakai Yoshifumi, who considers that the major impact of the 'China threat' argument came only with Samuel Huntington's 'The Clash of Civilizations' in 1994 (Nakai Yoshifumi, 'Comments on Your Draft', e-mail, 3 October 2001).

356 Yokoyama Hiroshi, *Chugoku o muda ni shita eiyu tachi*, Tokyo: Kodansha 1999, pp. 227–8.

357 Murai, Tomohide, *Gendai Chugoku no seiji. Sono riron to jissen*, Tokyo: Keio University Press, 2000, p. 371.

358 For a good analysis of the Western discussion on China as a successor to the Soviet Union as a threat, see Denny Roy, 'The "China Threat" Issue. Major Arguments', *Asian Survey*, vol. XXXVI, no. 8, August 1996, pp. 758–71.

359 Akio Watanabe, 'First Among Equals', *Washington Quarterly*, vol. 24, no. 3, summer 2001, p. 78.

360 Osaki, Yuji, *China and Japan in Asia Pacific: Looking Ahead*, in Kokubun, Ryosei (ed.), *Challenges for China–Japan–US Cooperation*, Tokyo: Japan Center for International Cooperation, 1998, pp. 91–2.

361 *Daily Yomiuri*, 30 September 1999. See also translated public opinion polls on the website of the Roper Center, available at http://www.ropercenter.uconn.edu/JPOLL/.

362 *Yomiuri Shimbun*, 17 March 1997, reproduced in Hideo Sato, 'Japan's China Perceptions', op. cit., p. 21. In a similar poll by the *Asahi Shimbun* in 1997, 29 per cent of the Japanese mentioned North Korea as a military threat; China came next with 18 per cent, followed by the US (*Asahi Shimbun*, 22 September 1997). In a poll in October 1996, 78.6 per cent (30.8 per cent of Americans) still named the Korean Peninsula and only 25.1 per cent China (50.5 per cent of Americans) (*Yomiuri Shimbun*, 19 December 1996).

363 Polls conducted by *Yomiuri Shimbun*, reproduced on the website of the Roper Center, op. cit.

364 *Asahi Shimbun*, 6 June 1998.

365 *Yomiuri Shimbun*, 30 September 1999.

366 *Jieitai, Boei mondai ni kansuru yoron chosa*: Tokyo: Prime Minister's Office, January 2000, available at http://www8.cao.go.jp/survey/bouei/index.html.

367 See, for example, the views of military analysts in *Japan Times*, 4 January 1996.

368　*International Herald Tribune*, 12 July 1994.
369　Akio Takahara, 'The Present and Future of Japan–China Relations', op. cit., p. 47.
370　Akihiko Tanaka, 'Hegemony, Chaos, Interdependence: Three Scenarios for China', *Japan Echo*, vol. XXI, no. 3, autumn 1994, p. 43.
371　Murai Tomohide, interview in *Yomiuri Shimbun*, 9 January 2001.
372　Hiramatsu, Shigeo, 'China's Naval Advance: Objectives and Capabilities', op. cit., p. 122.
373　Nakai Yoshifumi, *Chugoku no 'kyoi' to Nitchu, Nichi Bei kankei*, in Amako Satoshi (ed.), *Chugoku wa kyoi ka*, Tokyo: Keiso Shobo, 1997, p. 106; Hideo Sato, 'Japan's China Perceptions', op. cit., p. 6. See also Ebata, Kensuke, '15 nen go ni Chugoku no kai, kugun wa Nihon ni totte okina kyoi to naru', *Sapio*, 22 March 2000, pp. 12–14.
374　Kayahara Ikuo, *Chugoku no gunjiryoku to kokubo seisaku no shinten*, op. cit., pp. 46–74; Amako Satoshi (ed.), *Chugoku wa kyoi ka*, pp. 6–9.
375　Amako Satoshi (ed.), *Chugoku wa kyoi ka*, pp. 6–13.
376　Nakai Yoshifumi, *Chugoku no 'kyoi' to Nitchu, Nichi Bei kankei*, op. cit., p. 106.
377　Interview, 20 April 1999.
378　Kokubun, Ryosei (ed.), *Challenges for China–Japan–US Cooperation*, Tokyo: Japan Center for International Cooperation, 1998, p. 11.
379　Kokubun Ryosei, *Reisengo no anzenhosho to Nitchu kankei*, op. cit., p. 20.
380　Tanaka Akihiko, *Chugoku to taito*, op. cit., p. 210.
381　*Ibid.*, p. 213. Interview with Tanaka Akihiko, 28 March 2001.
382　On the latter, see Reinhard Drifte, *Japan's Foreign Policy for the 21st Century*, op. cit., p. 27.

3　Between power balancing and enmeshment policies

 1　Kokusai Keizai Seisaku Chosakai (ed.), *Umi no baibaru 2000*, vol. 1, Tokyo: Kokusai Keizai Seisaku Chosakai, March 2000, p. 47.
 2　Speech at the East–West Center in Honolulu on 8 August 2000.
 3　Michael J. Green and Benjamin L. Self, 'Japan's Changing China Policy: From Commercial Liberalism to Reluctant Realism', *Survival*, vol. 38, no. 2, summer 1996, pp. 35–58.
 4　See, for example, Akihiko Tanaka, 'Hegemony, Chaos, Interdependence: Three Scenarios for China', *Japan Echo*, vol. XXI, no. 3, autumn 1994, pp. 41–7.
 5　Yoshihide Soeya, *Japan at the Crossroads: From Activism to Minimalism and Back*, in Yu, Bin (ed.), *The North Pacific Quadrangle Fifty Years After. Balance of Power and Back to the Future*, Commack, NY: Nova Science Publishers, 1997, pp. 29–45.
 6　Ozawa Ichiro, *Nihon kaizo no keikaku*, Tokyo: Kodansha, 1994, p. 158.
 7　*Japan's Strategy Towards the Asia-Pacific Region*, Liberal Democratic Party, 28 November 1997 (Japanese version *Nihon no Ajia Taiheiyo senryaku, henka e no chosen*), p. 22.
 8　*Ibid.*
 9　*Military Balance 1998/99*, London: IISS, 1999, p. 167. The Mid-Term Defence Build-up Plan FY1996–2000 was adopted by the Security Council and the Cabinet on 15 December 1995.
10　*Nikkan Kogyo Shimbun*, 21 December 1995.
11　For details on this plan, see *East Asian Strategic Review 2001*, Tokyo: National Institute for Defense Studies, 2001, pp. 312–13.
12　*Japan Times*, 16 December 2000. For more details, see *East Asian Strategic Review 2001*, op. cit., pp. 307–11.
13　The following figures are from *Military Balance 2000–2001*, op. cit.
14　'Japan's Naval Power', *Strategic Comments (IISS)*, vol. 6, issue 8, October 2000, p. 2.
15　Such changes are alleged by Heginbotham and Samuels but without any substantiation (Eric Heginbotham and Richard J. Samuels, 'Mercantile Realism and Japanese Foreign Policy', *International Security*, vol. 22, no. 4, spring 1998, p. 183.

16 Jeffrey S. Wiltse, *The 'China Factor' in Japanese Military Modernization for the 21st Century*, Monterey: MA thesis, Monterey Naval Postgraduate School, June 1997, p. 90.

17 Interview with a senior official of the Defence Agency, 16 May 2000.

18 *Nihon Keizai Shimbun*, 20 September 1995.

19 *Yomiuri On-line*, 20 February 2000.

20 *Yomiuri On-line*, 23 August 2000.

21 *Military Balance 2000–2001*, op. cit., p. 183; *Mainichi Shimbun*, 20 August 2000; *Japan Times*, 28 March 2002.

22 *Yomiuri On-line*, 12 August 1999; *Asahi Shimbun*, 29 March 1999.

23 *Yomiuri On-line*, 9 April 2000; *Japan Times*, 27 August 1999.

24 *Nihon Keizai Shimbun*, 6 August 2001; *Japan Times*, 18 August 2001; *Asahi Shimbun*, 4 September 2001.

25 Both documents are reproduced in the appendixes in Michael J. Green and Patrick M. Cronin, *The US–Japan Alliance. Past, Present, and Future*, Washington, DC: Council on Foreign Relations, 1999.

26 *A Strategic Framework for the Asian Pacific Rim: Looking Toward the 21st Century: The President's Report on the US Military Presence in East Asia*, Washington, DC: US Government Printing Office, 1990.

27 *The Modality of the Security and Defense Capability of Japan. The Outlook for the 21st Century*, Advisory Group on Defense Issues, chaired by Higuchi Hirotaro, 12 August 1994 (subsequently referred to as the Higuchi Report).

28 *Higuchi Report*, op. cit., p. 18.

29 *Higuchi Report*, op. cit., pp. 5–6.

30 Kokubun Ryosei, 'Reisengo no anzenhosho to Nicchu kankei', in Okabe Tatsumi, Takagi Seiichiro and Kokubun Ryosei (eds.), *Nichi-Bei-Chu. Anzen hosho kyoryoku o mezashite*, Tokyo: Keiso Shobo, 1999, p. 26.

31 Michael Green, 'Managing Chinese Power', in Alastair Iain Johnstone and Robert S. Ross, *Engaging China. The Management of an Emerging Power*, London: Routledge, 1999, p. 156. See also *Japan Times*, 4 January 1996.

32 Christopher W. Hughes, *Japan's Economic Power and Security. Japan and North Korea*, London: Routledge, 1999, pp. 192–3.

33 Tamura Shigenobu, *Nichi Bei ampo to kyokuto yuji*, Tokyo: Nanso sha, 1997, p. 33.

34 *Asahi Shimbun*, 18 November 1995.

35 Nye Report, *United States Security Strategy for the East Asia-Pacific Region*, Washington, DC: Office of International Security Affairs, US Department of Defense, February 1995. On the report, see Funabashi Yoichi, *Domei hyoryu*, Tokyo: Iwanami Shoten, 1997, p. 249. For Nye's own review of the report, see Joseph S. Nye, 'The "Nye Report": Six Years Later', *International Relations of the Asia-Pacific*, vol. 1, no. 1, 2001, pp. 95–104.

36 Tamura Shigenobu, *Nichi Bei ampo to kyokuto yuji*, op. cit., p. 62.

37 Lijun Sheng, 'China and the United States: Asymmetrical Strategic Partners', *Washington Quarterly*, vol. 22, issue 3, summer 1999, p. 159. For a critical review of the 27 July 1996 Australia–US Joint Security Declaration, see Thomas-Durell Young, *'Enhancing' the Australian–US Defense Relationship: A Guide to US Policy*, 17 November 1997, available at http://www.carlisle-www.army.mil/usassi/ssipubs/pubs97/enhanc.enhanc.html.

38 *Comparative Connections*, vol. 3, no. 1, 1st quarter 2001, April 2001, p. 50.

39 For an account on US concerns about the multilateral security leanings of the Higuchi Report, see Tamura Shigenobu, *Nichi Bei ampo to kyokuto yuji*, op. cit., p. 66.

40 Michael J. Green and Patrick M. Cronin, *The US–Japan Alliance*, op. cit., p. 7. See also Joseph S. Nye, 'The "Nye Report"', op. cit., p. 97.

41 Mike M. Mochizuki (ed.), *Toward a True Alliance. Restructuring US–Japan Security Relations*, Washington, DC: Brookings Institution Press, 1997, p. 12.

42 *Foreign Relations of the United States 1961–1963*, vol. XXII, Washington, DC: Government Printing Office, 1996, p. 354.

43 Funabashi, Yoichi, *Alliance Adrift*, Washington, DC: Council on Foreign Relations, 1999, p. 257.

44 Joseph S. Nye, 'The Case for Deep Engagement', *Foreign Affairs*, July–August 1995, pp. 90–102; Yoichi Funabashi, *Alliance Adrift*, op. cit., p. 255.

45 Joseph S. Nye, 'The Case for Deep Engagement', op. cit., p. 91; Yoichi Funabashi, *Alliance Adrift*, op. cit., pp. 256–7.

46 Joseph S. Nye, 'The Case for Deep Engagement', op. cit., p. 94.

47 Joseph S. Nye, 'The Case for Deep Engagement', op. cit., p. 100.

48 Nye rejects the terms 'superiority' or 'dominance': Joseph S. Nye, 'The "Nye Report" ', op. cit., p. 102.

49 Yoichi Funabashi, *Alliance Adrift*, op. cit., p. 270.

50 Yoichi Funabashi, *Alliance Adrift*, op. cit., p. 269.

51 Tamura Shigenobu, *Nichi Bei ampo to kyokuto yuji*, op. cit., p. 184. The paramount role of China in preparing the guidelines was also confirmed to the author by a high-ranking officer of the SDF (interview, 2 November 1999).

52 Tamura Shigenobu, *Nichi Bei ampo to kyokuto yuji*, op. cit., p. 135; also confirmed by Yoshihide Soeya, 'Taiwan in Japan's Security Considerations', *China Quarterly*, no. 165, March 2001, p. 144.

53 Ming Zhang and Ronald N. Montaperto, *A Triad of Another Kind. The United States, China, and Japan*, New York: St Martin's Press, 1999, p. 100.

54 For a discussion of these points, see Christopher W. Hughes, *Japan's Economic Power and Security*, op. cit., pp. 198–9.

55 See, for example, Muroyama Yoshimasa, 'Reisengo no Nichi-Bei ampotaisei', *Kokusai Seiji*, vol. 115, May 1997, pp. 126–43.

56 'Senryakuteki aimaisa to senjutsuteki aimaisa wa chigau' (dialogue between Akiyama Masahiro and Joseph Nye), *Gaiko Forum*, September 1999, p. 12.

57 *East Asian Strategic Review 2000*, Tokyo: National Institute for Defense Studies, 2000, p. 128.

58 *East Asian Strategic Review 1998–1999*, Tokyo: National Institute for Defense Studies, 1999, p. 73.

59 Christopher W. Hughes, *Sino-Japanese Relations and Ballistic Missile Defence*, Coventry: CSGR Working Paper no. 64/01, January 2001, p. 29.

60 Masako Ikegami-Andersson, *Military Technology and US–Japan Security Relations. A Study of Three Cases of Military R&D Collaboration, 1983–1998*, Uppsala: Department of Pace and Conflict Research, Uppsala University, 1998, p. 136.

61 Ryukichi Imai, *Ballistic Missile Defense, the Nuclear Non-Proliferation Treaty Review and a Nuclear Free World*, Tokyo: IIPS Policy Paper 254E, August 2000, p. 6. The account by Cronin *et al.* mentions three options of cooperation presented by the US in October 1993 (Patrick M. Cronin, Paul S. Giarra and Michael J. Green, *The Alliance Implications of Theater Missile Defense*, in Michael J. Green and Patrick M. Cronin, *The US–Japan Alliance*, op. cit., p. 172).

62 The Japanese government choose to refer to ballistic missile defence since it is to cover Japan, which from an American perspective of protecting US forces in Japan is merely a 'theatre'. See, for example, the April 1996 Joint Statement point 5 (e), which refers to Japan–US cooperation in the ongoing study on ballistic missile defence.

63 For details of the research, see *East Asian Strategic Review 2000*, op. cit., pp. 90–1.

64 For a good summary of these critical points by a professor of the National Defence University, see Kamiya Fuji, 'Kokueki no kanten kara no giron o', *Intellectual Cabinet*, no. 52, July 2001, pp. 6–7. See also Christopher W. Hughes, *Sino-Japanese Relations and Ballistic Missile Defence*, op. cit.

65 For a discussion of Japanese and US motives for TMD, see *Working Group Report. Theater Missile Defenses in the Asia-Pacific Region*, Washington, DC: Henry L. Stimson Center, Report No. 34, June 2000, pp. 63–9. For a Japanese explanation of the reasons for TMD, see *East Asian Strategic Review 1998–1999*, op. cit., pp. 73–6. For a comprehensive analysis of the TMD debate in Japan, notably under the aspect of technology, see also Masako Ikegami-Andersson, *Military Technology and US–Japan Security Relations*, op. cit., pp. 142–9.

66 Shinichi Ogawa, *TMD and Northeast Asian Security*, 28 September 2000 (distributed by http://nautilus.org/ on 19 October 2000).

67 For details, see Masako Ikegami-Andersson, *Military Technology and US–Japan Security Relations*, op. cit., pp. 138–42.

68 Michael J. Green and Patrick M. Cronin, *The US–Japan Alliance*, op. cit., p. 175.

69 Ryukichi Imai, *Ballistic Missile Defense*, op. cit., p. 6. According to Imai, the phrase 'key allies' was to include Japan and Taiwan.

70 For these obstacles, notably the Three Non-Nuclear Principles, see Reinhard Drifte, *Japan's Rise to International Responsibilities: The Case of Arms Control*, London: Athlone Press, 1990. The Japanese government has always refused, however, to put the cabinet's Three Non-Nuclear Principles into law.

71 Selig S. Harrison and Clyde V. Prestowitz (eds.), *Asia After the 'Miracle'. Redefining US Economic and Security Priorities*, Washington, DC: Economic Strategy Institute, 1998, p. 21.

72 Morton H. Halperin, *The Nuclear Dimension of the US–Japan Alliance* (distributed by http://nautilus.org/ on 9 July 1999).

73 Some officials, however, did support the inclusion of Taiwan in the guidelines (Qingxin Ken Wang, 'Japan's balancing act in the Taiwan Strait', *Security Dialogue*, vol. 31, no. 3, summer 2000, p. 340).

74 For an overview of the discussion by Chinese Japan analysts of improved Japan–US military cooperation planned under the revised Guidelines see Rex Li, 'Partners or Rivals? Chinese Perceptions of Japan's Security Strategy', *Journal of Strategic Studies*, vol. 22, no. 4, December 1999, pp. 7–9.

75 Xinbo Wu, 'The Security Dimension of Sino-Japanese Relations', *Asian Survey*, vol. 40, no. 2, 2000, p. 303. In 1961 Prime Minister Ikeda even tried, though he was unsuccessful, to convince President John F. Kennedy of the merits of allowing the PRC to enter the UN as well as letting Taiwan continue as a member, thus proposing a 'two-China policy' in order to make Taiwan's UN membership more sustainable in the long run in view of the discrepancy of population between the two Chinese parts (*Asahi Shimbun*, 14 June 1998).

76 Yong Deng and Fei-Ling Wang (eds.), *In the Eyes of the Dragon. China Views the World*, Boston, MA/Lanham: Rownan & Littlefield Publishers, 1999, p. 201.

77 *East Asian Strategic Review 2000*, op. cit., p. 140.

78 On the former, Funabashi quotes a high US official involved in talks with Beijing officials (Yoichi Funabashi, *Alliance Adrift*, op. cit., p. 422). On the latter, see Bojiang Yang, 'Closer Alliance With Washington: Tokyo's Strategic Springboard for the New Century', *Contemporary International Relations*, vol. 9, no. 6, June 1999, p. 17.

79 For an US explanation of the need for ambiguity, see Nancy Bernkopf Tucker, 'China–Taiwan: US Debates and Policy Choices', *Survival*, vol. 40, no. 4, winter 1998, p. 162.

80 *East Asian Strategic Review 2000*, op. cit., pp. 128–9.

81 Article 6: 'For the purpose of contributing to the security of Japan and the mainte-nance of international peace and security in the Far East, the United States is granted the use by its land, air, and naval forces of facilities and areas in Japan.' There is also reference to the Far East in the treaty's Preamble and Article 4. For the argument that *shuhen* may go beyond the 'Far East', see, for example, Aurelia George Mulgan, 'Beyond Self-Defence? Evaluating Japan's Regional Security Role Under

the New Defence Cooperation Guidelines', *Pacifica Review*, vol. 12, no. 3, October 2000, p. 228.

82 Yoshihide Soeya, 'Taiwan in Japan's Security Considerations', op. cit., p. 142.

83 Jieqi Zhao, ' "Redefinition" of Japan–US Security Arrangements and its Repercussions', *Foreign Affairs Journal*, no. 41, September 1996, p. 35.

84 Okabe Tatsumi, Takagi Seiichiro and Kokubun Ryosei (eds.), *Nichi-Bei-Chu. Anzen hosho kyoryoku o mezashite*, Tokyo: Keiso Shobo, 1999, p. 77.

85 John Welfield, *An Empire in Eclipse. Japan in the Postwar American Alliance System*, London: Athlone Press, 1988, p. 47.

86 Bojiang Yang, 'Paving the Way for Friendship in the 21st Century', *Contemporary International Relations*, vol. 7, no. 8–9, August/September 1997, p. 32, quoting Gotoda Masaharu, then deputy prime minister, in *Asahi Shimbun*, 2 August 1997. See also *Tokyo Shimbun*, 21 August 1997.

87 *Asahi Shimbun*, 15 August 1997.

88 *Japan Times*, 21 December 1978.

89 *Japan Times*, 24 December 1978.

90 Jianwei Wang and Xinbo Wu, *Against Us or With Us? The Chinese Perspective of America's Alliances with Japan and Korea*, Stanford, CA: Asia/Pacific Research Center, Stanford University, May 1998, available at http://www.stanford.edu/group/APARC/publications/papers/Wangfu.pdf., p. 32.

91 Akaha Tsuneo, *US–Japan Relations in the Post-Cold War Era: Ambiguous Adjustment to a Changing Strategic Environment*, in Jain Purnendra and Takashi Inoguchi (eds.), *Japan's Foreign Policy Today*, London: Palgrave, 2000, p. 187.

92 Yoichi Funabashi, *Alliance Adrift*, op. cit., p. 399.

93 *Ibid.*, p. 428.

94 *Ibid.*

95 *Ibid.*

96 *Ibid.*, p. 429.

97 Tsuneo Akaha, *US–Japan Relations in the Post-Cold War Era*, op. cit., p. 188. For more quotes from US officials on Taiwan's inclusion in the guidelines, see Qingxin Ken Wang, 'Taiwan in Japan's Relations With China and the United States After the Cold War', *Pacific Affairs*, vol. 73, no. 3, fall 2000, pp. 367–8.

98 Kay Möller, *Sicherheitspartner Peking? Die Beteiligung der Volksrepublik China an vertrauens- und sicherheitsbildenden Maßnahmen seit Ende des Kalten Krieges*, Baden-Baden: Nomos Verlagsgesellschaft, 1998, p. 128.

99 Feng Ni, 'Enhanced US–Japanese Security Alliance: Cause for Concern', *Beijing Review*, 16–22 June 1997, pp. 7–8.

100 Yoichi Funabashi, *Alliance Adrift*, op. cit., p. 423.

101 Rex Li, 'Partners or Rivals? Chinese Perceptions of Japan's Security Strategy', *Journal of Strategic Studies*, vol. 22, no. 4, December 1999, p. 11.

102 Masahiro Akiyama, 'Japan's Security Policy Toward the 21st Century', *RUSI Journal*, April 1998, p. 8.

103 *Japan Times*, 18 July 1997; *Yomiuri Shimbun*, 1 August 1997.

104 Yoichi Funabashi, *Alliance Adrift*, op. cit., p. 399.

105 *Asahi Shimbun*, 31 May 1998. The same had also been stated by Akiyama Masahiro, the deputy defence director-general, in July 1997; he added that the Defence Agency had been preparing for such a case (*Yomiuri Shimbun*, 29 July 1997).

106 *Asahi Shimbun*, 23 January 1999.

107 *Nihon Keizai Shimbun*, 1 March 1999.

108 *Japan Times*, 19 June 1999. The Japanese government took a rather reserved position on NATO's intervention in Kosovo with a view to China (*Asahi Shimbun*, 29 June 1999).

109 *Asahi Shimbun*, 10 July 1999; *Nittchu Geppo*, 1 August 1999.

110 Interview with a senior official of the Defence Agency, 31 January 2001.

111 Hendrik Spruyt even writes that high-ranking officers have in public, but off the record, 'suggested that the US and Japan have contingency plans should a military conflict erupt over Taiwan' (Hendrik Spruyt, 'A New Architecture for Peace? Reconfiguring Japan Among the Great Powers', *Pacific Review*, vol. 11, no. 3, 1998, p. 368). On China's firm conviction about Taiwan's inclusion, see also Yoshihide Soeya , 'Japan's Future Direction: What the Neighbors Think', *Look Japan*, January 2000, p. 23.

112 Xinbo Wu, 'The Security Dimension of Sino-Japanese Relations', op. cit., p. 301.

113 Bonnie Glaser, 'Chinese Missiles and Taiwan Theater Missile Defense: Can a New Round in the Cross Strait Arms Race Be Averted?', *American Foreign Policy Interests*, vol. 21, no. 6, December 1999, pp. 20–9. For an official version of the Chinese position, see Jian Taojie, 'TMD-Source of Tension in the World', *Beijing Review*, 21 June 1999, pp. 9–10.

114 Banning Garrett and Bonnie Glaser, 'Chinese Apprehensions About Revitalization of the US–Japan Alliance', *Asian Survey*, vol. XXXVII, no. 4, April 1997, p. 393.

115 Dean A. Wilkening, *Ballistic-Missile Defence and Strategic Stability*, London: IISS, Adelphi Paper 334, 2000, p. 47.

116 Zbigniew Brzezinski, 'Living with China', *The National Interest*, spring 2000, p. 18.

117 *Daily Report of Nautilus*, 25 July 2001, quoting Deutsche Presse-Agentur of 25 July 2001.

118 *Washington Times*, 21 January 2000.

119 Martin Wagener, 'Raketenabwehrsysteme und die strategische Gleichung der Taiwan-Strasse', *Österreichische militärische Zeitschrift*, April 2000, p. 417.

120 *Working Group Report. Theater Missile Defenses in the Asia-Pacific Region*, op. cit., p. 68.

121 For a list of the Chinese literature, see Jing-Dong Yuan, 'Asia and Nonproliferation After the Cold War: Issues, Challenges, and Strategies', *Korean Journal of Defense Analysis*, vol. XI, no. 1, summer 1999, p. 35, fn. 89. For the reasons for China's opposition, see also Morimoto Satoshi, 'TMD no seijigaku', *Toa*, no. 385, July 1999, p. 16.

122 For some of these arguments, see Kori Urayama, 'Chinese Perspectives on Theater Missile Defense: Policy Implications for Japan', *Asian Survey*, vol. XL, no. 4, July/August 2000, pp. 602–4.

123 Patrick M. Cronin, Paul S. Giarra and Michael J. Green, *The Alliance Implications of Theater Missile Defense*, op. cit., pp. 170–1, 178–9.

124 See, for example, *Working Group Report. Theater Missile Defenses in the Asia-Pacific Region*, op. cit., p. 70.

125 William Perry, former secretary of defence, predicts a sharpening of the arms race if Japan uses TMD (*Asahi Shimbun*, 22 December 1999).

126 For a critical appraisal of US intentions, see Charles Ferguson, 'Sparking a Buildup: US Missile Defense and China's Nuclear Arsenal', *Arms Control Today*, March 2000, pp. 13–18.

127 See Michael O'Hanlon, *US Missile Defense Programs*, available at http://www.nautilus.org/nukepolicy/TMD-Conference/ohanlonpaper.txt, p. 7.

128 Kori Urayama, 'Chinese Perspectives on Theater Missile Defense', op. cit., p. 606.

129 Patrick M. Cronin, Paul S. Giarra and Michael J. Green, *The Alliance Implications of Theater Missile Defense*, op. cit., p. 176.

130 This point is made, for example, in Kori Urayama, 'Chinese Perspectives on Theater Missile Defense', op. cit., p. 607. China's opposition to Japan's research into ballistic missile defence is called 'misguided and unacceptable' in *East Asian Strategic Review 2000*, op. cit., p. 91.

131 Takagi, Seiichiro, 'Reisengo no Nichi-Bei domei to Tohoku Ajia', *Kokusai Mondai*, no. 474, September 1999, p. 8.

132 Barry Buzan, 'Japan's Defence Problematique', *Pacific Review*, vol. 8, no. 1, 1995, pp. 36, 41.

133 Kenneth N. Waltz, 'The Emerging Structure of International Politics', *International Security*, vol. 18, no. 2, fall 1993, p. 61; Christopher Layne, 'A House of Cards: American Strategy Toward China', *World Policy Journal*, fall 1997, pp. 77–95.

134 For this argument, see, for example, Yoshihide Soeya, *Japan at the Crossroads*, op. cit.

135 On this, see Reinhard Drifte, *Japan's Foreign Policy for the 21st Century. From Economic Power to What Power?*, Basingstoke: Macmillan, 1998.

136 On this development, see Yamazaki Ryuichiro, 'Reisengo no shuyo kokkan no boei koryu', *Gaiko Forum*, no. 128, April 1999, pp. 70–5.

137 Japan is holding regular bilateral security talks with Australia (since 1996), Singapore (since 1997), Indonesia (since 1997), Thailand (since 1998) and Malaysia (since 1999) (Nobuo Okawara and Peter J. Katzenstein, 'Japan and Asia-Pacific Security: Regionalization, Entrenched Bilateralism and Incipient Multilateralism', *Pacific Review*, vol. 14, no. 2, 2001, p. 172).

138 *Yomiuiri Shimbun*, 20 January 1998 and 24 August 1998.

139 The strengthening of ties with Australia also has to be seen in this light, as is expressed, for example, in *Japan's Strategy Towards the Asia-Pacific Region*, Tokyo: Liberal Democratic Party, 1997, p. 22.

140 For support of this front-building with the US as well as Asian countries, see, for example, Aichi Kazuo, former director-general of the Defence Agency, in Ito Kenichi (ed.), *21 seki Nihon no daisenryaku. Shimaguni kara kaiyo kokka e*, Tokyo: Nihon Kokusai Foramu Fuoresuto Shuppan, 2000, pp. 168–9.

141 *Asahi Shimbun*, 8 January 2000. For other Southeast Asian voices suggesting Japan as a counterbalance against China, see Sueo Sudo, *Toward a Japan–US–ASEAN Nexus*, in Masashi Nishihara (ed.), *The Japan–US Alliance. New Challenges for the 21st Century*, New York: Japan Center for International Exchange, 2000, p. 115.

142 *International Herald Tribune*, 15 March 2001.

143 For a background to this, see Donald M. Seekins, *Japan's "Burma Lovers" and the Military Regime*, San Diego: Japan Policy Research Institute, September 1999.

144 For a semi-official Japanese explanation, see Yamaguchi Yoichi, *Myanmar. The Present Situation and Future Prospects*, in *Nichi Bei gaiko seisaku kyocho project*, Tokyo: PHP Sogo Kenkyusho, April 1999, pp. 124–31; and Takeda Isami, 'Nihon no tai Myanmar gaiko no yon gensoku to wa', *Gaiko Forum*, May 2001, pp. 72–8. For an academic evaluation, see Akio Watanabe, *Japan's Position on Human Rights in Asia*, in S. Javed Maswood (ed.), *Japan and East Asian Regionalism*, London: Routledge, 2000, pp. 79–80; and Eiichi Hoshino, *Economic Sanctions Against Myanmar*, in Masashi Nishihara (ed.), *The Japan–US Alliance. New Challenges for the 21st Century*, New York: Japan Center for International Exchange, 2000, pp. 123–60.

145 *Japan Times*, 17 May 2001.

146 For an excellent explanation of the contrasting US policy, see David S. Steinberg, 'Burma/Myanmar and the Dilemmas of US Foreign Policy', *Contemporary South East Asia*, vol. 21, no. 2, August 1999, pp. 283–311.

147 The private Sasakawa Peace Foundation, part of Japan's richest foundation, has devoted a great part of its aid in recent years to this purpose (see *Annual Report* 1998 and 1999, available at http://www.spf.org.).

148 'China's Ambitions in Myanmar', *Strategic Comments* (IISS), vol. 6, issue 6, July 2000.

149 Eiichi Hoshino, *Economic Sanctions Against Myanmar*, op. cit., p. 144; interview with Hashimoto Kohei, PHP Research Institute, 19 May 1999. See also Akio Watanabe, *Japan's Position on Human Rights in Asia*, op. cit., p. 80.

150 Interview, 28 April 2000.

151 Tennichi Takahiko, 'Nihon no gaiko ronso', in Kokubun Ryosei (ed.), *Nihon, Amerika, Chugoku. Kyocho e no shinario*, Tokyo: TBS Britannica, 1997, p. 81. For a comprehensive analysis, see Keiko Hirata, *Reaction and Action. Analysing Japan's Relations with the Socialist Republic of Vietnam*, in S. Javed Maswood (ed.), *Japan and East Asian Regionalism*, London: Routledge, 2000, pp. 90–117.

152 *Japan Times*, 5 May 2000.
153 Gaimusho Press Conference, 14 March 2000, available at http://mofa.go.jp/index.html.
154 For an overview, see Purnendra Jain, *Japan and South Asia: Between Cooperation and Confrontation*, in Inoguchi Takashi and Purnendra Jain (eds.), *Japanese Foreign Policy Today*, New York: Palgrave, 2000, pp. 266–82.
155 For India's negative reaction to Japan's sanctions in 1998 and its proposal for dealing with the Kashmir conflict, see Purnendra Jain, *Japan and South Asia*, op. cit., pp. 269–70.
156 *East Asian Strategic Review 1998–1999*, op. cit., p. 63.
157 Press Conference of the Ministry of Foreign Affairs, Tokyo, 25 February 2000, available at http://mofa.go.jp/index.html.
158 See Isabelle Cordonnier, *Japan and India: Are There Inter-related Security Concerns?*, Tokyo: JIIA Fellowship Occasional Paper, 1999, p. 5.
159 *Japan Times*, 2 February 2001.
160 *Asahi Shimbun*, 26 March 2002.
161 See, for example, *China Daily*, 8 December 2000.
162 Quoted in Kojima Tomoyuki, 'Kyocho gaiko ni fukki sezaru o ezu', *Toa*, no. 400, October 2000, p. 27.
163 For the argument about India feeling that Japan does not want to understand the nuclear test as a reaction to China's nuclear arsenal, and not just to Pakistan's test, see Purnendra Jain, *Japan and South Asia*, op. cit., p. 269.
164 See the remark by Nishihara Masashi, in *Gaiko Forum*, August 2000, no. 144, p. 22.
165 See, for example, Miyamoto Nobuo, 'Nichi-Ro kankei wa naze "Nichi-Bei" no tsugi ni juyo ka', *Chuo Koron*, February 1999, pp. 244–51.
166 What follows relies on Reinhard Drifte, *Japan's Eurasian Diplomacy: Hard-nosed Power Politics, Resource Diplomacy, or Romanticism?*, in Arne Holzhausen (ed.), *Can Japan Globalize? Studies on Japan's Changing Political Economy and the Process of Globalization. In Honour of Sung-Jo Park*, Heidelberg: Physica Verlag, 2001, pp. 257–74.
167 These concerns are also shared by Western policy-makers and academics. See, for example, Bruce Russett and Allan C. Stam, 'Courting Disaster: An Expanded NATO vs Russia and China', *Political Science Quarterly*, vol. 113, no. 3, 1998, pp. 361–82. Russett and Stam even propose including Russia in NATO to prevent a Sino-Russian alliance.
168 For doubts about the long-term viability of the relationship, see Shiping Tang, 'Economic Integration in Central Asia. The Russian and Chinese Relationship', *Asian Survey*, vol. 40, no. 2, 2000, p. 361, fn. 2.
169 Kokubun Ryosei, 'Shuno gaiko to Chugoku', *Kokusai Mondai*, January 1999, p. 8.
170 Robert D. Blackwill and Paul Dibb, *America's Asian Allies*, Cambridge, MA: MIT Press, p. 47.
171 *Asahi Shimbun* website, 3 August 1998, available at http:www.asahi.com/english/index.html.
172 For a very positive Russian appreciation of these exchanges, including military exchanges, see Victor Pavliatenko and Alexander Shlindov, 'Russian–Japanese Relations: Past Achievements and Future Prospects at the Start of the 21st Century', *Far Eastern Affairs*, no. 4, 2000, pp. 3–32. For a Japanese overview of Japanese–Russian military exchanges, see the relevant appendixes in consecutive issues of *East Asian Strategic Review* by the National Institute for Defense Studies in Tokyo.
173 *Comparative Connections*, April/May/June, vol. 3, no. 2, 2001, pp. 115–16.
174 For China's problems with its Uighur minority in Xinjiang and the links to the Uighurs in Kazakhstan, see Larry M. Wortzel (ed.), *The Chinese Armed Forces in the 21st Century*, Carlisle: Strategic Studies Institute, US Army War College, December 1999, p. 20.
175 Interview with Professor Sato Seizaburo, 7 May 1999.

176 Michael Pillsbury, *China Debates the Future Security Environment*, Washington, DC: Institute for National Strategic Studies, National Defense University, 2000., pp. xlii, 47–8. See also Amy Myers Jaffe and Robert Manning, 'Russia, Energy and the West', *Survival*, vol 43, no. 2, summer 2001, p. 144.

177 Udo B. Barkmann, *Mongolisch-japanische Beziehungen (1990–1998)*, in Manfred Pohl (ed.), *Japan 1998/99. Politik und Wirtschaft*, Hamburg: Institut für Asienkunde 1999, pp. 129–57.

178 Ishii Akira, 'Shiren ni tatsu "Sekai no naka no Nitchu kankei"', *Kokusai Mondai*, January 1995, pp. 32–3.

179 *Japan Times*, 21 March 2002.

180 *Asahi Shimbun*, 25 August 1999.

181 *Recent Developments in China and Japan–China Relations*, Tokyo: Ministry of Foreign Affairs, January 1999, available at http://www.mofa.go.jp/region/asia-paci/china/relations.html.

182 Kawashima Yutaka *et al.*, 'Looking Back at the 20th Century (Round Table Discussion)', *Gaiko Forum* (English edition), summer 2000, p. 28.

183 *21 seki ni muketa tai Chu keizai kyoryoku no arikata ni kansuru kondankai*, Tokyo: Ministry of Foreign Affairs, December 2000.

184 On this issue, see Masuda, Masayuki, 'Chugoku no taikoku gaiko', *Toa*, December 2000, pp. 85–104.

185 Mel Gurtov and Byong-Moo Hwang, *China's Security. The New Roles of the Military*, Boulder, CO: Lynne Rienner, 1998, p. 68.

186 Tomoyuki Kojima, 'The Sino-Japanese Relationships', *China Perspectives* (Hong Kong), no. 30, July–August 2000, p. 13.

187 Liu Jiangyong, 'International Partnerships Facing Challenges', *Contemporary International Relations*, vol. 9, no. 4, April 1999, p. 4. For an official confirmation of this position, see 'Takumin shuseki rai-Nichi no igi to seika', *Gaiko Forum*, March 1999, p. 63.

188 *Asahi Evening News*, 16 December 1998.

189 For the official document on Zhu's Tokyo visit, see *Visit to Japan by Premier Zhu Rongji of the People's Republic of China*, Japan–China Leaders Summit Meeting (Summary), 13 October 2000, available at http://mofa.go.jp/index.html. See also the comment by Iokibe Makoto about his impressions from talks with Chinese experts, in Kawashima Yutaka *et al.*, 'Looking Back at the 20th Century', op. cit., p. 28. For a discussion of the partnership between Japan and China, see Kojima Tomoyuki, *Ajia no keizai kiki to Chugoku*, Tokyo: GFRS Seisaku Series, no. 7, May 1998, pp. 15–6.

190 *Asahi Shimbun*, 14 May 2000.

191 *Far Eastern Economic Review*, 4 November 1999.

192 Kenneth W. Allen and Eric A. McVadon, *China's Foreign Military Relations*, Washington, DC: Henry L. Stimson Center, October 1999, p. 20.

193 For the agreement on port calls in February and November 1998, see *Asahi Evening News*, 27 November 1998. One obstacle seems also to be the relative junior rank of the Maritime People's Liberation Army (MPLA) within the PLA.

194 *The Daily Yomiuri*, 9 December 1984; *Jane's Defence Weekly*, 23 February 1985; *The Japan Economic Journal*, 25 April 1987.

195 *Financial Times*, 27 May 1993 and 1 June 1993.

196 *Financial Times*, 11 January 1994.

197 Kay Möller, *Sicherheitspartner Peking?*, op. cit., p. 125.

198 Seiichiro Takagi, 'China as an "Economic Superpower": Its Foreign Relations in 1993', *Japan Review of International Affairs*, vol. 8, no. 2, spring 1994, p. 109.

199 Kay Möller, *Sicherheitspartner Peking?*, op. cit., p. 126.

200 The meeting in 1993 had only civilian members and the one in 1994 only military officials. For this reason the Japanese side counts both as the first meeting, with the one in 1995 counted as the second meeting.

201 Yang Bojiang of the China Institute of Contemporary International Relations writes that China suspended military contact with Japan in August 1995 after Japan froze grant aid to China in response to its nuclear tests (Bojiang Yang, *Sino-Japanese Relations and Measures to Enhance Mutual Trust*, in Michael Krepon (ed.), *Chinese Perspectives on Confidence-Building Measures*, Washington, DC: Henry L. Stimson Center, Report no. 23, May 1997, p. 74).

202 On the importance given to these exchanges, see *Asahi Shimbun*, 23 June 1998. Akiyama Masahiro (director-general of defence policy from April 1995 to June 1997 and thereafter deputy director-general of the Defence Agency, until 1999) was the main drive behind the expansion of contacts with Asian countries and confidence-building measures (Benjamin L. Self, *Confidence-Building Measures and Japanese Security Policy*, in Ranjeet K. Singh (ed.), *Investigating Confidence-Building Measures in the Asia-Pacific Region*, Washington, DC: Henry L. Stimson Center, Report no. 28, May 1999, p. 46).

203 *Asahi Evening News*, 25 November 1998.

204 For an overview, see *East Asian Strategic Review 2000*, op. cit., pp. 254–5.

205 *East Asian Strategic Review 1998–1999*, op. cit., pp. 148–9.

206 Kenneth W. Allen and Eric A. McVadon, *China's Foreign Military Relations*, op. cit., p. 64; *East Asian Strategic Review 2000*, op. cit., p. 209.

207 *East Asian Strategic Review 2000*, op. cit., p. 209.

208 Bojiang Yang, *Sino-Japanese Relations*, op. cit., p. 75.

209 For China's changing views on bilateral and multilateral confidence-building measures, see Kenneth W. Allen, *China's Approach to Confidence-Building Measures*, in Ranjeet K. Singh (ed.), *Investigating Confidence-Building Measures in the Asia-Pacific Region*, Washington, DC: Henry L. Stimson Center, Report no. 28, May 1999, pp. 1–24.

210 Jianwei Wang, *Confidence-Building Measures and China–Japan Relations*, in Benjamin L. Self and Tatsumi Yuki (eds.), *Confidence-Building Measures and Security Issues in Northeast Asia*, Washington, DC: Henry L. Stimson Center, Report no. 33, February 1999, p. 89.

211 Yamazaki Ryuichiro, 'Reisengo no shuyo kokkan no boei koryu', op. cit., p. 74; interview with a senior SDF officer in Washington, 2 November 1999; Michael Krepon (ed.), *Chinese Perspectives on Confidence-Building Measures*, Washington, DC: Henry L. Stimson Center, Report no. 23, May 1997, pp. 7, 17.

212 Harry Harding, 'The Uncertain Future of US–China Relations', *Asia-Pacific Review*, vol. 6, no. 1, 1999, p. 15. See also Yoichi Funabashi, *Alliance Adrift*, op. cit., pp. 429–33.

213 *Asahi Shimbun*, 16 March 1997.

214 Bates Gill, *Two Steps Forward, One Step Back: The Dynamics of Chinese Nonproliferation and Arms Control Policy-Making in an Era of Reform*, in David M. Lampton (ed.), *The Making of Chinese Foreign and Security Policy in the Era of Reform*, Stanford, CA: Stanford University Press, 2001, p. 278.

215 There had been a delay due to technical problems on the Chinese side because Japan's proposed specifications were too high. It is using normal telephone lines and technically corresponds to the one between Beijing and Washington (Interview with Miyamoto Yuji, Ministry of Foreign Affairs, 3 April 2001).

216 Reinhard Drifte, *China and the NPT*, in Joseph Goldblat (ed.), *Non-proliferation: The Why and the Wherefore*, London and Philadelphia: Taylor & Francis, 1985, pp. 45–55.

217 *Yomiuri Shimbun*, 26 February 1999.

218 *Sankei Shimbun*, 28 November 1995.

219 Michael J. Green and Benjamin L. Self, 'Japan's Changing China Policy', op. cit., p. 52.

220 Interview with a senior official of the Ministry of Foreign Affairs in Tokyo, 14 April 1999, and an officer of the SDF in Washington, 2 November 1999.

221 Interview with Sugawa Kiyoshi, deputy general manager of the DPJ, 16 February 2001.

222 For a proposal for an international training centre for PKO between Japan, China and the US, see Hisanori Kato, *China's Military Modernization and Japan–China Relations*, Tokyo: IIPS Paper 209E, June 1999, p. 24. For a proposal for cooperation with China on PKO in a multilateral framework, see Japan Forum on International Relations (ed.), *Japan's Initiatives Towards US, China and Russia*, Tokyo: Japan Forum on International Relations, April 1999, p. 17.

223 For a good overview, see 'Japanese Chemical Weapons in China', *Strategic Comments*, vol. 6, no. 10, December 2000.

224 For criticism of this slow process, see Funabashi Yoichi and Tanaka Akihiko, 'Nichi Bei Chu shinjidai', *Ushio*, October 1998, p. 88.

225 Press Conference of the Ministry of Foreign Affairs, 5 December 2000, available at http://mofa.go.jp/index.html.

226 Nobuo Okawara and Peter J. Katzenstein, 'Japan and Asia-Pacific Security', op. cit., pp. 174–5.

227 *Agence France Presse*, 18 October 2000.

228 For a list of Japanese complaints about China's attitude in this matter, see Yoichi Funabashi, *Alliance Adrift*, op. cit., p. 430.

229 *Asahi Shimbun*, 24 May 1999, available at http:www.asahi.com/english/index.html.

230 Jianwei Wang, *Confidence-Building Measures and China–Japan Relations*, op. cit., pp. 81, 86.

231 Kori Urayama, 'Chinese Perspectives on Theater Missile Defense', op. cit., p. 616.

232 Kenneth W. Allen and Eric A. McVadon, *China's Foreign Military Relations*, op. cit., p. 19.

233 Eric A. McVadon, *The Chinese Military and the Peripheral States in the 21st Century: A Security Tour d'Horizon*, in Larry M. Wortzel (ed.), *The Chinese Armed Forces in the 21st Century*, Carlisle: Strategic Studies Institute, US Army War College, December 1999, p. 44.

234 Email to the author, 30 July 2000.

235 Incidentally he also confessed ignorance of the fact that the Chinese crime rate in Japan is very high.

236 For a directory of exchange organizations, see Sasaka Heiwa Zaidan Sasaka Nitchu Yuko Kikin (ed.), *Nitchu koryu dantai meikan*, Tokyo: Toho Shoten, 1996.

237 *The Sasakawa Peace Foundation. 1999 Annual Report*, Tokyo: October 2000.

238 Osaki Yuji, *China and Japan in Asia Pacific: Looking Ahead*, in Kokubun Ryosei (ed.), *Challenges for China–Japan–US Cooperation*, Tokyo: Japan Center for International Cooperation, 1998, pp. 101–2.

239 Wada Jun, *Applying Track Two to China–Japan–US Relations*, in Kokubun Ryosei (ed.), *Challenges for China–Japan–US Cooperation*, Tokyo: Japan Center for International Cooperation, 1998, p. 179.

240 Osaki Yuji, *China and Japan in Asia Pacific: Looking Ahead*, in Kokubun Ryosei (ed.), *Challenges for China–Japan–US Cooperation*, Tokyo: Japan Center for International Cooperation, 1998, pp. 93–4; Numata Norio, 'Futoi paipu ga naku natte kita Nitchu kankei', *Digital Colum*, 9 October 1997, available at http://www.telecom21.nikkeidb.or.jp.

241 *Yomiuri-on-line*, 30 July 2001.

242 Report of the Prime Minister's Commission on Japan's Goals in the 21st Century (*The Frontier Within: Individual Empowerment and Better Governance in the New Millennium*, January 2000).

243 John G. Ruggie, quoted in Jörg Dosch, *The United States and the New Security Architecture of the Asia Pacific – A European View*, Stanford, CA: Asia/Pacific Research Center, Stanford University, April 1998, available at http://www.stanford.edu/group/APAR/publications/papers/Dosch.html, p. 83.

244 Reinhard Drifte, *Japan's Quest for a Permanent Security Council Seat. A Matter of Pride or Justice?*, London/Oxford: Macmillan/St Antony's College, 2000, pp. 53–62.

245 On the neo-liberal school's view of multilateral security, see Robert Keohane, 'International Institutions: Can Interdependence Work?', *Foreign Policy*, no. 110, spring 1998, pp. 82–94.

246 Interview with a senior official of the Ministry of Foreign Affairs, 31 July 1997.

247 Peter Van Ness, 'Alternative US Strategies With Respect to China and the Implications for Vietnam', *Contemporary Southeast Asian Studies*, vol. 20, no. 2, August 1998, p. 163.

248 Michael J. Green and Benjamin L. Self, 'Japan's Changing China Policy', op. cit., p. 52.

249 Wada Jun, *Applying Track Two to China–Japan–US Relations*, op. cit., p. 167.

250 For a discussion of Japanese 'Realists', 'Idealists' and 'Realistic Liberals' on security multilateralism, see Nobuo Okawara and Peter J. Katzenstein, 'Japan and Asia-Pacific Security', op. cit., p. 177.

251 Osaki Yuji, *China and Japan in Asia Pacific*, op. cit., p. 104.

252 Kosaka Masataka, *Kosaka Masataka gaiko hyoronshu*, Tokyo: Chuokoronsha, 1997, p. 438.

253 Tennichi Takahiko, *Debates on Japan's Foreign Policy*, in Kokubun Ryosei (ed.), *Challenges for China–Japan–US Cooperation*, Tokyo: Japan Center for International Cooperation, 1998, p. 81.

254 Ishii Akira, 'Shiren ni tatsu "Sekai no naka no Nitchu kankei" ', *Kokusai Mondai*, January 1995, pp. 30–42; Nakai Yoshifumi, 'Chugoku no "kyoi" to Nitchu, Nichi Bei kankei', in Amako Satoshi (ed.), *Chugoku wa kyoi ka*, Tokyo: Keiso Shobo, 1997, p. 119. See also Yoshihide Soeya, *Japan. Normative Constraints Versus Structural Imperatives*, in Muthiah Alagappa (ed.), *Asian Security Practice. Material and Ideational Influences*, Stanford, CA: Stanford University Press, 1998, p. 205.

255 Quoted in *Diplomatic Bluebook 1992*, Tokyo: InfoPlus, 1993, p. 183. For the intention of doing away with the special relationship, see Takagi, Seiichiro (ed.), *Datsu Reisen ki no Chugoku Gaiko to Ajia Taiheiyo*, Tokyo: Kokusai Mondai Kenkyusho, 2000, pp. 107–9.

256 Interview with a senior official of the Ministry of Foreign Affairs, 7 May 1999.

257 For an account of the development of Japanese approaches to multilateral security approaches, see Anne M. Dixon, 'Can Eagles and Cranes Flock Together? US and Japanese Approaches to Multilateral Security after the Cold War', in Michael J. Green and Patrick M. Cronin, *The US–Japan Alliance. Past, Present, and Future*, Washington, DC: Council on Foreign Relations, 1999, pp. 139–69.

258 For further historical and domestic circumstances accounting for Japan's 'ambivalent multilateralism', see G. John Ikenberry and Jitsuo Tsuchiyama, *Between Balance of Power and Community: The Future of Multilateral Security Cooperation in the Asia Pacific*, May 2000, pp. 8–9, available at http://rice.edu/projects/baker/Pubs/...publications/jescgem/fmscap4/fmscap.html.

259 'U.S.–Japan Joint Declaration on Security: Alliance for the 21st Century', Appendix 5 in Michael J. Green and Patrick M. Cronin, *The US–Japan Alliance*, op. cit.

260 Benjamin L. Self, *Confidence-Building Measures and Japanese Security Policy*, op. cit., p. 39.

261 On the latter discussion, see Mike Mochizuki, *Japan: Domestic Change and Foreign Policy*, Santa Monica: RAND National Defense Research Institute, 1995.

262 Reinhard Drifte, *Japan's Foreign Policy for the 21st Century*, op. cit., p. 84. For a general overview of Japan's gradual involvement in regional security dialogue, see Paul Midford, 'Japan's Leadership Role in East Asian Security Multilateralism: The Nakayama Proposal and the Logic of Reassurance', *Pacific Review*, vol. 13, no. 3, 2000, pp. 367–98.

263 On the Japanese discussion, see Paul Midford, 'Japan's Leadership Role', op. cit., p. 380; and Robyn Lim, 'The ARF: Building on Sand', *Contemporary South East Asia*, vol. 20, no. 2, August 1998, p. 117.

264   *Far Eastern Economic Review*, 24 September 1992.
265   Paul Midford, 'Japan's Leadership Role', op. cit., pp. 383–4 and fn. 48.
266   Reinhard Drifte, *Japan's Foreign Policy for the 21st Century*, op. cit., p. 85; Akiko Fukushima, *Multilateral Confidence Building Measures in Northeast Asia: Receding or Emerging?*, in Benjamin L. Self and Yuki Tatsumi (eds.), *Confidence-Building Measures and Security Issues in Northeast Asia*, Washington, DC: Henry L. Stimson Center, Report no. 33, February 1999, p. 38.
267   Reinhard Drifte, *Japan's Foreign Policy for the 21st Century*, op. cit., p. 85.
268   For Chinese opinions, see Chu Shulong, *China and the US–Japan and US–Korea Alliances in a Changing Northeast Asia*, Stanford, CA: Asia/Pacific Research Center, Stanford University, June 1999, available at http://www.stanford.edu/group/APAR/publications/papers/Chu2.pdf, pp. 10–11; and Jianwei Wang, 'Chinese Perspectives on Multilateral Security Cooperation', *Asian Perspective*, vol. 22, no. 3, 1998, pp. 103–32.
269   *East Asian Strategic Review 2000*, op. cit., p. 33.
270   Takagi Seiichiro, *Tayosei no kanri. Higashi Ajia anzenhosho no mondai*, in Okabe Tatsumi, Takagi Seiichiro and Kokubun Ryosei (eds.), *Nichi-Bei-Chu. Anzen hosho kyoryoku o mezashite*, Tokyo: Keiso Shobo, 1999, p. 189.
271   The positive effect of ARF on China's position on confidence-building measures and the South China Sea is also accepted by Japanese experts like Professor Nishihara Masashi who are critical of China (Nishihara Masashi, 'Chiiki anzenhosho no atarashii chitsujo o mezashite', *Gaiko Forum*, November 1997, p. 38).
272   For an excellent discussion of the extent and scope of this involvement, see Elizabeth Economy, *The Impact of International Regimes on Chinese Foreign Policy-making: Broadening Perspectives and Policies ... But Only to a Point*, in David M. Lampton (ed.), *The Making of Chinese Foreign and Security Policy in the Era of Reform*, Stanford, CA: Stanford University Press, 2001, pp. 230–53.
273   Assistant Secretary Stanley O. Roth, Presentation at Henry L. Stimson Center on Multilateral Approaches to Regional Security, 21 July 21 1998, available at http://www.stimson.org/cbm/china/resource.htm.
274   Although Bates Gill mentions the circumstance that China announced its intention to publish a White Paper on Defence in its bilateral security talks with Japan in January 1996, he does not give any credit to what this says about Japan's role in bringing this development about (Bates Gill, *Two Steps Forward, One Step Back*, op. cit., p. 278).
275   For a discussion of these papers, see Bates Gill, *Two Steps Forward, One Step Back: The Dynamics of Chinese Nonproliferation and Arms Control Policy-making in an Era of Reform*, in David M. Lampton (ed.), *The Making of Chinese Foreign and Security Policy in the Era of Reform*, Stanford, CA: Stanford University Press, 2001, pp. 257–88.
276   Michael Krepon (ed.), *Chinese Perspectives on Confidence-Building Measures*, Washington, DC: Henry L. Stimson Center, Report no. 23, May 1997, pp. 5–6.
277   James Shinn (ed.), *Weaving the Net. Conditional Engagement with China*, New York: Council on Foreign Relations Press, 1996, p. 19.
278   *Asahi Shimbun*, 29 November 1999.
279   *Yomiuri On-line*, 25 November 2000.
280   Quoted in Benjamin L. Self and Yuki Tatsumi (eds.), *Confidence-Building Measures and Security Issues in Northeast Asia*, Washington, DC: Henry L. Stimson Center, Report no. 33, February 2000, p. 47.
281   For a very guarded account of the significance of these regional efforts in the face of the 'fundamental differences' of the involved parties, see *Defense of Japan*, Tokyo: Defence Agency, 1998, pp. 57–8.
282   Ang Cheng Guan, 'The South China Sea Dispute Revisited', *Australian Journal of International Affairs*, vol. 54, no. 2, 2000, p. 210.
283   *Agence France Presse*, 11 October 2000.

284 Selig S. Harrison and Masashi Nishihara (eds.), *UN Peacekeeping. Japanese and American Perspectives*, Washington, DC: Carnegie Endowment Foundation, 1995, p. 10.

285 *Far Eastern Economic Review*, 13 April 1995.

286 Interview with Osuga Hideo, Maritime Safety Agency, Tokyo, 11 May 2000.

287 Information provided to the author by the Maritime Safety Agency, Tokyo.

288 *Asahi Shimbun*, 10 August 2000.

289 'Piracy in South-east Asia. Obstacles to Security Cooperation', *Strategic Comments* (IISS), vol. 6, issue 5, June 2000.

290 *Mainichi Daily News*, 30 April 2000.

291 Nobuo Okawara and Peter J. Katzenstein, 'Japan and Asia-Pacific Security', op. cit., p. 179.

292 Sheldon Simon, 'Asian Armed Forces: Internal and External Tasks and Capabilities', *NBR Analysis*, vol. 11, no. 1, 2000, pp. 10–11, available at http://www.nbr.or/publications/analysis/vol11no1/essay.html.

293 *Yomiuri Shimbun*, 19 June 2001; Press Conference of the Ministry of Foreign Affairs, 3 October 2000, available at http://mofa.go.jp/index.html.

294 Associated Press, 9 May 2000.

295 *Comparative Connections*, April/May/June, vol. 3, no. 2, 2001, p. 57.

296 Nobuo Okawara and Peter J. Katzenstein, 'Japan and Asia-Pacific Security', op. cit., p. 176.

297 Anne M. Dixon, *Can Eagles and Cranes Flock Together?*, op. cit., p. 153.

298 For an overview of these fora and their membership, see Table 4 in *Gaiko Forum* Special Issue 1999, p. 156.

299 For a critical evaluation of the meeting by Okamoto Yukio, see *Mainichi Daily News*, 16 March 2000 .

300 For the latest meeting in Sapporo, see *Japan Institute of International Affairs Newsletter*, no. 100, October 2000.

301 The results of the first meeting were published as Morton I. Abramowitz, Funabashi Yoichi and Wang Ji-Si (eds.), *China–Japan–US. Managing the Trilateral Relationship*, Tokyo: Japan Center for International Cooperation, 1998.

302 See Kokubun Ryosei (ed.), *Challenges for China–Japan–US Cooperation*, Tokyo: Japan Center for International Cooperation, 1998; and Japan Center for International Exchange (ed.), *New Dimensions of China–Japan–US Relations*, Tokyo: Japan Center for International Exchange, 1999.

303 Interview with Sakanaka Tomohisa, director of RIPS, 20 April 1999. Another trilateral Track III conference was organized by the Jon Sigur Center at George Washington University with Keio University and the China Institute of Contemporary International Relations, 1994–7. See their report *Toward the 21st Century. The Roles of the United States, China and Japan in the Asia-Pacific. Findings and Recommendations of American, Chinese and Japanese Experts*, Washington, DC, June 1997.

304 Okabe Tatsumi, Takagi Seiichiro and Kokubun Ryosei (eds.), *Nichi-Bei-Chu. Anzen hosho kyoryoku o mezashite*, Tokyo: Keiso Shobo, 1999; Ralph A. Cossa and Jane Skanderup, *U.S.–Japan–China Relations: Can Three Part Harmony Be Sustained?*, Honolulu/Washington, DC: Pacific Forum CSIS, September 1998.

305 Wada, Jun, 'Ajia Taiheiyo no chiteki koryu. Torakku 2 no Nichi-Bei-Chu kyoryoku ni mukete', in Kokubun Ryosei (ed.), *Nihon, Amerika, Chugoku: Kyocho e no shinario*, Tokyo: TBS Britannica, 1997, p. 173.

306 *Japan Times*, 2 October 1997. William Perry mentioned in a panel discussion in 1999 that as secretary of defence he had wanted to create a forum for government-level talks between Japan, the US and China, but neither the Japanese nor the Chinese government showed interest (*Asahi Shimbun*, 22 December 1999).

307 *Asahi Shimbun*, 11 October 1997.

308 *Ibid.*

309 Press Conference by the Press Secretary, 30 September 1997.

310 *Daily Yomiuri*, 13 November 1997.
311 *Asahi Shimbun*, 7 May 1999.
312 Interview with a senior official of the Japanese Ministry of Foreign Affairs, 7 October 1997.
313 Yoichi Funabashi, *Alliance Adrift*, op. cit., p. 435.
314 Lu Zhongwei, 'On China–US–Japan Trilateral Relations', *Contemporary International Relations*, vol. 7, no. 12, December 1997, p. 13.
315 David Arase, *US–Japan Relations After the Clinton Visit to China: The End of Innocence?*, Japan Association for Cultural Exchange, available at http://wwww.nichibei.org, 16 August 1998.
316 Aaron L. Friedberg, 'Will Europes's Past be Asia's Future?', *Survival*, vol. 42, no. 3, autumn 2000, p. 153.
317 Akiko Fukushima, *Multilateral Confidence Building Measures in Northeast Asia*, op. cit., p. 63.
318 The points are based on Elizabeth Economy, *The Impact of International Regimes on Chinese Foreign Policy-making*, op. cit., p. 230.
319 Jing-Dong Yuan, 'Culture Matters: Chinese Approaches to Arms Control and Disarmament', *Contemporary Security Policy*, vol. 19, pt 1, April 1999, p. 97.
320 Press Conference of the Ministry of Foreign Affairs, 4 March 1997.
321 Bates Gill, *Two Steps Forward, One Step Back*, op. cit., p. 280.
322 For the weakness of the private sector and its dependence on the government in Japan, see Osaki, Yuji as well as Wada Jun in their respective chapters in Kokubun Ryosei (ed.), op. cit., pp. 105, 169.
323 Christopher B. Johnstone, 'Japan's China Policy. Implications for US–Japan Relations', *Asian Survey*, vol. XXXVIII, no. 11, November 1998, p. 1080.
324 On Japanese–Chinese environmental cooperation, see Anna Brettell and Yasuko Kawashima, 'Sino-Japanese Relations on Acid Rain', in Miranda Schreurs and Dennis Pirages (eds.), *Ecological Security in Northeast Asia*, Seoul: Yonsei University Press, 1998, pp. 89–113.
325 For the latter, see, for example, Nishihara Masashi, 'Stronger US–Japan Ties Can Bolster Asian Stability' *International Herald Tribune*, 22 April 1999.
326 Ozawa Ichiro. *Nihon kaizo no keikaku*, op. cit., p. 132.
327 *Yomiuri Shimbun*, 17 March 1997, reproduced in Hideo Sato, 'Japan's China Perceptions and Its Policies in the Alliance with the United States', *Journal of International Political Economy*, vol. 2, no. 1, March 1998, p. 21.
328 Quoted in Stuart Harris, 'China and the Pursuit of State Interests in a Globalising World', *Pacifica Review*, vol. 13, no. 1, February 2001, p. 27.
329 Wayne M. Morrison, *Congressional Research Service Issue Brief*, IB91121, 5 March 2001.
330 For Chinese trade statistics, see http://www.fmprc.gov.cn/english/. For a discussion of the reasons for this discrepancy, see the analysis of the discrepancy between Chinese and American figures in K.C. Fung and Lawrence J. Lau, 'New Estimates of the United States-China Bilateral Trade Balances', paper for the Asia/Pacific Research Center, Stanford University, April 1999, available at http://www.stanford.edu/group/APARC/publications/papers/laufung.pdf. These results can also partly be attributed to the difference between Japanese and Chinese statistical methods.
331 *Sentaku*, July 2001, p. 77.
332 Hanns-Günther Hilpert 'Wirtschaftliche Teile meines Buches', e-mail (3 October 2001).
333 Frank Ching, *Economic Dimensions of Tripartite Relations*, in Susan C. Maybaumwisniewski and Mary A. Sommerville (eds.), *Blue Horizon. United States–Japan–PRC Tripartite Relations*, Washington, DC: National Defense University, 1997, p. 180.
334 Takahara Akio, 'Nihon to Chugoku. Sono fukabun naru kankei', *Gaiko Forum*, October 1999, p. 16. Japanese statistics give a higher FDI amount than their Chinese counterparts because of transfer pricing complexities and other differences.

335 Nihon Kokusai Boeki Sokushin Kyokai (ed.), *Nitchu Boeki Hikkei 2000*, p. 22.
336 *Nihon Keizai Shimbun*, 8 January 2001.
337 See Walter Hatch and Kozo Yamamura, *Asia in Japan's Embrace. Building a Regional Production Alliance*, Cambridge: Cambridge University Press, 1996.
338 Kamiya Matake, *Japanese Foreign Policy Toward Northeast Asia*, in Inoguchi Takashi and Purnendra Jain (eds.), *Japanese Foreign Policy Today*, New York: Palgrave, 2000, p. 232.
339 For a critical overview of Japan's ODA to China, see Komori Yoshihisa, 'Machigai darake no Chugoku enjo', *Chuo Koron*, March 2000, pp. 94–109. For an official view, see Miyamoto Yuji, 'Tai Chu keizai enjo o do suru ka', *Gaiko Forum*, no. 144, August 2000, pp. 78–83.
340 'Recent Trends and Prospects for Major Asian Economies', *East Asia Economic Perspectives*, vol. 12, February 2001, special issue (International Centre for the Study of East Asian Development, Kitakyushu), ch. 3; Saori N. Katada, 'Why Did Japan Suspend Foreign Aid to China? Japan's Foreign Aid Decision-making and Sources of Aid Sanction', *Social Science Japan Journal*, vol. 4, no. 1, April 2001, p. 48. For the share in state investments, see Kojima Tomoyuki, 'Tai Chu kyoryoku wa yokushi to hyori ittai de', *Sankei Shimbun*, 16 January 2001.
341 For a list of such functions and goals, see Margaret M. Pearson, *The Major Multilateral Economic Institutions Engage China*, in Alastair Iain Johnstone and Robert S. Ross (eds.), *Engaging China. The Management of an Emerging Power*, London: Routledge, 1999, p. 211.
342 *The Second Country Study for Japan's Official Development Assistance to the People's Republic of China*, Tokyo: Japan International Cooperation Agency, February 1999, pp. 25–6.
343 Takagi Seiichiro, 'The Chinese Approach to Multilateral Security Cooperation in the Asia-Pacific Region', *Ajia Taiheiyo sekai to Chugoku. Kaihatsu no naka no ningen*, Series Chugoku ryoiki kenkyu no. 10, p. 27.
344 Christopher B. Johnstone, 'Paradigms Lost: Japan's Asia Policy in a Time of Growing Chinese Power', *Contemporary Southeast Asia*, vol. 21, no. 3, December 1999, p. 377; Thomas G. Moore and Yang Dixia, 'China, APEC and Economic Regionalism in the Asia-Pacific', *Journal of East Asian Affairs*, vol. XIII, no. 2, fall/winter 1999, p. 408.
345 Margaret M. Pearson, *The Major Multilateral Economic Institutions Engage China*, op. cit., p. 207.
346 The following figures are based on 'Recent Trends and Prospects for Major Asian Economies', *East Asia Economic Perspectives*, op. cit., ch. 3.
347 OECD report, as quoted on the website of the Chinese embassy, UK, 14 October 2000.
348 Interview with Ke Long, economist at Fujitsu Research Institute, 30 January 2001.
349 The Commission's Communication 'EU Strategy Towards China: Implementation of the 1998 Communication and Future Steps for a More Effective EU Policy', 15 May 2001.
350 Tomoyuki Kojima, 'The Sino-Japanese Relationships', *China Perspectives* (Hong Kong), no. 30, July–August 2000, p. 9.
351 Stuart Harris speaks of foreign involvement in two-thirds of China's total exports (Stuart Harris, 'China and the Pursuit of State Interests in a Globalising World', op. cit., p. 17).
352 *Ibid.*, p. 19.
353 *Financial Times*, 22 January 2002.

4 The dynamics of engagement

1 Charles Horner, 'The Third Side of the Triangle. The China–Japan Dimension', *The National Interest*, no. 46, winter 1996–7, p. 23.

2 For a good overview of the discussion between the two schools, see Rex Li, 'The China Challenge: Theoretical Perspectives and Policy Implications', *Journal of Contemporary China*, vol. 8, no. 22, 1999, pp. 443–76.

3 Kay Möller, *China und Weltordnung: Prinzipien und Praxis*, Ebenhausen: Stiftung Wissenschaft und Politik, May 1999, p. 40. For another less pessimistic evaluation of China's economic reforms, see Elizabeth C. Economy, 'Reforming China', *Survival*, vol. 41, no. 3, autumn 1999, pp. 21–42.

4 On some of these uncertainties, see, for example, James Shinn (ed.), *Weaving the Net. Conditional Engagement with China*, New York: Council on Foreign Relations Press, 1996, pp. 35–9.

5 Paul A. Papayoanou and Scott L. Kastner, 'Sleeping With the (Potential) Enemy: Assessing the US Policy of Engagement with China', *Security Studies*, vol. 9, no. 1/2, autumn 1999–winter 2000, pp. 157–87.

6 EU Commission's Communication 'EU Strategy Towards China: Implementation of the 1998 Communication and Future Steps for a More Effective EU Policy', 15 May 2001, p. 6.

7 Mike Smith and Nicholas Koo, *China and US Foreign Policy in the Asia Pacific: Living With American Dominance*, Briefing Paper New Series no. 22, June 2001, London: Royal Institute of International Affairs, p. 4.

8 Bates Gill, *Two Steps Forward, One Step Back: The Dynamics of Chinese Nonproliferation and Arms Control Policy-making in an Era of Reform*, in David M. Lampton (ed.), *The Making of Chinese Foreign and Security Policy in the Era of Reform*, Stanford, CA: Stanford University Press, 2001, p. 287.

9 Thomas J. Christensen, *Pride, Pressure, and Politics*, in Yong Deng and Fei-Ling Wang (eds), *In the Eyes of the Dragon. China Views the World*, Boston, MA/Lanham: Rowman & Littlefield Publishers, 1999, p. 240. This point is also made by Rex Li, 'The China Challenge: Theoretical Perspectives and Policy Implications', *Journal of Contemporary China*, vol. 8, no. 22, 1999, pp. 464–65.

10 Margaret M. Pearson, *The Major Multilateral Economic Institutions Engage China*, in Alastair Iain Johnstone and Robert S. Ross, *Engaging China. The Management of an Emerging Power*, London: Routledge, p. 208.

11 Paul A. Papayoanou and Scott L. Kastner, 'Sleeping With the (Potential) Enemy', op. cit., pp. 157–87.

12 Tanaka Akihiko, 'Chugoku to taito', in Ito Kenichi (ed.), *21 seki Nihon no daisenryaku. Shimaguni kara kaiyo kokka e*, Tokyo: Nihon Kokusai Foramu Fuoresuto Shuppan, 2000, p. 212.

13 Interview with a senior official of the Ministry of Foreign Affairs, 3 April 2001.

14 For an official admission of this feeling, see, for example, remarks by Kawashima Yutaka, vice-foreign minister at the Ministry of Foreign Affairs, in Kawashima Yutaka *et al.*, 'Looking Back at the 20th Century (Round Table Discussion)', *Gaiko Forum* (English edition), summer 2000, p. 28. Also Akio Watanabe, 'First Among Equals', *Washington Quarterly*, vol. 24, no. 3, summer 2001, p. 79.

15 Yokoyama Hiroshi, *Nitchu no shoheki*, Tokyo: Simul Press, pp. 17–19.

16 For a discussion of Japanese academic writing on the failure scenario, see Hideo Sato, 'Japan's China Perceptions and its Policies in the Alliance with the United States', *Journal of International Political Economy*, vol. 2, no. 1, March 1998, pp. 11–13; Ito Kiyoshi, 'China and Hong Kong are Headed Toward Collapse', *Japan Echo*, vol. 25, no. 3, June 1998, pp. 38–42; Takahara Akio, 'The Present and Future of Japan–China Relations', *Gaiko Forum* (English edition), summer 2000, p. 47.

17 For critical Western evaluations of China's economy, see Callum Henderson, *China on the Brink*, New York: Mc Graw-Hill, 1999; Kay Möller, *China und Weltordnung*, op. cit.; Jack A. Goldstone, 'The Coming Chinese Collapse', *Foreign Policy*, no. 99, summer 1995, pp. 35–52. Carsten A. Holz, Economic Reforms and State Sector Bankruptcy in China, *China Quarterly*, no. 166, June 2001, pp. 342–67.

18 Tanaka Akihiko, 'Forming a New East Asia', *Japan Echo*, August 2000, p. 9.

19 Kokubun Ryosei, *Nichi-Bei-Chu kyoryoku no genkai to kanosei*, in Okabe, Tatsumi, Takagi Seiichiro and Kokubun Ryosei (eds), *Nichi-Bei-Chu. Anzen hosho kyoryoku o mezashite*, Tokyo: Keiso Shobo, 1999, pp. 295–300. For failed economic development having led to an increase in crime, see Nakai Yoshifumi (ed.), *China's Roadmap as Seen in the 15th Party Congress*, Tokyo: Institute of Developing Economies, March 1998, pp. 62–4.

20 For this re-evaluation and its various motivations, see Miyamoto Yuji, 'Tai Chu keizai enjo o do suru ka', *Gaiko Forum*, no. 144, August 2000.

21 *The Second Country Study for Japan's Official Development Assistance to the People's Republic of China*, Tokyo: Japan International Cooperation Agency, February 1999, pp. 20–7. For a critical evaluation of state enterprise reform, see also Nakai Yoshifumi (ed.), *China's Roadmap as Seen in the 15th Party Congress*, op. cit., ch. 5.

22 Christopher W. Hughes, *Japanese Policy and the East Asian Currency Crisis: Abject Defeat or Quiet Victory?*, Warwick: Centre for the Study of Globalisation and Regionalisation, Warwick University, Working Paper no. 24, February 1999, p. 35.

23 For an official expression of this awareness, see Diplomatic Bluebook 1993, *Striving for a More Secure and Humane World*, Tokyo: Ministry of Foreign Affairs, pp. 99–128.

24 On a review of such opinions, see Michael J. Green, 'State of the Field Report: Research on Japanese Security Policy', *Access Asia Review*, vol. 2, no. 1, September 1998, available at http://www.nbr.org/publications/review/vol2no1/essay.html.

25 See, for example, Takagi Seiichiro, 'Zadankai. Fukoku Kyohei paradaimu kara ikani kaiho sareru ka', *Gaiko Forum*, May 1994, p. 33.

26 Interview with a senior official of the Defence Agency, 31 January 2001.

27 *The Modality of the Security and Defense Capability of Japan. The Outlook for the 21st Century*, Advisory Group on Defense Issues, chaired by Higuchi Hirotaro, 12 August 1994, pp. 4, 6.

28 Interview with a senior Defence Agency official, 6 May 1999. The official told the author that the growth rate was officially given as 7.5 per cent, but the Defence Agency really estimated it at –6–7 per cent. This pessimism in the Defence Agency was confirmed by Professor Kokubun Ryosei in an interview on 11 May 1999.

29 Communication from Shaun Breslin, Tokyo, 18 January 2001. See also the news report about a book edited by the CCP in 2001 on civil unrest: *International Herald Tribune*, 2–3 June 2001.

30 Kato Hisanori, *China's Military Modernization and Japan–China Relations*, Tokyo: IIPS Paper 209E, June 1999, p. 13.

31 For a general discussion, see Kensuke Ebata, *The Role of Technology Transfers in Economic Development*, in Sverre Lodgaard and Robert L. Pfaltzgraff (eds), *Arms and Technology Transfers: Security and Economic Considerations Among Importing and Exporting States*, New York/Geneva: UNIDIR/UN, 1995, pp. 177–207.

32 Yuan Jing-Dong, 'Asia and Nonproliferation after the Cold War: Issues, Challenges, and Strategies', *Korean Journal of Defense Analysis*, vol. XI, no. 1, summer 1999, p. 29. See also Report to the Chairman, Joint Economic Committee, US Senate, *China. Military Imports from the US and the European Union since the 1989 Embargoes*, Washington, DC: General Accounting Office, June 1998.

33 Hiramatsu makes the case for the dual use of railway, road and air traffic systems, to which Japan has given considerable ODA (Hiramatsu Shigeo, 'Tai Chu ODA "Gunmin ryoyo" no jittai', *Toa*, October 2000, pp. 6–21.

34 *China Daily*, 18 January 1998.

35 On the intensifying competition from China, see the report on the White Paper on International Trade 2001 as reported in *Japan Times*, 19 May 2001.

36 Denny Roy, *Hegemon on the Horizon? China's Threat to East Asian Security*, in Michael Brown *et al.*, *East Asian Security*, Cambridge, MA: MIT Press, 1996, p. 122.

37   Paul A. Papayoanou and Scott L. Kastner, 'Sleeping with the (Potential) Enemy', op. cit., pp. 157–87.

38   Tanaka Akihiko, *Nitchu kankai, 1945–1990*, Tokyo: Tokyo Daigaku Shuppankai, 1991, p. 112.

39   Reinhard Drifte, *Arms Production in Japan: The Military Use of Civilian Technology*, Boulder, CO: Westview Press, 1986, ch. 6.

40   Miyamoto Yuji, 'Tai Chu keizai enjo o do suru ka', op. cit., p. 82.

41   For such illustrations, see Wenran Jiang, *Competing as Potential Superpowers: Japan's China Policy 1978–1998*, Carleton University, Ph D thesis, 1999, pp. 256–7. A private think tank called in 1994 for a strict application of the four 1992 ODA principles (Japan Forum on International Relations, Policy Recommendations on 'The Future of China in the Context of Asian Security', Tokyo, 1994, p. 9).

42   Jin Xide, 'Enjo de wa nakute, "gaishi donyu" ', *Asahi Shimbun*, 2 February 2001.

43   *Asahi Shimbun*, 10 October 2000.

44   *Japan Times*, 13 May 2000.

45   Even the media more inclined towards China have made this link (*Mainichi Shimbun*, 17 December 1999; *Asahi Shimbun*, 8 February 1999).

46   *Asahi Shimbun*, 8 September 2000.

47   *Financial Times*, 20 June 2001; *Japan Times*, 9 August 2001.

48   Murai Tomohide, 'Ajia no anzenhosho to Nitchu kankei', *Gaiko Jippo*, January 1998, p. 18. On the wastage inherent in Japan's ODA to China, see Christopher B. Johnstone, 'Japan's China Policy. Implications for US–Japan', *Asian Survey*, vol. XXXVIII, no. 11, November 1998, p. 1,079.

49   For details of the future direction, see the recommendations in *The Second Country Study for Japan's Official Development Assistance to the People's Republic of China*, op. cit. See also Miyamoto Yuji, 'Tai Chu keizai enjo o do suru ka', op. cit., pp. 82–3. See also '21 seki ni muketa tai Chu keizai kyoryoku no arikata ni kansuru kondankai', available at http://www.mofa.go.jp/mofaj/gaiko/oda/seisaku/seisaku_1/sei_1_13_1.html. For the loans in 2001, see *Japan Times*, 30 March 2002.

50   *Yomiuri Shimbun*, 25 November 2000.

51   The Japanese side had demanded the switch to an annual basis back in 1993 but had to give it up in the face of strong Chinese opposition (Zhao, Quansheng, *Interpreting Chinese Foreign Policy: The Micro–Macro Linkage Approach*, Oxford: Oxford University Press, 1996, pp. 169, 173).

52   For the dispute over yen loans for the next few years, see *Japan Times*, 27 July 2001.

53   For a report on such an expression of changing interest by Foreign Minister Tang Jiaxuan, see *Sankei Shimbun*, 26 December 1999.

54   *Asahi Shimbun*, 8 February 1999.

55   *Zadankai*, op. cit., p. 32.

56   For 'competitive coexistence', see Wu Xinbo, 'The Security Dimension of Sino-Japanese Relations', *Asian Survey*, vol. 40, no. 2, 2000, p. 296.

57   Denny Roy, *Hegemon on the Horizon?*, op. cit., p. 129.

58   Polls conducted by *Yomiuri Shimbun*, reproduced on the website of the Roper Center, available at http://www.ropercenter.uconn.edu/JPOLL/.

59   Quoted in Sharif M. Shuja, 'China After Deng Xiaoping: Implications for Japan', *East Asia*, vol. 17, no. 1, spring 1999, p. 83.

60   *Zadankai*, op. cit., p. 32.

61   Polls conducted by *Yomiuri Shimbun*, reproduced on the website of the Roper Center, op. cit.

62   '21 seki ni muketa tai Chu keizai kyoryoku no arikata ni kansuru kondankai', op. cit., p. 11.

63   Hanns-Günther Hilpert, *Japan und China im ostasiatischen Wirtschaftsraum: Komplementaritäten und Konflikte*, in Markus Taube and Anton Gälli (eds), *Chinas Wirtschaft im Wandel*, Munich: Weltforum Verlag, 1999, p. 29.

64 Nakai Yoshifumi, 'Chugoku no "kyoi" to Nitchu, Nichi Bei kankei', in Amako Satoshi (ed.), *Chugoku wa kyoi ka*, Tokyo: Keiso Shobo, 1997, p. 106.

65 For a thorough analysis of this complementarity, see Laura Newby, *Sino-Japanese Relations. China's Perspective*, London: Routledge, 1988.

66 For a discussion of the influence of the wider political and historical climate between the two countries on Japanese FDI, see Rong Xiaomin, 'Explaining the Patterns of Japanese Foreign Direct Investment in China', *Journal of Contemporary China*, vol. 8. no. 20, 1999, pp. 123–46.

67 The irony is, however, that these imports are generated by Japanese FDI in China, which is motivated by good profits, prevention of future Japanese–Chinese competition for agricultural goods on the world market and diversification of imports (Hanns-Günther Hilpert ,'Wirtschaftliche Teile meines Buches', e-mail, 3 October 2001).

68 For some earlier critical business opinions, see Michael J. Green and Benjamin L. Self, 'Japan's Changing China Policy: From Commercial Liberalism to Reluctant Realism', *Survival*, vol. 38, no. 2, summer 1996, fn. 57 and 58.

69 Kokubun Ryosei, 'Nichi-Bei-Chu kankei no genjo to tenbo', *Toa*, no. 402, December 2000, p. 47.

70 *Asahi Shimbun*, 19 January 2000.

71 For a list of Japanese complaints, see Tanaka Naoki, *The Outlook of Japanese–Chinese Relations in the 21st Century*, Tokyo: 21st Century Public Policy Institute, 2000.

72 On the former, see Kokubun Ryosei, 'Nichi-Bei-Chu kankei no genjo to tenbo', op. cit., p. 47.

73 This became particularly apparent during Prime Minister Zhu Rongji's visit to Japan in October 2000 (*Yomiuri Shimbun*, 18 October 2000).

74 Hanns-Günther Hilpert, *Japan und China im ostasiatischen Wirtschaftsraum*, op. cit., pp. 54–5.

75 *Nihon Keizai Shimbun*, 23 November 2000.

76 Gaye Christoffersen, 'China and the Asia-Pacific. Need for a Grand Strategy', *Asian Survey*, vol. XXXVI, no. 11, November 1996, p. 1,074.

77 For a report on such incidents involving Toshiba, Japan Airlines and Mitsubishi Motors, see *Asahi Shimbun*, 5 April 2001.

78 Xu Zhixian, 'Forecasting Sino-Japanese Relations in the 21st Century', *Contemporary International Relations*, vol. 8, no. 9, September 1998, p. 4. He and other experts seem to be rather out of step with how the Chinese public feels: asked in 1999 to choose between Japan's ODA being given to traditional infrastructure projects or to environmental protection projects, 80.8 per cent of the Chinese polled chose the latter (*Yomiuri Shimbun*, 30 September 1999).

79 Rex Li, 'The China Challenge', op. cit., p. 1.

80 On the tacit understanding in the 1970s, see Kokubun Ryosei, 'Reisen shuketsugo no Nitchu kankei', *Kokusai Mondai*, no. 490, January 2000, p. 50 (translation in *Japan Echo*, vol. 28, no. 2, April 2001, p. 13). On Deng Xiaoping making this link in 1987 in order to receive more Japanese ODA, see Takahara Akio, 'The Present and Future of Japan–China Relations', op. cit., p. 43. See also Michael H. Armacost and Kenneth B. Pyle, 'Japan and the Engagement of China: Challenges for U.S. Policy Coordination', *NBR Analysis*, vol. 12, no. 5, 2001, p. 14, available at http://www.nbr.org/publications/analysis/vol12no5/essay.html.

81 For examples of these Chinese accusations, see Tomoyuki Kojima, 'The Sino-Japanese Relationships', *China Perspectives* (Hong Kong), no. 30, July–August 2000, pp. 4–16.

82 On 'joint economic programme' and 'introduction of foreign capital', see *Sankei Shimbun*, 14 September 2000, and Jin Xide, 'Enjo de wa nakute, "gaishi donyu"', op. cit.

83   Mori Kazuko, 'Posto reisen to Chugoku no anzenhoshokan "Kyochoteki anzen-hosho" o megutte', in Yamamoto Takehiko (ed.), *Kokusai anzenhosho no atarashii tenkai*, Tokyo: Waseda Daigaku Shuppansha, 1999, p. 47. For the quote by Miyamoto Nobuo, see Zbigniew Brzezinski, 'Living with China', *The National Interest*, spring 2000, p. 17.

84   Gerald Segal, 'The Coming Confrontation Between China and Japan?', *World Policy Journal*, vol. 10, no. 2, summer 1993, pp. 27–32.

85   David Shambaugh, *China and Japan Towards the Twenty-First Century: Rivals for Pre-eminence or Complex Interdependence?*, in Christopher Howe (ed.), *China and Japan. History, Trends, and Prospects*, Oxford: Clarendon Press, 1996, p. 97.

86   Mel Gurtov and Byong-Moo Hwang, *China's Security. The New Roles of the Military*, Boulder, CO: Lynne Rienner, 1998. p. 73.

87   Shinkichi Eto, *Evolving Sino-Japanese Relations*, in Joshua D. Katz and Tilly C. Friedman-Lichtschein, *Japan's New World Role*, Boulder, CO: Westview Press, 1985, p. 55.

88   Hidenori Ijiri, *Sino-Japanese Controversy since the 1972 Diplomatic Normalization*, in Christopher Howe (ed.), *China and Japan. History, Trends, and Prospects*, Oxford: Clarendon Press, 1996, p. 60.

89   Amako Satoshi, 'Nihon kara mita Taiwan mondai to tenkanki no Nittai kankei', *Kokusai Mondai*, no. 488, November 2000, p. 47.

90   On Japan's changing perception of Taiwan, see, for example, Yokoyama Hiroshi, *Chugoku o muda ni shita eiyu tachi*, op. cit., pp. 195–204. On all these points, see also Qingxin Ken Wang, 'Taiwan in Japan's Relations with China and the United States After the Cold War', *Pacific Affairs*, vol. 73, no. 3, fall 2000, pp. 353–73.

91   Amako Satoshi, 'Nihon kara mita Taiwan mondai to tenkanki no Nittai kankei', op. cit., pp. 49–50.

92   Takahara Akio, 'The Present and Future of Japan–China Relations', op. cit., p. 41.

93   Qingxin Ken Wang, 'Taiwan in Japan's Relations with China and the United States after the Cold War', op. cit., p. 358.

94   Amako Satoshi, 'Nihon kara mita Taiwan mondai to tenkanki no Nittai kankei', op. cit., pp. 51, 54. The decrease is probably due to the different effect of the Asian economic crisis as well as to the rise in the number of Japanese visitors to South Korea.

95   *Yomiuri Shimbun*, 26 April 2000. For a journalistic analysis of the Taiwan lobby, see Honzawa Jiro, *Taiwan robii*, Tokyo: Data House, 1998.

96   For details, see Amako Satoshi, 'Nihon kara mita Taiwan mondai to tenkanki no Nittai kankei', op. cit., pp. 50–1.

97   The book was even reviewed in the Gaimusho-edited journal *Gaiko Forum*, no. 137, January 2000, p. 92.

98   *Sankei Shimbun*, 17 July 2000.

99   Qingxin Ken Wang, 'Taiwan in Japan's Relations with China and the United States After the Cold War', op. cit., p. 363.

100 He visited Taiwan as the first head of the metropolitan government since 1972, and in his talks with Taiwan's President Li Denghui referred to the island as the 'Republic of China' (*Yomiuri Shimbun*, 16 November 1999).

101 *Sankei Shimbun*, 14 October 2000.

102 Amako Satoshi, 'Nihon kara mita Taiwan mondai to tenkanki no Nittai kankei', op. cit., p. 55.

103 *Japan Times*, 25 September 1999; Interview with the Kyodo journalist Tsukayoshi Toshihiko, 6 October 1999.

104 *Nikkei Weekly*, 25 April 1992.

105 Takagi, Seiichiro (ed.), *Datsu Reisen ki no Chugoku Gaiko to Ajia Taiheiyo*, Tokyo: Kokusai Mondai Kenkyusho, 2000, pp. 106–25.

106 Rex Li, 'Partners or Rivals? Chinese Perceptions of Japan's Security Strategy', *Journal of Strategic Studies*, vol. 22, no. 4, December 1999, p. 6. For opinions from Chinese military research institutes, see Michael Pillsbury, *China Debates the Future Security Environment*, Washington, DC: Institute for National Strategic Studies, National Defense University, p.130.

107 Kokubun Ryosei (ed.), *Challenges for China–Japan–US Cooperation*, Tokyo: Japan Center for International Cooperation, 1998, p. 14.

108 David Shambaugh, 'The Insecurity of Security: The PLA's Evolving Doctrine and Threat Perceptions Towards 2000', *Journal of Northeast Asian Studies*, spring 1994, p. 6.

109 On China's opposition to Japan's proposal of a US–China–North Korea–South Korea–Russia–Japan group for solving the tensions on the Korean Peninsula, see Xiaoxiong Yi, 'A Neutralized Korea? The North–South Rapprochement and China's Korea Policy', *Korean Journal of Defense Analysis*, vol. XII, no. 2, winter 2000, p. 104.

110 *China Daily*, 26 May 1997.

111 Jianwei Wang, 'Confidence-building Measures and China–Japan Relations', in Benjamin L. Self and Yuki Tatsumi (eds), *Confidence-Building Measures and Security Issues in Northeast Asia*, Washington, DC: Henry L. Stimson Center, Report no. 33, February 1999, p. 86.

112 See the interview with the US Deputy Secretary of State Strobe Talbott in *Asahi Shimbun*, 23 June 1998. According to Limaye (quoting Funabashi), Japan itself had requested participation in the Geneva conference, but according to *Japan Echo* it was indeed Washington which had urged Japan (and Germany) to attend the Geneva meeting (Satu P. Limaye, 'Tokyo's Dynamic Diplomacy: Japan and the Subcontinent's Nuclear Tests', *Contemporary Southeast Asia*, vol. 22, no. 2, August 2000, pp. 325, 333). Aoki Shuzo, 'A New Nuclear Arms Race?', *Japan Echo*, vol. 25, no. 5, October 1998, p. 26.

113 For a typical critical Chinese opinion on Japan's regional leadership ambitions, see Tian Peiliang, 'The Rise of ASEAN and Japan's ASEAN Strategy', *Foreign Affairs Journal*, no. 37, September 1995, pp. 64–71.

114 Jianwei Wang, *Confidence-building Measures and China–Japan Relations*, op. cit., p. 73.

115 Yoichi Funabashi, *Alliance Adrift*, Washington, DC: Council on Foreign Relations, p. 423.

116 Denny Roy, 'China's Threat to East Asian Security', *International Security*, vol. 19, no. 1, summer 1994, pp. 119–20.

117 *Financial Times*, 30–31 August 1997.

118 Ishii Akira, 'Shiren ni tatsu "Sekai no naka no Nitchu kankei" ', *Kokusai Mondai*, January 1995, p. 35.

119 Yang Bojiang, *Sino-Japanese Relations and Measures to Enhance Mutual Trust*, in Michael Krepon (ed.), *Chinese Perspectives on Confidence-Building Measures*, Washington, DC: Henry L. Stimson Center, Report no. 23, May 1997, p. 63.

120 Reinhard Drifte, *Japan's Quest for a Permanent Security Council Seat. A Matter of Pride or Justice?*, London/Oxford: Macmillan/St Antony's College, 2000, pp. 150–1. For a negative Chinese voice, see Zhu Feng, 'Kokuren kaikaku. Chugoku no shiten', in Mushakoji Kinhide (ed.), *Kokuren no zaisei to chikyu minshushugi*, Tokyo: Meiji Gakuin Daigaku Kokusai Heiwa Kenkyusho, 1995, pp. 219–41. See also Takagi, Seiichiro (ed.), *Datsu Reisen ki no Chugoku Gaiko to Ajia*, op. cit., pp. 114–5.

121 Xu Zhixian, Zhang Minqian and Hong Jianjun, 'On the Foreign Strategy and the Trend of China Policy of the US, Western Europe, and Japan at the Turn of the Century', *Contemporary International Relations*, vol. 8, no. 3, March 1998, p. 16; Ishii Akira, 'Shiren ni tatsu "Sekai no naka no Nitchu kankei" ', op. cit., pp. 36–9.

122 Before the 1993 Tokyo Summit senior members of the Mitsuzuka faction called for the government to petition for the participation of China in the summit as an

observer (*Japan Times*, 23 June 1993; *Japan Times*, 6 July 1993). In 1997 a foreign-policy panel of the LDP, headed by Takemi Keizo, suggested that Japan 'may also propose that the G-7 should accept China into its membership in addition to Russia' (Liberal Democratic Party (ed.), *Foreign Policy, Part 1: Japan's strategy towards the Asia-Pacific Region*, Tokyo, 1997, p. 25).

123 *Asahi Shimbun*, 11 October 1997.

124 *Asahi Shimbun*, 3 March 2000.

125 For some speculation on China's reasons, see *Asahi Shimbun*, 3 November 1999.

126 At APEC China is represented by Jiang Zemin, but at ASEM by Zhu Rongji.

127 On China great-power ambition, see Gilbert Rozman, 'China's Quest for Great Power Identity', *Orbis*, summer 1999, p. 385. For a criticsm of China's duplicity on this subject, see Michael Yahuda, 'Future Uncertain', *China Quarterly*, no. 159, September 1999, pp. 650–1.

128 Mel Gurtov and Byong-Moo Hwang, *China's Security*, op. cit., p. 5.

129 Amako Satoshi (ed.), *Chugoku wa kyoi ka*, Tokyo: Keiso Shobo, p. 8.

130 See, for example, Prime Minister Obuchi's speech in Beijing in July 1999, when he said 'Gunji taikoku ni wa naranai' (not become a military big power), quoted in *Nitchu Geppo*, 1 August 1999.

131 Ross even argues that the implications of geography are pointing to stability (Robert S. Ross, 'The Geography of Peace. East Asia in the 21st Century', *International Security*, vol. 23, no. 4, spring 1999, pp. 81–118). Betts and Christensen are much more pessimistic and point to the rising costs of deterring China (Richard K. Betts and Thomas J. Christensen, 'China: Getting the Questions Right', *The National Interest*, winter 2000/1, pp. 17–29). G.D. Foster points to China's attempt to increase its asymmetrical fighting advantage by using unconventional warfare – that is, seeking to cripple, intimdate and confuse (Gregory D. Foster, 'China as Great Power: From Red Menace to Green Giant?', *Communist and Post-Communist Studies*, vol. 34, 2001, p. 163.

132 On Japan seeing the threat from China as arising earlier than the US, see Michael J. Green and Benjamin L. Self, 'Japan's Changing China Policy', op. cit., p. 45.

133 *Asahi Shimbun*, 6 June 1998.

134 Yoichi Funabashi, *Alliance Adrift*, op. cit., p. 270.

135 Hideo Sato, 'Japan's China Perceptions and Its Policies in the Alliance with the United States', op. cit., p. 17.

136 Christopher B. Johnstone, 'Japan's China Policy', op. cit., p. 1083. On the lesser Japanese interest in human rights in comparison to the US, see Wan Ming, 'Human Rights and US–Japan Relations in Asia: Divergent Allies', *East Asia*, vol. 16, no. 3/4, autumn/winter 1998, pp. 137–168.

137 Christopher B. Johnstone, 'Japan's China Policy', op. cit., p. 1070.

138 Sharif M. Shuja, 'China after Deng Xiaoping', op. cit., p. 92.

139 Qingxin Ken Wang, 'Recent Japanese Economic Diplomacy in China', *Asian Survey*, vol. XXXIII, no. 6, June 1993, p. 638.

140 Johnstone, op. cit., p. 1,079.

141 On US attitude on World Bank loans to China, see Wakisaka Noriyuki, *Nichi Bei no tai Chu Keizai kyoryuoku*, in Kokubun Ryosei (ed.), *Japan, United States and China. A Scenario for Cooperation*, Tokyo: TBS Britannica, 1997, pp. 249–53.

142 Kurt M. Campbell, 'Energizing the US–Japan Security Partnership', *Washington Quarterly*, vol. 23, no. 4, autumn 2000, p. 128.

143 For a simulation of a PRC–ROC crisis bearing this out, see PHP Sogo Kenkyusho (ed.), *Taiwan yuji no shimyureshon. Kannenteki amporon kara gutaiteki kodo ron e no tenkan*, Tokyo: PHP Sogo Kenkyusho, 2000.

144 Nakanishi, Hiroshi, *Sogo anzen hosho senryaku no saikosei*, in Kokubun Ryosei (ed.), *Nihon, Amerika, Chugoku: Kyocho e no shinario*, Tokyo: TBS Britannica, 1997, p. 115.

145 Interview with a senior official of the Defence Agency, 6 May 1999.

146 Nakai Yoshifumi, *Policy Coordination on Taiwan*, in Nishihara Masashi (ed.), *The Japan–US Alliance. New Challenges for the 21st Century*, Tokyo: Japan Center for International Exchange, 2000, pp. 80–1.

147 Nakai Yoshifumi, *Policy Coordination on Taiwan*, op. cit., pp. 87–8.

148 On the whole history of the 'Three Nos', which goes much further back than June 1998, see James Mann, *About Face. A History of America's Curious Relationship with China, from Nixon to Clinton*, New York: Alfred A. Knopf, 1999, pp. 330, 358, 366–7. The 'Three Nos' are: a promise that the US would not support Taiwan's independence, its admission to the United Nations or the creation of two Chinas.

149 For this concern, see Nishihara Masashi, who is otherwise known for his Realist opinion about China's security policy (Nishihara Masashi, 'Japan's Receptivity to Conditional Engagement', in James Shinn (ed.), *Weaving the Net*, op. cit., pp. 185–6).

150 Interview with a senior official of the Defence Policy Bureau of the Defence Agency, 6 May 1999. This evaluation is supported by recent disclosures about secret high-level contacts between the Taiwanese and Chinese governments in the early 1990s (Ijiri Hidenori, 'Nitchutai kankei e no shin shikaku', *Chugoku21*, vol. 10, no. 1, 2001, p. 62).

151 *Asahi Shimbun*, 23 March 1999; *Sankei*, 2 December 1997.

152 Nishihara Masashi, *Japan's Receptivity to Conditional Engagement*, op. cit., p. 187.

153 Ralph A. Cossa and Jane Skanderup, *U.S.–Japan–China Relations: Can Three Part Harmony Be Sustained?*, Honolulu/Washington, DC: Pacific Forum CSIS, September 1998, p. 8.

154 Edward N. Luttwak, 'Why We Need an Incoherent Foreign Policy', *Washington Quarterly*, winter 1998, pp. 21–31.

155 For a critical analysis of US unilateralism, see Charles Maynes, 'US Unilateralism and its Dangers', *Review of International Studies*, vol. 25, no. 3, July 1999, pp. 515–18.

156 US ambassador Meyer reportedly warned the administration in 1972 of Japanese fears about the possibility of Nixon offering to China the non-armament of Japan (Morinosuke Kajima, *The Road to Pan-Asia*, Tokyo: Japan Times Ltd, 1973, p. 107).

157 On Nixon and Kissinger's views, see Allen S. Whiting and Jianfei Xin, 'Sino-Japanese Relations: Pragmatism and Passion', *World Policy Journal*, winter 1990–1, p. 131. On similar views both in the US and Europe, see Gerald Segal, 'Keeping East Asia Pacific', *Korean Journal of Defense Analysis*, vol. V, no. 1, summer 1993, pp. 9–26.

158 James Mann, *About Face*, op. cit., p. 227.

159 Michael J. Green, 'The Forgotten Player', *The National Interest*, summer 2000, p. 42.

160 Tennichi Takahiko, 'Nihon no gaiko ronso', in Kokubun Ryosei (ed.), *Nihon, Amerika, Chugoku. Kyocho e no shinario*, Tokyo: TBS Britannica, 1997, p. 80.

161 On Shiina, see Wakamiya Yoshibumi, *The Postwar Conservative View of Asia*, Tokyo: LTCB International Library Foundation, 1998, pp. 242–3. The most famous public statement by the US on this containment function of the alliance is by Major-General Henry Stockpole, who spoke of the US being a cap in the bottle (*Daily Yomiuri*, 20 March 1990).

162 Interview with former State Foreign Secretary Takemi Keizo in *Asahi Shimbun*, 22 October 1999.

163 *International Herald Tribune*, 6–7 March 1999.

164 Ralph A. Cossa and Jane Skanderup, *U.S.–Japan–China Relations*, p. C-2.

165 Christopher B. Johnstone, 'Japan's China policy', op. cit., p. 1082.

166 *Dispatch Magazine*, (Department of State), June 1999, p. 6, quoting a speech on 20 May 1999.

167 *Asahi Shimbun*, 19 April 1998.

168 *Far Eastern Economic Review*, 25 June 1998. For a very critical comment on Clinton's alleged China bias, see Yoichi Funabashi, 'Tokyo's Depression Diplomacy', *Foreign Affairs*, November–December 1998, p. 32.

169 For a good summary of Japan's ill feelings, see Japan Center for International Exchange (ed.), *New Dimensions of China–Japan–US Relations*, Tokyo: Japan Center for International Exchange, 1999, pp. 79–83. For a critical US comment, see also Ralph A. Cossa and Jane Skanderup, *U.S.–Japan–China Relations*, pp. 19–20.

170 For US arms exports before Tiananmen, see Research Institute for Peace and Security (RIPS) (ed.), *Asian Security 1990–91*, London: Brassey's, 1991, p. 95; Nishihara Masashi, *Japan's Receptivity to Conditional Engagement*, op. cit., pp. 185–6.

171 Yuan Jing-Dong, 'Asia and Nonproliferation After the Cold War', op. cit., p. 29. See also Report to the Chairman, Joint Economic Committee, US Senate, *China. Military Imports from the US and the European Union since the 1989 Embargoes*, Washington, DC: General Accounting Office, June 1998.

172 *Washington Times*, 19 February 1999.

173 Press Conference by the Press Secretary, 30 June 1998.

174 *Washington Post*, 30 June 1998.

175 Soeya Yoshihide, 'Short Side of the Triangle', *Look Japan*, August 1998, p. 23.

176 *Asahi Shimbun*, 6 June 1998.

177 *Yomiuri Shimbun*, 29 December 2000.

178 For the US frustration about this, see Yoichi Funabashi, *Alliance Adrift*, op. cit., pp. 441, 452.

179 Kurt M. Campbell, 'Energizing the US–Japan Security Partnership', op. cit., p. 127; Christopher B. Johnstone, 'Japan's China Policy', op. cit., p. 1082, fn. 24.

180 *Asahi Shimbun*, 30 June 1998.

181 William R. Hawkins, 'For All the Tea in China: The "Commercial Temptation" in US Foreign Policy', *Strategic Review*, vol. XXIV, no. 4, fall 1996, p. 7.

182 Kurt Campbell refers to a split between the 'China first' and the 'Japan first' wings of the Asianist school inside the US policy-making circle, and says that this rift had become more explicit and exacerbated after the 1996 Joint Declaration (Kurt M. Campbell, 'Energizing the US–Japan Security Partnership', op. cit., p. 127).

183 *The United States and Japan: Advancing Toward a Mature Partnership*, National Defense University, Institute for National Security Studies, 11 October 2000, p. 3, available at http://www.ndu.edu//ndu/SR_JAPAN.htm.

184 Ming Zhang and Ronald N. Montaperto, *A Triad of Another Kind. The United States, China, and Japan*, New York: St Martin's Press, 1999, p. 100.

185 For the US–China agreements, see Harry Harding, 'The Uncertain Future of US–China Relations', *Asia-Pacific Review*, vol. 6, no. 1, 1999, p. 9. For the Japan–China projects, see http://mofa.go.jp/index.html.

186 For the former, see Ralph A. Cossa and Jane Skanderup, *U.S.–Japan–China Relations*, p. 30; for the latter, see Gilbert Rozman, 'China's Quest for Great Power Identity', op. cit., p. 391.

187 Michael Pillsbury, *China Debates the Future Security Environment*, op. cit., p. 128. Sutter quotes Prime Minister Hosokawa to that effect (Robert G. Sutter, *Chinese Policy Priorities and their Implications for the US*, Lanham: Rowman & Littlefield Publishers, 2000, p. 82).

188 Yoichi Funabashi, *Alliance Adrift*, op. cit., p. 423.

189 Lu Zhongwei, 'On China–US–Japan Trilateral Relations', *Contemporary International Relations*, vol. 7, no. 12, December 1997, p. 2.

190 For example criticizing Japan for the strengthening of the Japan–US alliance and not the US, putting more pressure on Japan over Taiwan (see Chapter 3), and intimating that Japan as an Asian country is expected to perform a different role. On the latter, see Yoichi Funabashi, *Alliance Adrift*, op. cit., p. 423.

191 China is also trying to win US sympathies by recalling both countries' war against Japan (James Miles, 'Chinese Nationalism, US Policy and Asian Security', *Survival*, vol. 42, no. 4, winter 2000–1, p. 71, fn. 32; Yoichi Funabashi, 'Tokyo's Depression Diplomacy', op. cit., p. 32).

192 Xu Zhixian, 'Forecasting Sino-Japanese Relations in the 21st Century', op. cit., p. 8.

193 Chinese often try to convince the US that it is naive about Japan's 'true' nature and that Japan only accepts US demands for a greater military role in order to become later independent of the US. On this point, see David Shambaugh, 'China's Military Views the World. Ambivalent Security', *International Security*, vol. 24, no. 3, winter 1999/2000, p. 69. See also Michael Pillsbury, *China Debates the Future Security Environment*, op. cit., p. 116.

194 For a good review of the immediate Chinese official statement on 18 April 1996 and the following Chinese press reports and comments, see Takagi Seiichiro, 'Reisengo no kokusai kenryoku kozo to Chugoku no taigai senryaku', *Kokusai Mondai*, no. 454, January 1998, pp. 7–14. See also Chu Shulong, *China and the US–Japan and US–Korea Alliances in a Changing Northeast Asia*, Stanford, CA: Asia/Pacific Research Center, Stanford University, June 1999, pp. 13–5, available at http://www.stanford.edu/group/APAR/publications/papers/Chu2.pdf.

195 Zhao Jieqi, ' "Redefinition" of Japan–US Security Arrangements and Its Repercussions', *Foreign Affairs Journal*, no. 41, September 1996, p. 36. It was alleged that Kurt Campbell, then US deputy assistant secretary of defence for Asia and the Pacific, even stated in September 1997 that the guidelines were to push NATO to the East (*Mainichi Shimbun*, 10 May 1999).

196 Kokubun Ryosei, 'Shin gaidorain. Keikai suru Chugoku', *Mainichi Shimbun*, 11 April 1999.

197 This Chinese concern is also mentioned in Yoichi Funabashi, *Alliance Adrift*, op. cit., p. 422.

198 This metaphor was also used in an article in the *Jiefang Ribao*, 6 May 1996, quoted in Okabe Tatsumi, Takagi Seiichiro and Kokubun Ryosei (eds), *Nichi-Bei-Chu. Anzen hosho kyoryoku o mezashite*, Tokyo: Keiso Shobo, 1999, p. 79.

199 *Asahi Evening News*, 2 February 1999, quoting the Chinese ambassador to Japan, Chen Jian.

200 Jiang Wenran refers to a consensus among well-informed Chinese academics and diplomats that the new Japan–US security partnership is aimed at containing China (Wenran Jiang, *Competing as Potential Superpowers*, op. cit., p. 270. This is also confirmed by Yoichi Funabashi, *Alliance Adrift*, op. cit., pp. 420–1.

201 See, for example, Shen Guofang, PRC Foreign Ministry spokesman, quoted in the *New York Times*, 19 April 1996.

202 On this point, see also *Beijing Review*, 14 August 1999, p. 9.

203 *Japan Times*, 1 April 1996.

204 Okabe Tatsumi, Takagi Seiichiro and Kokubun Ryosei (eds), *Nichi-Bei-Chu*, op. cit., p. ii; *East Asian Strategic Review 1997–1998*, Tokyo: National Institute for Defense Studies, 1998, p. 20; Amitav Acharya, 'A Concern of Asia?', *Survival*, vol. 41, no. 3, autumn 1999, p. 91; Wang Jisi, 'The Role of the US as a Global and Pacific Power: A View from China', *Pacific Review*, vol. 10, no. 1, 1997, p. 12.

205 Michael Yahuda, 'Future Uncertain', op. cit., p. 657.

206 Thomas J. Christensen, 'China, the US–Japan Alliance, and the Security Dilemma in East Asia', *International Security*, vol. 23, no. 4, spring 1999, p. 63. Fan Xuejiang of the National Defence University in China argued in 1999 that the possibility of a Sino-Japanese conflict over the Taiwan issue cannot be ruled out (quoted in Rex Li, 'Partners or Rivals? Chinese Perceptions of Japan's Security Strategy', *Journal of Strategic Studies*, vol. 22, no. 4, December 1999, p. 25, fn. 69.

207 *Yomiuri Shimbun*, 6 September 1997.

208 *International Herald Tribune*, 10 March 1999.

209 *China Daily*, 6 March 1999; *People's Daily*, 11 March 1999; *China Daily*, 9 March 1999.

210 *Japan Times*, 14 July 1999.

211 Among the Chinese security analysts there seems to be a wider spectrum of opinion which includes greater understanding of Japan's security interests. For a summary of this spectrum, see Rex Li, 'Partners or Rivals? Chinese Perceptions of Japan's Security Strategy', *Journal of Strategic Studies*, vol. 22, no. 4, December 1999, pp. 18–19.

212 Thomas J. Christensen, 'China, the US–Japan Alliance', op. cit., p. 70.

213 Interview with a diplomat of the Ministry of Foreign Affairs, 7 May 1999.

214 *Sankei Shimbun*, 14 July 2000.

215 Michael Yahuda, 'Future Uncertain', p. 657.

216 Wang Jisi, 'Building a Constructive Relationship', in Morton I. Abramowitz, Funabashi Yoichi and Wang Jisi (eds), *China–Japan–US. Managing the Trilateral Relationship*, Tokyo: Japan Center for International Cooperation, 1998, p. 29.

217 Liu Jiangyong, 'Clinton's China Visit and the New Trends in Sino-US–Japanese Relations', *Contemporary International Relations*, vol. 8, no. 7, July 1998, p. 10.

218 Yoichi Funabashi, *Alliance Adrift*, op. cit., p. 421.

219 Wang, Jisi, *Building a Constructive Relationship*, op. cit., p. 34. See also David Shambaugh, 'China's Military Views the World. Ambivalent Security', *International Security*, vol. 24, no. 3, winter 1999/2000, p. 66.

220 A senior diplomat involved in Japan's China policy-making confirmed to the author that it was a deliberate policy to avoid the use of the word engagement (interview with a senior Japanese diplomat, 14 April 1999).

221 'Nihon no Ajia Taiheiyo senryaku, henka e no chosen', Liberal Democratic Party, 28 November 1997 (English version: 'Japan's Strategy Towards the Asia-Pacific Region') , p. 23. However, Tamura Shigenobu, a key member of staff for security policy in the LDP, clearly refers in his book to engagement policy (mentioning the English as well as the Japanese version of the term); see Tamura Shigenobu, *Nichi Bei ampo to kyokuto yuji*, Tokyo: Nanso sha, 1997, p. 45.

222 For examples of private deference, see the *Sankei Shimbun* series on Japanese–Chinese relations from 6 February to 18 February 2001.

223 The Gaimusho now uses 'Donghai' (Tokai) for the East China Sea (for example in the old as well as the new Japan–China Fisheries Agreement), but other agencies (the coastguard or the National Land Agency) use 'Higashi Shina Kai' (*Sankei Shimbun*, 12 October 2000). On the Falungong case, see *Yomiuri Shimbun*, 9 March 2000. On the Dalai Lama visit, see a critical comment in *AERA*, 1 May 2000.

224 On the role of the Leftist intellectuals, see Chalmers Johnson, 'The Patterns of Japan's Relations with China', *Pacific Affairs*, vol. 59, no. 3, fall 1986, p. 409. On a recent critical account of China exploiting Japan's war guilt, particularly towards the Gaimusho, see Suzuki Masayuki and Takubo Tadae, 'Beijing "Nihon taishikan" dogeza gaiko no ichibu shiju', *Shokun!*, January 1997, pp. 38–49. For China's astute handling of pro-China organisations in Japan, see the series in *Sankei Shimbun* between 6 and 18 February 2001, op. cit.

225 Yokoyama Hiroshi, *Chugoku o muda ni shita eiyu tachi*, Tokyo: Kodansha, 1999, pp. 250–3.

226 On the impact of the notion of hierarchy on Japan's international relations, see, for example, G. John Ikenberry and Jitsuo Tsuchiyama, *Between Balance of Power and Community: The Future of Multilateral Security Cooperation in the Asia Pacific*, May 2000, available at http://rice.edu/projects/baker/Pubs/...publications/jescgem/fmscap4/fmscap.html.

227 Thomas J. Christensen, *Pride, Pressure, and Politics*, op. cit., p. 252.

228 See, for example, Miyamoto Yuji, 'Tai Chu keizai enjo o do suru ka', op. cit., p. 82. He incidentally uses the expression '*kanyo*' in his article. When I mentioned the official policy of avoiding the expression, he responded that he had not consulted with the China Division about it.

229 Ozawa Ichiro, *Nihon kaizo no keikaku*, Tokyo: Kodansha, 1994, p. 156.

230 *Japan Times*, 17 July 2001.
231 *Sankei Shimbun*, 28 August 2000.
232 *Asahi Shimbun*, 31 October 1999.

Conclusions

1 Quoted in Eto Shinkichi, 'Recent Developments in Sino-Japanese Relations', *Asian Survey*, vol. XX, no. 7, July 1980, p. 740.

2 William Perry, 'The Cost of American Military Strategy in Northeast Asia', *Gaiko Forum* (English edition), winter 2001, p. 14.

3 For this assertion, see Eric Heginbotham and Richard J. Samuels, 'Mercantile Realism and Japanese Foreign Policy', *International Security*, vol. 22, no. 4, spring 1998, pp. 172–3.

4 Richard K. Betts and Thomas J. Christensen, 'China: Getting the Questions Right', *The National Interest*, winter 2000/1, p. 22.

5 For an analysis of these developments, see Wakabayashi Masahiro, 'Taiwan ni okeru kokka, kokumin zaihen to Chu-Tai kankei', *Kokusai Mondai*, no. 488, November 2000, pp. 2–15.

6 Tanaka Akihiko, 'Chugoku to taito', in Ito Kenichi (ed.), *21 seki Nihon no daisenryaku. Shimaguni kara kaiyo kokka e*, Tokyo: Nihon Kokusai Foramu Fuoresuto Shuppan, 2000, pp. 213–18.

7 See, for example, Cho Koi, 'Chugoku no Taiwan seisaku no kettei', *Kokusai Mondai*, no. 488, November 2000, pp. 16–29.

8 Richard K. Betts and Thomas J. Christensen, 'China: Getting the Questions Right', op. cit., p. 23.

9 Paul Wolfowitz, *Managing Our Way to a Peaceful Century*, in Bill Emmott, Koji Watanabe and Paul Wolfowitz, *Managing the International System Over the Next Ten Years: Three Essays*, New York: Trilateral Commission, 1997, p. 52.

10 G. John Ikenberry, 'America's Ambivalent Economic and Security Multilateralism', *East Asian Economic Perspectives*, vol. 12, March 2001, pp. 40–1.

11 *Mainichi Daily News*, 16 March 2001.

12 Former Prime Minister Takeshita Noboru suggested that Japan should assume an intermediary role between China and the West (*Yomiuri Shimbun*, 14 January 1997; quoted in Tennichi, Takahiko, 'Debates on Japan's Foreign Policy', in Kokubun Ryosei (ed.), *Challenges for China–Japan–US Cooperation*, Tokyo: Japan Center for International Cooperation, 1998, p. 83). The Japan-based Chinese scholar Zhu Jianrong also suggests such an intermediary role for Japan, in 'Dai 136 kai Kokkai. Sangiin Gaimuiinkai Kaigiroku dai juichi go', House of Councillors, Foreign Affairs Committee, 16 May 1996. p. 45.

13 Hideo Sato, 'Japan's China Perceptions and its Policies in the Alliance with the United States', *Journal of International Political Economy*, vol. 2, no. 1, March 1998, p. 15.

14 Tennichi, Takahiko, *Debates on Japan's foreign Policy*, in Kokubun Ryosei (ed.), *Challenges for China–Japan–US Cooperation*, Tokyo: Japan Center for International Cooperation, 1998, p. 83.

15 Christopher P. Twomey, 'Japan, a Circumscribed Balancer: Building on Defensive Realism to Make Predictions about East Asian Security', *Security Studies*, vol. 9, no. 4, 2000, p. 168.

16 Aaron L. Friedberg, 'Will Europe's Past Be Asia's Future?', *Survival*, vol. 42, no. 3, autumn 2000, p. 157.

17 Kenneth B. Pyle, 'Old New Orders and the Future of Japan and the United States in Asia', *International House of Japan Bulletin*, vol. 17, no. 2, summer 1997, p. 6.

18 Samuel P. Huntington, *The Clash of Civilizations and the Making of World Order*, New York: Simon & Schuster, 1996, pp. 225, 229, 231–8.

19 Denny Roy, 'The "China Threat" Issue. Major Arguments', *Asian Survey*, vol. XXXVI, no. 8, August 1996, p. 766.

20 Murai Tomohide interview, *Yomiuri Shimbun*, 9 January 2001.

21 Tennichi Takahiko, *Nihon no gaiko ronso*, in Kokubun Ryosei (ed.), *Nihon, Amerika, Chugoku. Kyocho e no shinario*, Tokyo: TBS Britannica, 1997, p. 154.

22 Inoguchi Takashi, 'Nichi-Bei-Chu 3 koku kara mita sekai', *Nihon Keizai Kenkyu Centa Kaiho*, 15 September 1999, pp. 8–9.

23 For a Japanese Realist expert recognizing that explaining US–Japan defence cooperation is not enough, see Takagi Seiichiro, 'Tayosei no kanri. Higashi Ajia anzenhosho no mondai', in Okabe Tatsumi, Takagi Seichiro and Kokubun Ryosei (eds), *Nichi-Bei-Chu. Anzen hosho kyoryoku o mezashite*, Tokyo: Keiso Shobo, 1999, pp. 189–90.

24 Japan will have to decide to proceed from the research phase to the development phase, and the decision to procure and to deploy a TMD system is five or more years away. See Working Group Report, *Theater Missile Defenses in the Asia-Pacific Region*, Washington, DC: Henry L. Stimson Center, Report no. 34, June 2000, p. 63.

25 This is also argued by Kori Urayama, 'Chinese Perspectives on Theater Missile Defense: Policy Implications for Japan', *Asian Survey*, vol. XL, no. 4, July/August 2000, pp. 599–621; and by Thomas J. Christensen, 'Correspondence. The Author Replies', *International Security*, vol. 24, no. 4, spring 2000, p. 197.

26 For a good discussion of these issues, see Kori Urayama, 'Chinese Perspectives on Theater Missile Defense', op. cit., pp. 612–20. For a US proposal to abandon TMD and use a suspension of TMD to discuss arms control and confidence-building measures with China, see also Selig S. Harrison and Clyde V. Prestowitz (eds), *Asia After the 'Miracle'. Redefining US Economic and Security Priorities*, Washington, DC: Economic Strategy Institute, 1998, pp. 71–2.

27 *Asahi Shimbun*, 19 April 1998.

28 Mike Mochizuki and Michael O'Hanlon, 'Rethinking Alliances. A Liberal Vision for the US–Japanese Alliance', *Survival*. vol. 40, no. 2, summer 1998, p. 127.

29 Ikenberry and Tsuchiyama suggest a regional security organization which might include formal security commitments and collective security guarantees and which should involve China with the US, Japan and South Korea (G. John Ikenberry and Jitsuo Tsuchiyama, *Between Balance of Power and Community: The Future of Multilateral Security Cooperation in the Asia Pacific*, May 2000, available at http://rice.edu/projects/baker/Pubs/...publications/jescgem/fmscap4/fmscap.html

30 *Asahi Shimbun Asia Network Report 2000*, Tokyo: Asahi Shimbun, 2000, p. 59.

31 This has also been suggested by Thomas Berger, 'Set for Stability? Prospects for Conflict and Cooperation in East Asia', *Review of International Studies*, vol. 26, no. 3, July 2000, p. 427.

32 *Asahi Shimbun*, 22 December 1999.

33 Hideo Sato, 'Japan's China Perceptions and its Policies in the Alliance With the United States', op. cit., p. 18.

34 Hashimoto Kohei, *Asia's Energy Security and the Role of Japan*, Conference paper, May 2000.

35 Michishita Narushige, 'Security Arrangements After Peace in Korea', in Nishihara Masashi (ed.), *The Japan–US Alliance. New Challenges for the 21st Century*, New York: Japan Center for International Exchange, 2000, p. 59.

36 *Asahi Shimbun*, 22 September 2000; *Yomiuri Shimbun*, 7 January 2000.

37 *Yomiuri Shimbun*, 7 January 2000.

Index

abandonment and entrapment 9–10, 90–1, 121, 157, 161–3, 167
Acheson, D. 19
acid rain 72
Acquisition and Cross-Servicing Agreement 92, 161
Aegis destroyer 86, 93, 99–100
Afghanistan 71
Air Self-Defence Force 52, 58, 86, 169
air tankers 38
aircraft carrier 44
Akiyama, M. 97
Alagappa, M. 2, 36
Albright, M. 164
Allen, K. 119
'Alondra Rainbow' 106, 127
Amako, S. 73, 82, 157
Anti-Ballistic Missile Treaty 101, 179
anti-hegemony clause 24
anti-nuclear movement 45
ARF 4, 8, 36, 103, 110–11, 122–7, 129, 131–2, 142, 154
Armenia 107
Armstrong, D. 35
Asahi Shimbun 46, 67, 81
ASEAN 9, 61–2, 102–5, 132, 150, 154–5
ASEAN+3 110, 126
ASEAN Institutes of Strategic and International Studies 122
ASEAN Post-Ministerial Conference 124, 126
Asia-Europe Meeting 122
Asia-Pacific Forum of Defence Officials 113
Asia-Pacific Economic Cooperation 91, 111, 122, 124, 137
Asian Development Bank 60
Asian economic crisis 103, 136, 143, 164, 166

Asian Monetary Fund 138, 155
Association of East Asian Relations 70
Austin, G. 49
Australia 49, 89, 125, 129, 155
Azerbaijan 107

Baker, J. 31
Bandung Conference 20
Beijing Review 98
Berger, S. 130
Betts, R. 178
Bintuku 62
Bismarck, O. 64, 186
Bitzinger, R. 41
Blair, D. 84
Boao Asia Forum 129
Bolton, J. 100
Brown, L. 71
Brunei 61, 127
Burma *see* Myanmar
Bush, G. (Jun) 100–1, 107, 178–9, 184
Bush, G. (Snr) 30–1, 77, 88, 163
Buzan, B. 101

C3I 41
Cabinet Research and Information Office 66
Cairo Declaration 49
Calder, K. 49
Cambodia 77, 102, 104–5, 114, 118, 123–4, 127
Cambodian conflict 76
Campbell, K. 97, 108, 160
Canada 125, 137
Carnegie Endowment for International Peace 129
Center for Strategic & International Studies 130
Central Asia 39, 101–2, 107–8

Chemical Weapons Convention 118
Chen, J. 47
Chen, S. 153
Chi, H. 37, 113, 115, 118
China Daily 169
'China School' diplomats 19, 79, 83, 179
China: airforce 53; Beijing Institute of
    Strategic Studies 130; China–US
    relationship 26, 39; Chinese Academy
    of Social Sciences 34, 75, 129, 146,
    168; Chinese Reform Forum 129;
    Communist Party 34, 50, 117;
    Communist Party School 68; energy
    49–50, 109, 70–1; Institute of
    American Studies 129; Institute of
    International Studies 129; military
    budget 41–5, 81, 116–17, 174; Ministry
    of Foreign Affairs 50–1, 53, 95, 114,
    120, 168–9; missile exports 45–7;
    National Defence University 113; navy
    43, 48, 57–8, 61, 63, 69, 81–2, 118,
    158; nuclear deterrent 44–5, 94, 101,
    106, 172, 179; nuclear testing 44–8, 56,
    78, 83, 89, 95, 101, 114, 116–17, 146,
    174; People's Liberation Army 35, 39,
    42, 50–2, 61, 65, 82, 119–20, 154;
    tanker aircraft 58; territorial law 50,
    52–3, 61; threat 3, 13, 35, 46, 80–3,
    120, 132, 147, 155, 158
Christensen, T. 40, 142, 169, 171, 178
Chu, S. 37
Chuang, M. 70
Chun, Y. 169
civilian power 28, 37, 74, 133, 158, 162,
    176
Clark Air Force Base 77
Clemins, A. 65
Clinton administration 9, 22, 31, 64,
    89–92, 97, 128, 130, 156, 160, 164,
    166, 170–1
CNOOC 59
Coast Guard (*formerly* Maritime Safety
    Agency) 51, 53, 57, 73, 87, 106, 119,
    127–8
COCOM 21
Cohen, W. 103
Cold War 2, 9, 33–4, 54, 76–7, 86, 88–90
compensation 16
comprehensive national power 3, 39, 41,
    43, 133, 134
comprehensive national security 2, 41
comprehensive security (comprehensive
    national strength) 41

Comprehensive Test Ban Treaty 46–7,
    106, 117
confidence-building measures 108,
    113–14, 116–18, 121, 124–5, 133, 151,
    155, 183–4
constitution (Japan) 38, 80, 92–3, 169
constructivism 4, 6–7, 15; perspective 15,
    52, 84, 170, 175
containment 21, 35, 91, 101, 108, 122,
    134, 141, 158, 168, 184, 186
Cossa 162
Council for Security and Cooperation in
    Asia-Pacific 122, 129
crime 4, 70, 72–4, 83, 118, 175
cruise missiles 41
CSS-N-3 (JL-1) 47
Cui, T. 53
cultural revolution 17

Dalai Lama 171
Danjo Island 57
Davos World Economic Forum 129
Defense Academy 26, 61
Defense Agency 26, 44, 52, 66, 87, 93, 97,
    102, 112–3, 115, 118, 120, 125, 131,
    144, 154, 161, 169
deference 3–4, 6–7, 9, 18–19, 170–2, 177
democracy 19, 29, 33, 91, 140
Democratic Party of Japan 118
Democratic People's Republic of Korea *see*
    North Korea
Deng, X. 22, 23, 24, 41, 50, 53–4, 136
desertification 72
DF-3 (CSS-2) 47–8
DF-4 (CSS-3) 47
DF-15 (CSS-6/M-9) 47, 65
DF-21(CSS-5) 45, 47–8
dual-use technology 144
Dulles J. 14

East Asian economic crisis 9
East China Sea 43, 48–50, 52, 55–61, 63,
    65, 69, 71, 82–3, 109–10, 114, 177,
    183; Chinese incursions 50, 56–60,
    120; Chunxiao 59; oil/gas exploration
    58–60; Okinawa Trough 55; Pinghu
    59–60; pollution 72; Xihu 59
East Timor 9
ECAFE 49
economic interdependence 5, 8
EEZ 7, 50–1; 55–60, 62, 87, 118, 120,
    128, 158, 171, 175, 177, 183
Ema, S. 115

emperor (tenno) 16, 30, 50, 81
enlargement policy 91
environmental degration 72
Esaki, M. 27
Eto, S. 72, 152
Eurasia Diplomacy 107–8
Europe 2, 39–40, 71, 84, 86, 104, 119, 123, 179, 186
European Union 103, 125, 183
Export–Import Bank 60

F-2 86
F-15 52, 87
F-4EJ 52
Falungong 171
FDI 8, 70, 102, 133–8, 143–5, 149–50
Feigenbaum, E. 63
Fernandes, G. 106
food 71
Ford Foundation 83
Four Party (Power) talks 110, 126
France 137
Free Trade Agreement: ASEAN–China 126; Japan–South Korea 109
Friedberg, A. 181
Fujian 74
Fukushima, A. 131
Fukuyoshi, S. 66
Funabashi, Y. 54–5, 66, 90–1, 97, 167, 184
Futami, Nobuaki 51
Futemna 66

Gaoxiong 65
Georgia 107
General Agreement on Tariffs and Trade 137
Germany 28, 34, 137
Gill, B. 41, 132
'Global Mars' 127
Goh, C. 155
Gotoda, M. 120
Green, M. 84, 88
Gross Domestic Product 61, 75, 138, 148
Gross National Product 149
Ground Self-Defence Force 71, 87, 105, 144
Group of Seven (Eight) Industrialized Countries 30, 47, 99, 101, 156–7
Guangdong International Trust and Investment Corporation 150
Gulf War 32, 34, 41, 76, 79, 88, 90
Guomindang 13–14, 153
Gurtov, M. 152, 157

Hainan 62, 129
Halperin, M. 94
Harrison, S. 94
Hashimoto, H. 50, 53, 65, 92, 98
Hashimoto, K. 186
Hashimoto, Y. 37, 47, 56, 66–7, 95, 106–8, 130, 155–6; Hashimoto–Clinton Joint Declaration *see* Japan–US Joint Declaration
Hata, I. 114
Hatoyama, K. 154
Hatoyama, Y. 118, 186
Hawke, B. 129
Hayashi, Y. 172
hegemonic stability 5
high-technology warfare 41
Higuchi Report 44, 88–90, 123, 144
Hiramatsu, S. 55–6, 59–60, 82, 84
Hiroshima 45; Asian Games 153
'history card' 17–18, 47, 79, 155, 175, 177, 184
Hokkaido 87
Holbrooke, R. 10
Hong Kong 23, 50–2, 73–4, 88, 127, 136–7, 154, 178
Hosokawa, M. 44, 88
House of Councillors (Upper House) 67
Hu, Y. 25–8
Hua, G. 24
Hualian 65
Hughes, C. 89
human rights 6, 8, 30–1, 36, 39, 91, 103–4, 145, 159, 167
human security 143
Huntington, S. 182
Hwang, B. 152, 157

Ikeda, Y. 66–7, 106
IL-76 41, 62
illegal immigration 61, 70, 72–4, 83, 141, 176
'Independence' 65–6
India 41, 46, 48, 61, 84, 105–8, 127–8, 154–5
Indian Ocean 41, 82, 104, 106
Indochina 28
Indonesia 61–3, 102, 105, 125, 127, 132, 136–7, 143
information-technology warfare 43
Inoguchi, T. 182
Institute for Defense Analysis 84
Institute of Developing Economies 43, 69

Institute of Foreign Affairs and National
    Security (ROK) 129
Institute of International Affairs (Japan)
    128–30
International Atomic Energy Agency 49
International Maritime Bureau 63
International Military Education and
    Training 90
International Monetary Fund 75
International Peace Cooperation Law 123
Iran 46, 48, 71
Iraq 90
Iriye, A 20
Ishigaki Island 57
Ishihara, S. 75, 80, 154
Ito, M. 120

Japan: mediator 180; military force
    structure and expenditures 85–7;
    Imperial Army 118
Japan Centre for International Exchange
    129
Japan–China: Dietmen's Friendship
    League 172; establishment of
    diplomatic relations 21–3, 96, 112–13,
    121, 129, 134, 152; fishing agreement
    56; opinion polls 38–9, 46, 72, 80–1,
    134, 148, 158, 165; Peace and
    Friendship Treaty 24, 53, 96; Public
    Security Authorities Consultations 119;
    removal of chemical weapons 118;
    security dialogue 57, 99, 111–33;
    telephone hotline 117; trade 134–6,
    182–3; war reparations 16, 133
Japan Communist Party 14
Japan Export Trade Organization 135
Japan International Cooperation Agency
    143
Japan National Oil Company 62
Japan Socialist Party 17
Japan–South Korea Joint Development
    Zone 55
Japan–US Joint Declaration
    (Hashimoto–Clinton) 35, 47, 68, 88,
    91–3, 95–8, 112, 115, 123, 131, 166–9,
    171
Japan–Vietnam Petroleum 62
Japanese–American security alliance 3,
    7–10, 13, 15, 19–21, 24–5, 27, 29, 32,
    36–7, 39, 45, 47–8, 54–5, 64, 66, 69,
    74, 76–8, 80, 83–101, 108, 110, 112,
    121, 123, 125, 134, 139, 146, 157–70,
    174, 176–7, 179–81, 184; Far Eastern

Clause 60, 96–7; guidelines (revision) 9,
    51–2, 73, 89, 92, 95, 99, 108, 116,
    130–1, 155, 160–1, 167–8, 184;
    Investment Promotion Organization
    135; nuclear umbrella 20, 45, 47, 77,
    101; prior consultations 66–7; security
    guarantee 76; 'situations in areas
    surrounding Japan' 73, 92–3, 95–101;
    Trade Expansion Council 135
Japanese–American trade conflict 34, 88
Ji, G. 61
Jiang, J. 16
Jiang, Z. 17, 39, 41, 50, 53, 58, 79–80, 98,
    112, 117, 130, 157, 160, 163–4, 166,
    172
Jilong 65
Jin, X. 146
Jiyuto 51
Johnson, C. 10
Johnston, A. 1, 5
Johnstone, C. 159
Justice Ministry 73

Kaifu, T. 30, 109, 123, 154
Kajiyama, S. 98
Kakizawa, K. 43
Kan, Naoto 163
Kastner, S. 141, 145
Kato, H. 144
Kato, K. 67, 98, 121
Katzenstein, P. 119
Kawashima, Y. 111
Kayahara, I. 67, 82
Kazakhstan 107
KEDO 78
Kilo-class submarine 41
Kim Dae-jung 79
Kim Ilsung 109
Kishi, N. 96
Kissinger, H. 163
Kitakojima 51
Koizumi, J. 115, 121, 129, 151, 153
Kojima, T. 80, 111
kokaryo 27
Kokubun, R. 41, 76, 82, 88, 154
Kono, Y. 57–8, 60, 68, 89, 98, 105
Korea (Korean Peninsula) 13, 21, 23, 39,
    47, 50, 72, 76, 80, 81, 87, 89, 94, 96–9,
    109–10, 116, 121, 124, 130, 161, 174,
    181, 183, 185
Korean War 9, 14, 17, 19
Kosaka, M. 122
kowtow diplomacy (*dogeza gaiko*) 7, 171

Kurihara, Y. 25–26, 113
Kyoto University 153, 160
Kyrgyzstan 107
Kyuma, F. 115
Kyushu 73, 87

Lake, A. 164
Laos 127
lasers 41
Layne, C. 10
Lee, K. 103
Li, Denghui 55, 64, 69, 92, 100, 113, 151, 153, 166, 178
Li, Ding 128
Li, P. 56, 130, 132
Li, R. 154
Liberal Democratic Party (LDP) 21, 22, 43–4, 52, 57–8, 67, 75, 78–9, 85, 89, 98, 120–1, 146, 153–4, 171–2; Foreign Affairs Committee 58; International Economic Policy Special Research Committee 27; Security Treaty Committee 67
Liberal Party 99
Liberal School (liberalism) 4, 6, 8, 9, 84, 133, 140–2, 144–5, 170, 172, 175
Libya 48
light-water reactors 78
liquified natural gas 60, 62
London School of Politics and Economics 168
L-T Trade 21
Lu, Z. 131
Luttwak, E. 162

M-9 46, 65
McVadon, E. 119
Malaysia 61–2, 106, 127
Manchukuo 13
Manchurian incident 13
Marco Polo bridge 13
Maritime Safety Agency *see* Coast Guard
Maritime Self-Defence Force 48, 53, 57, 65, 67, 82, 87, 110, 112, 154
Matsu Islands 65
Matsunaga, N. 130
Maull, H. 28
median (equidistant) line 52, 55, 57, 59–60
Meiji 13, 156
Michishita, N. 186
Middle East 28, 60–1, 71, 81
militarism (Japan) 25–6, 38–9
Military Armistice Commission 78

Ministry of Education 26
Ministry of Finance 105, 119
Ministry of Foreign Affairs (Gaimusho) 46, 48, 51, 60, 66–7, 69, 79, 83, 98, 102, 111, 114, 119–20, 132, 143, 147, 158, 164–5, 171–2, 179–80
Ministry of Health and Welfare 119
Ministry of Justice 119
Ministry of Trade and Industry 23, 60
minsei taikoku 28
Mischief Reef 62–3
Missile Technology Control Regime 114
Mitsubishi Corporation 62
Mitsuzaka, H. 44
Miyakojima 60
Miyamoto, N. 152
Miyamoto, Y. 146
Miyazawa, K. 50, 53, 78
Mochizuki, M. 124, 185
Möller, K. 141
Mondale, W. 54, 66
Mongolia 109
Montaperto, N. 66, 166
Mori, K. 152
Mori, Y. 106–7
'Moskit' missiles 42
most-favoured nation 31
Mount Pinatubo 77
multilateral security 88, 90, 103, 174
multilateralism 4, 8, 35, 121–33, 141, 159, 168, 176, 178–9
Mumbai (formerly Bombay) 106
Murai, T. 80, 82, 182
Murayama , T. 46, 78, 88–9, 92
Muto, K. 114
Myanmar 102, 104–5, 127

Nagasaki 45
Nagatomi, Y. 105
Naha 58
Nakai, Y. 43, 69, 82, 149, 160
Nakanishi, H. 160
Nakanishi, T. 148
Nakasone, Y. 24, 26–7, 73, 129, 186
Nakayama, T. 124
Nanjing massacre 15, 121
National Defence Programme Outline of 1995 87–9, 102, 174
National Defence University (Japan) 115
National Graduate Institute for Policy Studies 96, 125
National Institute for Defense Studies 41, 47, 57, 67, 94, 113

National Missile Defense 94, 100–1, 184
National Party Congress 40–1
National Police Agency 73, 119
National Security Council 93
Natuna D-Alpha gas field 62
natural prolongation theory 55
naval ship visits 113, 118
Navy Theatre-Wide Defence 93, 99–100
New Frontier Party 79
New York terror attack 106–7
New Zealand 49, 125
Nihon Keizai Shimbun 87
Nikaido, S. 25
Nikka Giin Kondankai 153
'Nimitz' 65–6
Nippon Mitsubishi Oil Corporation 62
Nishihara, M. 61, 82, 115, 127, 134
Nishimura, S. 51
Nitchukan Sankyoku Forum 129
Nixon, R. 9, 96, 163
Nodong-1 93, 169
Nomura Research Council 152
Nonaka, H. 48, 121, 172
Norota, H. 154, 168–9
North Atlantic Treaty Organization:
    bombing of Chinese embassy 52, 164;
    eastward expansion 107–8, 168;
    Kosovo bombing 99, 171; NATO
    Russia Permanent Joint Council 186
North Korea 44, 48, 76–8, 81, 87, 93–4,
    97, 101, 109–10, 114, 117, 126, 139,
    161; drug smuggling 74; missiles 47, 94,
    100, 161, 169, 184; missile exports 48;
    missile test 48, 94, 169; nuclear crisis
    76–8, 89, 92, 161
North Pacific Cooperative Security
    Dialogue 129
Northeast Asia Cooperation Dialogue 129
Northern Territories 24, 81, 107–8
nuclear non-proliferation 36, 45, 47, 94,
    114, 117
Nuclear Non-Proliferation Treaty 45, 78,
    117, 123; NPT Extention Conference 46
Nye, J. 97
Nye Report (initiative) 35, 77, 88–92, 97

'Observation Island' 67
Obuchi, K. 58, 99, 109, 121, 126–7, 130,
    156, 166
ODA 4, 7 , 8, 28, 30–1, 43, 46–7, 51, 67,
    70, 79, 85, 102, 104–5, 108, 109,
    133–7, 143–51, 159, 177, 180; grant

aid 46–7; guidelines 46; yen loans 46,
    58, 108, 136–7, 147, 172
Ogawa, S. 47, 93
O'Hanlon, M. 185
Ohira, M. 26–7, 96, 99, 136, 146
Okamoto, Y. 129, 179
Okawara, N. 119
Okinawa 49, 54, 65–6, 68–9, 73, 86–7, 89,
    91, 184; Okinawa G-8 summit 2000
    156–7
omnidirectional diplomacy 27
Osaka Keizai Hoka University 66
Osaki, Y. 81
Ozawa, I. 79, 85, 99, 134, 171

P-3C 86–7
Pacific Economic Cooperation Council
    122, 137
Pacific Forum Hawaii 130
Pacific Ocean 82
Pacific War 46, 104
pacifism 6, 9, 17, 83, 88, 161
Pakistan 46, 48, 106–7, 155
Panama Canal 61
Panyarachun, A. 124
Papayanou, P. 141, 145
Paracel Islands 61–2
Partnership for Peace 185
Patriot system 93, 99
Pax Sinica 182
Perry, W. 65, 89–90, 98, 124, 185
Pertamina 62
Petronas 62
PHP Research Institute 186
Philippines 28, 61–2, 69, 73, 77, 90, 96,
    127, 129
Pillsbury, M. 35
piracy 61, 63–4, 73, 88, 106, 127–8, 155
PKO 38, 77, 88, 114, 118, 123, 156
post-Cold War 9, 32, 34–5, 40, 82, 106–7,
    111, 123, 134, 144, 161, 168, 170, 184
Potsdam Declaration 22, 49
Powell, C. 104
precision-guidance 41
preventive diplomacy 125
Primeline Petroleum Corporation 59
Prime Minister's Office 65, 81
Public Security Investigation Agency 119
Purchasing Power Parity 75
Pyle, K. 181
Pyongyang 77, 109

Qian, Q. 31, 39, 66, 114, 127, 130, 185

Ramos, R. 129
Rang Dong field 62
Reagan, R. 26, 93
Realism 3, 4, 5, 6, 7, 8, 9, 35, 38, 80, 84–5,
    91, 101, 133, 139–42, 144, 170, 172,
    175–6; structural 3; Realist scholars in
    Japan 83, 85, 108, 142, 161
refugees 4, 29, 72–3, 81, 96, 144
rekishi ninshiki 15
Renmin Ribao 169
Renminbi 143
reparations 16–17
Report on Comprehensive National
    Security 27
Research Institute for Peace and Security
    83, 130, 164
RimPac 38
Rosecrance, R. 28
Ross, R. 1, 5
Roy, D. 145, 148, 155, 182
Royama, M. 83
Russia 13, 32, 39–40, 44, 52, 63, 76–7,
    81–2, 84, 93, 99, 101, 107–9, 115, 119,
    124, 144, 154, 157, 165, 185; Chinese
    weapon imports from Russia 41–2, 61,
    108, 125

S-300 41
Sakamoto, M. 43, 53
Sakanaka, T. 82, 164
SALT III 77
San Francisco Peace Treaty 49, 61
Sankei Shimbun 57, 63, 79, 153
Sasakawa Japan–China Friendship Fund
    120
satellite-based navigation systems 41
Sato, E. 96
Sato, H. 19, 21, 159, 185
Sato, K. 127
Sato, S. 108
Sato–Nixon Communique 21, 68, 96
Scowcroft, B. 31
scramble sorties 52–3
sea lanes 48, 60, 63, 68–9, 71, 82, 102,
    104, 106, 186
Second World War 45
Segal, G. 152
seikei bunri 21
Seinensha 51
Self, B. 84
Self-Defence Forces 24, 28, 39, 66–8,
    77–8, 86–8, 119, 154, 174; SDF Law
    92

semiconductor supply 69
Senkaku (Diaoyu) Islands 24, 26, 38,
    47–56, 58, 60–1, 82, 89, 95, 118, 146,
    156, 158, 171, 177, 183; Chinese
    incursions 50, 56–8; oil exploration 53,
    59–60; US context 54–5, 164
Sha, Z. 169
Shambaugh, D. 40, 152, 154
Shanghai 59–60, 74
Shanghai Five (*later* Shanghai Cooperation
    Organization) 108
Shigemitsu, S. 20
Shiina, E. 163
Shikata, T. 71
shinryaku 26
Shinshinto 51
shinshutsu 26
Shiokawa, M. 172
Shizuoka Prefectural University 148
Siberia 39
Silk Road Diplomacy 107–8
Sing, J. 106
Singapore 127–8, 155
Sinopec Star Petroleum Corporation 59
Sino–Soviet Treaty of Friendship and
    Alliance 14
Skanderup 162
Social-Democratic Party 78–9, 88, 92
Soeya, Y. 22, 46, 67, 69, 85, 96, 164
Sonoda, S. 96–7
South Asia 41
South China Sea 8, 36, 41, 43, 48, 50, 52,
    60–3, 71, 73, 82–3, 89, 102, 105, 109,
    124–8, 144, 175; Code of Conduct 127
South Korea (ROK) 44, 49, 61–2, 68, 71,
    73–4, 76, 82, 96, 109–10, 119, 125,
    127–9, 154, 161, 186; East China Sea
    55; fishing agreement with China 56
Soviet Union 19, 20, 24–6, 31–2, 34, 41,
    45, 76–7, 80, 86, 88, 90, 96, 146, 181
Sovremenniy-class destroyer 42
Spratly Islands 61, 98
State Law and Order Restoration Council
    104
Straits of Malacca 40
Strategic Defence Initiative 93
Subic Bay 77
Suez Canal 61
SU-27 41, 53, 61, 87
SU-30 41
Suzuki, Z. 27
Syria 48

Taepodong-1 48, 94
Taiwan 3, 8–10, 13–16, 20–3, 26–7, 41,
    44, 46, 53, 55, 62, 68–70, 73–4, 81–3,
    95–101, 111, 124, 127, 136–7 140–1,
    144–5, 152, 152–4, 158, 160, 163,
    167–8, 175, 177–8, 181, 184; Senkaku
    49–52; Taiwan Relations Act 161, 168;
    Taiwan Strait 39, 44, 47–8, 68–9, 87–8,
    95–9, 160, 162, 181; Taiwan Strait
    crisis 64–70, 80, 91–2, 94, 153; 'Three
    Nos' 160
Tajikistan 107
Takagi, S. 96, 125, 137, 147
Takahara, A. 75, 82
Takasaki, T. 20
Takeshima (Dokto) 52
Takeshita, N. 120
Tamura, S. 67, 89
Tanaka, A. 69, 82, 142–3, 178
Tanaka, H. 98
Tanaka, K. 24, 53, 96
Tanaka, M. 180
Tang, J. 58, 146
Teikoku Oil 60, 62
Teikyo University 71
Tennichi, T. 122, 163, 180, 182
'Tenyu' 63
textbooks 16–17, 26, 37, 113, 115, 121,
    183
Thailand 63, 105, 127, 136–7
thermal imaging guidance 41
Tiananmen 2, 10,17–18, 29–32, 43, 51,
    73, 79, 81, 85, 112–13, 120, 123, 137,
    153, 164, 166
Tibet 8, 99
TMD 10, 15, 38, 47, 68, 93–5, 99–101,
    110, 116, 118, 139, 167, 169, 177, 184
Tokyo University 74
transboundary pollution 4, 70, 72, 133,
    141, 175–6
Treaty of Good Neighborliness and
    Friendly Cooperation 107
Truman, H. 14
Tsuruga Strait 57
Turkey 71, 154
Turkic minorities 108
Turkmenistan 107
Twenty-First Century Committee 25
Twomey, C. 181

Uighur 108
UN General Assembly 21, 46

UN Security Council 21, 165; seat for
    Japan 79, 106, 156, 167, 177
UNCLOS 51, 55–6
United Kingdom 137
UNTAC 38–9,
Uno, S. 30, 53
USA 74–5, 78, 80, 81–3, 86, 89, 97, 102,
    106, 109, 119, 121, 125, 127–31, 134,
    137–8, 142, 144–6, 148, 152, 154, 157,
    178, 182–6; anti-Communist strategy
    19; Bottom-Up Review 89; Congress
    94; Democratic Party 164; Department
    of Defense 77, 89, 91, 160, 164;
    Department of State 54, 94, 97–8;
    forces in Japan 39, 45, 81, 155;
    hegemon 34, 185; hegemony 40, 45,
    82, 90, 171; International Sea Power
    Symposium 128; leadership 32;
    National Intelligence Council 72, 163;
    nuclear umbrella 45, 47, 94; Pacific
    Reach 2000 128; preponderance 36,
    91, 103, 181; unipolarity 32; US–China
    relations 30, 54–5, 76–7, 145, 157–70,
    179–80; US–China trade 135;
    US–Chinese talks 1972 23;
    US–Japan–China triangle 10, 34, 54,
    85, 129–30, 157–70, 178; US–Soviet
    confrontation 13; Western Pacific Naval
    Symposium 128
Urayama, K. 101
Uzbekistan 107

Vajpayee, A. 106
Vietnam 25, 61, 102, 105, 125, 127
Vietnam War 9, 65

Wang, J. 168
war prostitutes 16
Watanabe, A. 80
Wenzhou 59
Western Pacific Mine Countermeasures
    Exercise 128
WESTPAC 93
Whiting, A. 31, 40
Wiltse, J. 87
Wolfowitz, P. 178
Woodrow Wilson Center 84
World Bank 30, 75
World Trade Organization 111, 137, 142,
    144, 150, 178–80, 183
Wu, X. 24–5, 39, 95, 148

Xia SSBN 47
Xiandai Jianchuan 38
Xin, J. 31, 40
Xiong, G. 115
Xu, Z. 151

Yahuda, M. 168–9
yakuza 73, 84
Yalta regime 34
Yamagata, A. 13
Yamazaki, T. 98
Yan, X. 34
Yanai, S. 97
Yang, B. 116, 156
Yang, D. 113
Yangtze River 63
Yao, Y. 27
Yasukuni shrine 15, 26, 37, 47, 95, 115, 121, 151, 183

Yasutomo, D. 30
Yokohama 67
Yokosuka 66
Yokoyama, H. 7, 80, 143, 171
Yomiuri Shimbun 38, 81, 87, 134
Yonaguni 65, 67
Yongxing Island 61
Yoshida, S. 14, 20–1, 28
Yuan, J. 132
Yugoslavia bombing 156
yuko 78

Zhang, A. 25–6, 113
Zhang, M. 66, 166
Zhao, J. 168
Zhao, Z. 25
Zhou, E. 20, 24, 33, 53, 96, 163
Zhou, J. 34
Zhu, R. 99, 112, 117, 120, 126, 146, 157